The Legal Guide for
Museum Professionals

The Legal Guide for Museum Professionals

Edited by Julia Courtney

ROWMAN & LITTLEFIELD
Lanham • Boulder • New York • London

Published by Rowman & Littlefield
A wholly owned subsidiary of The Rowman & Littlefield Publishing Group, Inc.
4501 Forbes Boulevard, Suite 200, Lanham, Maryland 20706
www.rowman.com

Unit A, Whitacre Mews, 26-34 Stannary Street, London SE11 4AB

British Library Cataloguing in Publication Information Available.

Library of Congress Cataloging-in-Publication Data

The legal guide for museum professionals / edited by Julia Courtney.
pages cm
Includes bibliographical references and index.
ISBN 978-1-4422-3041-5 (cloth : alk. paper) — ISBN 978-1-4422-3042-2 (pbk. : alk. paper) — ISBN 978-1-4422-3043-9 (electronic)
1. Museums—Law and legislation—United States. 2. Museums—United States.—Employees—Handbooks, manuals, etc. I. Courtney, Julia Hollett, editor.
KF4305.L44 2015
344.73'093—dc23

2014048207

Printed in the United States of America

Contents

Preface   ix
  Julia Courtney

Acknowledgments   xiii

I: Collections and Exhibits   **1**

  1 Found in Collections: How to Use Museum Property Statutes to
     Resolve Abandoned Property Issues in Museums   3
     Gilbert Whittemore, Ph.D., Esq.

  2 Stolen Cultural Property: A Risk Management Primer   13
     David L. Hall and Ivana D. Greco

  3 Museums and Museum Curators: Caught in the Cross-Hairs of
     Authenticity Disputes   27
     Ronald D. Spencer and Judith Wallace

  4 Nazi-Looted Art: Risks and Best Practices for Museums   41
     Nicholas M. O'Donnell

  5 A Brief Guide to Provenance Research   55
     Sharon Flescher

  6 A Native American Graves Protection and Repatriation Act
     (NAGPRA): A Case Study from Western Massachusetts   73
     Dr. Ellen Savulis

  7 Creating and Negotiating Contracts for Traveling Exhibits   85
     Julia Courtney

  8 Managing Historic Firearms in Museum Collections   99
         Alex Mackenzie and David Arnold

II: Museum Government and Finance   **125**

  9 Monetizing the Collection: The Intersection of Law, Ethics, and
         Trustee Prerogative   127
         Mark S. Gold

 10 Keeping Deaccessioned Objects in the Public Domain: Legal
         and Practical Issues   135
         Stefanie S. Jandl and Mark S. Gold

 11 There's No Such Thing as the Public Trust, and It's a Good
         Thing, Too   151
         Donn Zaretsky

 12 Endowments and Restricted Gifts: Accessible or "Hands Off"?   157
         Anita Lichtblau, Esq.

 13 The Fresno Metropolitan Museum Story: Assignment for
         Benefit of Creditors   171
         Riley Walter

 14 The Higgins Armory Museum and Worcester Art Museum
         Integration: A Case Study in Combining and Transforming
         Mature Cultural Institutions   179
         James C. Donnelly, Jr., and Catherine M. Colinvaux

III: Museum Operations   **203**

 15 Employee and Independent Contractor Issues in the Museum
         Context   205
         Ethan S. Klepetar, Esq.

 16 To Train or Not to Train. Is That a Question?: The Training of
         Security Officers in Museums   213
         R. Michael Kirchner, CPP

IV: Digital Technology and Social Media in Museums   **223**

 17 Social Media: Use Responsibly   225
         Katherine E. Lewis

 18 Digital and Information Technology in Museums   241
         Katherine E. Lewis

 19 Crowdfunding for Museums   255
         Alyssa L. Reiner, Esq.

 20 Rights and Reproduction: The Rapidly Changing Landscape   269
         Julia Courtney and Katherine E. Lewis

Index	285
About the Editor	293
About the Contributors	295

Preface

Julia Courtney

Since the first American museum debuted in 1786, in Philadelphia, when Charles Willson Peale was presented with a mastodon bone found in Kentucky and displayed it in his painting gallery,[1] museums have been an important source of public and private education and entertainment. Over the years museums have been charged with remarkable responsibility and multiple missions: to acquire, care for, and maintain collections; to preserve objects for future generations; to be a place of community, entertainment, and scholarship; and to withstand continuous reinvention that align with interests in popular culture. This is by no means a complete list. In fact, it merely scratches the surface of concerns the cultural institutions face.

Not only did Charles Willson Peale create the first museum in the eighteenth century, but he unknowingly formed what could be the first membership and marketing campaigns, as well as the first solicitations for museum donations. Peale's venture was a community museum, an annual ticket cost a dollar, and early members included everyone from presidents to congressmen to merchants and skilled laborers.[2]

Much of the funding came from ticket sales, Peale's exhibits had to be crowd-pleasers. His museum enjoyed a fifty-year legacy, and remained open even after Peale's death in 1827. At that juncture it fell under the management of Peale's sons, and disbanded in the 1840s. Once closed, the museum's collection was sold off, and buyers included the infamous showman, P. T. Barnum.[3]

Between 1841 and 1868, Barnum was the proprietor of the American Museum in New York City. The museum advertised that it contained more than 850,000 "interesting curiosities," and over 4,000 people visited daily and 20,000 visited on holidays.[4] The entrance fee was twenty-five cents. Barnum later traveled his show and it eventually evolved into a pure entertainment enterprise known as the Ringling Bros. and Barnum and Bailey Circus.[5]

By the middle of the nineteenth century, museums were springing up in cities large and small. Personal collections developed into cabinets of curiosity, reflecting the Victorian quest for knowledge and beauty. Over time, cabinets of curiosity inspired larger, public museums. The founding mission of these early institutions was to "educate and uplift the public and to improve the skills and taste of those who worked with their hands."[6] As American cities became principal centers of commerce, they formed large art museums as a way of demonstrating their economic and cultural power. As a result, museums began to shift focus from building and maintaining audiences to the care of their valuable and quickly expanding collections.[7] The dichotomy of attending to both of these important missions endured into contemporary times.

Museum missions have vacillated along with numerous cultural trends since this early period. Museums have transformed, transmuted, and transcended all of American history including early research expeditions, World Wars, the Great Depression, art market fluctuations, governments that did and did not support the arts, the digital and information technology age, and in recent times, a serious economic downturn that cost many museums their endowment. Consequently, about twenty museums of different disciplines and sizes folded during 2010 according to Dewey Blanton, then spokesperson for the national professional museum organization, the American Association of Museums (now the American Alliance of Museums).[8]

In addition to financial and operational challenges, museums have braved legal and ethical obstacles with regard to collections care including the repatriation of cultural objects, the restitution of artwork looted by the Nazi regime, art and object theft, forgery, fraud, and other crimes—all of which have kept museums vigilant.

As these institutions search for ways to navigate challenges they face, the legal system comes to their aid, in an effort to resolve, in a reasonable and impartial manner, both the simple and complex issues of the past and present day. Although museum ethics and legalities are different, the two inform each other and provide a resource in best practices for resolving difficulties for museums.

The essays that follow represent a sampling of compelling, contemporary challenges that museums encounter, and propose strategies for resolution and guidance for museum professionals. The authors, to whom I am immensely indebted, include renowned attorneys in the field of museum and art law, as well as museum professionals and supporters. Their suggestions offer an approach to a variety of legal problems, possible next steps, and resources for further research. The recommendations should be used only as a guide on how to best negotiate these challenges. Museum professionals may find the need to contract with legal experts who can assist them in more specific ways as each circumstance has its own implications.

The essays are divided into the following areas: Collections and Exhibits, Museum Government and Finance, Museum Operations, and Digital Technology and Social Media in Museums. Each section covers a myriad of subjects intended to inform museum professionals on the topics and their relation to the law. Hopefully, museums of all disciplines and sizes will benefit from their content. Although museums continue to transform, it is our hope that this publication will endure as a resource for many years to come.

NOTES

1. Liane Hansen, "Philadelphia Museum Shaped Early American Culture," National Public Radio website, July 13, 2008, www.npr.org/templates/story/story.php?storyId=92388477, accessed October 5, 2014.

2. Hansen, 2008.

3. Hansen, 2008.

4. The JBHE Foundation, "The Phineas T. Barnum Freak Show," *Journal of Blacks in Higher Education*, no. 23 (Spring, 1999): p. 44, www.jstor.org/stable/2999302, accessed December 10, 2014.

5. JBHE Foundation, 1999.

6. Harold Skramstad, "An Agenda for American Museum in the Twenty-First Century," *Daedalus: America's Museums*, vol. 128, no. 3. (Summer, 1999): p. 109–28.

7. Skramstad, 1999.

8. Reed Johnson, "The Fresno Metropolitan Museum of Art & Science Closes Its Doors," *Los Angeles Times*, January 12, 2010.

Acknowledgments

The Legal Guide for Museum Professionals publication was inspired by a conference session hosted by the American Alliance of Museums entitled, "Can You Stump the Lawyer." A panel of art and museum law attorneys made themselves available to field questions and guide conference participants with their particular challenge, either making suggestions on a course of action or advising participants to seek further legal counsel. When the panel members, listed below, invited me to facilitate the session, I enthusiastically accepted. I had the good fortune of coming to know these three attorneys—Mark Gold, Katherine E. Lewis, and Gilbert Whittenmore—through Harvard University's Museum Studies Program. Each of them generously assisted in bringing the book to fruition. I am grateful to them for their ideas, support, and friendship throughout the project.

I am also indebted to the Springfield Museums Association, a consortium of museums located in Springfield, Massachusetts, where I have been privileged to serve as guardian of their exceptional collections as curator of art for the Michele and Donald D'Amour Museum of Fine Arts and the George Walter Vincent Smith Art Museum.

Many thanks to my family, friends, and colleagues for their encouragement and enthusiasm. Finally, this book is dedicated in memory of my father, David; my sister, Patricia; and my sweet little nephew, Brian, all of whom departed this world far too early. They continue to inspire me.

I

Collections and Exhibits

INTRODUCTION: COLLECTIONS AND EXHIBITS

American museums and their collections are as varied as the collectors who have amassed them through the years and entrusted them to the watchful care of our cultural institutions. Museum collections represent and chronicle human history in the form of material culture, often separated into the art, science, and history disciplines. Some of the largest and oldest museum collections in the country include the Philadelphia Museum of Art, the Smithsonian Institution, the Metropolitan Museum of Art, and the Boston Wadsworth Atheneum Museum of Fine Arts.

As museums began to appear across the country, in 1881 Professor William Stanley Jevons, an early museum studies specialist, articulated the purpose of museums, and formulated a general mission statement, which outlined their purpose:

> The special function of the museum is to preserve and utilize objects of nature and works of art and industry; to guard the written records of human thought and activity; to discuss facts and theories as a learned society; to educate the individual, while all meet together on common ground in the custodianship of learning and extending the boundaries of existing knowledge. [1]

Jevon's words are just as true today as they were in 1881, and they continue to apply to contemporary museums, many of which have adopted missions based on these early insights. Museum conservators, collections managers, registrars, curators, and educators work to safeguard, preserve, interpretate, and display collections objects in museums today. From a legal perspective, collections issues are intriguing and include topics such as abandoned property, art theft and forgery, authenticity disputes, Nazi-era looted art, provenance research, repatriation of Native American objects, and the management of historic firearms collections.

These topics represent a sampling of the legal concerns that museum professionals navigate in their work. The authors of the following essays offer extensive information and suggestions on how best to approach these subjects, and provide museum professionals with sound advice and information.

NOTE

1. G. Brown Goode, "The Relationships and Responsibilities of Museums," *Science*, vol. 2, no. 34 (August 23, 1895): p. 198.

Chapter One

Found in Collections

How to Use Museum Property Statutes to Resolve Abandoned Property Issues in Museums

Gilbert Whittemore, Ph.D., Esq.

Have you become inspired by the power of new technology to inventory and record details regarding your collection, only to be surprised—even shocked—at the number of objects that computer databases report as having inadequate provenance documentation? You are not alone. Collections databases now make inadequacies in collections records readily visible through software programs such as PastPerfect, TMS, EmbARK, Argus, and so forth, so that records that used to lay buried in dusty file-card drawers and folders are now readable from computer databases.

This situation is not unusual. Through the many years that large and small museums have been acquiring collections, professional standards of record keeping have changed dramatically. Museum personnel have become increasingly more professional and standards of documenting provenance have become more rigorous. As a result, computer technology now makes gaps in the collection records much more apparent.

One serious—but fortunately rare—problem is that someone may come forward claiming to be the owner of an underdocumented object. But more common is the challenge of deaccessioning an object, as clear provenance must be shown for an object to be deaccessioned and sold or transferred to another museum. Additional problems may arise if an underdocumented object in the museum collection is in need of conservation treatment: before making an investment in restoration or preservation, more information may be required about the history of the object.

The fact that a museum has custody of such an object indicates that at some point the owner intended the museum to display or possess the object, but does not reveal whether it was for a limited time or intended as a permanent gift. The challenge is to discover and document the actual circumstances in a way that provides a museum with a clear legal title (ownership), or returns the object to whoever is identified as the rightful owner.

In the past, lawyers could only squeeze the unique situations museums encounter into laws designed for abandoned or lost property. This essay outlines some of the steps a museum should follow—and questions they should ask—when dealing with abandoned property. As the laws in each state may differ, it is important that museum staff read their own state's specific statute early in the process. By now, however, in most states museums have been successful in persuading state legislatures to enact statutes that specifically address the museum's situation. You will find a list of state statutes at the end of this chapter.

1. Read the actual statute for your state.

This is a crucial step. Do not rely on the conveyance of information through workshop presentations, paraphrases in articles such as this, or other shortcuts when beginning the research process. The statutes are not that long and, though sometimes the language is a bit convoluted, can be readily interpreted with a careful reading. Be sure to read the entire statute as laws often have internal cross-references or definitions in one section that answer questions raised by another section.

Statutory language is often further interpreted by the published opinions of courts applying the statute to a specific case. As of this writing, I have not found any such court opinions in the New England states. This is good news as it indicates that this process rarely results in extensive litigation, but it also means only the statutory language is available as a guide.

2. How much time does the museum wish to spend on an extensive documentation effort for an abandoned property?

Museums vary greatly in the thoroughness of their current collections inventory. Ideally, museum inventories should be perfect and complete, but the reality is that they are often works in progress. Depending on the extent of your inventory, museums may have a complete list of all underdocumented objects from a detailed inventory, or a small list of objects of special concern from an inventory still in progress. Perhaps you have only one object of immediate concern. There is something to be said for learning the process by attempting to document one or a small number of abandoned objects, before undertaking a large-scale project.

3. Assign staff responsibility and prepare an explanation for the public.

To avoid confusion, assign responsibility for the abandoned property documentation project to one person on staff. All staff should understand what is being done and why, but all inquiries should be directed to a single staff member. This will simplify the process and assure that one person holds accurate and up-to-date information on the status of the research.

Prepare a simple explanation for members of the public about what the museum is undertaking. It is easy for the public to misunderstand when a museum seeks to document abandoned property, especially if newspaper ads are placed (as explained below). Do not be surprised if people conclude the museum is closing down, especially if the abandoned property is a candidate for deaccessioning.

4. Which objects have been in the possession of the museum long enough for the statute to apply?

Your state's abandoned property statute applies only if the museum has had the object in its possession for a specific number of years. The museum must be able to document this. For loaned objects, the loan documentation provides this. For undocumented objects, inventories are the best resource, but datable photographs, catalogues, or records of past exhibits may also suffice.

You can only proceed with the objects that have been in the possession of the museum for the applicable number of years. Set aside the others, perhaps flagging them for consideration once the time requirement has been met.

5. Which objects have documentation of the identity of who provided the object?

Some objects may have an actual loan document, correspondence or notes indicating a loan, but any contact information is likely out of date. The statutes treat these objects differently than those with no such documentation.

6. For the objects with a named source, follow the statute's notice provision.

If an object has a known source, but no other documentation, the presumption should be that this was an undocumented loan. Obviously, if there is documentation of a loan, but no up-to-date contact information, this object should also be presumed to be a loan. For such objects, each statute provides a process for terminating the loan by providing some form of written notice with documented attempt at delivery.

If this process succeeds in "waking up" the lender, the museum can then proceed to deal directly with the lender—either securing a deed of gift to transform the loan into a gift or, if the museum does not wish to keep the object, arranging for its return. At this point, the statutory process is superseded by the more customary application of tact and persuasiveness needed in dealing with potential donors.

7. For objects with no known source, or a source that cannot be found, proceed with published notification.

Clearly the best approach is to succeed in contacting the source of the object. But if this fails, each statute provides a process for "notice by publication." This is a long-standing legal practice of providing notice to unknown persons through publication (usually in the form of an advertisement) in a widely read newspaper. Each statute specifies what the advertisement must contain and where it must be published.

The only ambiguous part of the statutory requirement is how detailed a description of the object must be when included in the ad. Typically, this is the most frequently asked question that arises with regard to these statutes. Unfortunately, the laws do not provide any specific requirements for a "description," nor are there any court cases or state regulations that provide guidance.

Remember that the purpose of the advertisement is to provide notice and alert a possible owner that they should contact the museum for further information. It does not have to contain all the detailed information a museum may have regarding an object. Keep in mind that longer descriptions entail greater advertising expense—perhaps not a major concern for one object, but an important factor if you are seeking to "clean up" the documentation for all the undocumented objects in your collection. At the very least, museums should provide more detail in their inventory catalogue.

Within the ad, provide clear and easy instruction for readers to acquire additional information about the object. A museum can provide deeper detail, images, and dimensions on its website or to those who inquire directly about a specific object. Museums need to strike a balance between giving adequate notice to potential legitimate owners or donors, without offering so much detail that it invites scam artists to pursue false ownership claims (although admittedly the author has not yet heard of this situation).

8. Respond to inquiries according to a procedure planned in advance.

Depending on the type of museum and its abandoned objects, you may receive very few or quite a number of inquiries. In any case, it is crucial that you plan in advance how to handle all questions.

Treat general inquiries about "what is happening at the museum?" as an opportunity to educate supporters about the museum's efforts to improve the documentation of its collection. Tell them how important the project is to fulfilling the museum's responsibilities as trustee of its collection. Sometimes such general inquiries provide an opportunity to renew ties with a supporter who has become inactive.

Treat claims of ownership in a considerate, thoughtful, and careful manner that has been planned in advance. At the very least, ask for any documentation the claimant may have, which could include photos, correspondence, or even a formal agreement that is no longer in the museum's records. The entire purpose of notice by publication is to inform an actual owner, so do not be disappointed when the process succeeds and an actual owner comes forward. At this point, the object should be returned to the owner, unless the owner elects to donate the object and the museum is willing to accept it.

9. Require clear documentation from anyone claiming to be an heir of an owner.

An heir of the original owner who delivered the object to the museum may make a claim. Require the heir to provide clear documentation that they are not only "an heir," but also "*the* heir" to the object in question. This need not be a bequest of a specific object; it could, for example, be documentation that the owner's probate estate transferred title to "all personal property" to the claimant/heir. This may be a situation where it is wise to consult an attorney to review the documentation. It may seem overly rigorous, but it serves two purposes: fulfilling the museum's obligations as the trustee of objects in its care, and protecting the museum from a later claim by another heir.

If there is more than one heir claiming ownership, under no circumstances should a museum decide between them. The museum should never try to act as a probate court in deciding between two rival claimants. The burden should be on the claimants to resolve their dispute through negotiation or litigation. The museum should simply retain and care for the object until it is presented with a legally binding document determining title, such as a binding agreement among the heirs, or a court order.

10. Carefully document the process for each object.

If no legitimate owner appears, then at some point under each statute the museum will have title to the object. Remember that this title arises from the fulfillment of several requirements, including the time of possession, attempts at mailed notice, notice by publication, and a waiting period following publication. Each of these steps should be documented as part of the file for each object.

By adhering to the steps outlined in this chapter, museums should be able to avoid many issues associated with abandoned property in their collection. Through referring to their own state's laws early in the process, museums will be provided with helpful guidance. As discussed, resources summarizing the basic aspects for each state and a reference to the complete text of each state's statute can be found in the following pages. These steps will assist museums with the challenge of discovering and documenting clear legal title (ownership), or direction in returning the abandoned property to its rightful owner.

ABANDONED PROPERTY STATUTES

The list below is a verification and updating with additional annotations of the list found in Melinda Simms, *"Found in Collections": Reconciling Undocumented Objects in Historical Museums*, assembled by Melinda Simms in partial fulfillment of the requirements for the degree of master of arts in museum studies, John F. Kennedy University, Orinda, CA, Spring 2003. Links to state statutes can also be found at www.lawsource.com.

"Holding period" refers to the length of time undocumented property must have been in possession of a museum for the statute to apply.

Alabama: Ala. Code Section 41-6-72; applies only to Alabama Department of Archives and History of the State of Alabama; five-year holding period; alisondb.legislature.state.al.us/acas/ACASLoginie.asp.

Alaska: Alaska Stat. 14-57-200 through 14-57-290: "Property Held by Museums"; seven-year holding period; www.legis.state.ak.us/basis/folio.asp.

Arizona: Ariz. Rev. Stat. Ann. Sections 44-351 through 44-356: "Unclaimed Property in Museums"; seven-year holding period; www.azleg.state.az.us/ArizonaRevisedStatutes.asp.

Arkansas: Arkansas Code 13-5-1001 through 1013: "Museum Property Act" (enacted 2005); ten-year holding period for loans; seven-year holding period for undocumented property; www.lexisnexis.com/hottopics/arcode/Default.asp.

California: Cal. Civ. Code [Title IV, Ch. 1.5] Sections 1899.1 through 1899.11: "Loans to Museums for Indefinite or Long Terms" (enacted 1983); defines the term "loan" to include undocumented property: "(c) The terms 'loan,' 'loaned,' and 'on loan' include all deposits of property with a museum which are not accompanied by a transfer of title to the property" (1899.1(c)); title acquired three years after actual notice of termination of loan or twenty-five years after last contact with lender (1899.10); leginfo.legislature.ca.gov/faces/codes_displayText. xhtml?lawCode=CIV&division=3.&title=4.&part=4.&chapter=1.5.& article.

Colorado: Colo. Rev. Stat. [Title 38 Article 14] Sections 38-14-101 through 38-14-112: "Loans to Museums"; seven-year holding period; www.lexisnexis.com/hottopics/Colorado/.

Connecticut: Connecticut General Statutes [Title 11, Chapter 194] Sections 11-80 through 11-89; five-year holding period; search.cga.state .ct.us/dtsearch_pub_statutes.html.

Delaware: None as of 2014.

Florida: Fla. Stat. Ann. [Title XVIII] Chapter 265.565: "Property loaned to museums; obligations to lenders; notice; loan termination; acquisition of title; liens; conservation or disposal"; five-year holding period after termination of loan or twenty-five years from date of beginning of loan for an indefinite term; archive.flsenate.gov/Statutes/Index. cfm?Mode=View+Statutes&Submenu=1&Tab=statutes.

Georgia: Georgia Statutes [Title 10 Article 17B] Sections 10-1-529.1 through 10-1-529.7: "Georgia Museum Property Act" (enacted 2006); seven-year holding period after expiration of loan or last contact with lender; www.lexisnexis.com/hottopics/gacode/Default.asp.

Hawaii: None as of 2014; www.capitol.hawaii.gov/.

Idaho: None as of 2014; www.legislature.idaho.gov/idstat/TOC/ IDStatutesTOC.htm.

Illinois: Ill. Comp. Stat. Chapter 765 Sec 1033/1 through 1033/999: "Museum Disposition of Property Act"; upon termination of loan or holding period of seven years of possession; www.ilga.gov/legislation/ilcs/ ilcs3.asp?ActID=2230&ChapterID=62.

Indiana: Ind. Code. Ann. [Title 32, Article 34, Chapter 5] Section 32-34-5-1 through 32-34-5-16: "Property Loaned to Museums"; seven-year holding period; www.in.gov/legislative/ic/2004/title32/ar34/ch5.html.

Iowa: Iowa Code [Title 7, Chapter 305B] Chapter 305B Sections 1-1: "Museum Property Act"; seven-year holding period; search.legis .state.ia.us/nxt/gateway.dll/acts?f=templates&fn=default.htm.

Kansas: Kan. Stat. Ann. [Chapter 58, Article 40] 58-4001 through 4013: "Museum Property Act"; seven-year holding period; kansasstatutes. lesterama.org/Chapter_58/Article_40/.

Kentucky: Ky. Rev. Stat. Ann. [Title 141, Ch. 171] 171.830 through 171.849; "Property on Loan to Museums"; seven-year holding period; www.lrc.ky.gov/statutes/chapter.aspx?id=37947.

Louisiana: Museums established by statute each have their own statutory provision; see La. Rev. Stat. Ann. [Title 25] Sections 25:345, 377, 379.5, 380.4, 380.14, 380.25, 380.45, 380.55, 380.65, 380.75, 380.85, 380.95, 380.105, 380.115, 380.125, 380.135, 380.145, 380.155, 380.166; ten-year holding period; www.legis.state.la.us/lss/lss.asp?folder=99.

Maine: Me. Rev. Stat. Ann. Title 27, Chapter 19, Sections 601: "Property Deposited with Museums and Historical Societies"; three-year holding period; www.mainelegislature.org/legis/statutes/27/title27sec601.html.

Maryland: None as of 2014; www.dsd.state.md.us/comar/SubtitleSearch.aspx?search=34.04.08.

Massachusetts: Mass. General Laws [Part II, Title II] Ch. 200B: "Disposition of Museum Property," seven-year holding period; malegislature.gov/Laws/GeneralLaws/PartII/TitleII/Chapter200B.

Michigan: Mich. Comp. Laws 399.601 through 399.613: "The Museum Disposition of Property Act"; thirty-five-year holding period; www.legislature.mi.gov/(S(knxepmbplr5vck45lwceismf))/mileg.aspx?page=getObject&objectName=mcl-399-601.

Minnesota: Minn. Stat. [Chapter 345] Sections 345.70 through 345.74: "Minnesota Museum Property Act"; seven-year holding period; www.revisor.leg.state.mn.us/statutes/?id=345.70.

Mississippi: Miss. Code Ann. [Title 39, Chapter 19] Section 39-19-1 through 39-19-21: "Museum Unclaimed Property Act"; five-year holding period after expiration of loan for definite term or twenty-five years after last contact regarding indefinite loan or undocumented property; www.lexisnexis.com/hottopics/mscode/.

Missouri: Mo. Rev. Stat. [Title XI, Chapter 184] Section 184-101 through 184.122: "Museum Property Act"; seven-year holding period; law.justia.com/codes/missouri/2011/titlexi/chapter184/section184112.

Montana: Mont. Code Ann. [Title 22, Chapter 3, Part 5] Sections 22-3-501 through 22-3-523: "Museum Loan Act"; twenty-five-year holding period; leg.mt.gov/bills/mca_toc/22_3_5.htm.

Nebraska: Neb. Rev. Stat. Section 51-701 through 51-712: "Museum Property Act"; seven-year holding period; nebraskalegislature.gov/laws/browse-chapters.php?chapter=51.

Nevada: Nev. Rev. Stat. Ann. [Chapter 381] Section 381.009; three-year holding period; applies only to state museums of the Division of Museums and History created by Section 391.004; three-year holding period; www.leg.state.nv.us/NRS/NRS-381.html#NRS381Sec009.

New Hampshire: N.H. Rev. Stat. Ann. [Title XVI] Section 201-E:1 through E:7; five-year holding period; www.nh.gov/government/laws .html.

New Jersey: New Jersey Permanent Statutes [Title 46; Chapter 30D] Sections 46:30D-1 through 46:30D-11: "Museum Unclaimed Loan Act"; five-year holding period after termination of definite loan or ten years after beginning of loan for indefinite term; www.njleg.state .nj.us/.

New Mexico: N.M. Stat. Ann. [Chapter 18, Article 10] Sections 18-10-1 through 18-10-5: "Abandoned Cultural Properties Act"; seven-year holding period; public.nmcompcomm.us/NMPublic/gateway.dll/?f= templates&fn=default.htm.

New York: NY [Education, Title 1, Article 5, Part 1] EDN Sec. 233-AA: "Property of Other [Non–State Owned] Museums"; ten-year holding period; public.leginfo.state.ny.us/menugetf.cgi?COMMONQUERY= LAWS.

North Carolina: N.C. Gen. Stat. [Chapter 121] Section 121-7(c) applies only to the state Department of Cultural Resources; five-year holding period; www.ncga.state.nc.us/gascripts/Statutes/StatutesTOC.pl? Chapter=0121.

North Dakota: N.D. Cent. Code [Title 47] Section 47-07-14: "Museum records—Disposition of loaned or donated objects"; two-year holding period; applies only to a museum that is closing or closed; www.legis .nd.gov/cencode/t47.html.

Ohio: Ohio Rev. Code [Title 33, Chapter 3385] Sections 33.3385.01 through 33.3385.10: "Property on Loan to Museum"; seven-year holding period; codes.ohio.gov/orc/3385.

Oklahoma: Okla. Stat. [Title 60] Section 683.2: "Museums shall not be subject to the provisions of the Uniform Unclaimed Property Act, but a museum may avail itself of the provisions of this act by complying with the requirements of this act"; www.oscn.net/applications/oscn/ DeliverDocument.asp?CiteID=86096.

Oregon: Or. Rev. Stat. [Vol. 9, Chapter 358] Sections 358.415 through 358.440: "Loans to Museums"; seven-year holding period after termination of loan or twenty-five years after last communication; www .oregonlegislature.gov/bills_laws/lawsstatutes/2013ors358.html.

Pennsylvania: None as of 2014; govt.westlaw.com/pac/Index?tran sitionType=Default&contextData=(sc.Default).

Rhode Island: RI General Laws [Title 34] Sections 34-44.1-1 through 1-8: "The Rhode Island Museum Property Act"; five-year holding period; webserver.rilin.state.ri.us/Statutes/TITLE34/34-44.1/INDEX. HTM.

South Carolina: S.C. Code [Title 27, Chapter 45] Sections 27-45-10 through 27-45-100: "Abandoned and Loaned Cultural Property"; ten-year holding period; requires certification by South Carolina Abandoned Cultural Property Board that museum followed the required notification procedures; www.scstatehouse.gov/code/t27c045.php.

South Dakota: S.D. Codified Laws [Title 43, Chapter 41C] 43-41C-1 through 43-41C-4: "Unclaimed Property Held by Museums or Historical Societies"; ten-year holding period; legis.sd.gov/Statutes/Codified_Laws/DisplayStatute.aspx?Type=Statute&Statute=43-41C.

Tennessee: Tenn. Code Ann. [Title 66, Chapter 29, Part 2] Sections 66-29-201 through 66-29-204: "Abandoned Cultural Property Act"; twenty-year holding period; www.lexisnexis.com/hottopics/tncode/.

Texas: Tex. Property Code [Title 6A, Chapter 80] Sections 80.001 through 80.008: "Ownership, Conservation and Disposition of Property Loaned to Museums"; fifteen-year holding period; www.statutes.legis.state.tx.us/Index.aspx.

Utah: Utah Code 9-8-801 through 9-8-806: "Preserve Our Heritage Act"; establishes a rebuttable presumption that any "reposited" materials held by a collecting institution are the property of that collecting institution; statute of limitations bars recovery by a claimant after twenty-five years; le.utah.gov/code/TITLE09/htm/09_08_040400.htm.

Vermont: Vermont Statutes Annotated [Title 27, Chapter 12] Sections 1151 through 1158: "Museum Property"; ten-year holding period; www.leg.state.vt.us/statutes/fullchapter.cfm?Title=27&Chapter=012.

Virginia: Va. Code [Title 55, Chapter 11.2] Section 55-210.31 through 55-210.38: "Property Loaned to Museums"; five-year holding period; leg1.state.va.us/cgi-bin/legp504.exe?000+cod+TOC5500000001100 0020000000.

Washington: Wash. Rev. Code [Title 63, Chapter 26] Sections 63.26.010 through 63.26.050: "Unclaimed Property Held by Museum or Historical Society"; five-year holding period; app.leg.wa.gov/rcw/default.aspx?cite=63.26&full=true.

West Virginia: None as of 2014; www.legis.state.wv.us/WVcode/code.cfm?chap=37&art=1.

Wisconsin: Wis. Stat. Ann. [Chapter 171, Subchapter II] Sections 171.30 through 171.33: "Property in Possession of a Museum or Archives"; seven-year holding period; docs.legis.wisconsin.gov/statutes/statutes/171.

Wyoming: Wyo. Stat. Ann. [Title 34, Chapter 23] Sections 34-23-101 through 34-23-108: "Museums—Loaned Property"; ten-year holding period; legisweb.state.wy.us/statutes/statutes.aspx?file=titles/Title34/T34CH23.htm.

Chapter Two

Stolen Cultural Property

A Risk Management Primer

David L. Hall and Ivana D. Greco

Destiny has called. You have been named the curator of the Astonishing Repository of Treasures (ART) Museum, and have been challenged by the board of directors to take ART to "the next level." The board did not provide specific expectations, but this sounds like the right direction for the ART Museum. First, you decide to upgrade the museum's Impressionist and Neo-Impressionist collections; you let it be known that you are in the market to purchase artwork and have a substantial budget. Your efforts are soon rewarded with an e-mail from a collector in Romania who is selling a painting by artist Georges Seurat (1859–1891) that recently came into his possession through an estate sale. At $100,000, the price is appealing, though suspect. The collector informs you that due to the vagaries of Romanian probate law, there is very little provenance information on the painting, as the decedent was not attentive to detail. The collector is anxious to sell and explains that he prefers payment in euros, in cash, as soon as possible.

You probably won't be surprised to learn that the Seurat painting was stolen from a collector in Nice. Hopefully not, as the red flags in this scenario are plentiful. The problem of stolen cultural property poses a serious and persistent challenge for museum professionals. When a museum acquires an object for its collection, it acquires only as much documentation of ownership, as the seller can convey. Although museums have become increasingly diligent, collections amassed in past years can be problematic. If the object is stolen, the seller does not have the right to convey title, and the purchaser's title is void ab initio.[1] The ART Museum curator might defend the acquisition of the stolen Seurat citing that he or she did not have knowledge of the theft. This may be true, but he or she certainly had reason to be suspicious:

the modest price alone was the tell, given that the market price for a Seurat painting would be in the million-dollar range. Regardless of whether the curator had knowledge of the theft, the ART Museum did not acquire clear title to the stolen Seurat. The painting no longer seems like it was a bargain.

When a museum acquires stolen cultural property, it can assume that the true owner will demand its return and likely initiate costly litigation if the demand is not satisfied. In some circumstances, the U.S. government might become involved, demanding forfeiture of the object. The expense of such litigation is significant, and the damage to the museum's reputation can be even more serious.[2]

How should museum professionals address the problem of stolen cultural property? Preventing the problem is obviously optimal, and the best means to that end is effective and rigorous due diligence prior to acquisition. However, sometimes even extensive due diligence will fail or an object has been in the museum's possession for years before record keeping was a priority. If this happens and the ownership is challenged, or the museum is accused of possessing stolen property, the museum should carefully consider all options, including a vigorous defense, the voluntary return of the object, and an affirmative action to clear title. These options are discussed in this chapter.

The best way to avoid problems associated with acquiring stolen artifacts is not to acquire them in the first place. However, this proves to be easier said than done. Theft of cultural property is a pervasive and global criminal activity, and its detection can be challenging. For this reason, the ill-gotten gains of criminal enterprise are sometimes invested in cultural property. As Brazilian judge Fausto Martin De Sanctis observed, the global cultural property market has become "an attractive sector for the practice of money laundering."[3]

The prevalence of stolen cultural property in the marketplace is exemplified in the contemporary case of Subhash Kapoor, a well-known New York dealer of Indian artifacts alleged to have sold stolen cultural property to prominent museums, falsifing provenance documents to create the appearance of legitimacy. Kapoor's gallery manager pled guilty to six criminal counts relating to the stolen artwork,[4] and Kapoor himself faces criminal charges in India as well as an open warrant from the Manhattan district attorney's office,[5] which has seized objects valued in excess of $150 million.[6] Among the victims of Kapoor's alleged scheme was the National Gallery of Australia, which purchased twenty-two pieces from Kapoor, including a $5 million statue that India has requested be returned.[7] The purchase was called "naïve" by an expert who claims the National Gallery failed to perform due diligence.[8]

Whether the result of inexperience, sloth, or bad luck, the failure to verify the suspicious provenance history of an artifact can result in criminal charges. Prosecution for possession or transportation of stolen property can be based on a theory of "willful blindness," under which knowledge that an object is stolen is imputed to a defendant who consciously closes his or her eyes to facts that would lead a reasonable person to realize the object was stolen. [9] The fictitious curator of the ART Museum who acquired the Seurat painting from the Romanian collector treads perilously close to this line.

PROVENANCE AND DUE DILIGENCE

Museums should insist that sellers and donors rigorously authenticate cultural property prior to its acquisition. [10] At a minimum, museums would be well advised to follow the general guidance provided by the Federal Bureau of Investigation (FBI):

1. Get a thorough provenance (history of ownership) on the work. Don't rely on a simple certificate of authenticity.
2. Carefully research the dealer. Check the Better Business Bureau for possible complaints. Find out if they sell only online or if they have a gallery.
3. For works you already own, go back to the gallery and ask for provenance documentation. Contact artists' foundations that provide side-by-side analysis/comparisons with originals for a fee.
4. Be cautious. You are most likely to let your guard down when you think you've found a treasure at a bargain price. [11]

How a museum conducts provenance research will vary depending on whether it is acquiring fine art or an archaeological object, each having special considerations that are outlined below.

Fine Art

The ultimate goal of provenance research in the context of fine art acquisition is to establish ownership that reaches all the way back to the artist. In the case of older works, this will be more challenging. Museums should take the following steps to assure due diligence.

What is the seller's basis for ownership? Demand complete documentation (such as invoices, receipts, import and export records, bills of lading, etc.) from the seller, and then verify them. If a seller will not comply with this request, or provides a vacuous explanation like the one offered by the Romanian collector in the ART Museum's Seurat transaction, walk away. If the seller provides a letter documenting provenance, contact the author of the letter. Then, go beyond the face of the letter and follow any clues that are revealed. If the letter refers to previous transactions, obtain records of those transactions. If the parties are still living, speak to them directly. Leave no stone unturned.

Has the work been reported stolen? Query stolen art databases, including the FBI's National Stolen Art File, INTERPOL's stolen-works-of-art database, and the Art Loss Register. Survey dealers and others who participate actively in the market for that type of work. Check public resources available through the Internet and news services.

Is the ownership of the work disputed? Determine whether there are any ongoing disputes over ownership, by examining relevant probate (the processes of administering the estate of a deceased person) and other court records. Obtain records relating to loans or sales of the object, and interview the parties involved. Identifying issues prior to acquisition—even if their merit is unclear—will save anguish and expense in the long run.

Was the object looted by Nazis? During World War II, the Nazi regime systematically plundered art from European museums, churches, and private collections, particularly those of Jewish families. As a result of the enormous scope of this effort, a significant number of stolen works in the market today are among those looted by the Nazis.[12] In addition, many questionable works of fine art, while not plundered by the Nazi regime directly, were acquired from Jewish owners under duress for a fraction of their value. Acquiring such works is obviously to be avoided.

One prominent example is *Republic of Austria v. Altmann*,[13] in which the ownership of several paintings by Gustav Klimt (1862–1918) was at issue. The plaintiff claimed the paintings had been owned by her uncle, who fled Austria prior to the Nazi invasion of 1938, leaving the paintings behind. She alleged the paintings were seized by the Nazis prior to being acquired by the Austrian Gallery. The gallery contended that the paintings had been bequeathed to it by the plaintiff's aunt. The plaintiff filed suit, first in Austria, and then in the United States. The case made its way to the U.S. Supreme Court, which ruled that the plaintiff could sue the Austrian government in U.S. court. Ultimately, the case went to arbitration, and the paintings were returned to the plaintiff.[14]

Archaeological Works

The challenges faced by museums in acquiring archaeological works differ in some ways from those involved in acquiring fine art—but are just as serious. Some issues to be considered include the following.

Is the object a protected Native American artifact? U.S. law protects certain Native American artifacts. The Archaeological Resources Protection Act (ARPA), 16 U.S.C. § 470aa et seq., prohibits removing or damaging "any archaeological resource" (as defined) located on federal and Native American lands without a permit, unless a specific exemption applies. ARPA also prohibits trafficking in such artifacts.[15] The Native American Graves Protection and Repatriation Act (NAGPRA), 25 U.S.C. § 3001 et seq., also protects Native American artifacts, particularly human remains and burial objects. Among other provisions, NAGPRA requires the return, under defined circumstances, of Native American human remains and artifacts.[16] Trafficking in Native American human remains or cultural objects contrary to NAGPRA's terms is a criminal offense under 18 U.S.C. § 1170. Federal prosecutors have a number of additional means to pursue those who illegally remove or traffic in Native American artifacts, including 18 U.S.C. § 641 (theft of government property), 18 U.S.C. § 1361 (damaging government property), 16 U.S.C.A. § 710 (Migratory Bird Treaty Act), 18 U.S.C. § 1163 (theft from a tribal organization), and 18 U.S.C. § 2314 (interstate transportation of stolen property).[17]

Does the object originate from a foreign nation? Looting of archaeological sites is an international scourge[18] that results in significant challenges for acquiring museums.[19] This problem is truly global in scope;[20] some recently looted sites, notably in Peru and Iraq, are so extensive they can be seen from space.[21] Proving that an object of cultural property has been looted can be factually challenging because no inventory of underground archaeological objects exists. Likewise, because looting has been so widespread and ongoing over the years, there is no comprehensive inventory of looted cultural property. Nevertheless, in evaluating whether an object might be stolen or looted, museums acquiring archaeological objects should consult resources such as the United Nations Educational, Scientific and Cultural Organization (UNESCO), the International Council of Museum's (ICOM) Red List, and the U.S. State Department Cultural Heritage Center.

Determining whether an object is looted can also be legally complex because it involves the analysis of international treaties—such as the Hague Convention of 1954, the UNESCO Convention of 1970, bilateral agreements between nations—and the laws of the object's country of origin.

Many nations, unlike the United States, have laws (sometimes called "patrimony laws") asserting national ownership of all cultural property that originated within the nation's borders.[22] These nations classify cultural objects removed without permission as stolen property.[23] In addition to cultural property ownership laws, many countries also have strict export laws for cultural artifacts; in fact, some countries prophylactically ban exports of certain kinds of cultural property.[24] An object brought to the United States in violation of these laws will be considered (by country of origin) to be an illegal export and might be considered an illegal import as well.

Does the object originate from a country or region in turmoil? Was it stolen from a foreign museum? One particularly egregious example of museum theft is the pillaging of the Iraqi National Museum of Antiquities immediately after the fall of Saddam Hussein—estimated by author Roger Atwood to involve the theft of 13,000 objects.[25] Of course, not every museum theft is so well publicized, and cultural property removed from museums sometimes enters the market long after it was stolen. Cultural property stolen from museums is generally more easily identified than looted artifacts, but the ease of identification depends on the quality of the museum's record keeping, which is highly variable.

Is the object subject to seizure by the U.S. government? A number of import restrictions can result in stolen cultural property being seized by the U.S. government for return to the country of origin.[26] One of these is the Convention on Cultural Property Implementation Act (CPIA),[27] which implements the 1970 UNESCO Convention and allows the U.S. government to restrict imports of certain cultural property,[28] including objects stolen from museums.[29] Under the CPIA, the U.S. government can enter into bilateral agreements and memoranda of understanding with foreign nations to restrict the importation of identified antiquities.[30]

The CPIA was the basis for the U.S. government's claim in *United States v. Eighteenth Century Peruvian Oil on Canvas Painting*,[31] which involved two paintings from the seventeenth and eighteenth centuries, imported into the United States from South America in 2005. Both paintings, which appeared to be cut from their original frames, were provided to a gallery in Washington, DC, to sell on consignment. The gallery was suspicious of their provenance, and they were seized by the FBI. The U.S. government filed a complaint under CPIA, obtained an order of forfeiture, and returned the paintings to Peru.[32]

Another basis for a U.S. government claim against an object is the National Stolen Property Act (NSPA),[33] which makes it a crime to knowingly transport a stolen object worth more than $5,000 across state or international boundaries. The leading example is *United States v. Schultz*,[34] a federal criminal prosecution against Frederick Schultz, a prominent antiquities dealer in New York. Schultz and a British confederate, Jonathan Tokeley-Parry, conspired to smuggle artifacts from Egypt to the United States through Britain, where they were altered to appear to be part of a fictional early twentieth-century collection called the Thomas Alcock Collection. Egypt has a patrimony law under which artifacts like those trafficked by Tokeley-Parry and Schultz are considered the property of the Egyptian government.[35] Tokeley-Parry was successfully prosecuted by British authorities and Schultz by U.S. authorities.

There are other statutes under which the U.S. government has sought forfeiture in addition to, or in combination with, the NSPA and the CPIA. These include 19 U.S.C. § 1595a and 18 U.S.C. § 545, which authorize seizure and forfeiture of merchandise imported into the United States "contrary to law." In these actions, the artifact at issue is usually first seized by the U.S. government, which then files a lawsuit against the object itself (as opposed to the object's purported owner). If the government prevails, the object is forfeited, meaning that the government takes exclusive title, usually with the goal of returning it to the country of origin.[36] One example is *United States v. A 10th Century Cambodian Sandstone Sculpture*,[37] in which the U.S. government brought a civil action seeking the forfeiture of a tenth-century statue—valued at $2 million—which had been consigned for auction at Sotheby's by a private collector in Belgium. The government contended that the statue had been looted from Cambodia and unlawfully imported into the United States, and sought its forfeiture under 19 U.S.C. § 1595a, 18 U.S.C. § 545, and the NSPA.[38] The case was eventually settled, after what one newspaper called a "long bare-knuckled court battle,"[39] and the statue was returned to Cambodia.[40]

Can the country of origin make a claim? Even without the aid of the U.S. government, foreign countries can seek the return of stolen objects through the U.S. legal system. For example, in 2008, the government of Peru sued Yale University, seeking the return of many artifacts from Machu Picchu.[41] The artifacts had been at Yale for approximately a hundred years—with the permission of the government of Peru, according to Yale. Peru contended they had been loaned to Yale in the early twentieth century, and never returned. The case was eventually resolved by a settlement, which is discussed below.[42]

When faced with acquisition decisions, museums should consider these critical questions:

- What is the object's country of origin?
- Does that country have a patrimony law?
- Is the object covered by CPIA and/or a bilateral agreement with the United States?
- When did the object leave the country of origin?
- If the date of exportation cannot be determined, can the earliest date of the object's presence outside the country of origin be determined (through sales records or family pictures, for example)?
- Can the object's presence outside the country of origin prior to the enactment of the patrimony law of the country of origin otherwise be determined?

WHEN DUE DILIGENCE FAILS

Even after careful due diligence on the provenance of an object, a museum might find itself entangled in an ownership dispute. When faced with a claim that an object in its collection is stolen, museums should consider taking the following steps.

Investigate the Basis for the Claim

Museums should carefully review the claimant's documents and records, and should conduct a thorough investigation of the claim, including interviewing witnesses such as dealers and prior owners. Just as a museum should carefully investigate provenance when making decisions about a possible acquisition, the museum should also conduct a thorough investigation of any claim that an object in its collection is stolen.

Consider Applicable Legal Defenses

There are a number of legal defenses to claims that cultural property has been stolen, including the following.

The statute of limitations—The "statute of limitations" is a time limit on when a claim can be brought. Often, accusations about stolen cultural property involve objects stolen many years prior to the claim. In such cases, the statute of limitations might be an effective defense. However, statute-of-limitations defenses can be complex, depending in part on the question of when the time period of the statute of limitations began running. One example is *Grosz v. The Museum of Modern Art*.[43] George Grosz escaped Germany after the Nazi rise to power. About seventy years later, his heirs filed a lawsuit against the Museum of Modern Art, alleging that three of Grosz's works in the museum's collection had been looted by the Nazis. The museum successfully argued that the lawsuit was barred by the statute of limitations.

Laches—Under this doctrine, if an owner of a stolen work of art is not sufficiently diligent in pursuing his or her claim, the court might not allow the owner to bring a lawsuit to recover the work. The point of the doctrine is to prevent plaintiffs from sitting on their rights and to protect defendants from lawsuits brought years after the events at issue occurred. *Bakalar v. Vavra*[44] provides an example of the successful use of the doctrine of laches as a defense. The case revolved around a drawing by Egon Schiele, among many owned by Austrian art collector Fritz Grunbaum, who died in a Nazi concentration camp in 1941. What happened to the drawing during World War II is unclear, but at some point it was sold to a gallery by Grunbaum's sister-in-law. It was subsequently sold to a collector in New York in the 1960s. In 2005, a lawsuit was filed to determine whether the drawing was owned by the New York collector or Grunbaum's heirs. After years of litigation, the court found that the Grunbaum heirs' claim was barred by the doctrine of laches because the heirs either knew or should have known the basis for their claim prior to 2005.

The act-of-state doctrine—Under this doctrine, "the courts of one country will not sit in judgment on the acts of the government of another done within its own territory."[45] The act-of-state doctrine applies where an object was taken by a government, rather than an individual, and was successfully employed as a defense in *Yale v. Konowaloff*.[46] In this case, Konowaloff alleged that Vincent Van Gogh's (1853–1890) painting *The Night Cafe* had been stolen from his family by the Soviet government. The work was sold to a private collector, and eventually became part of Yale University's collection after a bequest. A federal court in Connecticut found that the act-of-state doctrine barred Konowaloff's claim on the painting because the Soviet government had seized the painting pursuant to an act of state.[47]

Intervening or prior legal decisions—A plaintiff's claim might be barred by an intervening or prior judicial decision. There are a number of different legal doctrines that might bar a lawsuit that is substantially similar to an earlier,[48] or contemporaneous, lawsuit. In an ongoing case, *Meyer v. The Board of Regents of the University of Oklahoma*,[49] the plaintiff claims ownership of a painting by Camille Pissarro (1830–1903) given to the University of Oklahoma's Fred Jones Jr. Museum of Art in 2000. The plaintiff says that the painting—*Shepherdess Bringing in Sheep*—was stolen from her family by the Nazis, and she is entitled to its return.[50] The museum contends that the lawsuit is barred by an earlier decision by a Swiss court in the 1950s holding that the plaintiff's family could not recover the painting.[51] However, these doctrines do not automatically bar a lawsuit. In *Madanes v. Madanes*,[52] a federal court addressed a family dispute over inherited artwork (among other things) that "span[ned] one decade, three continents and an array of prior lawsuits,"[53] and nevertheless allowed the suit to proceed.

Consider Filing an Action to Quiet Title

Rather than waiting for a lawsuit to be filed against it, a museum should consider the possibility of a preemptive lawsuit to resolve a work's ownership. For example, in 2013, the J. Paul Getty Museum filed a preemptive lawsuit against a person claiming to be the real owner of a diptych (a pair of paintings), dating back to the 1300s, in the Getty collection.[54] That case is ongoing.[55] Such "quiet title" or "declaratory judgment" actions might result in final resolution of competing ownership claims, but under some circumstances can be costly and time consuming.

Consider Ethical Issues

In addition to legal issues, a museum should consider the ethics of keeping works that might be stolen—which is far from a simple matter. A prominent example is the long-running dispute over the Elgin Marbles, which were removed from the Parthenon in Athens in the early nineteenth century, and purchased by the British government under an act of Parliament. They have been on display at the British Museum for about two hundred years. The government of Greece has been officially seeking their return for decades,[56] contending that the Marbles, part of Greek heritage, belong to and in Greece. Others argue the British government acquired the Marbles lawfully in a purchase for value transaction, and that in any case, the Marbles are part of world heritage, owned by "the whole world,"[57] and are appropriately displayed in the renowned British Museum.

Factual uncertainty can add to the complexity of ethical issues. The Italian government asked the Getty Museum to return works looted by Giacomo Medici, who has been convicted of trafficking in antiquities in Italy.[58] The museum returned many pieces to Italy, but the sheer scope of Medici's looting poses challenges: Should the Getty return all objects in its collection connected with Medici, regardless of whether they are matched to specific, known looting crimes?[59]

Consider Public Relations Issues

Even if there is a valid legal defense to a lawsuit, a museum might conclude it is in its best interest to return objects alleged to have been stolen or looted. Indeed, museums can sometimes find creative solutions that benefit both the museum and the party seeking the return of the work of art or artifact. One example is the settlement of the 2008 lawsuit filed by Peru against Yale University seeking the return of Incan artifacts from Machu Picchu. Through an innovative agreement, those items were sent back to Peru, where they will be studied and preserved through a collaborative effort between Yale and the Peruvian Universidad Nacional de San Antonio Abad del Cusco.[60] The two universities created a new International Center for the Study of Machu Picchu and Inca Culture to house the pieces for research and public viewing.[61]

CONCLUSION

The best way to circumvent difficulty associated with stolen cultural property that has found its way into a museum collection, is to perform rigorous due diligence. Having said that, the provenance of objects, particularly objects of antiquity, can be complex and due diligence does not always guarantee a flawless title of ownership. When a claim is made against an object in a museum collection, carefully research the basis for the claim and consider appropriate legal defenses as well as ethical and public perception–related implications before deciding on a course of action. If a museum approaches these complex issues in a thorough, ethical, professional, and transparent manner, it will hopefully avoid the expense of litigation as well as reputational harm.

NOTES

This publication is a summary of legal principles. Nothing in this chapter constitutes legal advice, which can only be obtained as a result of a personal consultation with an attorney. The information published here is believed accurate at the time of publication, but is subject to change and does not purport to be a complete statement of all relevant issues.

1. "Void" title can be contrasted with "voidable" title. Under this doctrine, a party who acquires flawed—and therefore voidable—title to property does not automatically lose title when the flaw is discovered. The acquiring party might defend title on the ground, for example, that he or she is a "good faith purchaser." Generally speaking, this defense does not apply in the case of stolen property. See Patty Gerstenblith, *Art, Cultural Heritage and the Law* (Durham, NC: Carolina Academic Press, 2004), 423–24.

2. Of course, the legal rules of title cut in both directions. When an institution is the victim of theft and its stolen objects are discovered in someone else's possession, the institution can sue for the return of its property. For example, in *Brown University v. Tharpe*, a rare Civil War presentation sword was stolen from the Annmary Brown Memorial in the 1970s. In 2010, the museum sued to recover the sword from a private collector who claimed to have purchased it in good faith. Brown University contended that the sword was stolen, and therefore the collector's title was void. The court agreed, ordering the sword to be returned. No. 4:10-cv-167, 2013 WL 2446527 (E.D. Va. June 5, 2013).

3. Fausto Martin De Sanctis, *Money Laundering through Art* (Cham, Switzerland: Springer, 2013), 3.

4. Tom Mashberg, "Assistant to Accused Antiquities Smuggler Pleads Guilty to Possessing Looted Items," *New York Times*, December 4, 2013, artsbeat.blogs.nytimes.com/2013/12/04/assistant-to-accused-antiquities-smuggler-pleads-guilty-to-possessing-looted-items/?_php= true&_type=blogs&_r=0.

5. Robin Pogrebin and Kevin Flynn, "Museums Studying Dealer's Artifacts," *New York Times*, July 27, 2012, www.nytimes.com/2012/07/28/arts/design/us-asks-museums-to-ex amine-collections.html?_r=0.

6. Tom Mashberg, "In Queens Raid, Federal Agents Seize Artifacts They Suspect Were Looted," *New York Times*, March 5, 2014, artsbeat.blogs.nytimes.com/2014/03/05/in-queens -raid-federal-agents-seize-artifacts-they-suspect-were-looted/.

7. Rachel Kleinman and Amrit Dhillon, "The National Gallery of Australia Dances into Trouble with Shiva," *Sydney Morning Herald*, March 18, 2014, www.smh.com.au/national/the-national-gallery-of-australia-dances-into-trouble-with-shiva-20140317-34xui.html; Oliver Milman, "Indian Artworks: Brandis Considers Request for Their Repatriation," *The Guardian*, April 29, 2014, www.theguardian.com/world/2014/apr/29/indian-artworks-brandis-considers-request-for-their-repatriation.

8. "Expert Labels National Gallery 'Naïve' As It Sues over Allegedly Stolen Indian Shiva Statue," *ABC News*, February 13, 2014, www.abc.net.au/news/2014-02-13/national-gallery-sues-us-art-dealer-over-stolen-indian-shiva-st/5256568. See also Quentin McDermott et al., "Dancing Shiva: Brandis Slams National Gallery of Australia over $5M Purchase of Indian Artefact," *ABC News*, March 25, 2014, www.abc.net.au/news/2014-03-24/brandis-slams-nga-over-shiva-purchase/5342116.

9. "A defendant may not purposefully remain ignorant of either the facts or the law in order to escape the consequences of the law." *United States v. Schultz*, 333 F.3d 393, 413 (2d Cir. 2003).

10. When doing so, however, a museum must exercise caution to avoid publically casting doubt on the legitimacy of an object of cultural property. The Keith Haring Foundation was recently sued by art collectors following the foundation's determination that a large number of works—estimated at $40 million—attributed to Keith Haring were counterfeit. Associated Press, "Keith Haring Foundation Sued by Art Collectors Claiming Loss of $40M after 'Counterfeit' Label," *Daily* News, February 21, 2014, www.nydailynews.com/news/national/keith-haring-foundation-sued-art-collectors-counterfeit-label-article-1.1664422. Other foundations—such as the Andy Warhol Foundation, the Pollock-Krasner Foundation, the Calder

Foundation, the Basquiat Authentication Committee, and the Dedalus Foundation—have experienced similar adverse consequences.

11. FBI, "Art Crime: A Team Approach," www.fbi.gov/news/stories/2010/february/artcrime1_020210/art-crime-a-team-approach-part-1.

12. Michael Bazyler, *Holocaust Justice: The Battle for Restitution in America's Courts* (New York: NYU Press, 2003); Robert M. Edsel, *Monuments Men: Allied Heroes, Nazi Thieves, and the Greatest Treasure Hunt in History* (New York: Center Street Books, 2010).

13. *Republic of Austria v. Altmann*, 541 U.S. 677 (2004).

14. William Grimes, "Maria Altmann, Pursuer of Family's Stolen Paintings, Dies at 94," *New York Times*, February 9, 2011, www.nytimes.com/2011/02/09/arts/design/09altmann.html?pagewanted=all&_r=0.

15. See 16 U.S.C. § 470ee.

16. See 25 U.S.C. § 3005.

17. See generally Judith Benderson, Executive Office for U.S. Attorneys, *Native American Artifacts: The Archaeological Resource Protection Act and the Native American Graves Protection Act*, www.justice.gov/usao/briefing_room/ic/artifacts.html#artifacts3.

18. Matthew Bogdanos and William Patrick, *Thieves of Baghdad* (New York: Bloomsbury, 2005), 249; Peter Brems and Wilm Van den Eynde, *Blood Antiquities*, 2009, film. www.fandor.com/films/blood_antiquities.

19. Robert K. Wittman, *Priceless: How I Went Undercover to Rescue the World's Stolen Treasures* (New York: Crown Publishers, 2010), 82–86.

20. Roger Atwood, *Stealing History: Tomb Raiders, Smugglers, and the Looting of the Ancient World* (New York: St. Martin's Griffin, 2006).

21. Dan Contreras, "Using Google Earth to Identify Site Looting in Peru: Images," Trafficking Culture, accessed May 5, 2014, traffickingculture.org/data/using-google-earth-to-identify-site-looting-in-peru-images-dan-contreras/; Margarete Van Ess et al., "Detection of Looting Activities at Archaeological Sites in Iraq Using Ikonos Imagery," AGIT Symposium 18 (2006): 669.

22. U.S. Department of State, Bureau of Educational and Cultural Affairs, "Guide to Cultural Property Import Restrictions Currently Imposed by the United States of America," February 2013, eca.state.gov/files/bureau/chart-of-import-restrictions.pdf.

23. Leah Weiss, "The Role of Museums in Sustaining the Illicit Trade in Cultural Property," 25 *Cardozo Arts & Ent. L.J.* 837, 843 (2007).

24. Robert K. Paterson, "Moving Culture: The Future of National Cultural Property Export Controls," 18:1 *Sw. J. Int'l L.* 287, 287 (2012).

25. Atwood, *supra* note 17, at 1. See also Bogdanos and Patrick, *Thieves of Baghdad*.

26. Export restrictions might also be relevant. Under regulations by the U.S. Treasury Department's Office of Foreign Assets Control (OFAC), it would be difficult to return stolen cultural property to Iran, for example. 31 C.F.R. 560.204 (2014) (Prohibited exportation, reexportation, sale or supply of goods, technology, or services to Iran).

27. 19 U.S.C. § 2601 et seq. (2013).

28. 19 U.S.C. §§ 2602–2606 (2013).

29. 19 U.S.C. § 2607 (2013) (Stolen cultural property).

30. Applicable import restrictions can be found at the State Department website: eca.state.gov/files/bureau/chart-of-import-restrictions.pdf.

31. 597 F. Supp. 2d 618 (E.D. Va. 2009).

32. FBI, "18th-Century Paintings Returned to Peru," April 8, 2010, www.fbi.gov/news/stories/2010/april/peru_040810/restoring-cultural-heritage-18th-century-paintings-returned-to-peru/.

33. 18 U.S.C. §§ 2314–2315 (2013) (Transportation of stolen goods, securities, moneys, fraudulent State tax stamps, or articles used in counterfeiting; Sale or receipt of stolen goods, securities, moneys, or fraudulent State tax stamps).

34. 333 F.3d 393 (2d Cir. 2003). See also *United States v. McClain*, 545 F.2d 988 (5th Cir. 1977).

35. Ministry of Culture: Supreme Council of Antiquities, *Law No. 117 of 1983, as Amended by Law No. 3 of 2010 Promulgating the Antiquities' Protection Law*, available at www.unesco

.org/culture/natlaws/media/pdf/egypt/egypt_law3_2010_entof.pdf, accessed May 29, 2014.

36. Jennifer Anglim Kreder, "The Choice between Civil and Criminal Remedies in Stolen Art Litigation," 28 *Vand. J. Transnat'l L.* (2005): 1199, 1222–23.

37. *United States v. A 10th Century Cambodian Sandstone Sculpture*, No. 12-2600 (S.D.N.Y.).

38. The government also sought seizure of the sculpture under 18 U.S.C. § 981(a)(1)(C) (2013) (Civil forfeiture). See also *U.S. v. Mask of Ka-Nefer-Nefer*, No. 11-504 (E.D. Mo.).

39. Tom Mashberg and Ralph Blumenthal, "Disputed Statue to Be Returned to Cambodia," *New York Times*, December 12, 2013, www.nytimes.com/2013/12/13/arts/design/disputed -statue-to-be-returned-to-cambodia.html?_r=0.

40. *Id.*

41. *Republic of Peru v. Yale University*, No. 1:08-cv-02109 (D.D.C. July 30, 2009) (transferring case to Connecticut); *Republic of Peru v. Yale University*, No. 3:09-cv-01332 (D. Conn. Oct. 9, 2009); settlement agreement, No. 3:09-cv-01332 (D. Conn. Dec. 23, 2010).

42. Diane Orson, *Finders Not Keepers*, NPR, December 18, 2011, www.npr.org/2012/01/ 01/143653050/finders-not-keepers-yale-returns-artifacts-to-peru.

43. *Grosz v. Museum of Modern Art*, 772 F. Supp. 2d 473 (S.D.N.Y.), *aff'd*, 403 F. App'x 575 (2d Cir. 2010).

44. *Bakalar v. Vavra*, 819 F. Supp. 2d 293 (S.D.N.Y. 2011) *aff'd*, 500 F. App'x 6 (2d Cir. 2012). See also *DeWeerth v. Baldinger*, 836 F.2d 103 (2d Cir. 1987).

45. *Banco Nacional de Cuba v. Sabbatino*, 376 U.S. 398, 416 (1964) (quotation omitted).

46. *Yale v. Konowaloff*, No. 3:09CV466 AWT, 2014 WL 1116965 (D. Conn. March 20, 2014).

47. "Man's Claim to Yale's Van Gogh Painting Is Tossed," *Associated Press*, March 21, 2014, www.usatoday.com/story/news/nation/2014/03/21/yale-van-gogh-painting/6709441/. See also *Konowaloff v. Metropolitan Museum of Art*, 702 F.3d 140 (2d Cir. 2012).

48. These include the doctrine of res judicata and the doctrine of collateral estoppel. *Parklane Hosiery, Co, Inc. v. Shore*, 439 U.S. 322, 326 n.5 (1979).

49. No. 13-Civ-3128 (S.D.N.Y.).

50. David Ng, "Pissarro Painting at University of Oklahoma under Dispute," *Los Angeles Times*, February 27, 2014, www.latimes.com/entertainment/arts/culture/la-et-cm-camille -pissarro-painting-university-oklahoma-20140227,0,7756111.story#ixzz2xT7JMVRB.

51. "Holocaust Survivor Fights for Nazi-Looted Painting Displayed in Oklahoma," *Associated Press*, March 1, 2014, www.nydailynews.com/news/national/holocaust-survivor-fights-nazi-looted-painting-article-1.1707354.

52. *Madanes v. Madanes*, 981 F. Supp. 241 (S.D.N.Y. 1997).

53. *Id.* at 246.

54. Emma Kleiner, "Getty Seeks to Quiet Title of the Ansouis Diptych: Back to Legal Technicalities or End of an Era?" *Center for Art Law*, April 7, 2014, itsartlaw.com/2014/04/07/ getty_quiet_title_ansouis_diptych/.

55. *J. Paul Getty Trust v. Geraud Marie de Sabran-Ponteves*, No. 13-6561 (C.D. Cal.).

56. Gerstenblith, *supra*, n. 1, at 593–94.

57. Richard Dorment, "The Elgin Marbles Will Never Return to Athens—the British Museum Is Their Rightful Home," *Telegraph*, June 30, 2009, www.telegraph.co.uk/journalists/ richard-dorment/5699534/The-Elgin-Marbles-will-never-return-to-Athens-the-British-Museum-is-their-rightful-home.html.

58. Jason Felch and Ralph Frammolino, *Chasing Aphrodite* (Boston: Houghton Mifflin, 2011); "Antiquity Dealer's Conviction Stands," *Los Angeles Times*, July 16, 2009, articles. latimes.com/2009/jul/16/entertainment/et-quick16.S2.

59. Jason Felch, "Getty Studies Its Antiquities," *Los Angeles Times*, January 19, 2013, articles.latimes.com/2013/jan/19/entertainment/la-et-getty-ambers-20130119.

60. Sarah Nutman, "Yale and University of Cusco Sign Collaboration Agreement," *Yale Daily News*, February 11, 2011, yaledailynews.com/blog/2011/02/11/yale-and-university-of-cusco-sign-collaboration-agreement/.

61. Kianti Roman, "Peru-Yale Center for the Study of Machu Picchu and Inca Culture Opens," *Yale News*, October 6, 2011, news.yale.edu/2011/10/06/peru-yale-center-study-machu-picchu-and-inca-culture-opens.

Chapter Three

Museums and Museum Curators

*Caught in the Cross-Hairs of
Authenticity Disputes*

Ronald D. Spencer and Judith Wallace

INTRODUCTION

A core function of a museum curator's job is to make scholarly assessments of the authenticity, authorship, and date of creation of works of art. Such assessments may be expressed in museum exhibits and catalogues, in scholarly publications, or in communications with owners, collectors, and art merchants. The correctness of the artwork's historical record is rightly viewed as an issue of public interest, even when the art at issue is privately owned. Recently, however, there has been increased attention to the legal risks associated with issuing opinions, which has had the unfortunate effect of causing some foundations and independent scholars to hesitate to state opinions on the record, and may lead to increased number of requests to museum curators. Therefore, this chapter outlines the circumstances in which authenticity issues arise, the legal background, and suggested best practices for museum professionals.

CIRCUMSTANCES UNDER WHICH ART
AUTHENTICATION ISSUES ARISE

Art authenticity issues generally arise for museum curators in connection with retrospective exhibitions at universities, museums, or galleries. Nevertheless, to appreciate the distinct role of museums, it is essential to understand the range of other circumstances in which art authentication issues arise, and the different commercial practices and legal issues that govern in those other contexts. These include when art scholars author catalogues raisonnés; when artist-established foundations, authentication boards, and individual experts respond to requests for authentication; when, under French law, the holder of the *droit moral*, or moral rights, asserts the right of attribution; when auction houses and other art merchants sell works of art; when appraisers determine the value of an artwork for gift or for income or estate tax purposes; and when scholars or other experts make an unsolicited public comment about a work of art.

Despite the importance of a correct historical record, some experts (including curators) are constrained in rendering scholarly opinions by worry over their legal liability to owners, sellers, and buyers. Some U.S. museums have policies prohibiting their curators from expressing opinions on objects not already owned by the museum. Scholars often decline to express an opinion when they do not (and sometimes even if they do) believe a work is authentic, or exclude the work, without comment, from an exhibition or publication, for fear of provoking a lawsuit in response to a negative opinion.

Authentication is a unique factual scenario in that experts are constrained from charging a fee that reflects their litigation risk, if their opinion is disputed or if they turn out to be incorrect. An art scholar authenticating a work may not ethically charge a fee related to the value of the art. So why would an expert, for a modest fee of say $500 to $5,000, risk a million-dollar lawsuit for product disparagement or professional negligence from a disgruntled owner? Nevertheless, many experts are concerned about the accuracy of the art historical record and wish to be protective of the legacy of an artist. Accordingly, experts should be aware of the potential avenues to reduce their risk, including observing generally accepted procedures, obtaining contractual promises not to sue, securing insurance, and asserting constitutional protections for opinions.

THE AUTHENTICATION PROCESS—BACKGROUND AND GENERALLY ACCEPTED PROCEDURES

The authenticity of a work of art is *always* a critical issue. Whether the work is "real" or "original" is a perennial question in the art world and reflects an underlying intellectual respect for what is true and real and a rejection of what is not. "Authentication" is the process by which experts—art historians, museum curators, archaeologists, art conservators, and others—attribute a work of art to a particular artist or specific culture, era, or origin.

Fakes distort our understanding of an artist's work as well as our understanding of an era or a culture, and thereby the historical record itself. One important distortion is that many fakes (as well as malicious, fraudulent, negligent, or simply mistaken attributions) often contain current era-specific characteristics. Notwithstanding the common use of the word "forgery," a fake—a work created with intent to deceive—is but one facet of authenticity issues. The larger, more important and more frequent problem is the work of unknown or wrongly attributed authorship or origin.

Three lines of inquiry are basic to determining authenticity: (1) a connoisseur's opinion, (2) historical documentation or provenance, and (3) technical or scientific testing of the physical components of the work.[1] A "connoisseur" is an expert who evaluates the "rightness" of a work based on having looked hard and carefully at many works of the artist, combined with knowing the artist's usual manner of working and materials utilized during a particular time period of the artist's career. Thus, "connoisseurship" is the sensitivity of visual perception, historical training, technical awareness, and empirical experience needed by the expert to attribute the object. To determine an object's provenance, a researcher traces the physical object from the artist, culture, or geographic location (or all three) through a chain of ownership or possession (not necessarily the same thing) to the current owner or possessor. That's a simple enough concept, assuming the documentation is not faked or inaccurate. Its goal is to assure that the object under study is the same one that left the artist's hand.

The College Art Association (CAA) has adopted standards and guidelines for authentications and attributions, updated most recently in 2009 (one of the authors of this chapter, Ronald D. Spencer, was part of the task force that submitted these guidelines).[2] Many of its recommendations are common-sense prescriptions, including detailed guidance on remaining within one's area of expertise, carefully examining the work of art, and consulting other experts as needed.

First and foremost, the CAA guidelines emphasize that curators employed by museums should consider (taking into account museum policy) whether to issue an opinion at all.

Many scholars require the object being attributed to be physically available for visual examination to the connoisseur or other expert, should the expert wish to inspect it.[3] It is also possible that a curator may be able to determine that a work is *not* authentic from an image, but might need to see the work in person to confirm that it is authentic.

Documentary research can be performed on "provenance," that is, the historical chain of title, possession, ownership, and exhibition. But the most careful analysis of this provenance documentation is not helpful in attributing an object unless the expert can be reasonably sure that the documentation being examined is for the specific object in hand. So here again we are led back to the object itself.

This point is illustrated by a 1993 litigation involving an Alexander Calder (1898–1976) mobile in which the judge did not fully comprehend the attribution process or the experts' role.[4] An object, sold as a Calder mobile, had a well-documented ownership trail over twenty years, from the artist to the current owner/seller. But, because the mobile could not be made to hang as Calder intended, the buyer became convinced (probably correctly) that a fake had been substituted for the real mobile sometime during those twenty years. The judge of the federal district court, in deciding that the piece was authentic, relied largely on the apparently faultless provenance of the piece and heavily discounted the testimony of the leading expert on Calder, Klaus Perls, that the piece was a fake.[5]

Technical or scientific testing for age, structure, material, and method of manufacture is often longer on promise than result. Dating paint or wood samples, for example, can show that the painting was made in Rembrandt's lifetime, but cannot prove that it is by Rembrandt's hand. And, at a more technical level, testing of ancient pottery to determine the date of kiln firing assumes that the sample or samples tested are representative of the entire object. Conversely, repair or restoration work that is not obvious could, if inadvertently selected for materials testing, cause an object to be inaccurately found to be inauthentic.

AUTHENTICATION—SPECIAL ISSUES FOR VARIOUS CONTEXTS

Catalogue Raisonné

A "catalogue raisonné" is a definitive listing of the works of an artist. It identifies the artist's work (or one particular aspect, such as paintings, drawings, sculpture, or prints) and provides, for each work, an image, dimensions and date of creation, when and where it was exhibited or referred to in publications, and often, *some* ownership history—particularly if it has been owned by important collectors. An expert prepares the catalogue raisonné, often with involvement of a committee or foundation, which may include scholars, dealers, or members of the artist's family.

The basic decision to be made by the author of a catalogue raisonné is whether the artist created a work. If so, it is included. If not, generally it is not mentioned, though a minority of catalogues contain sections on false attributions or works for further study.[6] Inclusion or omission is generally understood to be a statement on the work's authenticity. When a catalogue is in progress, an author will sometimes respond to requests by an applicant for inclusion with the statement that the work "will" or "will not" appear in the forthcoming catalogue, which owners and others understand to be an expression of the author's *current* intention and opinion on the work's authenticity.

A reputable catalogue raisonné will usually gain acceptance in the industry as the authoritative source of information on an artist's oeuvre, and its author is often regarded as the definitive expert on the artist. Given the investment of time and resources required to adequately research and inspect each and every work, there is typically only one catalogue raisonné for an artist's work, unless there is good reason to question the scholarship or reliability of a publication. Its author may be consulted for opinions during the years or decades that the catalogue raisonné is in progress, and in the years afterward, when there is any question about a work being offered for sale or exhibition.

Artist-Established Foundations and Authentication Boards

Since approximately the 1980s, artist-established foundations and authentication boards have also increasingly undertaken the task of defining an artist's oeuvre, either by publishing a catalogue raisonné or by responding on a case-by-case basis to owners' requests for opinions. Generally, the foundation will require the owner to provide all information known by the owner about the work's history and previous owners, will require the owner to expressly waive the right to sue the foundation, will reserve the right to revise an opinion if new information surfaces, will reserve the right not to issue an opinion if it cannot make a determination based on the information at hand, will require permission to disclose or publish its opinion, and in some cases will insist on the right to mark a work of art so that it is not resubmitted repeatedly.

Foundations almost uniformly state that they will issue an opinion, and are not issuing a warranty or guarantee, although owners and purchasers of art sometimes resist this distinction. For some artists, a positive opinion from the artist's foundation is required as a condition of sale, and is relied upon by art merchants and purchasers. However, the foundations typically charge a nominal fee, or no fee at all, and therefore cannot underwrite the risks associated with particular art sales that may be worth millions of dollars. In contrast, warranties are usually and properly issued as a matter of law, under the Uniform Commercial Code and other applicable law, by the owners and merchants selling artwork, who retain the proceeds of the sales. Indeed, the New York arts and cultural affairs law specifies that an art merchant that provides a certificate of authenticity is deemed to have made a warranty of the facts stated in that certificate.

Nevertheless, foundations have for decades been targets of lawsuits by owners, perhaps because artist-established foundations sometimes have substantial assets that make them attractive targets, even when owners voluntarily signed a written no-sue agreement. Certain legal theories seem to have a persistent appeal to owners, despite their general lack of success in litigation against experts. When foundations own artwork by the artist (as artist-established foundations often do), disgruntled owners have claimed that the foundation was motivated to falsely deny an artwork's authenticity in order to increase the value of the foundation's own holdings, and have asserted (generally, far-fetched) allegations of fraud or antitrust or racketeering conspiracies.

Foundations (including the Basquiat and Calder foundations) have also been sued when they do *not* issue an opinion, either because they do not wish to evaluate a particular type of work, or because they cannot reach a decision based on the facts at hand. Some owners have asserted that by accepting the modest application fee, the foundation entered into a binding agreement to reach a decision. Foundations may also be reluctant to issue an opinion on notoriously controversial or disputed artworks. The work may be unsalable as authentic works of the artist without the foundation's (or a particular expert's) positive opinion, but a negative decision would at least allow the owner to assert a claim for damages for product disparagement to challenge the opinion in court and put the foundation's experts on trial. In any event, courts are hesitant to determine authenticity, and the art market is certainly *not* compelled to accept a court's determination, since in civil litigation, the general standard required to support a finding of fact is that it is "more likely than not" true. As a result, a court's decision that there is a 51 percent likelihood that a work is created by a named artist is far from sufficient to make art salable as such.

Suits against experts who give opinions that are not to the owner's liking are nothing new. In the famous case of *Hahn v. Duveen*,[7] Sir Joseph Duveen looked at a photograph of a supposed Leonardo da Vinci (1452–1519) painting owned by Mrs. Andrée Hahn, and told a newspaper reporter that it was only a copy, the "real one" being in the Louvre Museum. Mrs. Hahn sued Duveen, saying that because of Duveen's disparagement, she could no longer sell the painting for its real value. After a trial, and before the jury rendered its decision, Duveen settled out of court, paying Mrs. Hahn $60,000, "forever establishing in the minds of many people that opinions are dangerous things to give."[8]

Many foundations are extremely protective of the artist's legacy. Nevertheless, in response to the risk of litigation, even with no-sue agreements, some foundations have ceased evaluating the authenticity of artwork, especially after they have published a catalogue raisonné or otherwise evaluated the artist's known oeuvre. The works that surface for the first time, years after an artist's death, are more likely to be marginal or problematic. Instead of risking frivolous lawsuits over marginal works, many foundations opt to shift their focus to other activities to promote the visual arts. This has led to the ironic phenomenon of collectors who complain that the artist-established foundations (or the scholars who worked under their auspices) are abdicating their duty, since their previous opinions are considered authoritative. This leaves a void that museum curators may be asked to fill.

Professional Appraisers

Curators should understand the distinct and more limited findings typically made by an appraiser, especially since they are may arise in connection with gifts or bequests to a museum. Generally, though the Appraisers Association of America has a process for its appraisers to qualify to value works of a particular period, a professional appraiser of the value of art is most often not an art historian. This has led to the appraiser's practice, in many cases, of expressly assuming the authenticity of work, disclaiming an opinion on authenticity, and/or relying on an expert on the artist to render an opinion on authenticity. Museum curators may be asked to provide the opinion on authenticity, to complement the appraiser's work, especially when the work is proposed for a donation to the museum.

ISSUES FOR MUSEUM CURATORS

Often curators will, in effect, authenticate work owned by the museum, and in such cases the task is generally straightforward. In addition, curators express opinions about particular artworks in scholarly publications, essays, catalogues, and lectures.

Issues arise when owners of artwork seek the opinions of museum curators and independent scholars to fill the gap left by the lack of a catalogue raisonné or authentication committee for a particular artist. First, museum staff should consider whether they are being asked to express an opinion on their own or the museum's behalf, and, if the latter, whether they are authorized to do so. More likely than not the answer will be no, and the curators in such cases sometimes opt to issue off-the-record verbal opinions. Thus, owners may turn to independent scholars, who do not have these institutional constraints.

Despite strong legal defenses, curators and scholars have little interest in litigating these issues at their own expense, and sellers, auction houses, and dealers that benefit financially from art sales have thus far been unwilling to make it a general practice to fully indemnify experts they consult against any claims. Therefore, although scholars may care passionately about the accuracy of the record regarding an artist, and their reputations as experts on particular artists, they are increasingly reluctant to opine openly and on the record if they stand to gain little, yet risk litigation from deep-pocketed owners seeking damages or a humiliating retraction of the expert's opinion. Another unfortunate side effect of the fear of litigation is the increased likelihood that some experts will speak only off the record or in coded comments to the effect that they "like" or "don't like" a painting—a situation that is rife with potential for ambiguity and misunderstanding.

Safeguarding against the Risk of Litigation as a Result of Opinions

It is hoped that outlining the options for protecting scholarly opinion set forth below will encourage museum curators and independent scholars to speak on the record.

No-Sue Agreements

Scholars and curators issuing a formal opinion letter can obtain the same waivers that foundations require—such as a no-sue agreement and recognition that the opinion is not a warranty.

It is typical for art experts to obtain a written "no-sue" agreement from an owner/applicant. These agreements have been held legally enforceable since, at least, the year 2000, when the New York Supreme Court decided *Lariviere v. Thaw*.[9] (An owner who sues the expert in breach of a no-sue agreement would be liable for damages for breach of contract. The damages would be the expert's legal fees and costs in defending the owner's claim.) Some confusion and consternation, at least among nonlawyers, arose in 2009 when a federal district court in the case of *Joe Simon v. Andy Warhol Foundation for the Visual Arts et al.* allowed a lawsuit to proceed despite a no-sue agreement. In the *Simon* case (on a motion to dismiss, which procedurally, had to assume that everything the plaintiff alleged was true), the court merely held that the Warhol Foundation's no-sue agreement signed by plaintiff Simon might not be enforceable if the (otherwise legal and enforceable) agreement had facilitated an illegal antitrust conspiracy to manipulate prices in the market for Warhol paintings (which Simon alleged, but never proved).[10] The plaintiff later withdrew all his claims.

Thus, protection for expert opinion is unquestionably available by agreement (not to sue) with an art owner/applicant. The agreement should reserve the right *not* to issue an opinion at all, to *change* the opinion if new information becomes available, and to *publish* the opinion, and should state explicitly that the museum is entitled to attorneys' fees if the agreement is breached.

Insurance

Insurance against errors in authenticity opinions has become more available recently. For museums, this would generally be as a supplemental errors and omissions policy (older policies may include such coverage already). Galleries and scholars reviewing art for a fee would be covered by a professional services policy; there are also policies tailored to foundations.

Insurance is not a *substitute* for standardized, formal procedures and contractual agreements such as those discussed above. Rather, insurers will require such measures (and more), as a condition of the insurance coverage, and may insist on vetting the authentication program and the experts involved before agreeing to coverage.

The principal benefit of insurance for authentication services is that it can provide the cost of a legal defense if the expert is sued. Damage awards are exceedingly rare. When art experts are sued, the most immediate concern is the cost of litigation, which can rapidly mount to tens or hundreds of thousands of dollars, and the fact that experts and museums will not want to incur any legal fees can be used by owners to pressure experts into silence (or ambiguous statements about the art).

But, insurance carriers will not cover museum curators who informally provide opinions to private collectors at no charge without informing or involving museum administrators. Insurance companies will require, as a condition of coverage, that museums undertake safeguards to manage risk, such as requiring formal, written agreements before issuing opinions about art.

Museums should work with their insurers to clarify any policy conditions that are open ended or vague. These may include recommendations such as "keeping written documentation of all activity," "participating in peer review," or "screening new clients carefully."[11] Clarification is critical because noncompliance with the policy conditions can be a basis for a denial of coverage for legal defense. Helpfully, some insurers will provide (or insist on) a thorough review of museum procedures before the policy is issued. This review may be particularly useful to smaller museums that do not have in-house legal departments able to devote time to these issues.

Museums may be concerned about the cost of insurance, since the College Art Association guidelines discourage experts from charging a fee for authentication. However, it is generally acknowledged that fear of litigation is deterring some experts from issuing any opinions at all. A fee that covers the cost of the insurance that makes it possible for experts to feel comfortable issuing opinions should be viewed as an acceptable, and ethical, practice. Moreover, the charging of a fee may be necessary for some insurers to regard authentication as a "professional service" that they will cover.

Proposed Statutory Reform

Proposed legislation has been introduced in 2014 to amend the New York arts and cultural affairs law to offer some protections to experts issuing opinions on art.[12]

The proposed statute would also increase the burden on plaintiffs disputing the expert's opinion, requiring them to state their allegations with "particularity" (meaning, the plaintiff will need to state specific facts, such as who said what and when), and requiring plaintiffs to prove their claims at trial by "clear and convincing" evidence rather than (as usual) a mere preponderance of the evidence (i.e., that the claim is more likely than not true). The pro-posed new law does not categorically prohibit lawsuits over authentication of art. It also probably applies only to state-law claims such as product dispar-agement. A state statute may not be able to limit claims based on federal law, such as those for antitrust violations or racketeering.

If it becomes New York law, in its current form, it may deter *some* frivolous lawsuits, because it would allow "authenticators" who prevail in court to recover attorneys' fees. Nevertheless, many museums and indepen-dent scholars cannot afford to expend funds to take a case to trial in order to recover legal fees. In addition, if the plaintiff does not have the resources to pay a substantial judgment, the right to those fees will be a hollow victory.

The law does have some exceptions that disgruntled owners could take advantage of. The proposed law only applies to individuals who are "recog-nized in the visual arts community as having expertise regarding the artist or work of fine art" at issue or "recognized in the visual arts or scientific community as having expertise in uncovering facts that serve as a direct basis . . . for an opinion as to . . . authenticity." Scholars can therefore expect to be required to defend their credentials to obtain the protections of this proposed law, and less established experts may be vulnerable.

The proposed law applies only to authenticators who do not have a finan-cial interest in the artwork in question other than to receive a fee for their authentication services. This may allow plaintiffs to persist in raising the argument that foundations or individual experts (whose opinion those owners sought) improperly seek to exclude competing works because they own other works by the same artist. The same (arguably frivolous) allegation could be made against a museum that happens to have other works by the same artist.

Finally, while there is a strong case to be made that opinions about art are in the public interest and contribute to the art market that is an important part of the state economy, it may be challenging to convince the legislature of New York (or any other states contemplating such statutes) that art scholars are uniquely entitled to protection for their opinions in a way that journalists, financial analysts, medical doctors, or other professionals are not. The exam-ple of opinions rendered by medical doctors is instructive. It is apparent that doctors rarely, if ever, render unqualified diagnostic opinions. Such opinions are usually and properly of the "it is probably or likely" variety. But as a practical matter in the art world, this kind of medical opinion is (usually) not acceptable from an expert art historian. An owner or buyer will not be satis-fied with an opinion that "it is likely a Picasso but it could be by someone else"!

First Amendment Defenses

If, despite taking reasonable cautions, a curator or museum is faced with a lawsuit, a more promising defense is the First Amendment to the U.S. Constitution, since there is a well-established body of law concerning expressions of opinion generally, which is not limited to opinions concerning art. Courts have taken a variety of approaches, which provide some protection to scholars and curators. These decisions strongly suggest there is constitutional protection available for expert opinion if the expert is able and willing to set forth the factual information on which the expert relies for his or her opinion.

Taken together, the judicial decisions on this constitutional defense suggest that there is good reason for experts to make a reasonably full recitation of the facts upon which their opinion is based, including the major facts relied upon, following the usual three lines of inquiry: provenance, application of connoisseurship to the work's visual aspects, and the work's physical properties (that is, any available forensic analysis). Since many experts do not want to provide "road maps" for would-be forgers, providing "reasons" or facts to back up their private opinions is not common practice in art scholarship involving private opinions for owners. But, as discussed below, it appears that giving some "reasons" for their opinion is the procedure that will provide experts with the strongest First Amendment defense. In that circumstance, an unhappy owner would have the difficult task of proving that the expert did not believe his or her opinion or had no factual basis at all for his or her opinion.

It is the settled rule that expressions of an opinion "false or not, libelous or not, are constitutionally protected and may not be the subject of private damage actions."[13] This principle was established by the U.S. Supreme Court in 1974 in *Gertz v. Robert Welch, Inc.*[14] and later clarified in *Milkovich v. Lorain Journal.*[15] As the Supreme Court explained in *Gertz,* if the statements are held to be expressions of opinion that *cannot* be proved true or false, they are entitled to absolute protection of the First Amendment to the U.S. Constitution because "under the First Amendment there is no such thing as a false idea. However pernicious an opinion may seem, we depend for its correction not on the conscience of judges and juries but on the competition of other ideas."[16]

Of course, the challenge is that opinions about the authenticity of art are not "pure" opinion, but are, instead, "hybrid" statements that reflect the author's deductions or evaluations, but are laden with factual content.[17] A statement by an expert about the authenticity of a painting, even if preceded by the phrase "I think," "I believe," or "in my opinion," is not "pure opinion," but is at least "hybrid" opinion, in that it implicitly suggests the existence of specific underlying facts and conveys the author's judgment upon, or interpretation of, those facts. Of course, there often is also an intimation of personal aesthetic taste with respect to the art, but there can be no question that the judgment is based, in large part, on express or implied facts that can be proven true or false (and being so provable, the stated judgment could be actionable as negligence, defamation, product disparagement, etc.). Thus, scholars and curators will need to do more than *state* that their opinions are opinions to assure themselves of a constitutional defense.

Thus, it is important to have a defense that applies even if the expert could be proved to be wrong about the art in question. The answer may come from recent lawsuits against the credit-rating agencies that faced investor claims for their ratings of bonds backed by residential real estate mortgage loans, which, as demonstrated by the recent financial crisis, turned out to be quite wrong. The rating agencies' defense was that their statements about the creditworthiness of the rated bonds were protected, as opinion about a "matter of public concern," by the First Amendment to the U.S. Constitution guaranteeing freedom of speech, and these decisions offer some lessons for scholars and curators.

One federal court of appeals took a very deferential approach to these opinions—it analyzed "the credit rating itself" as pure opinion, and held that even where a statement *was* provably false, the First Amendment protection for a statement about a matter of public concern means that a plaintiff must prove that the defendant rendered the opinion with actual knowledge of its falsity or with reckless disregard of its truth, to wit, the so-called (constitutional) "actual malice" standard—something that it is almost impossible to prove. Moreover, reckless disregard is "not measured by whether a reasonably prudent man would have published . . . or would have investigated before publishing" but by whether "the defendant in fact entertained serious doubts as to the truth of its publication."[18]

The protection afforded by the actual-malice standard for matters of public concern is difficult to overstate. If a statement is of public concern it can be unreasonable, false, or dead wrong (as the bond ratings in the years 2000–2007 were, in fact), and even negligent, but the agency rating opinion is not legally actionable. Application of this standard to opinions about the authenticity of art would virtually insulate those opinions from legal challenges.

However, not all courts have taken this deferential approach. In a 2012 decision, *Abu Dhabi Commercial Bank et al. v. Morgan Stanley & Co. Incorporated et al.,* the federal court for the Southern District of New York took up the question of whether credit ratings are opinions and, if so, what kind.[19] The *Abu Dhabi* court treated credit ratings as hybrid "fact-based opinion" because they are understood to be "statements of creditworthiness based on an analysis of underlying facts." Accordingly, these opinions were not afforded the absolute protection provided to "pure" opinions. The *Abu Dhabi* court required that a credit rating opinion be (1) supported by reasoned analysis and (2) have a factual foundation or a basis in fact in order to receive First Amendment protection as nonactionable hybrid opinion. The lesson from this case for scholars and curators is that it can be helpful to set forth a reasoned basis for an opinion, in case a court evaluates the opinion under the "hybrid statement" standard.

Scholars and curators should also be aware of the distinction between "private" and "public" opinions—because opinions that are shared with only a select group have decreased constitutional protection. When the rating agency sent its report only to a select group of investors, and did not publicly disseminate its ratings report, courts have not required plaintiffs to demonstrate actual malice by the rating agency in order to prevail.[20] Curators and scholars should take note, because a private opinion is *precisely* what most art experts render to owners and buyers. By contrast, museum catalogues, lectures, and scholarly publications disseminated to the public would presumably be a matter of public concern, and therefore constitutionally protected.

There is also case law to suggest that "hybrid" opinions can be entitled to the protection typically afforded "pure" opinions, if the statement of the opinion is accompanied by a recitation of the facts on which it is based. New York's highest court, the Court of Appeals, explained its reasoning as follows:

> A "pure opinion" is a statement of opinion which is accompanied by a recitation of the facts upon which it is based. An opinion not accompanied by such a factual recitation may, nevertheless be "pure opinion" if it does not imply that it is based upon undisclosed facts. . . . When, however, the statement of opinion implies that it is based upon facts which justify the opinion but are unknown to those reading or hearing it, it is a "mixed opinion" and is actionable.[21]

This reasoning is supported by Justice Brennan's dissenting opinion in *Milkovich*, noting that a proffered hypothesis that is offered after a full recitation of the facts on which it is based is readily understood by the audience as conjecture.

CONCLUSION

Issuing opinions on valuable artwork owned by others inevitably involves some legal risk. However, museum curators can significantly reduce that risk by being mindful of generally accepted professional standards of practice, requiring owners to execute a written no-sue agreement, and providing a reasoned statement of the facts supporting their opinions.

NOTES

1. See Ronald D. Spencer, editor, *The Expert versus the Object: Judging Fakes and False Attributions in the Visual Arts* (New York: Oxford University Press, 2004).

2. College Art Association, "Standards and Guidelines, Authentications and Attributions," adopted October 25, 2009, available at www.collegeart.org/guidelines/authentications.

3. As obvious as that may be, though, difficulties of physical access by reason of distance, expense, or other impediments to direct visual examination by the expert result in many evaluations being based only on photographs, written descriptions, and measurements.

4. *Greenberg Gallery, Inc. v. Bauman*, 817 F.Supp. 167 (D.D.C. 1993), *aff'd.*, 36 F.3d U.S. (D.C. Cir. 1994).

5. The art market did not agree with the judge and voted with its checkbook; the piece sits today in the New York City basement of the gallery/buyer, quite unsalable.

6. See Francis V. O'Connor and Eugene Victor Thaw, *Jackson Pollock: A Catalogue Raisonne of Paintings, Drawings, and Other Works* (New Haven, CT: Yale University Press, 1978).

7. *Hahn v. Duveen*, 133 Misc. 871, 234 N.Y.S. 185 (Sup. Ct. N.Y. County 1929).

8. T. E. Stebbins, "Possible Tort Liability for Opinions Given by Art Expert," in Franklin Feldman and Stephen E. Weil, eds., *Art Law: Rights and Liabilities of Curators and Collectors*, vol. 2 (Boston: Little, Brown, 1986), p. 517.

9. *Lariviere v. Thaw*, Index No. 100627/99, 2000 N.Y. Misc. LEXIS 648 (Sup. Ct. N.Y. County June 26, 2000). Ronald D. Spencer represented the Pollock-Krasner Foundation in that case.

10. *Simon-Whelan v. The Andy Warhol Foundation for the Visual Arts et al.*, No. 07 Civ. 6423, 2009 WL 1457177 (S.D.N.Y. May 26, 2009) (Swain, J.). (The authors were among the attorneys representing the foundation and authentication board in this case.)

11. See, for example, Michael Fahlund, *Professional Liability Insurance for Art Authenticators*, CAA News, March 8, 2012, at www.collegeart.org/news/2012/03/08/professional -liability-insurance-for-art-authenticators/.

12. New York Senate Bill S06794, introduced March 11, 2014.

13. *Steinhilber v. Alphonse*, 68 N.Y.2d 283, 286 (1986); see also *Immuno AG v. Moor-Jankowski*, 77 N.Y.2d 235 (1991) (applying *Milkovich* to determine whether a statement is actionable based on it being capable of objective verification).

14. *Gertz v. Robert Welch, Inc.*, 418 U.S. 323 (1974).

15. *Milkovich v. Lorain Journal*, 497 U.S. 1 (1990). The constitutional doctrine referred to in *Milkovich* protects statements that cannot be proved false (which we might call "pure opinion") and statements that cannot be reasonably interpreted as stating actual facts, including name-calling, hyperbole, figurative language, and imaginative expression. *Milkovich* goes on to address how statements that can be proved false are protected by the actual-malice requirement.

16. *Gertz v. Robert Welch, Inc.*, 418 U.S. 323 (1974).

17. *Ollman v. Evans and Novak*, 750 F. 2d 970, 1021–1022 (D.C. Cir. 1984).

18. *St. Amant v. Thompson*, 390 U.S. 727, 731 (1968).

19. *Abu Dhabi Commercial Bank et al. v. Morgan Stanley & Co. Incorporated et al.*, No. 08 Civ. 7508, 2012 WL 3584278 at 1 (S.D.N.Y. Aug. 17, 2012).

20. *Abu Dhabi Commercial Bank et al. v. Morgan Stanley & Co. Incorporated et al.*, 651 F. Supp.2d 155 (S.D.N.Y. 2009).

21. *Steinhilber*, 68 N.Y.2d at 289.

Chapter Four

Nazi-Looted Art

Risks and Best Practices for Museums

Nicholas M. O'Donnell

The issue of artwork seized, stolen, or purchased under duress under Nazi auspices has affected U.S. museums as much as any other constituency. Related litigation in the last two decades has increased in U.S. courts, with cases that fell into two primary categories: those by private claimants asserting title to expropriated artwork against private individuals or museum defendants; and claims by private citizens against sovereign states or museums. In practice, both categories have met with courts receptive to jurisdiction over them, but hesitant to grant the ultimate outcome that they seek. Overlapping questions of museum governance and ethics have raised as many problems as they have solved.

The implications for museums are many. Existing collections should be scrutinized from a perspective that was unknown a generation ago, and any new acquisition must be scrutinized for possible connections to Nazi looting. Moreover, the history of recent litigation can provide some practical guidance for museums faced with a claim. This chapter will review the history of the issue, the course of litigation in the United States, and lessons that museums can learn in implementing best practices.

THE NAZIS AND ART

To understand the basis of these claims, a brief historical overview is essential. It is easy enough to understand that a stolen painting might be the subject of a claim, but the particulars of the Nazi regime and occupation complicate the subject. The Nazis assumed full control of the German government in

1933, after Hitler's appointment as chancellor and the Enabling Act. Overt encouragement of discrimination against Jewish people began right away. Then, successive laws (in particular the notorious Nuremberg Race Laws of 1935) restricted or abolished altogether the rights of Jews with regard to property. In 1937, Germany outlawed "degenerate art," which consisted of Modernist or Expressionist art that the Nazis deemed insufficiently German. Cynically, the art was not necessarily targeted for destruction. Instead, it was defined as contraband, and its purchase and sale created a monopoly in the hands of a small number of dealers, Karl Haberstock and Hildebrand Gurlitt in particular. This "degenerate art" was seized both from private owners (Jews and non-Jews), and from German state museums. It was sold internationally, through dealers like Curt Valentin in New York or the infamous Galerie Fischer auction in Lucerne that took place in 1938.

When Germany occupied the Sudetenland and annexed Austria in 1938, Jews in those countries were required to inventory and report their property, which served only to identify it as a target for enterprising party officials. By the late 1930s, Jews could not leave Germany or occupied territories with any of their property, which they often sold in advance of their departure. Worse yet, they were typically not allowed to keep the proceeds of those sales. Following the occupations of France and the Netherlands in particular, German agents and dealers fanned out to "buy" many of the great works of Western art for Nazi dignitaries or for the planned Führermuseum, slated to open in the city of Linz under the direction of Adolf Hitler.

When the war ended, an enormous quantity of art was not where it had been when the war began. Some artwork had been destroyed, some taken back east by the Soviet Union, and a great deal was in the Central Collecting Points set up by the Allies in Munich and Wiesbaden to facilitate the return of what the Nazis had plundered. This mission was extraordinarily successful, but not entirely. First and foremost, entire families had been murdered or fled Europe. And the restitution efforts were far from perfect. The Monuments, Fine Art and Archives (MFAA) organization returned most of Hildebrand Gurlitt's collection to him, for example, and accepted at face value his claim that the rest had been destroyed in Dresden, a commonly proffered explanation.

The MFAA work was the beginning of an important concept that carries through to present day: the idea that anything sold by Jews or other persecuted groups between 1933 and 1945 in Germany, or during any other period of German occupation, was presumptively done under duress. That is to say, an assumption that a Jewish collector in 1935 in Frankfurt, or 1939 in Vienna, or 1942 in Paris, could not have made an arm's-length bargain because the threat of seizure or worse hung over the entire transaction. Any sale under duress is no sale at all, and a legal presumption was born.

After the war ended, claimants made some effort to find their property, with varying degrees of success. Germany, of course, was divided and occupied, so anything related to the eastern zone was a lost cause by the late 1940s. Austria passed a restitution law, but forbade the export of any restituted artwork. Many collectors and owners sold their paintings at once-again artificially depressed prices. Much of the artwork was no longer in the occupiers' hands, as it had moved into the marketplace. Then, as now, most civil law countries in Europe recognized the good faith purchaser's title as superior to the person from whom the art had been stolen (the opposite of the law in the United States), and there are examples of litigation in Switzerland, for example, in which the Swiss court recognized that the painting had been stolen, but found that the possessor had purchased it in good faith. The University of Oklahoma recently cited such a decision in successfully moving to dismiss claims to the painting *La Bergere*, by Camille Pissarro (1830–1903), filing a copy of a Swiss decision that acknowledged the wartime history of the painting, but held that a Swiss man had acquired it in good faith, and good title accompanied it. As the Cold War settled in, and the trail grew colder, the issue simply faded from prominence, and provenance that overlapped with German or occupied territories was not widely regarded as problematic.

After five decades of inactivity, however, several developments in the 1990s fostered the rise of World War II restitution litigation. The first and most important of these milestones was the fall of the Soviet Union, which recast the alignment of all the countries involved. This was followed by the historiography of the 1990s. Beyond art specifically, long-accepted truisms about, for example, the distinctions between the Schutzstaffel (SS) and the Wehrmacht, or of the infiltration of the civil service were also challenged.[1] Combined with new post-Soviet information resources, the recognition that citizens of Eastern European countries may not have had a forum to pursue their claims until the fall of the Iron Curtain—and the creation of the Internet—and a new perspective on art restitution was inevitable.

The course of events raised the stakes still further. *Portrait of Wally*, by Egon Schiele (1890–1918), was loaned to the Museum of Modern Art but was seized by customs officials in 1998 on the theory that it was stolen property when it was imported into the United States—that is, that it had been wrongfully taken from Lea Bondi Jaray's predecessors. This was not a private lawsuit, but a civil forfeiture action brought by the U.S. government against the object itself, on suspicion of its having been already stolen at the time it was imported in violation of U.S. customs laws. The painting sat in a warehouse until a 2010 settlement on the eve of a trial over the competing claims to it. But at the time of its initial seizure, the painting galvanized the issue in the public consciousness in a new way, exposing in a very real sense that something had changed.

Later in 1998, the United States hosted the Washington Conference on Holocaust Era Assets to address the topic in a comprehensive manner among a wide array of stakeholders. That resulted in the now-famous Washington Principles on Nazi-Confiscated Art, which urged the identification of Nazi-stolen art, and the commitment of resources to researching and restituting them. The oft-cited principles are not a treaty, however, and they are not the law of the participating countries (including and in particular the United States). But they certainly established an aspirational standard, and the museum community soon followed.

In 1998, the Association of Art Museum Directors (AAMD) also published the *Report of the AAMD Task Force on the Spoliation of Art during the Nazi/World War II Era (1933–1945)*. The AAMD guidelines urged member museums to research their existing collections, and consider further acquisitions and gifts carefully under higher standards of provenance. They advised making collections records freely available, and if "after working with the claimant to determine the provenance, a member museum should determine that a work of art in its collection was illegally confiscated during the Nazi/World War II era and not restituted, the museum should offer to resolve the matter in an equitable, appropriate, and mutually agreeable manner."

The Washington Conference was a watershed event, and the principles still cast a long shadow over international relations, as claimants and nations question other countries' adherence to them.

PUBLIC AND PRIVATE DISPUTES

With the table set, litigation was inevitable, typically premised on the idea that art had either been stolen outright, or sold under duress. The most obvious obstacle to these claims, however—increased public awareness or not—was the passage of time. Most state property laws have three-year statutes of limitations for unlawful possession or theft. Other than New York, most states apply those statutes of limitations starting when a claimant knew, or reasonably could have known, of the existence of the claim. So, for example, if a claimant knew where the painting was shortly after the war, and lost track of its whereabouts, the claim might now be too late. By contrast, if a reasonable person searching diligently under the circumstances could not have known where it was and who had it, the claim could be considered timely.

New York is an exception that is important, both because the New York art market dwarfs all others in the United States, but also because of its conceptual differences. In New York, the statute of limitations does not begin until the true owner demands the return of his or her property from the possessor. So, using the same examples, whether or not the claimant lost track of the painting, or could have learned its whereabouts, if he or she did not demand the return until less than three years before bringing the claim, it would be timely. In other circumstances, a court may apply what is called "equitable tolling," meaning simply a delay in the application of the statute of limitations for reasons of fairness when a claimant has been prevented from knowing that he or she has a claim (like displaced or murdered family, or the Soviet Army). The application of that doctrine is purely discretionary, however, and the claimant has no specific right to it.

Some prominent examples, which are by no means exhaustive, are illustrative. After receiving notice of a claim to the painting, *Two Nudes* (1919) by Oskar Kokoschka (1886–1919), the Museum of Fine Arts, Boston sought a declaratory judgment claim in 2008 seeking quiet title to the painting. Dr. Claudia Seger-Thomschitz, the sole surviving heir of Oskar Reichel, a Viennese doctor and collector, argued that Reichel had sold the painting to a man named Otto Kallir in Paris, in 1939, under duress, consistent with the presumption in the Washington Principles that a sale by an Austrian Jew at that time could not have been at arm's length.

Unfortunately for Seger-Thomschitz, she brought the claim more than three years after her lawyer made a demand on the museum. Even "tolling" the statute of limitations to the date of her letter, the court ruled and the appeals court affirmed that she had waited too long.[2] It should be said, that the MFA has publicly defended its strategy, arguing that its own research showed that the sale had, in fact, been a voluntary one. Despite some criticism, it bears repeating that although the AAMD guidelines urge restitution when a claim is considered valid by a museum, that of course presupposes that validity. The MFA has been quite clear that it viewed the claim otherwise, and defended itself accordingly.

Claims by the heirs of George Grosz (1893–1959) failed on similar grounds to obtain the return of three disputed works from the Museum of Modern Art—the portraits *Poet Max Herrmann-Neisse* (1927) and *Self-Portrait with Model* (1928), and the watercolor painting *Republican Automatons* (1920).[3] In 2012, the Second Circuit Court of Appeals affirmed the judgment against David Bakalar concerning ownership of an Egon Schiele drawing, *Seated Woman with Bent Left Leg (Torso)*.[4] Bakalar is the current owner of the drawing, having purchased it in good faith in 1964. Fritz Grünbaum—who later died in Dachau—owned the 1917 work prior to the start of World War II. The question was the legitimacy of the various wartime and postwartime conveyances, the gaps in provenance, and whether a power of attorney signed in Dachau was any good.

Even though the court found the current owner could not prove good title (title that he argued he acquired when an intermediary owner bought the painting in good faith without any awareness of its wartime provenance), it also found that the delay by Bakalar and his predecessors after they had reason to believe they had a claim, prohibited them from seeking its return, a defense approach known as "laches." This case was also notable because it was one of the few to rule, as a matter of fact, on whether the painting had been stolen (it ruled that it was not).

ALTMANN AND THE FOREIGN SOVEREIGN IMMUNITIES ACT (FSIA)

Litigation in the United States has not been confined to art that ended up in private institutions. Art owned by European countries or state museums, claimed by survivors or heirs who settled in the United States, has also played a prominent role.

In 2001, Maria Altmann filed suit in Los Angeles against the Republic of Austria for the return of several Gustav Klimt (1862–1890) paintings that had belonged to her uncle. The legal question was whether the request by Adele Bloch Bauer (the subject of two of the paintings) before she died that the paintings be given to the Republic of Austria was binding on Altmann's uncle (Adele's husband), or whether Bauer's conveyance of the paintings by will to Altmann controlled. The problem for Altmann was that to sue in Austria, a prohibitively high filing bond was necessary, calculated as a percentage of the value of the claims (for art worth hundreds of millions of dollars). In bringing suit in the U.S. federal courts, Altmann argued that the Foreign Sovereign Immunities Act of 1976, 28 U.S.C. § 1602 et seq. (FSIA) gave the U.S. federal courts jurisdiction over her claims against Austria, the state sponsor of the Leopold Museum where the painting is hung (and whose director had acquired it when it could not be exported from Austria postwar). Sovereign immunity means that the sovereign, or later the state, cannot be sued without the sovereign's consent. Hundreds of individual laws in the United States, including the FSIA, determine when state or federal governments can be sued.

To satisfy the requirements of the FSIA, Altmann made what was a novel argument at the time: that because her uncle's paintings were taken in violation of international law (the "expropriation exception"), and that because Austria was engaged in commercial activity in the United States, the claim satisfied one of the exceptions to sovereign immunity under the FSIA and should be applied retroactively to wartime claims. In 2004, the Supreme Court of the United States agreed, also held that the 1976 statute should be applied retroactively to Altmann's claims, and sent the case back to Los Angeles for litigation.[5] The parties agreed to arbitrate in Austria, where Altmann won and the paintings were delivered to her.

The case was a revelation in that it seemed to offer the FSIA as a path to claimants unhappy with the adjudication processes available to them in Europe. Not surprisingly then, the heirs of Kasimir Malewicz sued the City of Amsterdam in 2005, similarly invoking the FSIA and the expropriation exception. In that case, however, the only commercial activity by Amsterdam (necessary to satisfy the FSIA as *Altmann* had) was the loan of the disputed painting itself by the Stedelijk Museum (a second-level instrumentality of the Dutch state via the City of Amsterdam). The court agreed, and the case was allowed to proceed even though the painting itself could never be ordered returned.[6] Yet that loan was protected by the Immunity from Seizure Act. The Immunity from Seizure Act (IFSA), 22 U.S.C. § 2459 (1965) creates a program under which exhibition organizers or any other recipient of a loaned object from abroad can apply to the federal government for a prospective declaration that the culturally significant object is immune from seizure. Any loaned objects given an IFSA grant of immunity may not be seized while in the United States to enforce an unrelated judgment. Largely as a result of the *Portrait of Wally* affair, museums had come to apply for IFSA immunity for international loans as a matter of course. So including the FSIA case set up the strange circumstance in which the plaintiffs, even if successful, could never have won the return of the painting. The *Malewicz* case settled, but it proved a harbinger of the complications of FSIA litigation.

CASSIRER AND VON SAHER

Not surprisingly, these cases have raised the question of whether the issue can be resolved legislatively. California led the way, and two cases have repeatedly tested the limits of state power in the federal system, in particular the proper role of U.S. foreign policy. Jacques Goudstikker was a well-known Dutch art dealer during the interwar period, who purchased two paintings by Lucas Cranach the Elder, *Adam* and *Eve* in 1931. Goudstikker fled the Netherlands in 1940, and a major part of his collection was appropriated by Hermann Göring himself, including the two works by artist Lucas Cranach der Ältere (c. 1472–1553). The U.S. Army recovered the Cranachs after the war, and they were returned to the Dutch government. Ultimately the paintings were sold and ended up in the Norton Simon Museum in Pasadena, California.

The second case, *Cassirer v. Kingdom of Spain*, was brought by plaintiffs who are the great-grandchildren of Lilly Cassirer, whose citizenship and property rights were stripped pursuant to the notorious 1935 Nuremberg Laws. Faced with a coercive offer to "buy" the painting, she relented and left Germany. The painting was sold by that buyer to an anonymous purchaser in 1943. After the war, Lilly obtained some compensation from the German courts. The painting was purchased in 1976 by Baron Hans Heinrich Thyssen-Bornemisza, who later sold it to the collection bearing his name, which is in fact an agency of the Kingdom of Spain. Claude Cassirer (Lilly's grand-son) discovered the whereabouts of the painting in 2000, and filed suit against the Collection and the Kingdom of Spain in U.S. district court in 2005 by invoking the Foreign Sovereign Immunities Act.

As part of the growing publicity over wartime art claims, California en-acted Section 354.3 of its Code of Civil Procedure, which effectively abol-ished the statute of limitations for any claim to return Holocaust-era artwork. So, in 2007, relying on the amended statute, Saher sued the Norton Simon Museum in U.S. district court in California to return the Cranachs asserting claims that might otherwise be time barred but for the California law. The district court dismissed the case on preemption grounds, concluding that the law abolishing the statute of limitations for wartime artwork claims "intrudes on the federal government's exclusive power to make and resolve war, in-cluding the procedure for resolving war claims."[7] On appeal in 2010, the court of appeals ruled slightly differently, upholding the dismissal of those claims that would have survived under the extended statute of limitations, but holding instead that "the power to legislate restitution and reparation claims is one that has been exclusively reserved to the national government by the Constitution."[8] The question went back to the trial court to see if Von Saher could prove the revived statute of limitations should be tolled.[9]

In response to *Von Saher I*, California amended § 338(c). In lieu of the old, universally applicable three-year statute of limitations and an exception for Holocaust claims, the State of California enacted a six-year statute of limitations, triggered only by the "actual discovery" of the whereabouts of a work of fine art, applicable to all claims then pending or filed before 2017, so long as the artwork had been taken in the one hundred years prior.

The *Cassirer* defendants' initial motion to dismiss under the FSIA had earlier been denied (citing *Altmann*, and making the important point that to rely on the FSIA all that was required was that the defendant was a sovereign entity, not that it had necessarily committed the taking in violation of interna-tional law—since Germany had done that, not Spain). After *Von Saher I*, however, the *Cassirer* defendants again moved to dismiss, arguing that § 338(c) was still an impermissible intrusion on foreign affairs. After Von Saher's claim was dismissed in early 2012 for that very reason (*Von Saher II*), the Thyssen-Bornemisza Collection cited that decision as a basis to dis-miss the *Cassirer* claims, and the district court agreed.[10] The 9th Circuit reversed the district court in December 2013, however, and sent the Cassir-ers' claim back for litigation. Reviewing the standards of "field preemption," or when "a state law has no serious claim to be addressing a traditional state responsibility and (2) intrudes on the federal government's foreign affairs power," the appeals court held that the revised statute did not create an independent remedy for wartime injuries of the sort that would intrude on the federal government's authority in that area, nor was it "functionally equivalent" to the § 354.3 that was struck down in *Von Saher I*.

First, the court noted that the extension of limitations for artworks was unrelated to wartime claims on its face. It applies equally to artworks taken under far more mundane circumstances. Indeed, the law is silent on matters of foreign affairs. Critically (see more below), the court rejected the idea that allowing the claim to proceed was necessarily an adjudication of the fairness of what Lilly had been paid by Germany, citing the important decision concerning the Hans Sachs painting collection. In that case, the high German commercial court (Bundesgerichtshof) restituted a collection to the heirs of Hans Sachs from the Deutsches Historisches Museum, notwithstanding the compensation paid to Sachs after the war. Had the newer California statute provided a method to attack those German payments collaterally, it might well have intruded on the foreign affairs function, but this law does not, said the court. Second, the court gave short shrift to the argument that the six-year limitations law was functionally equivalent to the one already struck down. The latter addressed Holocaust claims specifically, while the former is silent, as noted above.

Although argued on the same day as *Cassirer*, the next *Von Saher* decision did not come out until many months later. On June 6, 2014, the 9th Circuit reversed the district court and sent the case back to the trial court for litigation and to determine if the claims were nonetheless barred under the "act-of-state doctrine."[11] Notably, the 9th Circuit posed the question like this: Do Von Saher's claims conflict with the foreign policy of the United States with regard to restitution? In answering that question "no," the 9th Circuit shifted its analysis from its earlier decisions in the same case about whether the revised statute of limitations was itself a restitution mechanism (also answered in the negative by *Cassirer*), but whether claims either revived by the California law generally, or Von Saher's case specifically, conflict with the actual current foreign policy of the United States. That is a significant difference, because it required the court to reach a conclusion as to what the nation's foreign policy is. Here, for the first time in the holding of a U.S. decision, the 9th Circuit invoked the Washington Conference Principles on Nazi Stolen Art. The court summarized the policies evident in the Washington Principles as they relate to foreign policy as follows:

> (1) a commitment to respect the finality of "appropriate actions" taken by foreign nations to facilitate the internal restitution of plundered art; (2) a pledge to identify Nazi-looted art that has not been restituted and to publicize those artworks in order to facilitate the identification of prewar owners and their heirs; (3) the encouragement of prewar owners and their heirs to come forward and claim art that has not been restituted; (4) concerted efforts to achieve expeditious, just and fair outcomes when heirs claim ownership to looted art; (5) the encouragement of everyone, including public and private

institutions, to follow the Washington Principles; and (6) a recommendation
that every effort be made to remedy the consequences of forced sales.

Viewed in this light, the court found Von Saher's claims consistent with that
policy, and thus not preempted by it. Indeed, the court identified Von Saher's
claims as just those that the Washington Principles were intended to advance,
or at least permit to have their day in court. The court noted the hostility that
Goudstikker's widow *could* have faced had she filed a claim earlier in Holland, a significant recognition.

In its instructions on remand to the district court, the 9th Circuit identified
one theory that might yet defeat the claims, however: the act-of-state doctrine. This legal doctrine holds that notwithstanding a U.S. court's jurisdiction to hear claims, it should avoid as a matter of prudence any case that
concerns the act of a sovereign nation against one of its subjects. In the
restitution context, *Yale University v. Konowaloff* is the clearest application
of this. Yale sued preemptively to confirm its title to the iconic painting by
Vincent Van Gogh, *The Night Café*, from claims by Konowaloff. Earlier in
2014, the District of Connecticut awarded summary judgment to Yale, arguing that whatever the lawlessness of Soviet declarations of the abolition of
private property, the harm suffered by Konowaloff's predecessor was unquestionably the result of an official Soviet act against a Soviet citizen, and
thus beyond the review of the U.S. courts.

In the 2014 *Von Saher* opinion, the court posited that the act of returning
the paintings to Stroganoff-Scherbatoff might itself constitute an act of state
beyond review. In effect, the argument would go, even if returning the Cranachs to Stroganoff-Scherbatoff deprived Goudstikker's widow of what was
otherwise her property, that deprivation was an act by the Dutch government
to the detriment of a Dutch citizen, and thus beyond review.

One of the more interesting aspects of the *Altmann* case is that in hindsight, had Austria litigated in the United States, it may well have won. Here it
is important to remember what the Supreme Court did, and didn't, do. It did
send Altmann back to the trial court with the right to press her claim. It did
not rule that she was correct, or that Austria's defenses failed. Given the
recent invocation of the act-of-state doctrine in 2014 in *Von Saher*, could
Austria have prevailed in that argument (that the Austrian government took
property from an Austrian citizen, in Austria)? Distinctions could be made,
but the result could have been complicated.

NEW THEORIES, SAME RESULTS?

If *Altmann*, *Cassirer*, and *Von Saher* teach anything, it is the importance of
evolving legal theory. The District of Columbia Circuit Court of Appeals
reinstated in April 2013 the entire set of claims brought by the Herzog heirs

against the Hungarian National Gallery, the (Hungarian) Museum of Fine Arts, the Museum of Applied Arts, and the Budapest University of Technology and Economics. The appellate decision focuses on the claim that a bailment agreement was reached *after* WWII to hold the paintings for their owners, not the claims relating to their wartime fate.[12] In so doing, the court pushed to the side the whole range of defenses for sovereign defendants addressed above that have been increasingly successful.

David de Csepel, Angela Maria Herzog, and Julia Alice Herzog filed their case in 2010, citing the expropriation exception or, in the alternative, the "commercial exception"—the allegation that the defendants used the very property at issue in commercial activity that had an effect in the United States. In so doing, such a defendant is a commercial actor, and cannot invoke immunity for acts that are not uniquely sovereign in nature. The plaintiffs are the heirs of Baron Mór Lipót Herzog, a Jewish Hungarian collector who died in 1934, and whose collection was seized in German-occupied Hungary in 1944. After the war, say the plaintiffs, the Herzogs (who had fled the country) engaged in a series of correspondence about the collection. It is from the correspondence, the plaintiffs alleged, that what is known as a bailment resulted. "Bailment" is simply the act of entrusting an object to another; a coat or car check are the most common examples. Under a bailment, there is no ownership transfer, and the bailee (the person getting the property) is obliged to safeguard it and give it back upon demand.

In 2011 the Hungarian defendants moved to dismiss the complaint. The district court in Washington, DC, held it had jurisdiction under the expropriation exception. The appellate court took a slightly different approach and found that it was in fact the commercial exception that applied: "In their complaint, however, the Herzog family seeks to recover not for the original expropriation of the Collection, but rather for the subsequent breaches of bailment agreements they say they entered into with Hungary."[13]

In ruling that plaintiffs seek to recover against a commercial actor who breached a bailment contract, the DC circuit took away the defendants' arguments about acts of state and foreign affairs, arguments that have been increasingly successful in FSIA restitution cases. The plaintiffs will now have to prove, of course, that such an agreement existed, and they will no longer enjoy the presumptions that attach to defending their complaint.

PRACTICAL IMPLICATIONS FOR MUSEUMS

The importance of the foregoing for museums could scarcely be higher. Every case will be different, but some trends emerge of which to be mindful whether investigating or defending a claim.

There is no question that knowledge is the most important component of best practices. At the outset, and for many other reasons as well, collections management policies must be current and must address this subject specifically. Too many museums rely on institutional practice, and good governance is always a sign to claimants and the public alike that the topic is taken seriously. That alone can go a long way toward defusing some of the twists and turns described here. Although the AAMD guidelines directed its members long ago to review their existing collections, that is a minority of museums nationwide as a matter of compulsion. It need not take a significant investment of resources to review provenance. Here, the MFAA presumption is the guiding point. Did anything in the collection change hands in an occupied area between 1933 and 1945, or was everything in the United States before then? If not the first, or if the latter, there are unlikely to be any concerns. If there are exchanges or periods of ownership of concern, then existing databases like the Art Loss Register can be consulted.

Next, an understanding of these issues and of possible claims informs diligence. Here the marketplace has come a long way. No longer will "private collection, Switzerland, 1941–1949" suffice. If there are suspect periods or gaps, the object is simply not worth acquiring without complete provenance information.

If and when a dispute arises, the ups and downs of litigation prove nothing if not that there are few winners when it comes to museums and restitution lawsuits. As noted above, most museums have prevailed in the absolute sense, but often at great cost. Resolution by agreement may be impossible, but all parties involved will do well to consider the ultimate goals of the other. Claimants may simply want the artwork, but they may also (or more importantly) want recognition of the circumstances that their family suffered. Museums will be wary of their obligations to safeguard their collections, but with the right balance, the best resolution is usually a quick one.

NOTES

1. See, for example, Ian Kershaw, *Stalinism and Nazism: Dictatorships in Comparison* (Cambridge, UK: Cambridge University Press, first published 1997).

2. See *Museum of Fine Arts, Boston v. Seger-Thomschitz*, 623 F. 3d 1 (1st Cir. 2010).

3. See *Grosz v. Museum of Modern Art*, 403 Fed. App'x 575 (2010).

4. See *Bakalar v. Vavra*, 500 Fed. App'x 6 (2d Cir. 2012).

5. *Republic of Austria v. Altmann*, 541 U.S. 677, 677 (2004).

6. *Malewicz v. City of Amsterdam*, 362 F. Supp. 2d 298 (D.D.C. 2005).

7. *Von Saher v. Norton Simon Museum of Art*, 592 F.3d 954, 960 (2010) ("Von Saher I").

8. *Id.* at 967.

9. *Id.* at 970.

10. *Cassirer v. Thyssen-Bornemisza Collection Found., an Agency or Instrumentality of the Kingdom of Spain*, Case No. 2:05-cv-03459-GAF-E, (C.D. Cal. May 24, 2012), ECF No. 159; *Von Saher*, 862 F. Supp. 2d at 1052–53.

11. *Von Saher v. Norton Simon Museum of Art at Pasadena*, F.3d, 2014 WL 2535473, at *1(9th Cir. 2014).
12. *De Csepel v. Republic of Hungary*, 714 F.3d 591 (D.C. Cir. 2013).
13. *De Csepel*, 714 F.3d at 598.

Chapter Five

A Brief Guide to Provenance Research

Sharon Flescher

INTRODUCTION

Once the province of art historians and others dealing primarily with issues of attribution and authenticity, and still important in that respect, provenance research is now—or should be—also an essential step in a due diligence process before acquiring or exhibiting a work of art for anyone, and certainly any museum, concerned about adhering to the legal and ethical standards expected of art professionals.

Ownership claims by heirs of Holocaust victims whose artworks were looted or otherwise misappropriated by the Nazis, as well as claims by "source" countries for objects they believe were looted or otherwise taken from their countries in violation of cultural heritage laws, have raised awareness of the need to verify that objects entering collections have no taints in their ownership history. Of particular concern are works that reveal provenance gaps in the crucial years of Nazi occupation, 1933–1945.

If anything has brought home the importance and difficulty of provenance research, it is the recent discovery of a trove of more than 1,200 artworks in Munich and Salzburg secreted by the late Cornelius Gurlitt, the elderly and reclusive son of a German curator and art dealer, Hildebrand Gurlitt, who worked closely with the Nazis to market so-called "degenerate" art confiscated by the German government from its museums in the 1930s. Amongst the collection were works suspected of having been looted from Jewish owners during the Nazi era, as well as works legitimately owned (painted by Gurlitt's relatives, for example, or indisputably acquired prior to 1933), and also numerous works classified as "degenerate." A German government website posted a fluid list of works—initially 458—with questionable provenances, while an international team of provenance researchers was assembled to determine which works were looted and which not. Under German law, "degenerate" works confiscated from German museums are not considered "looted," but a "degenerate" work that had been misappropriated from a Jewish person and sent to a museum from which it was later confiscated, would be (or should). Hildebrand Gurlitt acquired many works through trades, and some apparently from the artists themselves. Documentation is scarce. The provenance team was given one year to complete the task, but it was/is an enormous assignment, and after six months, only two works out of an estimated dozens have been officially determined to have been looted and cleared for return to their rightful owners. [1]

It is important to note at the outset that

- Provenance research is often painstaking, time consuming, and difficult—as the Gurlitt situation indicates.
- Not every work has a fully discoverable provenance leading back to the artist. In fact, a complete provenance is the exception rather than the norm.
- Attributions and titles of artworks—even dimensions—may change over the years, complicating the research and identification process.
- Documentation or other evidence may conflict, requiring days and months of research to sort out.
- Previously published provenances may be incorrect, unclear, or incomplete and should be independently verified. The incorrect information may have been repeated elsewhere, compounding the initial error.
- Owners' names may be missing from a provenance, with dealers and other intermediaries named instead, or the more generic designation, "private collection."
- Ownership documents and proofs of sale may no longer exist; this is often the case for works of lower value, or works that have only recently appreciated in value.
- Provenance information and related documentation may be intentionally faked and like all documentation, need to be verified (see below). This is especially true with regard to authenticity, but also art theft.
- It is important to become familiar with "red flags," particularly in regard to the Nazi era, as the presence of a so-called "red-flagged" name in the provenance may indicate that an artwork was stolen, part of a forced sale, or otherwise misappropriated. [2]
- Not every gap in provenance indicates that a work was stolen or misappropriated. But gaps during the Nazi period do indicate that additional research should be undertaken.

There *is* some good news for provenance researchers. Digitization is rapidly altering the research environment. Over the last few years, many previously classified or inaccessible archives—particularly those relating to Nazi confiscations and postwar art recoveries and transfers—have been declassified and opened to researchers, if not the general public. Many have also been digitized. This includes millions of documents housed in the U.S. National Archives and Records Administration (NARA). Thus, what was once an enormously time-consuming task of navigating the NARA index card catalogues housed in College Park, Maryland, can now be accessed remotely via searchable keywords. It is, indeed, a new world!

The records of the Munich Central Collecting Point (MCCP), the largest art repository for postwar Allied recoveries, have also been digitized. Posted on a site maintained by the Deutsches Historisches Museum, they are searchable—in both English and German—under one of several categories (e.g., artist, archive number, subject). Many foreign language publications and archives—particularly in Germany, Holland, and Austria—have also been digitized and are being posted and translated into English. This includes wartime and postwar sales of major European auction houses, such as Dorotheum in Vienna and Weinmüller in Munich and Vienna, for whom business flourished during the war. The Weinmüller catalogues—ninety-three volumes covering 1933–1945, which until recently were believed to have been destroyed—are annotated with prices and the names of consignors and buyers. The catalogues will soon be posted on the website lostart.de, the same site hosting the Gurlitt material. It is a safe prediction that the site will become invaluable for investigating works transferred via forced sales or under duress during the Nazi era.

The following discussion provides a brief overview of and introduction to provenance research both in relation to authenticity, as well as to issues of legal title—in other words, verifying that a work was not misappropriated during the Nazi era or otherwise, or that it was/is being acquired in accordance with foreign cultural property ownership laws and U.S. law. It will include examples from research at IFAR—the International Foundation for Art Research, the nonprofit educational and research organization for which I currently serve as executive director, and which has a particular expertise in provenance research. It will also make reference to legal claims made against museums in recent years. But the subject is vast, so this essay should be viewed as a beginning, not an end. For a more extensive discussion, I refer readers to the Provenance Guide on IFAR's website (www.ifar.org) and to the resources and publications listed in this chapter and on our website.

The Importance of Provenance

Simply put, provenance is the history of ownership of a work of art, but it is actually much more. An ideal provenance provides a documentary record of owners' names going back to the artist's studio, and includes

- Dates of ownership.
- Methods of transfer, such as inheritance, gift, donation, trade (by the artist, collector, or dealer), or sale, whether through a dealer or auction house, and if the latter, with lot number.
- The location where the work was kept and also sold (city or country).

As already noted, such clarity and transparency, even when the facts are known and intentions honorable, are unusual. For reasons of privacy or custom, many owners request confidentiality. It is not uncommon to see "Private Collection, France" or Switzerland, United States, and so on, even several such listings, in a provenance. This may be fine under normal circumstances, but not when you are trying to clear up a problematic history.

Provenance research—like detective work or investigative journalism—must be approached with creativity, persistence, attention to detail, and the ability to think outside of the box. It is fundamentally interdisciplinary. While rooted in traditional art historical scholarship and methodology, research often leads to, and is frequently dependant upon, source material relating to history, economics, and political science. Often, provenance researchers encounter difficulties due to the state of extant records. Archives may suffer damage, destruction, or dispersal, and the records of smaller or short-lived galleries are not always preserved. But the rewards for persistence are great.

A work's provenance can often tell us much more than its ownership history; it helps verify authenticity, provides insight into the history of taste and collecting, and offers a record of economic, market, and even political conditions. Provenance indicating that a work was included in a major estate sale—such as that of Mrs. John Hay Whitney (Sotheby's 1999); Victor and Sally Ganz (Christie's 1997); Yves Saint Laurent (Christie's 2009)—lends credibility as well as value to the work, and tells us that it once belonged to an important and carefully pruned collection. A provenance that lists a work as having been in the "Sammlung [Collection] Stroganoff, Leningrad," sale at the Lepke Auction House, Berlin in May 1931, tells us that the work presumably came from the distinguished Stroganoff Collection, which was confiscated by the Bolsheviks during the Russian Revolution and later sold by the Soviet government to earn badly needed cash. A current legal dispute in federal court in California, however, has raised the possibility that two Lucas Cranach paintings sold at that sale and now in the Norton Simon Museum in California may not have actually belonged to the Stroganoff Collection, although the facts are still in dispute. (For a summary of this lawsuit and hundreds of others, see the Art Law and Cultural Property Database Section of the IFAR website.)

The Basics

There are a number of ways to get started on provenance research. In regard to World War II–era research, along with the online IFAR Provenance Guide noted above, a good basic reference tool for novice and experienced researchers alike is *The AAM Guide to Provenance Research* (by Nancy Yeide, Konstantin Akinsha, and Amy Walsh). If you can only purchase one reference book, this should be the one. The first part of the book discusses general provenance research, while the second part focuses on World War II–era provenance research. Replete with case studies and explanatory text, the *AAM Guide* is particularly valuable for its appendices containing often hard-to-find bibliographic and archival information, such as a bibliography on looting and restitution (which, given the book's 2001 publication date, needs updating); lists of names associated with Nazi-era looting; a list of wartime and postwar interrogation reports; and codes used by the Einsatzstab Reichsleiter Rosenberg (ERR)—the special Nazi task force based in Paris—in its confiscation of collections in France and Belgium. Appendix D on "Dealer Archives and Locations" is particularly valuable. Locating archival documents can, in itself, be a major undertaking, and this appendix alone can save a researcher days and weeks of wasted time. It is worth noting that since the publication of the *AAM Guide*, the records and photographs of objects confiscated by the ERR have been digitized and posted online, providing another major tool for the arsenal of provenance researchers.

Another basic resource is the special double issue of the *IFAR Journal*, vol. 3, nos. 3 and 4 (2000), devoted to "Provenance & Due Diligence," the proceedings of an IFAR/NYU workshop/conference. The journal contains still-useful information about navigating provenance resources at, for example, the Frick Art Reference Library and NARA.[3]

These resources and others are invaluable, but when conducting provenance research on a specific object, please don't forget the basics:

1. Start with the object itself. It is an important, and frequently the *most* important, source of provenance information:

   • Examine the front and back for any inscriptions, signatures, dates, or other distinctive marks, including blemishes, tears, or other signs of age. If the work is one of several similar works that an artist is known to have made, such markings will help determine whether the work in question is the one that was looted/stolen.
   • Carefully note the object's medium and support (e.g., oil on canvas or panel; gouache on paper, etc.).
   • You can glean other useful information from exhibition stickers, seals, dealers' and collectors' marks, and transport and customs

stamps, all of which are often found on the backs of paintings, or on the stretchers (but, remember, labels can be faked, so proceed with caution).

- Determine whether there are or have been significant changes to the object's condition, size, or support (e.g., relining).
- Indicate whether there are alternate titles for the work, and, if known, whether the artist's attribution may have changed.
- Take or obtain a good photograph of the work, front and back; this will allow you to compare it with illustrations in auction catalogues, newspaper clippings, or other documents.

The accuracy of the information you amass in the above exercises may be crucial in determining whether the artwork that you own or are researching is the same as a work whose ownership is questioned. That is what happened with a landscape painting by the nineteenth-century Austrian artist Ferdinand Georg Waldmüller, which belonged to the National Gallery in Berlin before World War II and disappeared from its hiding place in Berlin in May 1945. In 1999, the painting was consigned for auction to Sotheby's in New York. A routine due diligence search by the auction house determined that a similar Waldmüller painting was listed in a 1965 German postwar publication, *Verlorene Werke der Malerie,* with which all World War II–era provenance researchers need to be familiar.[4] But it wasn't certain that the two works were one and the same, both because Waldmüller painted several similar landscapes and also because there was a discrepancy about the date of the painting. The one listed in *Verlorene* was dated "1850." The consignors argued that theirs was dated "1830." Further research, however, showed that the discrepancy in the date was noted by scholars even before World War II—namely, that the date could be alternatively "read" as "1830" or "1850," or even "1860." More significant, however, was the presence of a crack in the paint on the right side of the consigned landscape. That very crack showed up in old photographs of the looted work. Armed with this evidence, the Berlin museum reached an out-of-court settlement with the consignors, and the painting was returned to the museum.

2. Gather the known object history:

- Begin compiling a list of all exhibitions or publications in which the object appeared. This list may change as your research progresses. You may find, for example, that the work listed in a publication was not yours but a similar one with a confusingly similar title, especially when dealing with subjects such as still lifes, generic landscapes, and odalisques. You may also find that an object listed as being in an exhibition, was not lent after all. Publication deadlines for exhibition catalogues are long in advance of the exhibitions themselves, and it is not uncommon to learn that intended loans didn't come to fruition.

- Prepare a list of the object's known provenance and, where possible, indicate the source of that information. You will want to go back to that source to double-check its accuracy or supplement missing information. You will, of course, be adding to (or at least trying to add to) this initial list.
- Note the previous owners of the object; you will want to try to contact them or their heirs. Even if they no longer have any records, their recollections could be helpful.

3. Examine the object file(s), if any, of the institution/museum in which the object is held. If it is your museum, so much the better, as you should have unrestricted access to both institutional and collection records, such as

- Registrarial records, which generally contain information on the acquisition, loan, sale, and transport of a work of art;
- Curatorial records, which contain research on and correspondence relating to the artwork;
- Conservation files, which may include X-rays, infrared photographs, and technical and condition reports (often a "match" with a stolen/looted work is missed because the work subsequently underwent restoration);
- Other institutional archives containing material beyond that in registrarial files—exhibition history, bequest or gift details, and additional donor correspondence;
- Loan files, which may be helpful regarding objects sent to a museum for long-term loan before entering the permanent collection.

The importance of examining all types of institutional records can be demonstrated by a recent example concerning the Baltimore Museum of Art (BMA), which in 2014 recovered a Renoir painting that had been stolen in 1951. The painting, a tiny, 1879 oil painting on linen, turned up in 2012, more than sixty years after the theft, when it was consigned to a small auction house in Virginia. A routine due diligence search by the auction house had uncovered nothing untoward, but the BMA noticed that a recent Renoir catalogue raisonné (see discussion below of catalogues raisonnés) listed one of the BMA's major benefactors in the painting's provenance, and began searching its *permanent* collection records to see whether the painting had ever been in its collection. It found nothing. An enterprising *Washington Post* reporter, however, had better luck and, dare we say, better research skills. He expanded his search to the museum's *loan* records and discovered that the painting had been *lent* to the museum in 1937 by the benefactor's wife, and that the painting remained at the museum until it was stolen in 1951. Armed with the loan number, the museum searched its records again and found that it had reported the work stolen to the police and had actually received an insurance payout. With that information, the BMA filed an ownership claim for the Renoir, as did the consignor to the auction house. The competing claims were adjudicated, and the painting was awarded to the museum by court order in 2014.[5]

Once a provenance has been established, it needs to be recorded in a clear, organized, and complete manner. A provenance may be organized in list or in paragraph form, and opinions vary as to whether the sequence of ownership should be given in chronological or reverse chronological order (IFAR prefers chronological order, oldest first.). But be consistent. Owners should be distinguished from dealers or auction houses. Ideally, the source of information about each owner or transaction should be documented in footnotes or, if the information is brief, in parentheses. This will help the next person who reads your material.

Art Historical Resources

After undertaking the steps above regarding the examination and study of the object itself and the institution's files, a researcher is ready to pursue outside research.

As stated earlier, provenance research is often interdisciplinary; this is especially true of Nazi-era research, which frequently requires navigating military and other government and historical records. Nonetheless, traditional art historical methodology is at the core of provenance research, and often all that is necessary. This is true whether faced with a Holocaust-era claim or simply verifying that a work in your collection was *not* looted during the Nazi period.

While as a matter of course, you should always check World War II–era reference materials to verify that the work doesn't appear on one of the many lists of looted works, or that its known provenance doesn't include a red-flagged name—whether it is the name of a known dealer in looted art, or a collector whose art was misappropriated (different resources need to be consulted for each)—you shouldn't neglect traditional art historical research as well. Let's take as an example a 1915 Cubist painting by Picasso that a university museum asked IFAR to research in order to determine whether it had a problematic Nazi-era history, or, rather, to assure them that it did not.

The museum had received the work as a partial gift, partial promised future donation; it had no provenance documents.

IFAR's research was multipronged—using both World War II–related and general art historical resources, but the latter was more useful, and the decisive information was provided by an art historian. A routine search of World War II–era reference resources, including ERR records and the *Répertoire des bien spoliés en France Durant la Guerre* 1939–1945, a 1947 publication listing works reported lost or missing in France, turned up nothing suspicious. Our Picasso was not among them. We also contacted the donors (never overlook the obvious), who had inherited the painting and who knew only that it had been purchased in a New York gallery in 1937 and that the gallery had purportedly acquired it directly from Picasso. They thought the gallery's name was something like "Valentine." Assuming that was correct, it was not immediately clear whether it referred to Curt Valentin or Valentine Dudensing, both of whom dealt in Picassos in New York in the 1930s. The first, Valentin, might have raised concerns, but it turned out to be the latter.

Routine research in the Frick Art Reference Library—an invaluable resource for art historical research, with an extensive collection of photographs, auction catalogues (many of which are annotated), and gallery records—turned up a 1937 exhibition catalogue from the Valentine Gallery, which mentioned the very Picasso painting at issue. Although the catalogue provided no additional information, it did at least verify that the painting was in New York in 1937—a good sign.

We wanted to know, how, when, and from where and whom the work got to New York. Standard reference materials turned up nothing. Through John Richardson, the noted Picasso specialist (then on IFAR's board of directors), we learned of a graduate student who was preparing a publication on the Valentine Gallery and had obtained all of the gallery's sales records. A search through those unpublished records provided the precise date the gallery sold the Picasso to the family of the museum's donors, as well as the date Dudensing had acquired the painting, from whom, and at what price. Although it turned out that his source was not Picasso, the information did assure us—and the museum—that there was no Nazi-era taint to the work.

Normally, the artist's catalogue raisonné—a scholarly documentation of an artist's entire body of work, or work in a given medium—would provide provenance and, ideally, other information about a work. Consulting a catalogue raisonné on the artist, therefore, assuming there is one, is an important early step for any provenance researcher. In this particular case, however, the painting was not listed in the monumental Zervos catalogue raisonné of Picasso's oeuvre.[6] While, that might otherwise have raised questions as to authenticity, the authenticity of this painting was never in doubt, nor is it that unusual for an authentic Picasso to be missing from Zervos.

This does, however, bring up the subject of catalogues raisonnés as indispensable tools for provenance researchers, whether regarding authenticity or ownership history. A cautionary note: catalogues vary in quality and comprehensiveness. The best are informed by meticulous scholarship and years of familiarity with the artist's work. In addition to a work's ownership and exhibition history and mention in bibliographic references, all of which should be independently verified and consulted for supplemental information, a good catalogue also provides descriptive information, such as medium, dimensions, condition, and identifying inscriptions, if any. Needless to say, it also provides a photograph of the work. Some also indicate whether variants of a work exist, and how they differ. It doesn't take much imagination to realize how helpful this can be to provenance researchers seeking, for example, to determine whether a particular landscape is the one missing from a looted collection.

To discover whether a catalogue raisonné for a specific artist already exists or is in preparation, and also to learn about the features of that catalogue, you can consult IFAR's online catalogues raisonnés database (www.ifar.org/cat_rais.php). This continuously updated and annotated bibliographic resource, which IFAR provides free to the public, contains information on, currently, more than 3,500 published catalogues raisonnés and hundreds of catalogues still in preparation—information virtually impossible to find elsewhere.

If more than one catalogue exists, it is best to begin with the most recent, but consult earlier publications as well. They may be very revealing. A case in point: the various catalogues raisonnés for the Austrian Expressionist Egon Schiele, which actually factored into the long restitution battle for a Nazi-appropriated painting by Schiele, the *Portrait of Wally*. The battle initially embroiled New York's Museum of Modern Art as well as the Viennese museum that lent the work to MoMA in 1997. Significantly, *Wally*'s World War II ownership history was laid out differently in the various catalogues raisonnés. Rudolph Leopold, a collector and founder of the museum in Vienna, wrongfully acquired the painting in 1954. In 1972, he compiled a Schiele catalogue raisonné, in which he eliminated the name of the rightful pre–World War II owner, Lea Bondi Jaray, from *Wally*'s provenance. But other catalogues raisonnés—in 1930 and in 1990—*did* include Bondi Jaray as the prewar owner. A lot would have been missed had only the 1972 catalogue been consulted.

When consulting a catalogue raisonné, keep in mind that many years of research go into its preparation. Thus, a catalogue published in 1948, for example, which lists the current owner of a painting, may be basing that information on scholarship compiled years before. The painting may have had other owners in the interim years; this may be significant when tracing the ownership of a work during the Nazi era.

Auction and exhibition catalogues, too, can provide critical information as to past and current owners of works, as well as locations. An owner who chose anonymity when *selling* a work, may have permitted his name to be used in a loan exhibition. As with all sources, however, treat these with caution, and cross-reference and verify. In a provenance project that IFAR undertook for the federal government and the FBI regarding a painting by Henri Matisse, for example, the work was listed in a 1959 gallery exhibition in London as being part of the "T. D. Barlow Collection, Manchester," although the gallery itself owned the work at the time and must have known that the painting hadn't been part of the Barlow Collection for several years. We were able to document with certainty at least two interim owners. It was never clear to us why the incorrect and clearly outdated information was put into the 1959 catalogue: Was it carelessness or laziness on the part of a gallery researcher? Was it intentional dissimulation (without, as far as we could see, any apparent motive)? Or something else? But it did reinforce our conviction that everything has to be verified.

Photo archives, containing photographs of works of art as well as clippings from sale and exhibition catalogues, are especially valuable resources for documenting whether a work has been altered, restored, or cut down. Annotations on the photographs can be particularly helpful, sometimes listing the owner or former owners and exhibitions where the work was shown.

Among the most important photo archives are the following:

- Archives of American Art, Smithsonian Institution, Washington, DC
- Frick Art Reference Library, New York
- Getty Research Institute, Los Angeles
- Louvre and Musée d'Orsay documentation centers, Paris
- National Gallery of Art, Washington, DC
- Rijksbureau voor Kunsthistorische Documentatie (RKD), The Hague
- Villa I Tatti, Florence
- Witt Library, The Courtauld Institute of Art, London
- Zentralinstitut für Kunstgeschichte, Munich

For a comprehensive list of art historical resources for conducting provenance research, please consult IFAR's online Provenance Guide (www.ifar .org), which also provides links to resources that have been digitized. The list is too long to present in this chapter, but here are four of the best:

- The Getty Provenance Index—a series of searchable databases of archival documents, sale catalogues, and works in public collections. The Getty has numerous other resources as well, including many dealer archives.
- The Archives of American Art headquartered in Washington, DC, with a research center in New York, houses an enormous collection of dealer and

artist archives. Some are digitized and searchable off-site. Those that have not been digitized or microfilmed must be searched in Washington.

- Rijksbureau voor Kunsthistorische Documentatie, The Hague—generally known as the RKD—is invaluable for researching Dutch and Flemish artists.
- Frits Lugt's *Répertoire des catalogues de ventes publiques intéressant l'art ou la curiosité* (4 vols; La Haye: M. Nijhoff, 1938–1987), available in hard copy and also now online for a fee, lists more than 100,000 art sales catalogues dating from 1600 to 1925. Lugt's other indispensable resource, *Les marques de collections de dessins & d'estampes* (originally published in 1921 and also available at www.fondationcustodia.fr/english/index.cfm), compiles the collectors' marks found on works on paper and identifies the collector associated with each mark.

World War II–Era Provenance Research

As already noted, provenance research has loomed particularly large for museums in recent years due to concerns about World War II–era looted art that may have entered their collections through purchase, bequest, or donation. From 1933 through the end of the war in 1945, the Nazi regime was responsible for the confiscation, looting, sale, and destruction of millions of artworks and other cultural objects (such as manuscripts, books, and decorative arts) at an unprecedented scale. While most items were taken from the private collections of Jews and other victims, objects were also taken from public collections in Nazi-occupied countries, and still others were seemingly "purchased" legitimately, but with payments at far below market value or against the wishes of the seller. These "forced sales" or sales made "under duress" are particularly thorny for provenance researchers, as it is not always easy (or possible given the passage of time and loss of documents and witnesses) to distinguish between a forced sale and a voluntary one during this period. Moreover, definitions as to what constitutes a forced sale or sale under duress have changed over the years. But absent convincing evidence that a work was voluntarily sold, it is wise and certainly more ethical to assume that it was not and to proceed accordingly.

Many stolen works entered the collections of Nazi officials (Reichsmarschall Hermann Göring, for example, was an avid collector and Hitler planned a museum in his hometown of Linz, Austria), but numerous stolen works were sold or traded for cash or other artworks; some were traded more than once. This can make it particularly difficult to trace the provenance of an object during the war. Perhaps the best overview of Nazi art looting is Lynn Nicholas's comprehensive and beautifully researched and written, *Rape of Europa* (New York: Alfred A. Knopf, 1994).

After the war—in fact, even during the war starting in 1943—the Allies made a Herculean effort to find, document, sort, and return stolen and otherwise misappropriated artworks. The military also had strict rules prohibiting the taking of objects as "spoils of war," but that didn't prevent the disappearance of many objects hidden by German museums and institutions for safekeeping. The Quedlinburg Treasures is a good example. These exquisite and enormously valuable jewel-adorned medieval manuscripts and liturgical objects were hidden for safekeeping by a church in eastern Germany, to which they had belonged for hundreds of years. A U.S. Army officer, Joe T. Meador, assigned to the unit that was supposed to guard the mineshaft where the Quedlinburg Treasures were found in 1945, instead, took the Treasures home to Texas, where they remained hidden for around forty years. They surfaced—and were recognized—after Meador died, when his family tried to market them. Eventually, they were returned to Germany in a story that played out in the media and the U.S. court system, but only after a monetary settlement was reached between the family and the German government.[7]

The Allied military forces charged with finding and protecting the looted art—the Monuments, Fine Arts, and Archives Section, better known now as "The Monuments Men"—succeeded in restituting millions of objects before they ceased their operations in 1951. Postwar Allied policy called for the restitution of confiscated works to the countries where their prewar owners resided (external restitution) for return by those governments to the rightful owners (internal restitution). While many countries did a good job at restitution, thousands of objects were kept in museums or were sold or otherwise dispersed. Some of these works have turned up in recent years—while on loan to exhibitions or on the marketplace. Still others have never been found. This does not even address the works taken east by Soviet troops, whose government had a very different idea about war booty than did the Western Allies. Some of the artworks that went to countries in the Soviet bloc were never restituted and are now starting to appear in the marketplace.

In the 1990s, the issue of looted and still-unrestituted works of art, while it had never truly gone away, broke into the public consciousness with the opening of previously classified archives, the fall of the Soviet Union, and the publication of new books on the subject, including the above-mentioned *Rape of Europa*. Heightened awareness prompted the museum community to enact more stringent guidelines regarding the handling of objects in their collections with Nazi-era gaps in provenance, and to undertake provenance research.

The number of archives and research resources to aid museums in World War II–era provenance research is too extensive to list here, beyond those already mentioned, but here are a few of the most essential:

- *AAM Guide to Provenance Research* (cited above)—a good basic guide and, as already noted, particularly useful for its appendices.
- National Archives and Records Administration (NARA) in College Park, Maryland, which holds millions of military and other government records concerning the war, including the Office of Strategic Services (RG226) and the Office of the Military Governor, United States (RG260). A 1999 publication, *Holocaust-Era Assets: A Finding Aid to Records at the National Archives at College Park,* compiled by Greg Bradsher and also available online, helps researchers locate and understand the NARA materials.
- Office of Strategic Services (OSS) Art Looting Investigation Unit's (ALIU) *Biographical Index of Individuals Involved in Art Looting.* This is an important list of so-called "red-flagged" names, which includes most of the people interrogated or investigated by the ALIU at the end of the war. As many of the individuals listed were middlemen who had legitimate art dealing operations before and even during the war, their name in a provenance does not necessarily mean the object in question was looted, but it does mean further investigating is necessary.
- *Cultural Plunder by the Einsatzstab Reichsleiter Rosenberg* (ERR) (www .errproject.org/jeudepaume/). This is a digitized resource for researching the more than 20,000 artworks confiscated in France and Belgium and stored by the ERR in the Jeu de Paume in Paris. Replete with images (where available) of the objects, it is searchable by artist, collection, medium, ERR code, and so on.
- Bernhard, Marianne. *Verlorene Werke der Malerei in Deutschland in der Zeit von 1939 bis 1945 zerstörte und verschollene Gemälde aus Museen und Galerien.* This book, published in 1965, lists works still missing from German museums twenty years after the war; organized by city and museum. (See above and footnote 4.)
- *Répertoire des biens spoliés en France durant la guerre, 1939–1945.* 4 vols. plus supplements (Berlin: Impr. nationale, 1947–1949). This indispensable multivolume, multilingual publication prepared soon after the war lists some of the property looted in France and not yet recovered. Although difficult to navigate and containing a limited number of mostly poor quality images, this publication is a must-check for World War II–era provenance researchers. Happily, it is now digitized and posted by the French government.

Just as France and Germany, in the publications above, published lists of artworks missing from their countries, so, too, did Poland, Italy, Belgium, and so forth. Lists of losses from private collections, such as the Schloss and Koenigs Collection (the latter claimed by the Netherlands), were also published. Depending upon the nature of your research, do not neglect to consult these works.

Antiquities

While this chapter is not focused on researching antiquities, the issue is so important for museums currently that the subject merits a brief mention. Let us start with a distinction: "provenance" (ownership history) and "provenience," a word with which provenance is often confused, are not one and the same, although both are important in researching archaeological artifacts/ antiquities. "Provenience" refers to the "findspot" of an object (e.g., where it was dug up), and knowing the findspot and detailing an object's position within the site and its proximity to other documented items—its archaeological context—helps specialists identify the object's function, date, and cultural origin. Looting, war, natural disasters, and other vicissitudes, however, destroy archaeological sites and cause damage to the objects.

In recent years, many countries have recognized the threat to their cultural heritage caused by the looting of archaeological sites and the illicit export of culturally significant objects. This has resulted in the enactment of many bilateral and international agreements, most notably the 1970 UNESCO Convention,[8] and also the enactment by many countries of so-called "patrimony" laws to vest ownership of antiquities in the state. Similarly, countries have enacted legislation to restrict the export of certain types of cultural objects. Until recently, trying to locate and navigate this mushrooming body of laws was an uphill battle. IFAR responded by creating a comprehensive website resource with complete texts (in original language and English translation) and summaries of the legislative documents. See IFAR's online Art Law and Cultural Property Database, www.ifar.org.[9]

As these agreements and laws are rarely retroactive, the enactment date of a national ownership law or an international or bilateral agreement may be significant in determining legal ownership of a cultural artifact. Therefore, a documented provenance, including the date the object left its country of origin, and its ownership and publication history are crucial for a current owner to demonstrate legal title, as well as the ethical acquisition of the object. At the least, it is important to show that the acquisition was not the result of recent looting (or any looting, for that matter) and will not be an inducement to further looting.

The United States became a party (with reservations) to the 1970 UNESCO Convention with the passage of the Cultural Property Implementation Act (CPIA) in 1983. Under the CPIA, countries that are signatories to the 1970 UNESCO Convention and whose cultural property is in "jeopardy of pillage" may ask the United States to restrict the importation of designated types of threatened objects as of a certain date. Such bilateral agreements last for five years, but are renewable. The types of restricted objects are listed in the Federal Register. Once the import restriction is put in place, an owner or importer must be able to prove that an object imported from that country left that country before the date the restriction went into effect. This puts additional pressure on owners to do appropriate provenance research.

In 2008, new guidelines for the Association of Art Museum Directors (AAMD) in the United States and Canada adopted the threshold date of 1970—the date of the UNESCO Convention and not the date of 1983 when the United States became a state party to the convention—for applying more stringent acquisition standards for archaeological objects. Member museums were mandated to undertake provenance research to substantiate that an object was "outside its country of probable modern discovery before 1970 or was legally exported after 1970."

In addition to IFAR's Art Law and Cultural Property Database, which has the most extensive information and legislation on this subject, there are many other resources for information about laws and provenance research concerning antiquities. See IFAR's online Provenance Guide, for a comprehensive resource list, with links, but three of the most useful are

- U.S. Department of State, Bureau of Educational and Cultural Affairs: Cultural Property Protection: eca.state.gov/cultural-heritage-center/;
- UNESCO—National Cultural Heritage Laws Database: www.unesco .org/; and
- ICOM (International Council of Museums) International Observatory on Illicit Traffic in Cultural Property: obs-traffic.museum/.

Some Words on Authentication—and Conclusion

I began this chapter with a mention of the art historical importance of provenance research in the context of authenticity/attribution, and then segued into a discussion of the importance of provenance as a means of verifying that a work has no taint on its ownership history. But I cannot end without returning, however briefly, to the importance of provenance research for confirming the authenticity of a work of art.

While many authentic works have gaps in provenance, and it is not inconceivable that a work without verifiable provenance is authentic, previously unknown works by major artists rarely just "turn up." Therefore, it is extremely important that a museum—or any collector—carefully research the provenance of a work offered to them. Provenance along with other scholarly documentation is part of the three-pronged approach that IFAR has always taken in its Authentication Research Service—the other two being careful examination (with specialists) of the work's material and stylistic properties.

Provenance research for purposes of verifying authenticity utilizes the same resources and approaches discussed in "Art Historical Resources" above, and the same cautionary notes prevail. Never accept information or documents without independently verifying them.

Fakers can be very clever and the best know how to exploit the system. The convicted German forger Wolfgang Beltracchi, for example, who admitted to creating hundreds of works that, he said, modern masters "would have liked to paint," and which fooled sophisticated collectors and specialists, was a master at exploiting provenance expectations. His wife, an integral part of his fraud scheme, claimed that she had inherited some of the works from her grandfather, Werner Jägers (thus, the concocted "Jägers Collection"), who in turn had obtained the works from Alfred Flechtheim, the renowned German Jewish art dealer, who died in 1937. Many of the fakes bore a paper sticker with the inscription "Sammlung [Collection] Alfred Flechtheim" on the back of the frame. The provenance was plausible in that Flechtheim died in exile and many works from his collection remain dispersed.

The ingenious art fraud scheme perpetrated by John Drewe in London in the 1990s is another example. Over a period of years, Drewe, with the help of a talented but poor artist, John Myatt, doctored archival records in various British libraries to help substantiate the phony provenances he concocted for Myatt forgeries. Drewe understood that people concerned or suspicious about a painting might want to verify its provenance, so he made sure that they would find in the archives what he wanted them to find. In that case, even a conscientious purchaser might have gotten fooled, suggesting that even more vigilant verification is needed than one might think. Caveat emptor: not all the fakes put on the market by Beltracchi or Drewe have been found.

Over the years, IFAR's Authentication Research Service has seen just about every type of falsification of provenance documents. A particularly large number have accompanied purported works by Jackson Pollock. An owner of an obviously fake "Pollock," for example, submitted a sales receipt dated 1952 supposedly from the Betty Parsons Gallery (Pollock's dealer in 1952). But examination revealed that the receipt was written with a type of pen that wasn't manufactured until ten years later. Moreover, the painting wasn't listed in Parsons's own handwritten list of works sold in 1952; nor was the receipt consistent with Parsons's known receipts. Another "Pollock" owner submitted a work with a stamp on the verso showing the name of a New York gallery and an inventory number. But a simple check with the gallery revealed that it had never used stamps and the number belonged to a work by a different artist. Still another purported "Pollock," which had recently been purchased from the long-established Knoedler Gallery in New York, came to us with the assertion that it had passed down from Pollock via Alfonso Ossorio. While Pollock knew Ossorio well, making the assertion initially plausible, extensive research caused us to conclude that the Ossorio provenance was "inconceivable." For that reason and many others, we could not accept the painting as a work by Jackson Pollock. Years later, the true artist of that work and more than sixty other paintings was revealed, through a government fraud investigation, to be a Chinese painter in Queens.

Thus, I will end with the following advice: no matter who offers an artwork to you, and no matter how plausible the backstory initially seems, "Trust but verify." This is a paraphrase of a statement by a former U.S. president, but it is good advice for museum professionals and anyone in the art world.

NOTES

1. For an in-depth discussion of the Gurlitt story, see among others, Sharon Flescher and Michele Wijegoonaratna, "The Tangled Web of a Munich Art Trove," *IFAR Journal*, vol. 14, no.4/vol. 15, no. 1 (2014), pp. 3–14.

2. See "Post-War Reports: Art Looting Intelligence Unit (ALIU) Reports 1945–1946 and ALIU Red Flag Names List and Index," lootedart.com: The Central Agency of Information on Looted Cultural Property 1933–1945, www.lootedart.com/MVI3RM469661.

3. Back issues of this particular *IFAR Journal* and other journal issues can be obtained through IFAR's website: www.ifar.org/publications_ifar_journal_php.

4. See Marianne Bernhard, Kurt Martin, and Klaus P. Rogner, *Verlorene Werke der Malerie* (Munich: F. A. Ackermann, 1965). This basic reference book, which lists all works still missing from German museums and public institutions as of 1965, is long since out of print. In 1998 and 1999, IFAR facilitated the printing of facsimiles of this book (and others) and made them available to researchers and libraries around the world at our cost. Thus, many libraries currently possess a copy.

5. The legal case is *In re: "Paysage bords de Seine," 1879 Unsigned Oil Painting on Linen by Pierre-Auguste Renoir*, Slip op., No. 1:13cv347 (LMB/ TRJ) (Jan. 14, 2014 E. D. Va.).

6. Christian Zervos, *Pablo Picasso,* 33 volumes (Paris: Cahiers d'Art, 1932–1978).

7. For a good discussion of the Quedlinburg Treasures, see "Case Study: The Quedlinburg Church Treasures," in *The Spoils of War: World War II and Its Aftermath: The Loss, Reappearance, and Recovery of Cultural Property*, ed. Elizabeth Simpson (New York: Harry N. Abrams, 1997), pp. 148–58.

8. The full title is the 1970 UNESCO Convention on the Means of Prohibiting and Preventing the Illicit Import, Export, and Transfer of Ownership of Cultural Property.

9. www.ifar.org/art_law.php. IFAR's Art Law and Cultural Property Database is a subscription-based resource comprising two main sections: a "Case Law and Statutes" section, featuring summaries of hundreds of legal cases in subjects such as World War II–era art looting, cultural property claims, and forgery and fraud, and a section devoted to "International Cultural Property Ownership and Export Legislation (ICPOEL)." The latter contains summaries of legislation for, currently, more than 115 foreign countries. The full texts of hundreds of international legislative documents in the original language and English translation are linked to their country summaries. This database is continuously updated and expanded by IFAR.

Chapter Six

A Native American Graves Protection and Repatriation Act (NAGPRA)

A Case Study from Western Massachusetts

Dr. Ellen Savulis

INTRODUCTION

This chapter presents a case study that illustrates the processes that museums go through in order to comply with the Native American Graves Protection and Repatriation Act (NAGPRA).[1] It follows the identification and documentation of NAGPRA-sensitive items, consultations with federally recognized tribes, the determination of cultural affiliation, and repatriation. It offers a discussion of resources available to museums to assist with NAGPRA compliance.

President George H. W. Bush signed the Native American Graves Protection and Repatriation Act (NAGPRA) into law in November 1990. This law requires federal agencies and institutions that receive federal funding to return specific cultural items to lineal descendants and culturally affiliated, federally recognized Indian tribes and Native Hawaiian organizations. Cultural items to be considered include human remains, funerary objects, sacred objects, and objects of cultural patrimony. It requires that museums and agencies compile inventories of these cultural items and provide them to potentially affiliated Indian tribes.

DESCRIPTION OF COLLECTIONS

The Springfield Science Museum, part of a five-museum consortium in Springfield, Massachusetts, has approximately 89,000 objects in its Native

American archaeological collection. Of these there are 2,040 human remains including complete skeletons and separate bones. The collection from the Connecticut River Valley contains eighty-four sets of human remains and 321 associated funerary objects. All of the burial ensembles appear to date to the Woodland and Historic periods, 2,700–275 BP ("before present" where "present" is 1950) based on mortuary practices consistent with Native American interments, or grave sites, of that time.

Collectors who did not keep field notes excavated many of the human remains. Critical information about spatial relationships between remains, artifacts, and their stratigraphic placement is not available. Because of this, some items identified as "associated funerary object" may not be accurately identified. Instead, they may be artifacts from habitations that were mixed into the matrix of burials at interment. They may also have been collected without regard to a direct burial association. However, these possible scenarios cannot be determined for several of the burials in the museum's collection. Because of this, the museum has included all possible objects in its inventory of associated funerary objects.

The collection of human remains from the Connecticut Valley was acquired over a period of one hundred years. They were recovered from agricultural fields, a rock shelter, and early twentieth-century road and bridge improvement projects. More than half were removed from known archaeological sites. Several were inadvertent discoveries.

Most of the burials did not contain associated funerary objects. However, those that did produced cultural material such as hammer stones, lithic flakes, projectile points, faunal remains, and undecorated pottery sherds (historic fragments of pottery). Diagnostic funerary objects suggest that interments occurred during the Middle to Late Woodland periods and possibly later (1,200–450 BP). Two burials from South Hadley, Massachusetts, may have been Early Woodland Period Adena interments (2,700–1,200 BP). One produced copper-stained bones; another produced forty-five copper beads.

CULTURAL AFFILIATION

King Philip's War of 1675–1676 forever altered the demographic landscape of the Connecticut River Valley. After the war, historical sources mention returning hunting parties or small encampments of native people in the valley.[2] Correspondence in 1696 and 1697 between Lieutenant Governor William Stoughton and John Pynchon of Springfield and Samuel Partridge of Northampton indicate that occasional hostilities continued.[3] However, King Philip's War caused a cultural upheaval for the native communities at Woronoco, Agawam, Chicopee, Norwottock, and Pocumtuc, which ceased to exist.

Under NAGPRA, it is necessary to identify culturally affiliated, federally recognized tribes. "Cultural affiliation" is defined as "a relationship of shared group identity that can be reasonably traced historically or prehistorically between a present day Indian tribe or Native Hawaiian organization and an identifiable earlier group."[4] In addition, "cultural affiliation is established when the preponderance of evidence—based on geographical, kinship, biological, archaeological, linguistic, folklore, oral tradition, historical evidence, or other information or expert opinion—reasonably leads to such a conclusion."[5]

In Massachusetts, there are four federally recognized tribes that might be affiliated with the museum's inventory of Connecticut Valley human remains and associated funerary objects. These include the Mashpee Wampanoag Tribe of Cape Cod, the Stockbridge-Munsee Band of Mohican Indians of Wisconsin, the Wampanoag Tribe of Gay Head (Aquinnah) of Martha's Vineyard, and the Narragansett Tribe of Rhode Island. Primary document research, the consultation process, and review of archaeological reports led the museum to determine that the Stockbridge-Munsee, Gay Head, and Narragansett tribes are culturally affiliated with its Connecticut Valley collections.

GUIDA FARM SITE

The Guida Farm site is located on the west bank of the Westfield River in Westfield, Massachusetts. The site was first discovered in 1937 during the removal of topsoil for commercial purpose.[6] Examination of the archaeological assemblage from the site and primary historical documents of Westfield provided tantalizing information about the site's history and the cultural affiliation of the museum's Connecticut Valley collection.

NAGPRA-sensitive material from the Guida site includes forty-nine sets of human remains and 176 funerary objects. These consisted of one adze blade tip, forty-six pieces of charcoal, seventeen faunal fragments, eleven lithic flakes, one burned nut hull, one quartzite projectile point, and forty-seven pottery sherds. Byers and Rouse describe the site as an Early to Late Woodland Period habitation site (2,950–450 BP) with burial components.[7] Grumet dates the occupation of the Guida Farm site up to the turn of the eighteenth century.[8]

The Massachusetts Historical Commission reports that the site was occupied as late as the Plantation Period (1675).[9] Westfield is identified as a potential major Native American settlement area. It was reputed to be the central location of the Woronocos, "a sub-group of the Pocumtucks, who by the seventeenth century loosely controlled territory encompassing most of the westernmost quarter of Massachusetts and extending south and north along the Connecticut River into northern Connecticut and southern Vermont."[10] Archaeological materials from the site suggest "local trade ties with natives inhabiting the Hudson River Valley (New York) and the southern portion of the Connecticut River Valley (Connecticut)."[11] This evidence supports a Stockbridge-Munsee oral tradition that maintains that there was connection between people of the Hudson and Connecticut River valleys during prehistoric times.

DEED RESEARCH

A series of land deeds establishes a cultural connection between the early historic native population of Westfield and the contemporary Stockbridge-Munsee community of Wisconsin. In 1905 Harry Andrew Wright published a series of Indian deeds from Hampden County, Massachusetts.[12] The first recorded deed dates to 1636. Land in what is now Agawam, Chicopee, Longmeadow, Springfield, and West Springfield, Massachusetts, was sold for eighteen fathom of wampum, eighteen coats, eighteen hoes, eighteen hatchets, and eighteen knives to William Pynchon, Henry Smith, and Jehu Burr. This marked the establishment of the first English settlement at what is now Springfield, Massachusetts. This deed reserved land planted in corn for Indian use, and gives them liberty to hunt, fish, and gather in the deeded parcel.[13] Peter Thomas notes that five years later in a deed conveying land in Chicopee to the English, "rights to these lands were held by (native) residents of both Woronoco (Westfield) and Norwottuck (Northampton)."[14] These two early deeds illustrate the persistence into the seventeenth century of native seasonal subsistence strategies and their continued presence along the Connecticut River Valley. Thomas further suggests that marriage alliances and other interactions likely occurred between these communities.[15]

In 1665, Spanesa and Poxonock sold a four-acre parcel of meadowland in Woronoco of what is now Windsor, Connecticut, to Daniel Clark and Samuel Marshall. The deed does not reserve land for native subsistence use. It does, however, state that both Clark and Marshall would be first in line for future land sales, indicating the continued native presence in the area. The deed also states, "And for the more full assurance of the said land unto ye said persons wee the Granters doe hereby Mortgage or fully engage that if wee make not the title of the land to these two Grantees, then Samuel Marshall is to have our little Daughter now about ffoure yeers old to enjoy her & dispose of her as his own estate."[16] Wright notes that there is no known legal acknowledgment of this deed.[17] We do not know if Spanesa and Poxonock (both noted as men) had to relinquish their daughter to Marshall for failure to comply with the conditions of the deed. However, including the conveyance of ownership of a child in a land transaction suggests that social and economic stress was increasing in the native community.

In 1669, several hundred acres were conveyed by "Aquat the Indian Sachem [chief] of Woronoak & Pojassick for & in Consideration of forty pounds."[18] It exempts "seven acres of meadow Land for Wollump, son of sd Alquat." The deed also reserved the "liberty for Indians to fish and take fowls."[19] The following year on April 25, Alquat and Wollump conveyed the seven-acre parcel to Mr. John Pynchon and Mr. Joseph Whiting in exchange for yearly access to five acres of planting land for Indian corn from Mr. Whiting.[20] On November 24, 1673, Wallump is identified as a resident and sachem of Pochaset, part of Westfield, Massachusetts. He conveyed a parcel of land yet reserved a meadow for himself, "before the Old Fort on the South Side of the River."[21]

These deeds indicate the dwindling presence of native people in the Westfield area. They also show that they continued to hunt and grow corn there. The deeds provide a glimpse into the genealogy of a prominent native family. Alquat was sachem of the Woronoco tribe until sometime between 1660 and 1673. His son, Wallump, was sachem in 1673 and lived in Westfield at least until November 1673.

Growing hostilities between the native population and the English culminated in King Philip's War of 1675–1676. The war lasted for fourteen months, and the remaining Woronocos likely moved to a refugee settlement at Schaghticoke, New York. According to Gordon Day, "Schaghticoke had been established beeen 1674 and 1676 by refugees from southern New England. Early Schaghticoke probably contained Woronoke, Agawam, and Narragansett tribes, forming a village of perhaps 1000 persons."[22] Patrick Frazier supports this report that Indians from the Westfield River area relocated to the Hudson River a year before the outbreak of the war.[23]

A deed dating to August 11, 1703, provides information on the last native land transaction in Westfield:

> Wallascoanoote, Nahhaisawolemett, Suckonsago & Petoawoacute of Albany alias Housatunuck all Indians Relations of Wolump who was formerly Chief Sachem of Pochassuck, for in Consideration of the Sum of five Pounds Current money & Two new Coates . . . [convey a parcel of] . . . forty acres . . . which WeLump Reserved to himself when he Sold his other land at Pochas-Suck, which land lyes before the old fort in a Place now Commonly known by the name of Welump Bottome.[24]

This document definitively establishes a "shared group identity" between the Woronoco of Westfield, Massachusetts, and the Housatonuck (Mohican) Indians of the Hudson River Valley. Memory of the Westfield homeland was still present in 1745. An important Mohawk chief, Hendrick, was the son of a Mohican chief and a Mohawk woman.[25] He spoke at Albany, New York, about fears of losing Mohawk lands to the English, citing Westfield, Massachusetts, as an example, and as the place where his father formerly lived.[26]

STOCKBRIDGE-MUNSEE BAND OF
MOHICAN INDIANS OF WISCONSIN

Scholars of the Stockbridge-Munsee tribe such as Dorothy W. Davids, Shirley W. Dunn, and Patrick Frazier have traced their origins to native populations from New England, the Mid-Atlantic, and the Hudson River Valley of New York. The original homeland of the Stockbridge (Mohican) encompassed the Hudson River Valley from Lake Champlain to Manhattan and extended into Connecticut, Massachusetts, and Vermont. By the 1730s most Mohicans had moved to the Christian missionary town of Stockbridge, Massachusetts.[27]

In 1780, the Stockbridge Indians moved to New Stockbridge on the Oneida Reservation in central New York. In the 1820s they began their migration to Wisconsin where the Munsee joined them in the 1840s. Today the Stockbridge-Munsee Reservation encompasses 22,139 acres in Shawano, Wisconsin.[28]

NAGPRA GRANTS

The Native American Graves Protection and Repatriation Act provides two types of grants for consultation/documentation and repatriation. Museums that may have NAGPRA-sensitive items, federally recognized Indian tribes, and Native Hawaiian organizations are eligible to apply. Application deadlines are posted on the National NAGPRA website.[29]

Consultation/documentation grants are competitive and are awarded annually. Grants range from $5,000 to $90,000. National NAGPRA staff provide a prereview period that allows applicants to fine-tune their proposals. Repatriation grants help defray the cost of decontamination, packaging, transporting, reburial, or storage of NAGPRA-sensitive items. These grants are noncompetitive and are awarded on a continuing basis up to $15,000.[30]

Consultation Grant

Upon determining cultural affiliation between the Stockbridge-Munsee and the museum's Connecticut River Valley archaeological collection, the museum applied for and received a NAGPRA consultation grant. The consultation had five objectives:

1. Identify the human remains and objects in the museum's collections that are culturally affiliated with the Stockbridge-Munsee Band of Mohican Indians.
2. Meet with authorized representatives from the Stockbridge-Munsee to examine collections, review museum records, and consult with museum staff about the proper care, treatment, and disposition of culturally affiliated human remains and objects.
3. Prepare a notice of inventory completion for the human remains and associated funerary objects.
4. Identify any items that meet the requirements for NAGPRA categories of unassociated funerary object, sacred object, and object of cultural patrimony, and prepare notices of intent to repatriate, if necessary.
5. Develop a care and treatment plan for material that will remain either temporarily or permanently at the museum.

Official representatives of the Stockbridge-Munsee Band of Mohican Indians visited the Science Museum in March 2002 to meet with staff members in order to review objects and their associated records. During consultation, tribal representatives determined what material was culturally associated with the Stockbridge-Munsee. The consultation resulted in the identification of eight sacred objects, all smoking pipes, and eighty-four sets of human remains and 321 associated funerary objects from the Connecticut River Valley.

Identification of this material was accomplished by first conducting a computer search of all museum archaeology records for western Massachusetts; second, reviewing all paper-catalogue entries; third, visually inspecting identified collection items; and finally, reconciling catalogue information with visual observations of material to generate a review list for consultation.

The Stockbridge-Munsee representatives decided that all human remains and associated funerary objects would be repatriated and reburied. The eight smoking pipes identified as sacred objects would also be repatriated. It was decided that no remaining NAGPRA-sensitive material would remain permanently at the museum.

Currently, the museum is temporarily curating Stockbridge-Munsee human remains and associated funerary objects pending reburial. A care and treatment plan was drafted during the consultation process. According to the plan this material is held in a separate storage area in a climate-controlled collection facility that meets museum industry curation standards. Only authorized representatives of the Stockbridge-Munsee, the curator of anthropology, and the director of the museum have access to the material. No research can be conducted on the material, including carbon 14 testing or photo documentation. When possible, items have been removed from plastic bags and kept only in acid-free cardboard boxes.

A notice of intent to repatriate the eight smoking pipes was published in the Federal Register on March 7, 2003.[31] On August 20, 2003, the Springfield Science Museum published a notice of inventory completion in the Federal Register.[32] This inventory describes in detail eighty-four sets of human remains of Native American ancestry and 321 associated funerary objects. The notice allowed for a thirty-day waiting period to allow additional claimants to come forward.

After publication of the notice the Narragansett Indian Tribe of Rhode Island and the Wampanoag Tribe of Gay Head (Aquinnah) contacted the museum and provided documentation of their cultural affiliation with the Connecticut River Valley human remains and associated funerary objects. Oral tradition and historic evidence indicate that the Narragansetts were involved in wampum production and distribution in western Massachusetts during the Contact and Early Historic periods. Historic evidence also indicates that the Narragansetts engaged in battles in western Massachusetts during King Philip's War (1675–1676). Oral tradition and historical evidence indicate that the Wampanoag Tribe of Gay Head also considered the Connecticut River Valley a sacred area, and that they participated in battles in western Massachusetts during King Philip's War. A correction to the notice of inventory completion was published in the Federal Register on September 14, 2004.[33] This notice added the Narragansett Indian Tribe of Rhode Island and the Wampanoag Tribe of Gay Head (Aquinnah) of Massachusetts to the Native American tribes that were consulted and to whom repatriation may proceed.

RESOURCES

The identification of objects that fall under NAGPRA can be challenging. Native American human remains, associated funerary objects, and unassociated funerary objects can be determined through examination of museum and archival records, collectors' field notes, and skeletal biology. These sources can provide information about the age of the remains, provenance, and mortuary practices. A list of further reading can be found at the end of this essay.

The NAGPRA consultation process is crucial to identifying objects of cultural patrimony, sacred objects, and unassociated funerary objects. The National NAGPRA website provides useful information to help with consultation and repatriation.[34] The Native American Consultation Database (grants.cr.nps.gov/nacd/index.cfm) offers a searchable list of official contacts for Native American tribes and Native Hawaiian organizations. The database also provides information about the locations of native land claims.

Two searchable databases are the Notices of Inventory Completion (NIC) and the Notices of Intent to Repatriate (NIR). NIC, for human remains and associated funerary objects, can be viewed at www.nps.gov/nagpra/FED_NOTICES/NAGPRADIR/index.html, while NIR, for unassociated funerary objects, objects of cultural patrimony, and sacred objects, can be found at www.nps.gov/nagpra/FED_NOTICES/NAGPRADIR/index2.htm. These databases contain all of the notices published in the Federal Register. They provide examples of objects subject to NAGPRA, their geographic origins, and the Native American tribes and Native Hawaiian organizations.

Many federally recognized Native American tribes have websites as well. These can provide a range of information about tribal history, migration routes, and land claims. Additionally, Tribal Historic Preservation Officers (THPO) can provide information on pending and completed NAGPRA claims at www.nathpo.org/.

CONCLUSION

This case study traces the steps that the Springfield Science Museum took to comply with NAGPRA and repatriate archaeological material and human remains from the Connecticut River Valley. It illustrates the value of researching primary documents, such as deeds and personal correspondence from the seventeenth and eighteenth centuries. These documents were enhanced with information obtained during consultation with federally recognized tribes. Oral tradition, archaeology, and primary and secondary historical sources all contributed to a determination of cultural affiliation. The NAGPRA consultation process clarified the areas of western Massachusetts of interest to different federally recognized and nonrecognized native groups. The NAGPRA consultation grant provided further support for museum staff by increasing awareness of repatriation protocol. Staff has also extended the care and treatment plan developed during consultation to the entire NAGPRA-sensitive collection held by the museum.

NOTES

1. Native American Graves Protection and Repatriation Act (NAGPRA) 25 U.S.C. 3001 et seq.
2. Patrick Frazier, *The Mohicans of Stockbridge* (Lincoln: University of Nebraska Press, 1992).
3. William Stoughton, "Letter from Lieutenant Governor William Stoughton to Colonel John Pynchon, of Springfield," Massachusetts Archives, vol. 30 (Boston, October 13, 1696), 383; and Samuel Partridge, "Letter from Samuel Partridge to Lieutenant Governor William Stoughton," Massachusetts Archives, vol. 30 (Boston, March 4, 1697), 401a.
4. NAGPRA 26 U.S.C. 3001 (2).
5. NAGPRA 43 CFR 102c.

6. Douglas S. Byers and Irving Rouse, "Re-Examination of the Guida Farm," *Bulletin of the Archaeological Society of Connecticut* 1960, 30:3–39.

7. Byers and Rouse.

8. Massachusetts Historical Commission (MHC), *MHC Reconnaissance Survey Town Report: Westfield* (Boston: MHC, 1982).

9. MHC, 4.

10. MHC, 4.

11. Harry Andrew Wright, ed., *Indian Deeds of Hampden County* (Springfield, MA, 1905).

12. Wright, 122.

13. "Deed to Lands along and North of the Chicopee River, Massachusetts" (Boston: Massachusetts Historical Society, 1641) cited in Peter A. Thomas, *In the Maelstrom of Change: The Indian Trade and Cultural Process in the Middle Connecticut River Valley, 1635–1665,* Ph.D. Dissertation (Amherst: University of Massachusetts, 1979), 142.

14. Thomas, 142.

15. Thomas, 142.

16. Wright, 55.

17. Wright, 56.

18. Wright, 69.

19. Wright, 70.

20. Wright, 72–73.

21. Wright, 82.

22. Gordon M. Day, *The History of the St. Francis Indians* (Ottawa: National Museums of Canada, 1981), 63–63.

23. Frazier, 5.

24. Springfield Registry of deeds, Book B (Springfield, MA, 1703), 133.

25. Frazier, 9.

26. Frazier, 75.

27. Dorothy W. Davids, *Brief History of the Mohican Nation Stockbridge-Munsee Band* (Bowler, WI: Stockbridge-Munsee Historical Commission, 2001); Shirley W. Dunn, *The Mohicans and Their Land, 1609–1730* (Fleischmanns, NY: Purplemountain, 1994); Shirley W. Dunn, *The Mohican World, 1689–1750* (Fleischmanns, NY: Purplemountain, 2000); Shirley W. Dunn, *The River Indians: Mohicans Making History* (Fleischmann, NY: Purplemountain, 2009).

28. Stockbridge-Munssee Band of Mohican Indians, 2009, www.mohican-nsn.gov; Stockbridge-Munsee Band of Mohican Indians, "Tribal Statistics," 2013, witribws.wi.gov/docview.asp?docid=19080&locid=57.

29. National NAGPRA, www.nps.gov/nagpra.

30. National NAGPRA.

31. Springfield Science Museum, "Notice of Intent to Repatriate Cultural Items: Springfield Science Museum, Springfield, MA," *Federal Register*, March 7, 2003 (FR Doc 3), 5511.

32. Springfield Science Museum, "Notice of Inventory Completion: Springfield, MA," *Federal Register*, August 20, 2003 (FR DOC 03), 21336.

33. Springfield Science Museum, "Notice of Inventory Completion, Correction, Springfield, MA," *Federal Register*, September 4, 2004 (FR DOC 04), 20652.

34. National NAGPRA.

FURTHER READING

Byers, Doulas S., and Irving Rouse, 1960, "Re-Examination of the Guida Farm," *Bulletin of the Archaeological Society of Connecticut* (30): 3–39.

Davids, Dorothy W., 2001, *Brief History of the Mohican Nation Stockbridge-Munsee Band.* Stockbridge-Munsee Historical Committee, Bowler, WI.

Day, Gordon M., 1981, *The Identity of the St. Francis Indians.* National Museums of Canada, Ottawa.

Dunn, Shirley W., 2009, *The River Indians: Mohicans Making History*. Purplemountain Press, Fleischmanns, NY.

Dunn, Shirley W., 2000, *The Mohican World, 1680–1750*. Purplemountain Press, Fleischmanns, NY.

Dunn, Shirley W., 1994, *The Mohicans and Their Land, 1609–1730*. Purplemountain Press, Fleischmanns, NY.

Frazier, Patrick, 1992, *The Mohicans of Stockbridge*. University of Nebraska Press, Lincoln.

Grumet, Robert S. 1995, *Historic Contact: Indian People and Colonists in Today's Northeastern United States in the Sixteenth through Eighteenth Centuries*. University of Oklahoma Press, Norman.

Massachusetts Historical Commission, 1982, *MHC Reconnaissance Survey Town Report Westfield*. Massachusetts Historical Commission, Boston.

National NAGPRA, www.nps.gov/nagpra/.

Partridge, Samuel, 1697, "Letter from Samuel Partridge to Lieutenant Governor William Stoughton," Northampton, March 4, 1697. Massachusetts Archives, vol. 30:401a.

Stockbridge-Munsee Band of Mohican Indians, 2013, Tribal Statistic: www.witribe.wi.gov/docview.asp?docid=19080&locid=57.

Stockbridge-Munsee Band of Mohican Indians, 2009 Official Website: www.mohican-nsn.gov.

Stoughton, William, 1696, "Letter from Lieutenant Governor William Stoughton to Colonel John Pynchon, of Springfield," Boston, October 13, 1696. Massachusetts Archives, vol. 30:383.

Thomas: Peter A., 1979, *In the Maelstrom of Change: The Indian Trade and Cultural Process in the Middle Connecticut River Valley, 1635–1665*. Ph.D. Dissertation, University of Massachusetts, Amherst.

Chapter Seven

Creating and Negotiating Contracts for Traveling Exhibits

Julia Courtney

Since the 1960s when the first group of objects from King Tutankhamun's tomb traveled to eighteen cities in the United States and six cities in Canada to stimulate public interest in the UNESCO-sponsored salvaging of Nubian monuments threatened by the Aswan Dam Project,[1] traveling exhibits have captured the public's attention. This early exhibit led to one of the most popular blockbuster exhibits in the United States in 1977 and 1978, *Treasures of Tutankhanum.*[2] These early megaexhibits attracted enormous crowds and created unprecedented income for art museums—from admissions and especially from the sales of related merchandise.[3] During the three years the exhibit toured the United States, more than seven million people saw objects from one of the most important finds in archaeological history, which was loaned by Egypt's Cairo Museum in celebration of the bicentennial of the United States.[4]

Traveling exhibits have been a mainstay for museums for over fifty years, and whether the purpose of the exhibit is to raise public awareness or increase attendance and revenue, traveling shows continue to fill the exhibit schedules of large, midsized, and small museums around the world. The information provided in this chapter was compiled as a result of scrutinizing, developing, and implementing numerous exhibit contracts. *On the Road Again: Developing and Managing Traveling Exhibitions* (Buck and Gilmore, Washington, DC: American Association of Museums, 2003) contains a chapter devoted to exhibit contracts, which provides a useful overview of various sections of a contract and includes sample language.

OVERVIEW

Contemporary traveling exhibits are organized and co-organized and marketed in several ways: by a museum(s) holding a large number of objects in a particular topic area in their collection(s), by independent/guest curators, or by traveling exhibit entities such as Smithsonian Institution Traveling Exhibit Service (SITES), International Arts and Artists, Landau Traveling Exhibits, Evergreen Exhibits, the Association of Science and Technology (ASTC), Independent Curators International, George Eastman House, and Exhibits USA, to name a few. There are also many small, regional traveling exhibit companies and specialty museums that offer a menu of exhibits, à la carte.

Most museums and exhibit organizers form and host traveling exhibits with several intentions: to highlight important or spectacular objects in a collection, to share objects and information to a large audience, to raise public awareness about a topic, to increase visitation and generate income, to showcase exhibit designs and curatorial connoisseurship associated with a collection or museum, to attract potential sponsors/donors, to increase national or international visibility of a collection or museum, and to add to the scholarship of a topic and its associated objects. Although museums are sometimes critiqued for becoming entertainment venues in addition to repositories for artifacts, the novelty and appeal of the blockbuster exhibit and traveling exhibits in general continue to grow.

Large museums with substantial endowments and generous supporters organize, host, and travel multiple blockbuster shows, but small to midsized museums or museums with limited resources look to organize and host exhibits that are more manageable in size, in order to keep offering novel experiences and presenting new information and objects with which to educate their visitors.

The rewarding task of organizing and offering traveling exhibits requires significant forethought and careful planning. One of the first steps in the process is to develop and negotiate a comprehensive, legally binding contract that articulates expectations, protects all involved parties, and assures the safe care and protection of the objects to be included in the exhibit. This chapter will outline the important features of a traveling exhibit contract and discuss reviewing or creating clear and reasonable contracts that safeguard objects on loan and articulate the expectations for involved parties. Whether a museum is developing and traveling an exhibit with its own objects, hosting the work of one or more artists, or borrowing a preorganized show, the suggestions that follow will assist museum professionals in creating and negotiating an exhibit contract that addresses important concerns.

As with any contract, traveling exhibit contracts set forth the expectations for each party involved. In this case it typically refers to a lender and a borrower, which are most often a museum or institution, a private collector, an artist, or a gallery. Carefully reviewing and negotiating contracts and ancillary materials generated for traveling exhibits up front can reduce potential issues that might arise when the exhibit is shipped, installed, and de-installed, as well as for the duration of the show.

Contracts for traveling exhibits vary in format; the language may be very clear, basic, and casual, or formal with a lot of legal terminology.[5] Regardless of approach, there should be a contract in place for each venue that is hosting an exhibit—an agreement between the lender and that particular venue that contains some pertinent information.[6] The contracts must be signed and approved by all parties listed on the agreement in order to be effective. Most contracts include the agreement and ancillary materials, some examples of which include

- An exhibit checklist (ideally one with images and measurements of each object and installation requirements),
- A list of pertinent staff members,
- A prospectus and promise of public relations materials.

Each section of the contract should delineate expectations relevant to the topic of the section and be easy for all participants to understand. In the following pages, each area of concern for an exhibit contract will be discussed and suggestions given as to how best to solidify expectations.

PREPARING TO LEND OR BORROW

Before pursuing an exhibit or creating and negotiating a contract, museum professionals should review the exhibit proposal to make sure that the exhibit is an appropriate size, subject, and price for their institution. If previous venues have hosted the exhibit, public relations, admissions, and curatorial personnel can be consulted to find out what can be expected and if their visitors responded favorably to the show. Keep in mind the following questions when assessing whether a particular traveling exhibit is right for your institution:

- Does the topic relate to the museum's permanent collection? Is there another compelling reason to host the exhibit (e.g., public appeal, discussion of a social issue, introduction of a subject or art form)?
- What is the expected attendance? Anticipated audience? Appropriate age?
- How much space does the exhibit require (usually given in linear or square feet)?
- What is the participation fee? Shipping costs? Courier fees, if applicable?

- Are there components that require electricity, hardware, equipment, or other technology?
- Is the exhibit available during the time frame the museum hopes to host it?
- How labor and resource intensive is the installation? How many people will be needed to accept shipment and install the exhibit?
- Does the exhibit come with display cases, furniture, and so forth, or must the borrower provide the means to display the objects?
- Will the museum charge an exhibition entry fee? Does the lender allow a fee to be imposed?
- Does the lender or artist have expectations for an exhibit opening, lectures, and other related programs?

GENERAL AGREEMENT-TO-BORROW
TERMS OR INFORMATION

Most exhibit contracts begin with recital paragraphs that name the borrowing and lending institutions or parties and with a description of the exhibit, objects, or artwork to be loaned or borrowed. It is important to include the legal name of both institutions, as it may vary from the museum's common name. In addition, the expected loan date, dates of the exhibit, and date of de-installation are typically included in these sections. The official title of the exhibit and any subtitles should also be included in this area.

So, the first part of the contract often looks something like this:

> The borrowing institution (museum name and location) requests to borrow from (organizer) and agrees to show the exhibit entitled (exhibit title) to be exhibited at the borrower's location for a participation fee of (amount in U.S. currency), shipping costs (outlined in another section), and courier fees (outlined later). Said exhibit will be shipped to the borrower no later than (approximate incoming shipment date) and will be received at the next venue no later than (approximate outgoing shipment date). The exhibit will be exhibited for XX weeks (time frame). A current, signed facility report (AAM has an ideal template to follow) must be provided to the lender within 30 days of the signed contract. A certificate of insurance must be provided to the lender 30 days prior to the shipment/arrival of the exhibit. [7]

Note that the overall loan period always extends beyond the exhibit's official open dates to provide time for shipping/transportation and installation, and de-installation and shipping after the exhibit closes. However, most contracts make that assumption and only list the exhibit dates in the front matter. Often, this extra time frame is outlined in the shipping portion of the contract.

After the exhibit description and particulars have been outlined, many exhibition contracts include a background or introduction section that articulates the "uses" of an exhibit and typically includes a statement of the lender's educational mission, a disclaimer against any potential conflict with sponsors, and whether or not a borrowing institution will be permitted to impose an exhibit fee on visitors. If the exhibit lender agrees to allow an exhibit fee, oftentimes the maximum amount a museum can charge will appear in the contract. When revising or creating a contract, you might find it helpful to include an "at a glance" table at the beginning of the document that outlines the basic information contained in the contract, including exhibit dates, participation fee, shipping costs, security level, insurance value, and square or linear footage requirements. This makes finding pertinent information quickly or disseminating it at an exhibit planning meeting much more efficient.

Following the background and/or introduction section of the contract, usually particulars such as participation fees, facility reports, and shipping and courier costs are described. In recent years, in addition to requiring a signed contract, exhibit companies have been reluctant to "hold" on an exhibit without a deposit, so deposit payments are becoming more of an industry standard. The participation fee (including the deposit) for the exhibit is typically accompanied by a payment schedule with agreed-upon dates that payments will be made. This information might be conveyed in a paragraph or in the form of a table. In addition, the expectation to pay shipping, either one way or both incoming and outgoing shipping, will be delineated, as well as any requirements for a courier who may accompany the exhibit and payment of their travel expenses. It is a good plan to request and document a limit on travel expenses for couriers, curators, or speakers when negotiating the contract. Museums typically book exhibits well in advance and travel expenses can fluctuate dramatically in terms of airfare, hotel fees, and fuel prices depending on the time of year and variants in the economy.

In addition, most lenders will not consider loaning art or objects without carefully reviewing the facility report from the borrowing institution. The contract should be and usually is contingent upon approval of the facility report.

The request for the borrowing museum's certificate of insurance, which delineates insurance coverage of objects on loan, is typically demanded under the general information area of the contract. The request for the certificate of insurance as well as other details mentioned in the recitals and background or introduction sections of the agreement, will be expanded upon deeper in the document.

Although exhibit dates, ship dates, courier fees, and payment schedule might be points to negotiate, the facility report and certificate of insurance are usually nonnegotiable.

PARTICIPATION FEE AND SHIPPING

The second section of the contract typically outlines the total exhibit participation fee and breaks the total down into incremental payments. It also should outline any late fees or charges that the borrower is responsible for in the event that a payment is delayed. For example, if an exhibit participation fee is $50,000, the payment schedule might be as follows:

Payment 1: Deposit $12,500 due upon signing of contract
Payment 2: (Date) $12,500
Payment 3: (Date) $12,500
Payment 4: $12,500 due prior to the exhibit opening

Shipping payments are often prorated and divided between all the exhibit venues; however, occasionally the organizer of an exhibit will ask the borrower to pay the shipping company directly. It is important to make sure this is articulated in the contract, too, so that no surprises surface late in the process.

CHECKLIST: EXHIBIT CONTENTS

Most exhibit contracts will include a checklist and description of all the objects that are to be loaned for the exhibition. Sometimes the checklist is part of the contract and other times it is included as a separate document, referred to as an "exhibit" or "appendix," along with other ancillary materials provided with the contract. In addition, a paragraph that describes the exhibit contents should appear in the contract. Such a paragraph may read:

> The exhibit will include XX (number) of objects including (paintings, works on paper, sculpture, antiquities, etc.) as listed in the exhibit checklist. If any changes are made to the checklist the borrower will be informed of the changes and an updated checklist will be provided. There may be circumstances that require the withdrawal of certain objects from the exhibit. The lender will keep the borrower updated about changes. The borrower may not omit any component from the exhibit without prior written approval from the lender. [8]

The flexibility of omitting an object or exhibit component is worth negotiating. Sometimes during installation of the exhibit it will become apparent that space will not allow an object or component to easily fit or it may impede on American Disabilities Act (ADA) requirements for maneuvering through a public space, such as a museum exhibit. Most lenders understand space limitations and will help find a solution if something in the show simply will not fit into the space. During initial conversations, if the square or linear footage requirement for the exhibit is close to a museum's capacity, it is wise to share floor plans and come up with a layout that both the borrower and lender agree on.

The contract, exhibit checklist, or installation guide should carefully outline what exhibit furniture or exhibit display mechanisms are required for the show and if the lender provides them. If the borrowing museum is charged with constructing specialized display cases, risers, or other display components, enough time should be allotted for the construction or fabrication of these items.

In addition to the objects and furniture, the contract should indicate if didactic information in the form of labels, panels, introductory panels, signage, catalogues, or cell-phone tour scripts is provided. Interpretation and educational information is not always addressed in the contract. It is important to ask this question as writing interpretive material for objects that are not part of a museum's permanent collection can prove to be time consuming. It is best to have this information in advance. This way museum staff can allot time before the exhibit opening to conduct research and write labels, brochures, or cell-phone tour scripts. Many traveling exhibits are reducing the amount of exhibit text that they provide, in favor of a catalogue or cell tour. This may work well for your institution, but it is best to have something in writing that articulates the expectations for both the borrower and lender with regard to interpretive materials.

INSURANCE AND SECURITY, CARE AND PROTECTION

In addition to a facility report, most lenders require a certificate of insurance before moving forward with an exhibit contract. The certificate of insurance delineates the museum's insurance coverage (usually fine art insurance) for objects on loan and the amount that is covered. This confirms that the loaned objects are covered under the museum's umbrella policy or will make evident the need for any additional insurance. Typically fine art insurance covers the exhibit on loan, its components and furniture from wall to wall, including while it is in transit.[9] In other words, the objects are insured from the time they leave the owner's premises until the time they return.[10] The total value of the exhibit or objects being loaned should be stated in the contract. Often the lender provides an itemized list, with the insurance value of each object. Sometimes the museum that organizes the exhibit will provide insurance coverage, but not always. They may require the borrower to cover the exhibit or purchase an additional policy. It is critical to know who is insuring the exhibit and what the policy covers. Providing all-risk, wall-to-wall insurance is a standard approach.

By nature, the handling of art objects or artifacts or moving them from one location to another inevitably puts them at higher risk than if they were to remain locked in a museum vault, display cases, or on a gallery wall. Therefore it is very important to be familiar with fine art insurance coverage and follow the requirements necessary to maintain the safety of the objects. Staff should be able to mitigate any issues that might arise that may put the objects at risk while they are not in their permanent location.

An example of wording that may be used for this portion of the contract:

> The borrower (or lender) will provide all-risk, wall-to-wall fine arts insurance coverage for the total insurance value of the exhibition, valued at $XX. A certificate of insurance must be received from the borrower (or provided by the lender) upon signing of the contract (or sometimes, prior to the delivery of the exhibit).[11]

Exclusions from the insurance that should be mentioned in the contract will normally include general wear and tear, gradual deterioration, acts of God or terrorism, and other exclusions that are standard to museum collections coverage.

According to Buck and Gilmore, if an exhibit is an international loan, the organizer may decide to insure the exhibit using the indemnification process offered by the U.S. government.[12] It is best for museum professionals to explore all insurance options and select the one that best applies to the situation. Museum registrars and attorneys are well versed in the topic and should be consulted as a matter of course.

FACILITY AND SECURITY REQUIREMENTS

Most times, the exact location in which the exhibit will be installed is spelled out in the contract. Listing the gallery, building, and so forth, is important as it represents the agreed-upon space, for which the approved facility report is provided. Security requirements are usually differentiated and listed as limited, moderate, or high security as defined in guidelines developed by the Smithsonian Institute Traveling Exhibits Service.[13] Expectations regarding how much security will be provided are included in the contract. A live security guard in the exhibit or in the vicinity of the gallery during public hours is a standard expectation, as is live, on-site, twenty-four-hour security, as well as security cameras that monitor all activity and are specific to the exhibit space.

Climate and lighting conditions are generally laid out in this section of the contract as well. Environmental requirements will vary depending on the nature of the objects being loaned. Generally, contracts will ask for a constant temperature of 68–72 degrees Fahrenheit, and relative humidity of 48–52 percent, as well as light levels of 15–20 foot candles or less for works on paper. Most contracts for fine art exhibits insist that objects are handled only by trained museum personnel and experienced art handlers (no interns or volunteers). Locked exhibit cases or pedestals are usually required as well as security plates or alarms for two-dimensional works. Eating and drinking in the gallery or exhibit space is generally prohibited. Most lenders will not permit photography of their objects by the public or amateur photographers, although this requirement is changing, especially as museums endeavor to use open-source image databases, and varies from exhibit to exhibit.

SHIPPING, HANDLING, AND INSTALLATION INSTRUCTIONS

Pay very close attention to this area of the exhibit contract as it articulates the shipping details, as well as detailed handling of objects, information on con-ducting condition reports, and whether a courier will accompany the exhibit to assist with condition reports, as well as important installation instructions.

The prorated cost for fine art shipping (and a cap), and whether the borrower is responsible for one way or both incoming and outgoing shipping, are important to know. This allows an accurate exhibit budget to be prepared in the beginning stages of exhibit planning. It may be necessary for the shipping vehicle used to have a liftgate (if borrower does not have a loading dock, this makes the delivery process much easier and faster). This should be negotiated along with the estimated day of delivery in relation to the exhibit opening, which is typically delineated in this section of the contract (two weeks before, ten days before, for example).

Not all exhibits provide/require a courier, but if a courier is required, the contract will indicate so in this section. Typically, it is stated as follows:

> The borrower will pay travel expenses for a courier who will be on site to conduct condition reports with the assistance of museum staff provided by the borrower upon unpacking the exhibit and repacking after de-installation of the exhibit.[14]

Sometimes the courier will also help with unpacking, installing, de-installing, and repacking the exhibit, but not always. The contract may indi-cate how many qualified art handlers are needed to install the exhibit in some cases. The length of time a courier will be on-site (usually one week) will determine some of the travel expenses (hotel and per diem), and whether the courier will drive or fly will impact the exhibit budget. It is wise to place a limit on the total travel expenses a borrowing institution will pay, as well as determine who will make the travel arrangements.

The exhibit checklist, whether part of the contract or as a separate docu-ment, should provide detailed instructions on how to install the objects, in-cluding measurements of each object, whether it should be on a display stand or not, or if it's a two-dimensional work, a description of the hardware that is included and what hardware might be needed.

A crate list and load diagram of how the crates fit into a truck, are both important documents and are not always included in the contract. If they are not, the borrower representative should try to obtain both from the lender. The crate list usually includes the measurements of the crates, which is critical information, as some crates may be too large to maneuver through entryways, in elevators, or to storage. Knowing what is in each crate is also important information for the lender as it determines appropriate placement of the crate in the museum in anticipation of installation. The crates can then be placed in proximity to where the objects will be on display. Ideally, an object should be moved the shortest distance possible and the fewest times possible during the installation and de-installation processes.

PUBLICITY AND CREDIT LINE

A list of publicity materials that are provided in advance usually appears in the contract, although documents themselves have yet to be created. For example, press kits, high-resolution images, image captions, artist biographies, education guide or materials, exhibit catalogue, and other materials are some of the common items included as part of the exhibit education and publicity kit that comes with an exhibit. Often, a curator or museum staff from the organizing institution will provide lectures, demonstrations, and the like. Their honorarium or fee and whether travel expenses must be covered by the borrower are occasionally identified in this section of the contract, but should also be included in the fees section of the contract.

As was mentioned previously, most lenders will not permit photography, in which case, it is best to post a public sign that states, "No photography (and/or video) permitted in the exhibit." In the age of cell phones, most of which have a camera and video recording capacity, it is a challenge to enforce this stipulation. Security guards should be informed of any limitations with regard to taking pictures, as they are usually the ones to enforce the policy. Some lenders are now articulating permissions with regard to images and content to be used on social media sites such as Facebook, Twitter, Pintrest, and Instagram. It is very important to obtain permission to post information on social media sites in advance as the lender can easily see what is being done on a borrower's website or social media account and a breach of contract in any area subjects the exhibit to potential closing.

The credit line and/or logo of the lending institution should be provided in the contract. Often the logo will be sent to the borrower via e-mail or on a CD along with high-resolution images of the objects included in the exhibit.

The expectations regarding use of the credit line is usually articulated in the publicity section.

Some lenders will request that the credit line be included on all publicity documents, interviews, press releases, signage, and invitations or brochures. If a local sponsor is supporting the exhibit, the borrower typically has permission to post that information as long as the organizer's credit line is included as well. Some lenders want their own public relations team to approve all signage, publicity materials, and advertisements. Note how far in advance they want to review the material and what their turnaround for approval might be. This information can be important to know when a museum is churning out information about an exhibit in anticipation of its opening.

CANCELLATIONS, RESOLUTION OF DISPUTES, FORCE MAJEURE

Although it is always the intention of both parties to uphold the exhibit agreement, a manner in which to resolve disputes should be described in the contract. Often the contract suggests that both parties will be willing to "negotiate in good faith, any claims, disputes, or controversies that arise or relate to the contract,"[15] and further describes the way in which to resolve a dispute through mediation or some other means.

In addition, the reality that some exhibits are cancelled is one that has to be addressed in the exhibit contract. Sometimes the lender will impose a cancellation fee or require the borrowing institution to incur all fees associated with the cancellation, such as storage of the exhibit during the time frame it would have been on view and shipping to another venue, as well as losing the deposit and any payments made in advance of the show. The language might read something like this:

> The borrower must notify the lender in writing of any need to cancel this contract. The exhibit participation fee represents all direct and indirect expenses for the production and maintenance of the exhibition, therefore the borrower must pay the full exhibition fee. In the event that an alternative venue is secured for the same time frame, the borrower will forgo any payments made by the date of cancellation plus any additional expenses incurred and legal fees required to collect payment, in the event the full amount is not covered by an alternate venue.[16]

Although it is in the best interest of the borrower to fulfill the contract obligations and make payments on time, it is helpful to understand the ramifications of cancelling the contract should circumstances arise that make it unavoidable.

Finally, most contracts have a loophole that renders both parties excused from contractual obligations in the event of circumstances beyond their control. Two examples of force majeure language you might see in an exhibit contract are below:

> Neither the Lender or the Borrower shall be responsible or liable for damages caused by a delay or failure in the performance of this agreement or any provision hereof, if such delay or failure is due to a cause beyond its control, including but not limited to fires, strikes, scarcity of materials or fuel, acts of terrorism, acts of war, acts of mobs or rioters, acts of public authorities, delay or defaults caused by public carriers, or earthquakes, storms, floods or other acts of God. [17]

And this shorter example covers the same concepts:

> To the extent that circumstances beyond the reasonable control of a party, including weather or other acts of God, war, terrorism or threats of terrorism, governmental actions, labor strife, conduct by third parties or curtailment of transportation facilities prevent, delay or make commercially impractical performance by that party, in whole or in part, then such performance will be excused. [18]

CONCLUSION

Traveling exhibits exemplify the age-old challenge of keeping objects safe and inspiring the public's quest for learning through the display and interpretation of objects. In order to make large and small exhibit loans feasible and safe for the objects, great care must be taken with regard to security, insurance coverage, preservation, climate control, art handling, and logistics when an object is moved, regardless of how far, or for how long. A well-executed exhibit contract and loan agreement can articulate the expectations regarding the care, interpretation, publicity, and security of the objects, as well as serve as a vehicle to document indemnification while exhibits are on the road.

All traveling exhibit contracts should set forth the expectations for each party involved, and be carefully reviewed and negotiated according to suggestions set forth in this essay. By following these guidelines from the beginning, museum professionals can reduce the number of potential issues that might arise when the exhibit is shipped, installed, and de-installed, as well as for the duration of the show.

NOTES

1. www.museum.upenn.edu/expedition.

2. Melanie McAlister, "'The Common Heritage of Mankind': Race, Nation and Masculinity in the King Tut Exhibit," *Representations*, no. 54, Spring, 1996, p. 80.

3. "Art History and the 'Blockbuster' Exhibit," Editorial, *The Art Bulletin*, vol. 68, issue 3, 1986, www.tepotech.com/Art_Bulletin/1986683SepEditorialTheBlockbuster.pdf, accessed October 3, 2104.

4. McAlister, p. 80.

5. Rebecca A. Buck and Jean Allman Gilmore, *On the Road Again: Developing and Managing Traveling Exhibitions* (Washington, DC: American Association of Museums, 2003), p. 39.

6. Buck and Gilmore, p. 39.

7. Exhibit Contract, Springfield Museums, Springfield, MA, Section 1, p. 1.

8. Exhibit Contract, International Arts & Artists, Washington, DC, Section 4, p. 2.

9. Buck and Gilmore, p. 44.

10. Buck and Gilmore, p. 44.

11. Exhibit Contract, Reading Public Museum, Reading, PA, Section 5, p. 4

12. Buck and Gilmore, p. 45.

13. Buck and Gilmore, p. 49.

14. Exhibit Contract, International Arts & Artists, Washington, DC, Section 5, p. 2.

15. Exhibit Contract, International Arts & Artists, Washington, DC, Section 13, p. 3.

16. Exhibit Contract, International Arts & Artists, Washington, DC, Section 7, p. 3.

17. Exhibit Contract, Wadsworth Athenaeum, Hartford, CT, Section 18, p. 10.

18. Exhibit Contract, International Arts & Artists, Washington, DC, Section 15, p. 4.

Chapter Eight

Managing Historic Firearms in Museum Collections

Alex Mackenzie and David Arnold

Many museums have historic firearms in their collections. Some may have only one or two; others may have thousands. Managing these as museum objects can be a challenge—particularly for smaller museums whose firearms make up only a small percentage of their overall collections. In addition to their care as historic mechanical artifacts and material culture, firearms present issues due to their use as weapons. Historic firearms can be found loaded. They can have laws or ordinances at the federal, state, and/or local level that regulate their possession and storage. Museums that have large firearm collections are likely well versed in these issues, though smaller museums or those with only a few firearms may not be.

What follows is a basic introduction to the early development of small arms and their ammunition. This description is in no way intended to be comprehensive—it is simply the minimum knowledge necessary not only for the safe handling of most firearms and ammunition, but also for their legal possession as well. Knowledge of the terms used to describe firearms is important not only for identification, cataloguing, and safe handling, but also to understand applicable laws and regulations that use these terms.

Additionally, there is basic guidance on the safe handling of a firearm— primarily how to tell if it is loaded (unsafe) or unloaded (safe), and what to do should a loaded firearm be discovered among museum collections. Ammunition can be a concern on its own, though perfectly acceptable to keep as historic items in and of themselves with the appropriate precautions. Finally, firearms can be unique in the way in which they are cared for and present challenges not seen in other mechanical objects. Guidelines and recommendations on preservation and storage wrap up the chapter.

A BRIEF EVOLUTION OF EARLY FIREARMS

The first step in managing firearms in museum collections is to know exactly what you have. Firearms have been around for centuries and come in a variety of forms, mechanisms, quality of manufacture, and condition. New curators can inherit collections with little to no information about each object. Firearms have been found among uncatalogued objects or donated as one unknown object within a much larger and varied collection. While a firearm can be easy to identify as a firearm, knowing exactly what kind of firearm it is and how it works is essential.

Early firearms were simple metal tubes with one sealed end. A touch-hole was drilled near the sealed end, called the breech, which enables the weapon to fire. For the most part, this configuration was the same with small or large projectiles. This is the primary difference between small arms, which fire projectiles about a half inch and smaller, and artillery, which fire large projectiles. Small arms include muskets, rifles, handguns, and later, machine guns. On the other side of the spectrum is artillery, being much heavier and larger than small arms primarily because of the amount of propellant needed to launch massive projectiles. These large cannons need to be fired from carriages or heavy mounts that require multiple people to operate, while many small arms can be fired by a single user.

Because one end of the barrel is sealed at the breech, early firearms were loaded from the other end of the barrel (the muzzle), and are generally known as muzzle-loaders. A measure of explosive propellant, usually black powder, is poured down the muzzle, and a projectile (in most cases a lead ball) is seated on the powder with a ramrod. Once ignited, the black powder rapidly turns into a gas, propelling the projectile back through the barrel toward the target.

Small arms are distinguished from one another by their size, the manner in which they ignite the propellant, and the manner in which they are loaded. Historic small arms are largely divided into two groups by size: handguns and long arms. Handguns include pistols and revolvers, while long arms include muskets, rifles,[1] and carbines. Each of these types—particularly in a given era—will have similar ignition systems.

The earliest ignition system involved setting off the main charge by touching a flame or burning cord against the touch-hole near the breech. In another early configuration, a small indentation or attachment (known as a "pan"), which held a small amount of black powder to prime the main charge, sat next to the touch-hole. Because it is difficult to do manually, mechanical "locks" were incorporated into small arms that mechanized the action of ignition.

- Matchlock—Matchlocks have a constant slow-burning cord that is lowered to the pan once the trigger is pulled. Upon contact with the smoldering cord, the priming powder in the pan ignites, which then ignites the powder within the barrel, discharging the weapon.
- Wheel Lock—Wheel locks incorporate a steel wheel that is wound with a key under tension, much like a clock. The top of the wheel is exposed in the pan. A cock with a piece of flint is lowered, touching the wheel. When the trigger is pulled, the wheel spins against the flint, creating a spark, igniting the priming powder, and discharging the weapon.
- Flintlock—Flintlocks keep the cock and flint from the wheel lock, but instead of a wheel under tension, the cock and flint are put under tension when pulled back. A pull on the trigger releases the tension, which drives the flint forward into a steel "frizzen" or "battery," creating the spark that ignites the powder in the pan and discharges the weapon. Related, earlier mechanisms are the snaplock and snaphaunce.
- Percussion—Wind and weather tended to limit the ways the early designs could be used—particularly with powder in the pan exposed to the outside air. This system uses a "nipple" or "cone," in place of the touch-hole and pan. The weapon is primed with a small top hat–shaped metal cap containing a disc of fulminate of mercury. To ignite the main charge, a percussion cap is placed on the nipple, and when the trigger is pulled, a hammer falls against the cap, creating a spark and discharging the weapon.

While the ignition systems improved and became more reliable, as illustrated above, all of these firearms remained, for the vast majority, muzzle-loaders. Muzzle-loaders were common through the mid-nineteenth century, but the drawbacks to this method of loading were likely known from the very first firearm. The loose powder presented issues with consistency of fire, mainly because it was exposed to the elements when loading. Also, once

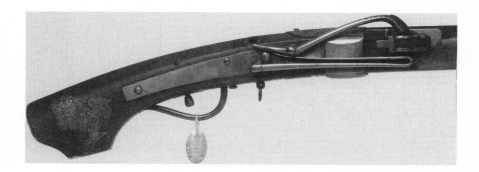

Figure 8.1. Matchlock. Springfield Armory National Historic Site.

loaded, muzzle-loaders are very difficult to unload without firing. There were several early ideas to load firearms from the breech (the opposite end of the barrel from the muzzle), which would solve a lot of these issues, but challenges resealing the breech after loading restricted the use of these designs until the development of self-contained ammunition.

THE DEVELOPMENT OF AMMUNITION

Initially, powder was stored in containers, such as powder horns, and poured into the pan and down the muzzle. In the case of soldiers who needed to fire quickly, powder was premeasured into paper tubes, which also included the projectiles. Early projectiles evolved into simple lead spheres (a ball), which were slightly smaller than the bore of the barrel, or several smaller lead spheres (buckshot). Some ammunition configurations included both buckshot and a ball.

One early firearm development that dramatically affected ammunition was rifling. "Rifling" is a series of lands and grooves cut into the bore of a barrel. The rifling will usually have a twist in order to impart a ballistic spin to the projectile, which dramatically increases accuracy over "smoothbores," weapons without rifling. A rifle is a long arm that has rifling.

Rifles had been around for centuries, but the limits of muzzle-loaders prevented their widespread use. In order for rifles to function properly, the projectile needs to bite into the rifling. Loading from the muzzle meant forcing the projectile through the bore and rifling in order to seat it near the breech. This was very time consuming (soldiers who carried rifles were often equipped with a mallet to help seat the projectile properly). Rifles were largely used by hunters and sharpshooters who had time to load carefully, whereas line infantry in the eighteenth and early nineteenth centuries used massed fire of less accurate but faster loading smoothbores.

The issues with loading a muzzle-loading rifle were major reasons for the attempts at developing a breech-loading firearm. Though breechloaders were not widely used until the mid-1800s, the answer that enabled the widespread use of muzzle-loading rifles was the minié ball. Shaped like a cone, the minié ball was actually undersized, and could be quickly loaded because it did not need to be forced down through the rifling in the barrel. The base of the minié ball was concave, which created a skirt at the base. When the rifle is fired, this skirt expands into the rifling. Simply reshaping this piece of lead from a sphere to a cone revolutionized firearms and warfare—but it wasn't to last long.

The development of metallic cartridges started in the mid-1800s. This ammunition contains the primer and a main charge, along with a projectile. This effectively did away with the loose powder, percussion cap, and projectile. Metallic, self-contained ammunition also dramatically increased reliability and operation in inclement weather, enabled the wide use of rifles, and allowed for a wide variety of firearm designs that load from the breech. Metallic cartridges rendered the muzzle-loader obsolete.

Self-contained ammunition went through some design changes as well—primarily in the priming operation. Until the late 1800s, this ammunition continued to use black powder and lead projectiles. As with firearms, there is a very, very wide variety of ammunition. Below are some of the major categories of ammunition.

- Paper Cartridge (with lead ball and minié ball)—Illustration of early cartridges, which required the use of a separate primer, whether loose powder poured into the pan of a flintlock, or a percussion cap on a percussion rifle or musket.
- Pinfire Ammunition—The primer is inside the casing and a pin extends outside the casing. When struck by a hammer, the pin hits the primer, igniting the charge. This type of ammunition should be handled carefully.
- Rimfire Ammunition—The primer is incorporated in the rim of the casing. The hammer or firing pin, integral to the weapon, strikes the rim, which sets off the main charge.
- Centerfire Ammunition—Once developed, this is the most widely used system for self-contained ammunition. It required a change in the design of firearms, which incorporated a firing pin to strike the primer.
- Breech-Loading Rifle—With the advent of self-contained metallic cartridges, breech-loading rifles rendered muzzle-loaders obsolete. Early breechloaders still used black powder and usually fired one shot at a time.

Figure 8.2a. Ammunition. Springfield Armory National Historic Site.

Figure 8.2b. Open Breech-Loading Weapon. Springfield Armory National Historic Site.

THE DEVELOPMENT OF MODERN SMALL ARMS

The continued advancements in designs for self-contained metallic ammunition reached a pivotal moment with the invention of smokeless powder in the late nineteenth century. Black powder, which had been the primary projectile propellant for centuries, does not burn efficiently. This results in a cloud of smoke coming from the muzzle (and from the pan, in early ignition systems like the flintlock). It also leaves residue in the barrel and other parts of the weapon. Complex small arm designs were limited by the fouling associated with black powder. It took a laboratory to develop synthetic propellant, which burns much more efficiently and rapidly with much less residue and smoke. Though the smoke wasn't completely eliminated, it is known as "smokeless" powder.

The widespread use of smokeless powder enabled much more advanced designs, and launched the modern period of firearms. Ammunition that used smokeless powder needed to withstand the higher velocities created by the new powder as the projectile exits the barrel, and to retain its ballistic properties. Some projectile designs retained a core of lead, which was jacketed in tougher metals, such as copper and tin. Other casing designs could also be stacked in magazines, or linked in belts for continuous firing.

Because of the improvements in propellants, the next several generations of firearms were able to increase the rate of fire, and mechanize the loading process. Smokeless powder burned cleanly and powerfully enough to consider more complicated mechanisms that might automate the loading and firing process. Semiautomatic weapons are those that go through the whole cycle (fire, eject, load) with each pull of the trigger after loading the first round. Fully automatic weapons will continue to fire, eject, and load as long as the trigger is held. Early machine guns (fully automatic weapons) tended to be very heavy and unwieldy. The earliest were mounted on carriages and managed like artillery. They needed to be bulky in order to cope with sustained firing. As materials were developed that were lighter and stronger, it became possible to create fully automatic weapons that could be carried and operated by one person. This occurred around World War II.

The introduction of smokeless powder and the introduction of the machine gun also mark the point that has been defined by federal and most state legislation as the line between antique and modern firearms.

- Bolt-Action Rifle—A bolt is manually rotated and moved to the rear to unlock the breech. Cartridges are either fed individually, or can be fed from a magazine below as the bolt is pushed forward. Each time the bolt-action is fired, it must be manually operated to eject the spent cartridge and insert a new one.
- Semiautomatic Rifle—After the first round is fed, each pull of the trigger fires the cartridge, ejects the spent cartridge, and inserts a new one until empty.
- Machine Gun—Holding down the trigger continuously operates the weapon (load, fire, eject) until the trigger is released or ammunition is depleted. Machine guns use belted or linked ammunition for sustained firing. Because of the heat and abuse generated by this high, continuous rate of fire, machine guns tend to be very heavy and solidly built. These machine guns are usually operated by a team of people.
- Fully Automatic Rifle—In the early twentieth century, it proved difficult to get the high rate of fire without making the weapon very heavy. With improved manufacturing and new materials, fully automatic weapons that could be carried by a single person were developed during and after World War II. These rifles use magazines instead of belts to hold the ammuni-

Figure 8.3. Fully Automatic Rifle. Springfield Armory National Historic Site.

tion, and many designs can be switched to fire semiautomatically, fully automatically, or in bursts.

LEGAL ASPECTS OF ANTIQUE FIREARMS IN MUSEUMS

In addition to knowledge about the evolution and mechanics of firearms, it is important for museums to know the legal requirements for their possession as well. Because there are varying laws, regulations, and ordinances at the federal, state, and local levels, firearm laws can be complex, change frequently, and be interpreted differently by courts. An in-depth overview is out of the scope of this chapter. This section is intended to be a brief and basic overview of the identification of antique firearms that will be kept inside a museum and permanently secured in exhibits or storage. Keep in mind that firearm laws apply to museums just as they apply to individuals and corporations.[2] These laws not only regulate the ownership, possession, and transfer of certain types of firearms, but also their security and storage—even on exhibit. These laws can require the registration of certain firearms and mandate the acquisition of a federal- or state-issued firearm permit. If you are unsure about the applicability of firearm laws to objects already in your collection or offered as a donation, to ensure total compliance, contact legal counsel that is well versed in all applicable federal, state, and local laws.

As discussed above, the date that marks the beginning of the modern firearm roughly coincides with the introduction of smokeless powder and the development of automatic firearms. This date is January 1, 1899. With some exceptions, firearms manufactured on or before December 31, 1898 are considered antiques and for the most part do not apply to federal, state, and local laws and regulations.[3] In many museums, the bulk of historic firearms are considered antiques. The federal definition of an antique firearm (which most states have also adopted) comes from 18 U.S.C. § 921 (a)(16), which states:

The term "antique firearm" means—

a. any firearm (including any firearm with a matchlock, flintlock, percussion cap, or similar type of ignition system) manufactured in or before 1898; or
b. any replica of any firearm described in subparagraph (A) if such replica—
is not designed or redesigned for using rimfire or conventional centerfire fixed ammunition, or uses rimfire or conventional centerfire fixed ammunition that is no longer manufactured in the United States and that is not readily available in the ordinary channels of commercial trade; or
c. any muzzle-loading rifle, muzzle-loading shotgun, or muzzle-loading pistol, which is designed to use black powder, or a black powder substitute, and that cannot use fixed ammunition. For purposes of this subparagraph, the term "antique firearm" shall not include any weapon that incorporates a firearm frame or receiver, any firearm that is converted into a muzzle-

loading weapon, or any muzzle-loading weapon that can be readily converted to fire fixed ammunition by replacing the barrel, bolt, breechblock,
or any combination thereof.[4]

With many early firearms, identification as an antique is straightforward. A
flintlock musket from the American Revolution is an antique, as is a muzzle-
loading rifle-musket, made in 1862 during the American Civil War. Per the
legal definition in 18 U.S.C. § 921 (a)(16)(A), any firearm with a matchlock,
flintlock, or percussion cap ignition is considered an antique. In addition,
replicas of these historic weapons are also considered antiques, as long as
they cannot be modified to fire modern, fixed (self-contained) ammunition.
This can be useful when using nonmuseum replicas for interpretive demonstrations.

Identification of antiques becomes a challenge the closer you get to the
1899 cutoff date. There are many models of arms from various manufactur-
ers where initial production started in the years before January 1, 1899, and
continued into the next century. Because the critical word in the federal
definition of antique firearm is "manufactured," a particular firearm made
before 1899 is considered an antique, and the same exact model firearm
made years later is not.[5] In cases like this, in addition to consultation with
legal counsel, research on a particular firearm may be necessary to determine
its date of manufacture. This is most often linked to the firearm's serial
number. Production records at factory archives can have information regarding the date that an individual firearm was made—or at least a range of serial
numbers that were manufactured during a given span of time.

SAFE HANDLING OF FIREARMS AND AMMUNITION

No matter what type of firearm is in your collection, any firearm should be
treated as if it were loaded. It's true that you know your collections well
enough, but it's a good habit to start, and it encourages safe handling no
matter what. While the firearms in museum collections will likely never be
fired, and may never be loaded again, it's worth following one of the cardinal
rules of firearm handling: don't point the muzzle of the weapon at anything
you wouldn't want to shoot. This is especially true when handling an unfa-
miliar arm, or one that is new to the collection. Always be aware where the
weapon is pointed so that if it does discharge, it does the least amount of
harm. Keep in mind people who work above, below, or to the side of where
you are.

Whether a weapon that has been in the collection forever, or a new donation, one of the most important things is to be able to identify it as loaded,
and personally verify that the firearm is safe or unsafe to handle. However, if
you are uncomfortable, put it down in a safe, secure spot, and contact a

qualified conservator or professional gunsmith to discuss options to make the firearm safe.

Muzzle-Loading Small Arms

Because the barrel of a muzzle-loader (whether it's a flintlock, percussion, or other early ignition system) is a long tube sealed at one end, there is no safe way to tell through simple visual inspection if the arm is loaded or if there is some other obstruction. Note: there are products called "bore lights" to help look down a barrel, mainly for the purpose of inspecting condition. Do not use these to check if a muzzle-loader is loaded. Not only will you likely not be able to see all the way to the breech, but you should never ever look down the muzzle of a firearm if you have a suspicion that it's loaded.

There is an easy method to determine if a muzzle-loading small arm is loaded or obstructed, and outlined nicely in the *NPS Museum Handbook*:

> You will need a wooden dowel smaller in diameter than the firearm's caliber and longer than its barrel.
>
> • Select a safe, dedicated work area. Place the firearm on a padded table. Point the muzzle so nothing will be harmed if it accidentally fires. *Never stand in front of a firearm's muzzle.*
> • Wear leather gloves and safety goggles.
> • Be sure the firearm is not cocked.
> • Standing to the side of the firearm, gently push the dowel into the muzzle until it stops. Hold the dowel between the thumb and forefinger so that the dowel will be propelled *between* the fingers should the firearm discharge. *Do not hold the dowel in such a way that it can be propelled into your hand.*
> • Place a pencil mark on the dowel where it just clears the muzzle of the barrel.
> • Gently withdraw the dowel from the barrel.
> • Place the dowel on top of the barrel with the pencil mark aligned with the muzzle. If the other end of the dowel extends the full length of the barrel, the weapon is not loaded. However, if the measurement indicates that the dowel stopped forward of the touch-hole, consider the firearm to be loaded with a live round. . . .
> • Label the firearm as unsafe and arrange to store it in a secure space.[6]

A few ways to deal with a loaded or obstructed muzzle-loader should all be performed by a qualified conservator or gunsmith.

A tool called a "wiper" or "worm," fastened to the end of a ramrod, acts like a corkscrew. The worm is put down the barrel and twisted into the lead ball, which can then be pulled out of the barrel.

Another option may be more appropriate, especially if the museum is interested in saving what is inside the barrel. The breech ends of many

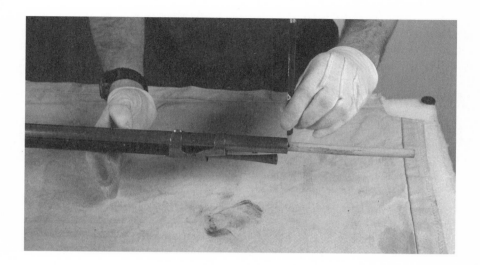

Figure 8.4. Marking dowel with a pencil. Springfield Armory National Historic Site.

muzzle-loading barrels are sealed with a threaded plug that, depending on condition, may be able to be removed. Once the breech plug is out, the obstruction can be carefully pushed out of the breech with a long dowel.

There are other alternatives, such as the use of compressed air blown through the touch-hole. Consider all options carefully as they may risk damage to the object, and can propel the object with velocity.[7]

Once verified as unloaded and safe, the muzzle-loader can be handled as appropriate.

Breech-Loading Small Arms

Breech mechanisms vary with design, but they all offer the ability to look directly at the breech with the firearm pointed in a safe direction to see if it is loaded. Simply opening the breech will show if there is a cartridge inserted in the chamber. Most breechloaders include a mechanism to eject cartridges, which should happen when the breech is opened. If the cartridge is stuck, and cannot be easily removed, contact a gunsmith.

If there is no cartridge, the weapon is not loaded. There may still be an obstruction in the barrel, but if the firearm will never be fired again, that may not be a big deal. A dowel can easily push the obstruction through the muzzle or breech.

Ammunition

Occasionally, ammunition is found in collections, and it can be important to retain as historic objects. In many cases, the only remaining item is the projectile, such as a lead ball or cone-shaped minié ball. Aside from being made of lead, these are harmless on their own, and can be safely handled—though with as much caution as needed for handling lead. Usually, the black powder propellant is long gone. However, in those instances where a complete cartridge is found, the best thing to do is to leave it alone and ensure appropriate environmental storage. As with most materials, the fluctuation of temperature and relative humidity—particularly high temp and relative humidity (RH)—can cause the materials to degrade.

The National Park Service provides the following guidance in its museum handbook for the safe handling of small arms ammunition:

> Small arms ammunition includes Revolutionary and Civil War paper musket cartridges; metallic cartridges used in the American West; and contemporary pistol, rifle, and machine gun ammunition from World Wars I and II. These small arms cartridges do not pose a serious risk unless they are damaged. Tests conducted by the U.S. Army, the National Rifle Association, the arms industry, and several fire and insurance companies have repeatedly demonstrated that such ammunition will not detonate by itself. This kind of ammunition requires a direct blow to its primer or a direct spark or flame to detonate the powder. If this ammunition is accidentally detonated when it's not confined within the barrel of a firearm, the pressure drops rapidly. The bullet will fly out of the cartridge with about the same velocity as a cork from a champagne bottle.
>
> Follow these general rules for safely handling small arms ammunition:
>
> - Never attempt to deactivate small arms ammunition. Procedures such as drilling holes in a cartridge case or pulling a bullet to remove the powder and charge can be extremely dangerous. If you must deactivate the ammunition, contact a specialist.
> - As with all museum collections, prohibit smoking.
> - In [museums] with large collections, store live cartridges in a separate museum specimen cabinet. Clearly label the cabinet with a warning sign to notify fire-fighting personnel.
> - If you want to put fixed ammunition on exhibit, it must be rendered inert. [Contact a qualified gunsmith to deactivate live ammunition.][8]

A NOTE ON ARTILLERY AMMUNITION

Ammunition fired by cannon and other forms of artillery is a very large topic, and it is outside the scope of this chapter. However, it is worth explaining that artillery ammunition not only is larger than that of small arms, but can be

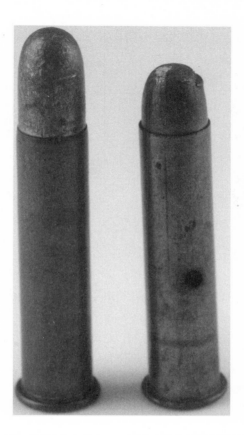

Figure 8.5a. Live and Inert Ammunition. Springfield Armory National Historic Site.

vastly more dangerous. With a few exceptions, small arm ammunition is simply a projectile and propellant. Many kinds of artillery ammunition, on the other hand, are designed to explode once they reach their target, so there is a secondary charge contained within the projectile beyond what is needed to propel it. Any artillery ammunition found in collections should be treated with an abundance of caution. If you are in doubt about the type and condition of any artillery ammunition in your museum, immediately secure the area and consult an expert to quickly identify the piece. It may be that it is solid shot, and simply a large, harmless ball of iron. But if it is identified as a potentially explosive shell, the safest course of action may be the removal and destruction of the item by a bomb squad. Tread carefully around any artillery ammunition, no matter how historic.

Figure 8.5b. Live and Inert Ammunition. Springfield Armory National Historic Site.

CONSERVATION AND CARE OF FIREARMS

Once formally in museum collections, firearms can be a challenge to care for. Antique firearms are largely wood and ferrous metal—two materials that have differing ideal environments. Other additional materials can be brass, ivory, bone, mother-of-pearl, plastic, fiberglass, and even precious metals. What follows is a basic introduction to some antique firearm conservation methods and guidelines should a museum decide to pursue the stabilization of its collection.

PRESERVING YOUR ANTIQUE ARMS COLLECTION, BY DAVID ARNOLD, NPS CONSERVATOR

The following are *guidelines* to help you care for a collection that will be preserved for as long as possible and will *never be fired.* It represents the *safest,* most conservative advice that can be given without thoroughly examining your specific firearm. Methods recommended here may *not* be the most efficient. There are many more treatment options available to conservators that cannot be responsibly shared in this forum. What may work beautifully in one situation can be a disaster in another. Every gun should be treated as a unique object and the treatments will vary considerably from the advice that follows that is limited in scope and cannot cover every possible situation. It is based on the author's training and experience as a conservator, and experience working mainly with military firearms made during the last three centuries. The author continues to learn more with every completed treatment. As a consequence, these guidelines remain a work in progress. The author appreciates your comments as by sharing them, you will contribute to the improvement of these notes. David Arnold, Conservator, National Park Service, Harpers Ferry Center, Museum Conservation Services.

A. Preventive Care

1. Environment

    *   Avoid dramatic swings in relative humidity (RH). Try to keep as stable as possible between 40 and 50 percent.
    *   Consistency is more important than precise maintenance of a specific RH reading.
    *   RH control is most critical because of an unusual physical property of wood called *anisotropy*. Wood cells expand or contract very differently in response to changes in relative humidity—*depending on their specific grain orientation* (axial, transverse, or radial) in the log from which they came. Large swings in RH can result in cracks caused by compression-set shrinkage.
    *   *If humidity remains fairly constant*, changes in temperature make little difference to either metal or wood; it's better to concentrate on controlling relative humidity. However, a rapid rise in indoor temperature can pull the moisture out of the environment (including your artifact), causing a sharp drop in RH. Cell shrinkage and cracking or splitting can occur.

2. Handling

    *   Wear gloves when handling your collection. No protective coating—appropriate for conserving an artifact—(see below) can stand up for long against repeated handling. It is best thing is to *always* wear gloves and handle as little as possible.
    *   Nitrile examination gloves[9] are recommended when cleaning and coating your collection.
    *   Once an item has been coated, wear plain, cotton gloves when handling.

3. Housekeeping

- Keep dust free. Dust can trap moisture increasing the likelihood of corrosion occurring.
- Do not use commercial dust cloths. They often leave an oil film behind. Oil films trap dust. Dust traps and collects water vapor in the air.
- When dusting, use a soft cotton cloth very lightly dampened with water. Without moisture, dust merely gets shoved around and will not be picked up.
- Do not use alcohol of any kind when dusting or cleaning a stock. It can permanently disturb a historic finish.
- Dry immediately with a clean cloth.
- Never use liquid or spray dusting products. Most leave mineral oil behind, which traps dust. Dust traps and collects moisture. Starting to see a pattern?

B. Cleaning and Coating Historic Firearms

1. Cleaning Wood Stocks

   - Separate wooden and metal parts. They are cleaned and coated differently.
   - Unless absolutely necessary, *leave unfinished interior wooden surfaces alone*.
   - Clean *exterior* of stock as follows:

     a. Use a few *drops* of a mild detergent[10] in a gallon of warm, distilled water, applied with a slightly damp soft cloth, and rinsed with clean cloths dampened with distilled water.
     b. Dry with soft cloths immediately after rinsing.
     c. Clean again with mineral spirits, using a soft cloth to apply. Work in fresh air or a well-ventilated area.

   - Avoid using "oil soaps" as their pH can be high enough to damage a historic oil finish.

2. Cleaning Barrels and Other Metal Parts
   Please note: *It is essential to practice any new technique on a sacrificial piece first*, before applying it to something irreplaceable.

   - Use nylon or animal-bristle bore brushes.[11] Wherever possible, avoid using brass or steel brushes. Such hard materials can scratch, but also might (under certain conditions) cause galvanic (bimetallic) corrosion (specifically when using a copper-alloy brush on ferrous metals) by leaving a slight metallic smear behind.

- Use mineral spirits to soften accretions. Work in fresh air or a well-ventilated area. Are there other solvents that are "stronger"? Yes, but they are difficult to work with *safe*ly.
- Swab clean with a cloth patch.
- Use only *extremely fine* abrasives such as oil-free 0000 steel wool.[12] In very tough cases, use nylon web pads—specifically Norton's *Bear Tex* #748 gray "final shine" pads.[13] Use *only if absolutely necessary* to remove stubborn rust deposits or other accretions. Work slowly and be alert to any changes in the surface. There is always an element of risk in such work. If you are at all uncertain, hire a conservator *before* causing irreversible damage.
- When cleaning brass parts *never* use metal-cleaning products that contain ammonia. Ammonia can damage old copper-alloy materials. In addition, such products often include abrasives that may damage surfaces. Elbow grease and mineral spirits should be tried first. If something slightly stronger is needed, try applying small amounts of wet tooth powder with a cotton swab and rinse with water.
- A general comment about commercial rust removers. To date, I have not found a rust-removal product that is entirely safe to use on historic metal surfaces. The problem is that *most* rust removers cannot "tell" the difference between iron oxide and iron metal, and will leave an etched surface even where there is no rust. Some new products seem to come close, however. Often they require extremely close attention and precision—too much so for most of us. In short, there are no magic solutions that are risk free and the author advises against their use on anything you value.
- Most surface rust can be removed by first lubricating the area with a light penetrating oil[14] and *cleaving* it off with a sharp scalpel held at a very low angle to the metal. It requires close attention, a steady hand, and some patience, but if you are careful, you will probably get most—if not all—of the surface rust off without leaving so much as a scratch. When done, remove any remaining oil with mineral spirits.

3. Disassembly and Reassembly

- If you are organized and systematic—you should be able to safely disassemble and reassemble most firearms successfully.
- Probe the floor of every external screw slot with a sharp point. It's amazing how much dirt can be packed into a "clean-looking" slot.

All foreign matter must be removed for the screwdriver to fill the slot completely and work safely.

- A good selection of screwdrivers is a must. Their tips must be matched perfectly to each slot in order to maximize the area of mechanical contact. Taking this precaution will minimize slippage and the scratching and scarring that can result. The internal shapes of screw slots have changed a lot since their invention[15] and screwdriver tips often have to be ground or filed in order to get a good match. Keep this in mind when regrinding a screwdriver's tip.
- There are many publications that offer exploded drawings and disassembly/reassembly tips.[16] There is also a brilliant website that illustrates with moving images how various types of firearms work.[17]

4. Coating Stocks

- Wood is neither thirsty nor hungry. It is usually covered by a finish that may have become corrupted in some way, making it look "dry." The wood beneath the finish does not need to be "fed" (despite what wood-care product commercials may claim).
- Never put oil of any kind on a historic finish. There may well be unintended, but permanently damaging, consequences to ignoring this advice.
- A cautionary word about linseed oil. While it may be an appropriate material to use to finish a modern historic replica, consider the following:

  a. Linseed oil takes forever to dry and will trap dust. (It will *not* stop water penetration either.)
  b. When linseed oil oxidizes, its molecules cross-link with one another, making it increasingly more difficult to remove as time passes.
  c. Oxidized linseed oil (linoleic acid) eventually becomes linoxin, better-known commercially as Linoleum! Repeated, or seasonal, applications eventually develop into a surface that can look like very dark brown alligator skin, and can become almost impossible to remove.
  d. Applying a modern coating over an identical historic finish can eventually, given enough time, confuse the finish "history" of a stock by making it difficult, if not impossible, to tell what is original, and what is a restoration material—even with an analytical microscope. So, for ex-

ample, you would not want to touch up a historic shellac finish with shellac.

- Use paste waxes only as a protective clear coating. Carnauba-based pigmented furniture paste waxes such as Kiwi Bois are preferred by the author or either Mohawk or Behlen on wood stocks.[18] Use only *pigmented* paste waxes on dark wood surfaces. "Clear" or light-colored waxes can collect in pores and appear as white specks against a dark background. Liberon's *Black Bison* in walnut is another good choice for dark stocks.
- Avoid wax mixtures that include a high percentage of bee's wax. These are not especially *harmful*, but are relatively soft (fingerprint easily) and can be slightly acidic.

5. Coating Metals (*This advice is strictly for guns that have been "retired" from use and will* never *be fired.*)

- Avoid using oils. They are not the best material for long-term protection of collection pieces as they trap dust and dirt, eventually break down, and have to be periodically replaced. A high-quality light oil is fine for maintaining a gun you still shoot, though.
- Use a microcrystalline wax as a protective coating on ferrous metals. Commercially available examples include Renaissance Wax or Conservator's Wax.[19] Such waxes are practically inert, remaining stable for a very long time. Apply and buff out with a soft cloth or brush. I coat all ferrous parts with this material—inside and out.[20]
- Ferrous metals (iron, steel) *should be preheated* for a half hour or so to a temperature between 210 and 230 degrees Fahrenheit before applying wax to them. Use either a convection oven or infrared lamps, depending on the size and type of part. Preheating assures us that the wax will be pulled by capillary action into every remote nook and cranny to form the most protective seal possible.
- Brass parts can also be coated with wax. I prefer, however, to use Incralac[21] acrylic spray lacquer because it can be removed with solvents but bonds especially well to copper-alloy metals, and should withstand more abuse and last longer than wax. It can be purchased in an aerosol can.

6. Minor Stock Repairs: *If a split or detached piece of a stock must be repaired, use an adhesive that is both strong and reversible (i.e., can be safely removed in the future). There is only one: traditional hide glue.*[22]

- Do not proceed if there is evidence that the damaged site has been previously repaired. In this case, consult a conservator.
- Unless you already work with hide glue every day, make it up fresh in small amounts as needed. It doesn't take long to prepare and it will do a better job than using old glue. Hot hide glue made from crystals is preferable to liquid hide glue as it is less affected by humidity.[23]
- Dampen the area to be glued with hot water. Blot the area and wait a few minutes. Then apply hot glue to both surfaces with a brush and clamp immediately. An appropriate clamp can be as simple as a few pieces of masking tape, rubber bands, bicycle tire strips, or small padded weights. Use the least force needed to do the job.
- Clamps can usually be removed in a few hours, but it takes at least twenty-four hours for the repair to fully harden.
- Excess glue can be removed with a lint-free cloth dampened with hot water. The best time to do this is usually right after removing clamps.

7. If you still need help:

- Seek the services of a professional conservator.
- Contact me or the American Institute for Conservation of Historic and Artistic Works (AIC)[24] for a referral.
- There are few, if *any*, conservators who treat only firearms. Look for an *objects* conservator with experience working with metal *and* the other materials (wood, bone, celluloid, leather, etc.) that are part of your artifact.

STORAGE AND DISPLAY OF FIREARMS

Security is paramount in the protection and preservation of historic firearms. Most museums will have overall security measures in place for the protection of their collection as a whole—whether on exhibit or in storage. In most circumstances, these measures should be quite strong and appropriate for the security of firearms as well. One caveat, though: modern firearms may have legal requirements depending on the state or locality for the security of the weapon—even when on display in an exhibit. Consult with appropriate law enforcement to ensure compliance.

MUSEUM ARMS STORAGE 101
BY DAVID ARNOLD, NPS CONSERVATOR

Almost all ready-made firearms storage systems are made specifically to meet the needs of military, police, or private arsenals—both large and small. They are intended to maximize storage density with little or no regard to the preservation needs of diverse historic arms collections that are kept in museums. Domestic storage solutions—usually gun safes—tend to serve the same need, that is, to secure as many guns as possible in a limited amount of space. Neither storage solution is intended to function as museum storage furniture.

Some commercial storage systems can be adapted or improved to meet museum standards for storing arms collections. Such accommodations must be specified by the collection manager or other purchasing agent. As an alternative, quality open racks can be fabricated using foam padding and tape fasteners from conservation supply sources and wood or metal components that are readily available in "big box" stores such as Home Depot or Lowe's.

Commercial gun safes or gun cabinets should not be necessary inside a properly secured museum storage room. If a museum storage facility already provides appropriate security for its collections, then installing a gun safe within a collection storage space is redundant and potentially harmful to its contents. High levels of security and restricted access should apply equally to *all* museum storage facilities and their contents—not just storage facilities that happen to include historic firearms.

One of the primary goals of preventive conservation is to passively eliminate the need for excessive handling of artifacts. Well-designed arms storage systems can dramatically reduce or eliminate the need for museum staff to handle collections—thus prolonging their life as museum objects. Museum staff should be able to access any single object without having to touch or remove a neighboring firearm.

Ideally, storage and exhibit environments for historic arms should include *good air filtration and circulation,* as well as adjustable mechanical systems to assure reasonable *control and consistency of relative humidity (RH) and*—to the degree that it affects RH—*temperature.* They should also provide *good lighting* throughout the storage area so that artifacts do not need to be moved to a brighter area to inspect their tags or labels. *Ample and adjustable spacing* is needed for varied collections that typically occupy museum storage. And finally, support and other *physical stabilization* systems are needed to assure that a historic firearm cannot accidentally come out of its assigned space.

Concerns about Using Gun Cabinets and Gun Safes for Preservation Storage

- *Environmental.* The air inside a gun safe is still. Mold outbreaks occur when any two of the following three conditions are met: (1) still air, (2) elevated temperature, or (3) elevated relative humidity (RH). A failure to control any two of the three conditions inside a safe puts its contents at risk for damage from a mold outbreak. Organic elements such as wooden stocks or leather slings are especially vulnerable to irreversible damage by mold in such an environment.
- *Visibility.* The interiors of gun safes are invariably dark spaces, often requiring that guns be removed to a brighter workspace in order to identify specific selections. Locating, inspecting, inventory, or routine accessing of collection artifacts are made inefficient and difficult when those objects have been hidden inside a locked cabinet or safe. It should be sufficient that they be kept in secured storage rooms where visibility is appropriate by design.
- *Susceptibility to damage from excessive or risky handling* is a major risk factor when using gun safes and cabinets for storing museum collections.

    a. Gun safes and cabinets are generally cramped inside. Commercial storage solutions aim to store as many guns as possible inside very small spaces—usually by arranging them in multiple rows—one in front of the other. The most common method used to do this is to install horizontal Plexiglas® organizer panels supported by small corner clips, with cutouts to separate and support barrels, fore stocks, and butts.

    b. Organizer panels require one to fill the safe up from back to front and to very carefully manipulate each gun during installation or removal—to avoid sliding its surfaces against the edges of its organizer panels and to avoid bumping one gun into another.

    c. It is impossible to inspect the contents of a filled gun safe without engaging in excessive handling.

STORAGE OF FIREARMS IN MUSEUM COLLECTIONS

Museum arms storage solutions should have the design flexibility to safely accommodate a physically diverse collection of firearms. They should provide physical stability, good visibility, good air circulation, and customizable spacing between stored objects. One of the biggest challenges to storing firearms can be their size. Pistols, revolvers, and other handguns are much easier to deal with and will be able to fit into readily available museum storage furniture such as drawers with appropriate padding, while long arms present a unique storage challenge—many can be over five feet long and only a few inches wide.

Overall Storage Recommendations

- *Separation/Spacing.* It should be possible for museum staff to maintain sufficient separation between firearms—regardless of their individual space requirements—to eliminate the likelihood of one object bumping into another. Spacing between firearms should be as generous as possible. Museum systems should include spacing schemes that allow its staff to set up ad hoc spacing to accommodate uniquely configured firearms in its collections. Closed-cell foam bars (made of dense Ethafoam, Volara, or similar materials), attached to the front surfaces of support bars—with notches individually cut for each firearm—can provide a soft, stable surface against which to prop a firearm, and, at the same time, facilitate the establishment of optimal spacing between firearms. If it becomes necessary to modify existing spacing, old notched foam pieces can easily be cut out, removed, and replaced with blank foam bars—which can then be notched and spaced as required.
- *Chemical Stability.* Only chemically stable materials should be used in the construction or finishing of museum storage furniture. For example, metal fixtures should be powder coated. Foam padding materials should be made of closed-cell poly foam materials such as Ethafoam or Volara.
- *Good Visibility.* Museum storage rooms should provide sufficient illumination for the collection staff to function without the aid of flashlights or other portable lighting fixtures.
- *Ample Air Movement* throughout the storage space mitigates against mold outbreaks.

Additional Considerations for the Storage of Long Arms

Because of their long, thin dimensions, long arms can be difficult to store appropriately. Whether a museum collection has two or three long arms or five thousand, the recommendations below outline a solution in which long arms are racked vertically, enabling the objects to be stored under ideal conditions.

- *Physical Stability.* In most cases, the most stable storage configuration for vertical racking of long arms is with the trigger guard facing the viewer and the barrel perpendicular. This configuration assures that the firearm's center of gravity is directed inward, toward the center axis of its rack, making it less likely to fall into an aisle or to flop from one side to the other.

- *Adjustability.* Long arms can vary considerably in length and in total width. It may be necessary to have several racks with crossbar supports of varying heights in order to achieve optimal support for all arms in a museum's collections.
- *Restraint.* Firearms should be gently but firmly restrained when resting against their support bars. A very simple way to achieve this is to install a Velcro (hook and loop) system that will use soft loop strips to secure each firearm by looping around the barrel and attaching itself to a Velcro hook strip located either on the support bar's upper surface—just behind the vee-notched foam padding—or on the back side of the support bar.
- *Rotational Stability.* Long arm butts should rest on a closed cell foam mat. Select a density of foam that will allow the butt to sink somewhat into the foam mat. In most cases this will supply all of the rotational stability necessary.
- *Adaptability.* For firearms having unusually shaped butts (such as those often used in competitive shooting), dense foam wedges (or other shaped inserts) can be added to improve their stability.

EXHIBITING FIREARMS

Narrow hooks or loops of wire should not be used to support collection pieces either in storage or on display. The weight of most long arms is sufficient to result in indentations in their stock at the points of contact with narrow supports.

Instead, use broad, padded supports. I recommend using thin sheets of a high-density, closed-cell Polyolefin foam material[25] for padding gun mounts.

And, as with the display of all museum objects, avoid at least two of the three conditions known to promote mold and mildew outbreaks: elevated temperature, still air, and elevated humidity.

NOTES

1. The term "rifle" refers to a long arm that has rifling—a series of twisting lands and grooves—inside the bore of the barrel. Handguns can also have rifling, but are never referred to as rifles.

2. There is a government exception to federal firearm laws, which enables the military and law enforcement to use and keep firearms that would otherwise be regulated. Federal, state, and local government museums may be exempted to some degree, but this should absolutely be confirmed after consultation with legal counsel.

3. Consult legal counsel to ensure complete compliance with local, state, and federal laws, as exceptions can occur. For example, some states and localities further refine laws regarding antique handguns.

4. 18 U.S.C. § 921 (a)(16), www.law.cornell.edu/uscode/text/18/921, accessed May 31, 2014.

5. For many firearms, the year that the model was adopted is different than the manufacture date. For example, the Model 1894 (or Model 94) Winchester was adopted and began manufacture in 1894, prior to the 1899 cutoff date, but continues to be produced today. The only way to identify if a particular firearm was manufactured before 1899 is by researching its serial number.

6. *NPS Museum Handbook*, Part I (2001), pp. 11:21 to 11:22.

7. On certain designs of revolving weapons, such as cap-and-ball revolvers and rifles, the rotating cylinder is what holds the loads. If there is a load or obstruction showing in the cylinder of a revolver, contact a qualified conservator or gunsmith to remove it.

8. *NPS Museum Handbook*, Part I (2001), p. 11:22.

9. Nitrile examination gloves come in several different sizes, and can be purchased from most medical supply stores and some pharmacies. I recommend them over latex for two reasons: (1) some people have serious allergic reactions to latex rubber; and (2) latex breaks down if it comes in contact with the solvents most commonly used to remove oils and grease, and those used in paste wax formulations.

10. *Kodak Photo-Flo* is a nonionic detergent available at photographic supply stores in a variety of sizes from four ounces up. *Orvus* is mildly anionic and available as a powder or paste.

11. *KleenBore* makes a stiff nylon bore brush that I like a lot. They even make a series of "black powder" brushes with bristles that extend to the tip. Contact Kleen-Bore, Inc., 16 Industrial Parkway, Easthampton, MA 01027, (800) 445-0301, or at www.safariland.com/more.../kleenbore/.

12. Liberon/Star markets an excellent 0000 grade of Belgian steel wool. It can be purchased from Rockler Woodworking and Hardware Stores (800) 279-4441. Another source is Conservation Support Systems in Santa Barbara, California. They can be reached at (800) 482-6299 or on the web at www.conservationsupportsystems.com.

13. *Bear-Tex#* 748 hand pads can be ordered from Grainger (www.grainger.com).

14. Choice of oil for this purpose is not critical. I happen to use CRC 3-36, but WD-40 or any similar product will work fine as a scalpel lubricant as long as it is removed before coating.

15. See Warren E. Roberts, "Wood Screws as an Aid to Dating Wooden Artifacts," *Chronicle of the Early American Industrial Association* 3/1978. Also see, the Canadian Conservation Institute's excellent *Technical Bulletin #17: Threaded Fasteners in Metal Artifacts* by George Prytulak, 1977. The latter includes useful information on cleaning metals.

16. The National Rifle Association is a very good source for books on firearms assembly. Their address is 11250 Waples Mill Road, Fairfax, VA 22030-9400, www.nrastore.com. Search their technical references.

17. Take a look at home.howstuffworks.com. Search for either "machine guns" or "flintlocks."

18. *Kiwi Bois* can be ordered from Hummer Capital, Inc., 1018 Stuyvesant Ave., Union, NJ 07083, (800) 552-9952, or at www.hummercap.com. It can also be ordered from Kingdom Restorations Ltd. And toll free # 252-955-0156, or at www.kingdomrestorations.com/catalog_i86616.html?catId=5272 Kiwi Bois comes in seven different wood tones. I frequently use "walnut." As far as I can tell, *Mohawk* and *Behlen* are either the same product with different packaging or are very close to being the same. Mohawk's Blue Label brown wax (#M860-12455) can be ordered directly from Mohawk Finishing Products, 4715 State HWY 30, Amsterdam, NY 12010-9921, (800) 545-0047, or at www.mohawk-finishing.com. Behlen Blue Label brown wax can be ordered from Olde Mill Cabinet Shoppe, 1660 Camp Betty Washington Road, York, PA 17402, (717) 755-8884, or at www.oldemill.com. Liberon can be found online.

19. *Renaissance Wax* comes in a 200-milliliter container and can be ordered from Woodcraft (formerly Woodcraft Supply), 560 Airport Industrial Park, P.O. Box 1686, Parkersburg, WV 26102-1686, (800) 225-1153, or at www.woodcraft.com. *Conservator's Wax* is packaged in a 125-milliliter container and can be ordered from Lee Valley Tools, LTD, P.O. Box 1780, Ogdensburg, NY 13699-6780, (800) 871-8158, or at www.leevalley.com.

20. I recommend reading "Preserving the Metal on Your Guns and Swords" in the October 2004 issue of *Man at Arms*. It is a very thorough, balanced discussion of options for coating historic arms.

21. *Incralac* acrylic lacquer is offered in twelve-ounce spray cans by Custom Aerosol Packaging, P.O. Box 1411, Piqua, OH 45356, (937) 773-1824.

22. Hide glue is actually made up of tendons and other connective tissues rather than hides. It is easier to make than oatmeal, and—unless used daily—should be prepared fresh in small batches whenever needed. It is available from Woodcraft, Olde Mill, and many other fine woodworking suppliers. It is the only adhesive I recommend as a conservation material for wood.

23. Susan Buck, "A Study of the Properties of Commercial Liquid Hide Glue and Traditional Hot Hide Glue in Response to Changes in Relative Humidity and Temperature," Winterthur/University of Delaware Art Conservation Program, Science Research Project, University of Delaware, 1990.

24. AIC, 1717 K Street NW, Suite 301, Washington, DC 20006, (202) 452-9545, fax (202) 452-9328. Best done initially on their website: aic.stanford.edu/. Click the "Find a conservator" button.

25. *Voltek* produces sheets of *Volara* in a range of thicknesses, colors, and hardnesses that have proven to be very stable, conservation-grade materials used in many museums for padding storage shelves and exhibit fixtures. For your nearest supplier, contact VOLTEK, Division of Sekisui America Corporation, 100 Shepard Street, Lawrence, MA 01843, (800) 225-0668, or at www.sekisuivoltek.com.

FURTHER READING

331 + Essential Tips and Tricks: A How-To Guide for the Gun Collector by Stuart C. Mowbray, published by Andrew Mowbray Inc., 2006. The author presents an unusually thoughtful, up-to-date, conservative approach to *all* aspects of arms collecting.

II

Museum Government and Finance

INTRODUCTION: GOVERNANCE AND FINANCE

Over 850 million people visit approximately 7,000 American museums each year, more than the attendance for all major league sporting events and theme parks combined (483 million people in 2011).[1] These statistics indicate that museums continue to be an important part of the cultural landscape of the country. Museums are complicated and unique institutions with boards of trustees, museum administrators, volunteer committees, and corporators leading them into the twenty-first century.

Each of these teams is assigned different responsibilities and, ideally, work in unison to face the fiscal realities and leadership concerns of modern museums. Museums are multifaceted entities from a financial standpoint as well, as their capital resources include anything from admission fees, endowments, private donations, corporate donations, grants, and sponsorships as well as monies secured through fundraising campaigns. Despite growth in the economy overall, more than two-thirds of museums reported economic stress at their institutions in 2012,[2] putting additional pressure on organizations for creative financing for operational expenses and special initiatives.

The authors in theis section grapple with new ways to address the business of museums including how to keep their doors open in challenging economic times. Examining the various options available to museums in times of crisis, the writers discuss many concerns including the monetizing of collections, keeping objects in the public domain, scrutiny of public trust, the appropriate use of endowments and restricted gifts, and finally, important

case studies describing how two prestigious institutions, the Fresno Metropolitan Museum of Art and Science (Fresno, California) and the Higgins
Armory (Worcester, Massachusetts), when all other options were exhausted,
made the heartbreaking decision to close their doors.

NOTES

1. American Association of Museums website: www.aam-us.org/about-museums/museum
-facts.
2. American Association of Museums website: www.aam-us.org/about-museums/museum
-facts.

Chapter Nine

Monetizing the Collection

The Intersection of Law, Ethics,
and Trustee Prerogative

Mark S. Gold

There is no greater flashpoint—real or imagined—in the relationship between trustees and museum professionals than the monetizing of the collection, defined as the use of the proceeds of deaccessioning for purposes other than the collection and its care or, even worse, deaccessioning to raise money for operations or other institutional expenses.

Underlying the distrust and disaffection, frequently, is a lack of appreciation for the legal status of the ethical rule that proscribes monetization and a lack of appreciation for the duties and responsibilities that are vested in trustees as a matter of law.

Although the language of the rule differs slightly from association to association, it is a universally accepted ethical principle of museums and museum professionals that the proceeds of deaccessioning may be used only for acquisitions or direct care of the collection. [1]

In the case of the American Alliance of Museums, the ethical rule was a reaction to an initiative of the Financial Accounting Standards Board to require the financial statements of museums to list their collections at fair market value. The enactment of the ethical rule was more about avoiding the capitalization of collections than it was about preserving collections. [2] Regardless, it has become sacrosanct, and condemnation of violators is swift and unequivocal. While the professional museum associations have no legal authority, they seek to turn the offending institution (even if not an association member) into a pariah, often encouraging other museums to refrain from intermuseum loans with the offender. [3]

With some very limited exceptions in a few states, and assuming there are no donor-imposed restrictions on any particular object, however, there are no laws or regulations on a federal or state level that prohibit the sale of objects from the collection nor restrict the use of the proceeds from those sales. There is nothing illegal about monetizing the collection.

If monetizing the collection were illegal, the attorneys general would be enforcing the prohibition. In the United States, oversight of public charities (and the decisions of their boards) is vested exclusively in the office of the attorney general of the state having jurisdiction over the institution. In performing that function, they are considered to act as guardian of the public's interest.[4] The very rare exception occurs in those situations in which someone has such an intimate relationship to the specific object at issue (the donor of a recently accessioned painting, for example) that the courts might allow that person to participate in the process. Generally, it is only the attorney general who has standing to challenge museums on their disposition-related decisions.

That oversight is limited to ensuring that the board, in taking the action at issue, has met its fiduciary duties and obligations to the institution and has complied with any applicable donor restrictions. It is not a matter of substituting the judgment of the attorney general for the judgment of the board in the good faith exercise of its decision-making power.[5]

If one examines the cases of monetization, a common thread is the very limited extent, if at all, to which attorneys general have entered the fray to oppose the transaction. Indeed, in the massive deaccessioning for operations by New-York Historical Society in 1994–1995, the attorney general of New York helped structure the transaction.[6] In the recent case of Fisk University's plan to sell a partial interest in its Stieglitz collection to Crystal Bridges Museum of American Art, the attorney general of Tennessee was a very active participant, but the dispute centered on an interpretation of a donative document and not on whether Fisk University otherwise had the legal authority to sell an interest in the collection to support the operations of the university.[7] When Randolph College undertook to sell paintings from its Maier Museum of Art, the only action by the attorney general of Virginia was to join in efforts to obtain an injunction while litigation relating to a specific donor was resolved, which effort failed when the requisite bond could not be posted.[8] Had the controversy over the planned sale of the collection and closing of the Rose Art Museum at Brandeis University not been resolved by abandoning the plan, the involvement of the attorney general of Massachusetts would ultimately have been limited to ascertaining if any of the objects to be sold were subject to donor restrictions.[9]

Unquestionably, professional associations have authority to create a system of rules for their members and impose sanctions on those that violate them. Although the associations, admirably, do not seek to confuse their members into believing that the rules have the force of law, one would be hard pressed to find any of the associations making the distinction. The mistaken perception as to the status of the rule does nothing to help museum professionals think about the issue of monetization and respond thoughtfully when it takes place.

The unwillingness of the museum community to recognize the legal right of museums to monetize their collections lies not just in the misconception that the ethical rule has somehow acquired the status of law but, more importantly, is encumbered by a failure to appreciate the legal obligation and prerogatives of the governing boards of museums—the trustees.

The principles are stunningly simple and logical. There are two duties of trustees that are relevant to this discussion—the duty of due care and the duty of obedience. Almost every articulation of the duty of due care shares the following language or concept:

> A director . . . shall perform his or her duties as such in good faith and in a manner he or she reasonably believes to be in the best interests of the corporation, and with such care as an ordinarily prudent person in a like position would use under similar circumstances. [10]

Marie C. Malaro and Ildiko Pogany DeAngelis describe the duty of due care as follows:

> At the very least, the board should be under obligation to institute policies reasonably designed to further the mission of the organization and should also be able to demonstrate good-faith efforts to monitor such policy. [11]

Malaro and DeAngelis further describe the duty of obedience as "the obligation to focus on the specific mission of the organization" and continue with the following elaboration:

> Also, although a museum board has discretion in deciding how its mission is to be accomplished, careful adherence to the duty of obedience means selecting goals carefully. The question should not be merely, "Is this goal relevant to our mission?" The harder question needs to be asked: "Is this a wise goal in light of our anticipated resources?" [12]

Both in theory and in practice, it is all about mission and the legal obligation of the trustees to deploy institutional resources to support the mission.

For most freestanding museums, the mission goes far beyond possession and care of a collection. The museum community is justifiably proud of the evolution of museums into sites for education and community dialogue. A museum without programming is little more than the proverbial cabinet of curiosities. The mission statements of most museums are expansive articulations of the several benefits that the institution provides to its defined community.

When the museum is part of a parent organization, the collection is of even less prominence. The typical college or university will cast its mission in terms of education and, in some cases, research. One is not likely to find a college or university that includes the collection, preservation, exhibition, and interpretation of objects in its mission statement. Although there may be a predilection on the part of a college or university to maintain a museum and its objects for the prestige it can bring to the institution, the only basis on which any academic museum will fit into the mission of a college or university is as part of the educational process.

That educational mission is the seminal justification for college and university trustees thinking about the museum and its collections differently than if they were museum trustees. The academic museum is just one component of an array of resources and strategies available to meet the mission of the organization, which is broadly educational and not limited to the care, preservation, and interpretation of the collection owned by the museum on campus.

Similar issues pertain to other parent organizations such as foundations, municipalities, and other governmental entities.

Regardless of whether a museum is freestanding or part of a parent organization, when there are insufficient resources to support its mission, a prudent board of trustees will, in addition to seeking other sources of revenue and reductions in expenses, look to programs that can be eliminated and, perhaps, assets that can be monetized—all within the context of fulfilling its mission.

When the Randolph College community was informed that the trustees were considering a monetization of the collection of its Maier Museum of Art, the interim president clearly articulated the legal obligation of the trustees, as follows:

> The art is, of course, an issue of great concern. By many valuations, the art collection is more valuable than the College's endowment. In carrying out their fiduciary duty, trustees must determine that the College is deploying all the assets available to it in a fashion that will best enable the College to fulfill its mission of educating students in the liberal arts and sciences. [13]

The tension between the law, the ethical rule, and trustee prerogatives has real-life implications. The Berkshire Museum in Pittsfield, Massachusetts, is an excellent example.

The Berkshire Museum hosts around 85,000 visitors per year with an array of exhibitions and programs. It boasts a natural science collection, objects from ancient civilizations, and a collection of American art. Few students leave the public schools of Berkshire County without experiencing at least one field trip to the Berkshire Museum.

In 2008, the museum deaccessioned three Russian paintings that had no relevance to the collection and had never been exhibited in more than fifty years of ownership. The museum netted about $7 million in proceeds at public auction—a significant event in the life of an institution with a $2 million operating budget. The proceeds were placed in an account restricted to acquisitions and the direct care of the collection, as the rule requires. [14]

Although the Berkshire Museum is lean, efficient, and well managed, staff reductions to meet budget shortfalls could impair the museum's ability to be the educational and cultural resource so valued by the community. The collection, on the other hand, is well cared for, and there is no interest in expanding it in a new direction.

The mission of the Berkshire Museum is to "bring people together for experiences that spark creativity and innovative thinking by making inspiring education connections among art, history, and natural science." Although the museum possesses a collection of over 30,000 objects, the word "collection" is not even mentioned in its mission statement. [15]

To date, the trustees of the Berkshire Museum have honored the restriction of the use of the proceeds from this sale, as required by the ethical rule. Since the proceeds are otherwise unrestricted as to use, if the trustees were to apply those proceeds to fund operating or capital expenses for the museum, all in support of its articulated mission, they would unquestionably be within their legal right to do so. Indeed, one might speculate that at some point, if conditions became dire, they would be violating their fiduciary duties to the institution by declining to do so.

In fact, there is no stronger case for the use of the proceeds of deaccessioning than when the survival of the museum hangs in the balance.

On March 26, 2014, the Delaware Art Museum announced that it would deaccession and sell four works of art from its collection of 12,500 objects. The museum's stated goal was to raise $30 million to pay off the bond debt of $19.8 million incurred in connection with renovation and expansion of its Kentmere Parkway building and to replenish the endowment to secure the financial future of the museum. [16]

The following statement issued by Elva Ferrari-Graham, president of the board of trustees, is an articulate expression of how thoughtful governing boards will weigh priorities and deploy resources:

> This decision was made with heavy hearts, but clear minds. While the Trustees fully understand and respect museum best practices, we couldn't bear voting to close our beloved Delaware Art Museum—a local treasure with a century-long legacy of uniting our community and cultivating a deep connection to art. This decision today will help us achieve financial stability and allow us to channel

all of our collective energy back into our tradition of being a cherished community. Our unique collections provide educational opportunities, access to art for all ages and the chance to experience learning and creativity. In addition, the Museum fosters innovation, drives economic development and tourism and adds to the quality of life in our region. The Trustees and staff will work tirelessly in 2014 to support our new educational initiatives, our thriving Studio Art program, our new Membership program and the exciting exhibition schedule.[17]

Mike Miller, chief executive officer of the Delaware Art Museum, could not have summarized the issue more precisely:

After detailed analysis, heavy scrutiny and the exhaustion of every reasonable alternative to relieve our bond debt, the Trustees had two agonizing choices in front of them—to either sell works of art, or to close our doors. While today's decision is certainly hard to bear, the closure of this 100-year-old museum would be, by comparison, unbearable.[18]

The Berkshire Museum and the Delaware Art Museum are situated at the intersection of law, ethics, and trustee prerogative. They are not alone.

The ethical rule is all about collections to the exclusion of all else. A thoughtful and informed trustee will put the collection into the context of the broader institutional mission. The trustee will recognize that the rule does not rise to the level of law and that the trustee's legal obligation is to deal with the collection as one of several resources to fulfill the mission of the museum and, indeed, ensure the survival of the museum. In being so transparent about their decision and in articulating their rationale so clearly, the trustees of the Delaware Art Museum have contributed significantly to highlighting how this can and should operate in the real world.

A failure by museum professionals to understand the legal obligations and prerogatives of trustees, and their persistent opposition to the use of the proceeds of deaccessioning to support the mission of the museum, risk rendering them irrelevant in the important discussion on the deployment of limited institutional resources.

NOTES

1. American Alliance of Museums. "Code of Ethics for Museums." 2000. www.aam-us.org/resources/ethics-standards-and-best-practices/code-of-ethics. See also Association of Art Museum Directors. "Code of Ethics." 2011. aamd.org/about/code-of-ethics.
2. Gold, Mark. "An Ethical Framework for the Pledge of Collections as Collateral for Financing Museums" (MLA thesis, Harvard University, 2005), 9.
3. See, for example, Association of Art Museum Directors. Statement on the National Academy Museum, December 5, 2008; and Association of Art Museum Directors. Statement on the Delaware Art Museum, June 18, 2014.

4. Kurtz, Daniel L. "The Role of the Attorney General in Regulating Museums." *Legal Problems of Museum Administration*. American Law Institute. 2004: 35.

5. Allen, Richard C. Personal Interview, August 5, 2004. See also cases cited in Forman, Laura. "Checklist of Cases Involving Breach of Museum Trustees' or Staffs' Fiduciary Duties." *Legal Problems of Museum Administration*. American Law Institute. 2004: 27–31.

6. Vogel, Carol. "Historical Society to Sell." *New York Times*, September 9, 1994.

7. Cooper, Robert, "Deaccessioning and Donor Intent—Lessons Learned from Fisk's Stieglitz Collection" (remarks delivered at the 2013 Columbia Law School Charities Regulation and Oversight Project Policy Conference on "The Future of State Charities Regulation," New York, February 7–8, 2013).

8. Kerns, Mason. "Selling the Picasso to Fix the Plumbing: An Analysis of Five High-Profile Deaccessioning Attempts." *Legal Issues in Museum Administration*. American Law Institute–American Bar Association. 2010: 219–223.

9. Kennedy, Randy, and Carol Vogel. "Outcry over a Plan to Sell Museum's Holdings." *New York Times*, January 27, 2009.

10. American Bar Association, Business Law Section, Subcommittee on the Model Nonprofit Corporation Law. *Revised Model Nonprofit Corporation Act*. Prentice Hall Law & Business. 1988. Section 8.30(a).

11. Malaro, Marie C., and Ildiko Pogany DeAngelis, *A Legal Primer on Managing Museum Collections*, 3rd Edition (Washington, DC: Smithsonian Books, 2012), 18.

12. Ibid. at 20.

13. Worden, Virginia Hill. Letter to Faculty, Staff, Alumnae, and Trustees. August 17, 2007.

14. Drew, Jack. "Art Nets $7M." *Berkshire Eagle*, November 4, 2008.

15. Berkshire Museum. Mission. berkshiremuseum.org/about/mission/.

16. Delaware Art Museum. Press Release, March 26, 2014.

17. Ibid.

18. Ibid.

Chapter Ten

Keeping Deaccessioned Objects in the Public Domain

Legal and Practical Issues

Stefanie S. Jandl and Mark S. Gold

INTRODUCTION

When the hammer fell on Lot #363 of the Sotheby's auction in New York City on January 29, 1995, the last item had been sold of 863 objects from the New-York Historical Society collection offered for sale over a three-day period. Unlike other auctions at Sotheby's, however, these sales were not final. For a period of forty-five days, museums, libraries, and archives chartered in the state of New York were given a rare opportunity: they had the right to preempt any sale and, in some cases, at a price less than the hammer price.

New York City was the site of another unique disposition of art objects in 2009 when the Brooklyn Museum's legendary costume collection was moved across the East River to the Metropolitan Museum of Art. The collection-sharing agreement between the two museums provided for the transfer from one museum to another—a gift, not a purchase—of the best objects from the Brooklyn costume collection, and the sale by public auction of the remaining objects.

These two cases were in part shaped by an ongoing, and perhaps increasing, public and professional discourse around keeping deaccessioned art objects in the public domain. These cases undoubtedly contributed to the conversation. For their efforts, the disposing museums in each instance received less in proceeds than the objects would have realized from a customary commercial sale. In each situation, the goal was to keep as many deacces-

sioned objects as possible in the public domain—an ideal shared by many
museum professionals and museum audiences. In some cases, it is a goal
embraced by the museum itself. In other cases, it may be a goal imposed
upon the museum by others.

In all circumstances, though, the goal would seem to be contrary to the
obligation of museum boards of trustees to realize the highest possible sale
price for the benefit of their institution. What are the implications of the
tension between the desire to keep deaccessioned objects in the public domain and the fiduciary—and perhaps legal—duty to ignore that desire and
achieve the best result for the selling museum? How have museums resolved
that tension? What are the legal and practical considerations, and costs, for
disposal in the public domain?

ETHICAL ENVIRONMENT

While the law informs museums about what they can and cannot do, ethical
standards are established by the profession to guide museums as to what they
should and should not do. Standards of conduct for the art museum community in the United States are articulated by two professional organizations,
the American Alliance of Museums (AAM) and the Association of Art Museum Directors (AAMD).

With its Code of Ethics for Museums, AAM states that a member museum will ensure that "acquisition, disposal, and loan activities conform to its
mission and public trust responsibilities"[1]—hardly a road map of ethical
conduct, but a succinct reference to its legal responsibilities. In a 2008 position paper on cutbacks and retrenchment, AAM advises that if a museum
determines it is unable to appropriately care for some objects in its collections, it should "carefully consider whether it is appropriate for the material
to remain in the public domain at another nonprofit institution."[2] AAM,
therefore, offers no truly helpful ethical guidance on the disposal of objects
removed from a museum collection.

AAM launched a Collections Exchange Center in 2003 to facilitate the
purchase, sale, or transfer of deaccessioned objects between member institutions, but the program never received great usage and was terminated. At
present the American art museum community has no practical support from
national professional organizations for the retention of deaccessioned art
objects in the public domain.

AAMD includes "sale or transfer to, or exchange with another public
institution" among the preferred methods of disposal, but does not seem to
endorse the concept enthusiastically, noting, "While it is understood that
museums must fulfill their fiduciary responsibilities and act in the museum's
best interests, museums may give consideration to keeping a deaccessioned

work in the public domain."[3] One could infer that while AAMD intended to make it ethical to keep objects in the public domain (presumably at some cost to the transferor museum), it was also ethical not to. And they expressed no preference.

As professional codes of conduct neither the AAM nor the AAMD positions are legally binding. They barely articulate what is undoubtedly a universal wish that objects remain in the public domain, but have little, if any, impact on the discourse.

LEGAL ISSUES

The legal environment in which museums operate in the United States is a product of state law enforced at the state level (the exception being restrictions imposed by virtue of federal tax-exempt status, which are not relevant here). While the statutes and judicial decisions may vary somewhat from state to state, there are some generally accepted principles that relate to the disposition of deaccessioned objects by museums.

Any decision to dispose of objects in a manner that results in the museum realizing less than full market value will be made by the board of trustees (sometimes designated as the board of directors) of the museum. The board is bound by law to fiduciary duties and obligations to the institution, and particularly the duty of due care and loyalty. Almost every articulation of that duty shares common language requiring a trustee/director to perform his or her duties in good faith, in a manner he or she reasonably believes to be in the best interests of the institution, and with such care as an ordinarily prudent person in a like position would use under similar circumstances.[4]

The issue is immediately raised, therefore, as to how the board of any museum might determine that the disposition of objects for no payment or at a price less than could have been received in an arm's-length transaction would be in the best interest of the museum.

Indeed, many states have statutory or case law that prohibits public charities such as museums from disposing of any assets for less than fair market value. Often that determination is made by the judiciary, with consideration given to the charitable purpose of the transferor and transferee.[5]

In the United States, the office of the attorney general of each state is responsible for oversight of public charities within the state. With very limited exceptions (such as the disposition of certain restricted assets), only the attorney general can challenge museums on their disposition decisions, and his or her review is limited to ensuring that the governing body has complied with its legal and fiduciary duties to the institution. The attorney general will usually not substitute his or her judgment for that of the board in the good faith exercise of its decision-making power.

The attorney general can take a more proactive stance if the survival of a nonprofit entity is at stake (and thereby the preservation of its assets), as it did with the New-York Historical Society to be discussed below.

The laws applicable to museums require that the board make decisions based upon the best interest of the museum. The board's obligation to do so would seemingly preclude the museum giving away, or selling for less than fair market value, objects that could be monetized for the benefit of the museum. This should be so regardless of whether the board feels a desire or an obligation to take a broader view and look at the benefit to be derived by the public at large rather than just their own institution. Indeed, it would seemingly be the duty of the attorney general to insist that only the disposal of assets at fair market value would be in the best interest of the museum for which they are responsible.

With rare exception, museums do just that. They sell their deaccessioned objects for the highest price possible, either through public auction or private sale. And yet there are still instances of museums opting instead—or being forced to opt instead—to realize less in proceeds in order to keep the objects in the public domain. How are the principles of law described above applied to permit or accomplish that outcome?

The answer to that question lays in the concept and definition of mission, coupled with the fact that the perspective and interest of an attorney general are very much limited to the state he or she serves.

Every museum has a mission—its charitable purpose. The mission is normally set forth in its organizational documents and can evolve, and even change materially, over time. Both AAM and AAMD require member museums to have a clearly articulated mission statement. A museum's mission is generally included in documents filed with the state or maintained internally, and it can be inferred from the organization's conduct.

The significance of mission is that it can be used to justify expanding the boundaries of "best interest of the institution" to encompass decisions and acts that are seemingly not. The expansion is most often of a geographic nature that would define the museum's constituency beyond those people who pass through its doors, take advantage of its collections and services, or live in the same community.

For example, if a museum's mission were articulated to be the education of the people of a rural county in Massachusetts by exposing them to objects from other cultures, its board could argue successfully that they have adhered to their mission by giving an object to another museum in the same county. If, however, the object was to be given for no consideration or at a discounted price to a museum in Bentonville, Arkansas, it could be anticipated that the Massachusetts attorney general would intercede to prevent the transaction as a breach of the board's duty to its institution and its mission.

Indeed, there seems to be a willingness—perhaps a propensity—on the part of attorneys general to be guided by geography. In the case of the New-York Historical Society, geography trumped the financial need of the institution. In the case of the Brooklyn Museum, also discussed below, a sense of geography apparently kept the attorney general from any concern about the transfer of a large collection of objects for no consideration—essentially for free.

It would not be unexpected that the way in which an attorney general would interpret the mission of a particular museum could be informed in part by the outcome desired by an attorney general—either for philosophical or political reasons.

One need only explore the pages of auction house catalogues to appreciate the paucity of efforts being made by museums to keep objects in the public domain by offering other museums a discount on pricing or other beneficial terms. Anecdotally, there are few cases in which museums turn over their objects to other museums for no payment unless the transfer is in the context of the closing of a museum without creditors seeking repayment.

In fact, the boards of most museums consider their museum and its viability to be their mission and the focus of their responsibility. This is a position supported by law. It is intriguing, then, to look at cases in which museums have taken steps—developed by them or imposed upon them, but always at a financial cost to themselves—to keep objects in the public domain.

NEW-YORK HISTORICAL SOCIETY

A low-water mark in the two-hundred-year troubled history of the New-York Historical Society was realized in early 1995, when it deaccessioned 863 objects and sold them at auction through Sotheby's.[6] The deaccessioning and sale were part of a multifaceted plan to stabilize the museum for the future. It was crafted with the office of the attorney general for the State of New York and encompassed governance issues as well. The high-profile auction represented the first time that an effort was made to give an advantage to institutions willing to keep the objects in the public domain.

The rules of the auction were the direct result of the involvement of the attorney general's office, acting pursuant to its power of oversight of charitable institutions in the state. Those rules provided that "qualifying institutions" would have the right to make a preemptive bid following the auction and purchase the object at a discount from the highest bid. The amount of the discount was 10 percent if the successful bid was $25,000 or less, 5 percent if the successful bid was more than $25,000, but less than or equal to $100,000, and 3 percent if the successful bid was greater than $100,000 and more than the high presale estimate by Sotheby's, exclusive of the buyer's premium that had to be paid on the successful bid without discount.

"Qualifying institutions" were defined as nonprofit museums, libraries, and archives formed or chartered pursuant to New York law that exhibited their collections or otherwise made them available to the public on a consistent basis. Each qualifying institution was required to agree to retain the purchased object in its collection for at least ten years. As an additional incentive, financing was made available by the museum to qualifying institutions.[7]

The intention implicit in this plan was to give qualifying institutions a financial advantage to acquire these objects and keep them in the public domain. The auction represents the singular model of this magnitude to make that effort. There is no doubt that it was imposed upon the museum by the attorney general and was not born of a desire on the part of the board to keep these objects in the public domain. The board was most assuredly focused on the survival of the museum, but dependent on the approbation of the attorney general to a long-term survival plan.

At auction, more than $12.2 million was realized from the sale of 183 old master paintings on January 12, 1995; $1.5 million was realized from the sale of paperweights on January 18, 1995; and $3.9 million was realized from the sale of Americana and decorative arts on January 29, 1995. Those numbers included the buyer's premium, with a net to the New-York Historical Society of $16 million.[8]

On January 19, 1995, the Metropolitan Museum of Art announced that, for $2.2 million, it had exercised its option to purchase Lo Scheggia's *Triumph of Fame*, a 1449 birth plate of Lorenzo de' Medici, which had been on view at the museum on a long-term loan from the New-York Historical Society. Because the highest bid was below the high estimate given by Sotheby's, the museum received no discount on its purchase, nor did it take advantage of the financing offered to qualifying institutions, so the New-York Historical Society lost no money on that preemption.[9]

The Loeb Art Center at Vassar College exercised its preemption rights to purchase a fifteenth-century painting from the Brussels school for $179,000, and the Brooklyn Museum, after the auction, purchased a fourteenth-century Florentine altarpiece by Nardo di Cione for $354,000.[10] Of the 863 lots in the auction, forty-three (fewer than 5 percent) of them were purchased by thirteen qualifying organizations.[11]

A thoughtful analysis of the process was offered by Beverly Schreiber Jacoby, cochair of the Community Advisory Board of the New-York Historical Society, shortly thereafter. Based on the number of objects preempted by qualifying institutions, she concludes that the preemption model did not achieve the desired result of keeping as much of the collection as possible in the public domain.[12] Although the loss to the New-York Historical Society by virtue of the preemption discount was minimal, it is notable that the institutions that took advantage of the discount were in a much more stable financial condition than the New-York Historical Society, resulting in the troubled museum essentially underwriting the purchase of its objects by more well-off institutions.

In addition, Jacoby concludes that the availability of preemption actually discouraged potential bidders from bidding on the more expensive pieces. There was no incentive for the qualifying institutions that may have engaged in the bidding to do so since they could purchase the object afterward; consequently, their absence depressed the final price and the money ultimately realized by the New-York Historical Society. Jacoby speculates that loss to be in the range of $1,500,000 to $2,650,000. [13]

The preemption model, which has not been replicated on this scale, appeared to seek a balance between the competing goals of maximizing the monies realized by a museum in distress with the possibility of its disposed assets to remain in the public domain. Its effectiveness at achieving those goals is not widely accepted. The preemption plan is also notable for its geographic bias. This plan was not about keeping objects in the public domain. It was about keeping objects in the public domain in New York.

BROOKLYN MUSEUM

New York City, the fashion capital of the United States, was the site of the largest, and probably the most ambitious, collection transfer between museums in recent American history. In January 2009 the Brooklyn Museum transferred ownership of its renowned collection of American and European costumes, composed of 23,500 objects, to the Costume Institute at the Metropolitan Museum of Art. [14] The most important objects were accessioned into the holdings of the Metropolitan Museum, where the collection retains its own identity as the Brooklyn Museum Costume Collection at the Metropolitan Museum of Art, while other objects have been sold at auction over a several-year period with proceeds benefiting the Brooklyn Museum. The combined holdings of the two museums have formed the preeminent collection of costumes in the world and are an unsurpassed resource for scholars, designers, and the public. The *New Yorker* magazine referred to this landmark collection transfer as "an unusually collegial open adoption." [15]

The Brooklyn Museum's costume collection was established in the first years of the twentieth century to serve the emerging American design community. [16] It features a depth of holdings from legendary American and European fashion designers, which together offer the most comprehensive narrative of any collection of fashion history from the late nineteenth century to the mid-twentieth century. Despite this wealth of holdings the Brooklyn Museum began questioning its ability to appropriately steward the collection in the early 1990s. Costume collections pose particular challenges with the fragility of the objects and the expense, staffing, and space needed to properly maintain them. The financially strained Brooklyn Museum had been criticized for neglecting and failing to exhibit the collection, which had not had its own curator since a 1990 budget crisis.[17] As best-practice standards evolved, the Brooklyn Museum realized that it was increasingly unable to care for the deteriorating collection.

By 2004 the board of the Brooklyn Museum was actively considering its options, which included transferring the costume collection to another museum within New York City. A core issue, however, was the fact that the collection was not fully inventoried and catalogued—a prerequisite for deaccessioning in compliance of AAM guidelines—and the museum had no resources to undertake such a project. When the program officer for museums and conservation at the Andrew W. Mellon Foundation learned of the Brooklyn Museum's predicament, she invited the museum to apply for a grant to catalogue the collection. After several months of work in which the Mellon Foundation helped shape the final proposal, the Brooklyn Museum was awarded $3,925,000 to inventory, catalogue, digitally photograph, and assess the Western costume collection.[18] The grant included making high-resolution images of the top 4,000 objects available to an international audience via the nonprofit digital image library ArtStor.

Implementation of the Mellon grant commenced in 2005 and took a team of twelve to fifteen people over three years to complete.[19] At the end of the project the collection was fully inventoried and catalogued, and its condition and storage needs were assessed. This collection review enabled the Brooklyn Museum to affirm that it was not in a financial position to be an effective steward of the collection, supporting a decision to deaccession.

In looking at its options, the board believed it had what its chairman characterizes as an "enormous responsibility" to keep the core of the collection intact and in New York City.[20] The museum then invited acquisition proposals from two city institutions and selected the Metropolitan Museum of Art as the collection partner because it presented the strongest proposal and because its mission was most closely in alignment with that of the Brooklyn Museum.[21] Although the board recognized the sale of the collection as an alternative, at no time was it considered seriously.[22]

In January of 2009, the Brooklyn collection was deaccessioned and physically moved to the Metropolitan Museum. In accordance with its agreement, the Metropolitan accessioned the best 4,000 objects and made arrangements to auction off a group of mutually agreed-upon non-museum-quality objects. Work is ongoing in the process of examining the remainder of the collection to make determinations for accession or auction based on quality and overlap with the Metropolitan's collection.[23] (Both museums must agree on each object selected for auction.) The Brooklyn Museum continues to have access to the collection for its own exhibitions.[24]

In accordance with their extensive acquisition proposal, the Metropolitan Museum organized an exhibition[25] of the Brooklyn collection that complemented a simultaneous exhibition held at the Brooklyn Museum.[26] A catalogue of the Brooklyn collection was published,[27] a two-day symposium was held that explored details and issues of the collection cataloguing and transfer,[28] and the Brooklyn collection was the focus of the Metropolitan Museum's 2010 Costume Institute Gala Benefit. Finally, the Metropolitan Museum has dedicated a curator and a fellowship to the Brooklyn collection for five years.[29]

A number of factors gave shape to this historic collection transfer and enabled the collection to remain in the public domain. The Brooklyn Museum, albeit challenged, was not in dire financial condition, but the costs of storing and conserving the collection were considerable. The Metropolitan Museum was in stable financial condition and able to assume the costs associated with the transfer and with the stewardship of the core of the collection. The proximity of the two museums meant that the collection would be located just across the river from its original home. The geography of this deal met the needs and desires of all stakeholders—including the attorney general of the State of New York, who seemingly had no interest in questioning or disrupting the transaction.

The costume collection transfer, which the two museums refer to as a "partnership,"[30] offered an innovative and expanded notion of what ownership means, one that was consistent with the Brooklyn Museum's mission statement—to "act as a bridge"[31] between the visitor and the collections.[32] Because the costume collection was rarely exhibited in Brooklyn, placing it at the Metropolitan Museum meant that the works could be properly cared for and exhibited, thus giving the public increased access to the collection. With two costume exhibitions and the publication of the collection catalogue, the Metropolitan immediately increased the visibility of the Brooklyn collection, which was elegantly consistent with the mission of the Brooklyn Museum.

Financial and practical considerations were also involved in the success of this collection transfer. The project could not have gone forward without the extensive financial commitment from two well-funded organizations, the Mellon Foundation and the Metropolitan Museum. At nearly $4 million, the Mellon Foundation grant offered a rare opportunity to address a collection need on a scale difficult for most museums to secure. As the receiving institution, the Metropolitan Museum of Art had an unparalleled ability to allocate staffing, expertise, and funding (which included securing corporate sponsorships) to receive, care for, and exhibit the collection.

As exemplary as this collection transfer was, it also demonstrates the inestimable value—and infrequent confluence—of third-party financial resources (Mellon), a willing and financially stable partner, the lack of financial urgency on the part of the transferor museum, and a broad view of mission on the part of its board to make a result like this possible. As with the New-York Historical Society, this plan was also not so much about keeping objects in the public domain. It was about keeping objects in the public domain in New York City.

OTHER EXAMPLES

In April of 2005 the New York Public Library announced that Sotheby's, as its agent, was accepting sealed bids for the purchase of Asher B. Durand's *Kindred Spirits*. A prominent work of the Hudson River School that had been donated to the library one hundred years earlier, the painting depicts the artist Thomas Cole and the poet William Cullen Bryant standing on an overlook in the Catskill Mountains of New York. The terms of the sale included a provision for a one-year deferral of payment for any New York institution. The Metropolitan Museum of Art was seen as a likely purchaser.[33]

The high bidder, however, turned out to be Alice L. Walton, for Crystal Bridges Museum of American Art, a museum then being built by her family's foundation in Bentonville, Arkansas. Purchased for a sum reportedly in excess of $35 million, the bid eclipsed the joint bid submitted by the Metropolitan Museum of Art and the National Gallery of Art.[34]

The departure of the painting from the state of New York was met with public criticism. However, since the library was not in fiscal or administrative crisis and the transaction was arm's-length and for fair market value, there was no role for the New York attorney general. The president of the library did acknowledge his delight (and undoubtedly some relief) that the work was remaining in the public domain—and in the United States, if not New York.[35] Criticism would no doubt have been much more vocal and sustained had the work vanished into a private collection.

On November 11, 2006, the board of trustees of the Thomas Jefferson University in Philadelphia, Pennsylvania, announced the planned sale to the National Gallery of Art and the Crystal Bridges Museum of American Art (an interesting partnership in light of the results of the sale of *Kindred Spirits*) of Thomas Eakins's *The Gross Clinic* for $68 million in a private sale arranged by Christie's.[36] The artist, the painting, and the subject matter—a legendary medical school teacher performing surgery—were deeply connected to the city of Philadelphia and the prospect of the painting's departure provoked local outrage.[37]

Since the sale presumably was an arm's-length transaction for fair market value, there was no role to be played by the attorney general for the Commonwealth of Pennsylvania. Nevertheless, and reportedly having learned from the criticism levelled at the New York Public Library for the sale of *Kindred Spirits*, the university included in the terms of sale a provision that local art museums and governmental institutions had an opportunity to match the offer with a preemptive bid. With loans and the support of hundreds of donors eager to keep this iconic work in Philadelphia, the painting was ultimately purchased jointly by the Philadelphia Museum of Art and the Pennsylvania Academy of the Fine Arts.[38]

The university lost no money by virtue of the preemption, but the sale does reflect a heightened sensitivity to the geographic affinity of some objects and the desire to avoid controversy. As seen before, this was not about keeping an object in the public domain. It was about keeping an object in Philadelphia.

The 2013 transfer of the core collection of arms and armor from the Higgins Armory Museum in Worcester, Massachusetts, to its neighbor, the Worcester Art Museum, although not technically a deaccessioning, presents an elegantly designed model of efforts to keep objects in the public domain—in this case, in the context of a museum destined for closure. A case study of this transaction appears elsewhere in this volume, but there are several aspects of the transaction that help inform our discussion here.

The Higgins had assets (a physical facility, the collection, and investments) that far exceeded its liabilities. It also had a governing body that appreciated that the condition of the physical facilities and the cost to repair or replace them, in the context of museum visitation and revenue, rendered the museum not sustainable for the long term. Higgins had the benefit of assets, engaged and thoughtful trustees, and time.

After years of considering all strategies for keeping the museum open, the trustees focused on trying to establish a strategic alliance that would perpetuate the mission of the museum. In pursuing alternatives, the trustees established the following four priorities:

a. ensuring the Higgins core collection continues to exist intact as the highest priority;
b. preserving the collection in the City of Worcester if reasonably possible;
c. seeking a transfer of assets and Higgins institutional culture, including the spirit of its very successful programs and educational activities; and
d. seeking an economically sustainable and transformative combination with the receiving institution.[39]

In articulating these priorities, the trustees highlighted principles similar to those that drive the efforts to keep deaccessioned objects in the public domain.

Strategic alliances were explored with several other institutions, including museums in Philadelphia, New York City, and Boston. Though just forty miles away and within the Commonwealth of Massachusetts, Boston was seen as an even farther distance in terms of demographics, access by public transportation, and in the context of the great pride in and affection for the Higgins that the people of Worcester had. [40]

Ultimately, a comprehensive document entitled "Covenants for the Transfer of Assets" was crafted with, and executed by, the Worcester Art Museum that preserved the core Higgins collection, kept it within the city of Worcester, and outlined the structure to preserve the collection and continue and enhance already robust programming. It also allowed for the deaccessioning and sale of objects outside of the core collection to support those activities in the collection's new home. [41]

It is reasonable to speculate that the attorney general of Massachusetts would not have happily embraced a transfer of the core collection to Pennsylvania or New York. But the confluence of geography, financial sustainability, and loyalty to mission made it easy for her to consent to the transfer. Court approval (required because the transfer was for less than fair market value) followed quickly. [42]

On March 28, 2014, just three months after the closing of the Higgins Armory Museum, the Worcester Art Museum opened *Knights!*, a critically acclaimed exhibition and the first step toward the meaningful integration of the two collections. Arms and armor from the Higgins collection were exhibited alongside Worcester artworks—including classical sculpture and Renaissance paintings—to illuminate the historical context in which the armor was made and used. Enhancing the exhibition's reach was ambitious programming that engaged numerous schoolchildren, families, and community members in the exhibition and its ideas. Though situated in a new home, the Higgins collection, its core intact, is still cared for, exhibited, interpreted, and enlivened by the same mission-driven values as before, and it is still very much at the heart of the Worcester community.

CONCLUSION

One goal of this essay was to explore how museums resolve the tension between the desire to keep deaccessioned objects in the public domain and the desire (and perhaps duty) to achieve the best financial result for the disposing museum. The reality is that any tension is almost always resolved by selling deaccessioned objects in a manner designed to maximize the proceeds to the selling museum without regard to whether or not the objects remain in the public domain as a result.

The New-York Historical Society and the Brooklyn Museum represent deviations from that normal practice of such magnitude as to make them watershed moments. Even as deviations, however, they provide lessons of greater applicability. This is so even though the effort to keep objects in the public domain was imposed upon the New-York Historical Society by the attorney general of the State of New York and the effort by the Brooklyn Museum was driven by its own board.

One of the lessons learned is that geography matters. It mattered to the New York attorney general that the collection of the New-York Historical Society remain in the state of New York. It mattered to the board of the Brooklyn Museum that its costume collection remain in the city of New York. Even the modest incentives offered by Thomas Jefferson University and the New York Public Library demonstrated at least a sensitivity to local concern and the potential for local criticism. And, clearly, the experience of the Higgins Armory Museum demonstrates the high priority given to—and facility of transaction provided by—geography.

In thinking about geography, it is probably more accurate to refer to political boundaries, rather than proximity. In four of the five instances cited, the neighboring state of New Jersey was equally convenient for public access, but likely a world away in terms of an acceptable outcome.

Mission is important as well. A board's sense of its mission informs its willingness to sacrifice proceeds for public access. There was clear and strong consensus on the part of the board of the Brooklyn Museum that its costume collection was of such significance—and so integral to—the city of New York as a capital of fashion that it was unthinkable that the highest quality and most important objects from the collection would be dissipated among smaller museums and private collections.

Similarly, the fact that the Higgins collection had its genesis in the obsessive collection of a local steel manufacturer whose business included the production of "doughboy helmets" during World War I, embedded the museum and its collection in the history of the city. To have it moved even down the turnpike to Boston would have been a blow to the city that had been its home since it opened to the public in 1931. Likewise, protecting the core of the collection was perceived to be at the heart of the museum's mission for both the Brooklyn Museum and the Higgins Armory—of higher priority than the incremental monetary benefit of selling it to the highest bidder.

Mission is also what informs an attorney general of his or her role in the transaction. It can be used to justify support for or opposition to a particular plan, even if the position taken is based on political or other considerations.

One would be hard pressed to find support in the museum community or within the general public that deaccessioned objects depart the public domain and end up in private collections. Yet the legal and ethical duties of board members, in almost all instances, require them to subordinate their personal preferences in that regard to the best interest of their museum. In fact, it is near imperative that they do so in an institution under financial siege unless museum closure is certain.

In other instances, however, the financial sacrifice can be ethically and legally made, but only when the board concludes that the public domain alternative is clearly within the mission of the museum and the attorney general agrees. It is a rare museum that is blessed with the confluence of sufficient finances, a broad enough mission, and the agreement of both the board and the attorney general that the gift or incentive crafted to keep the object in the public domain is in the best interest of the museum and serves its mission.

NOTES

The original version of this essay first appeared in *Museums and the Disposals Debate* (Davies, Ed.), MuseumsEtc., 2011, www.MuseumsEtc.com.

1. American Alliance of Museums, "Code of Ethics for Museums," 2000, www.aam-us. org.

2. American Alliance of Museums Accreditation Commission, *Considerations for AAM Accredited Museums Facing Retrenchment or Downsizing*, 2008, www.aam-us.org/resources/assessment-programs/accreditation/commission.

3. Association of Art Museum Directors, *Policy on Deaccessioning*, 2010, aamd.org/sites/default/files/document/AAMD%20Policy%20on%20Deaccessioning%20website.pdf.

4. American Bar Association, Business Law Section, Subcommittee on the Model Nonprofit Corporation Law, *Revised Model Nonprofit Corporation Act* (Clifton, NJ: Prentice Hall Law and Business, 1988), Section 8.30(a).

5. See, for example, *Massachusetts Charitable Mechanic Ass'n v. Beede et al.*, 320 Mass. 601 (1947), cited in Commonwealth of Massachusetts, Office of the Attorney General, *Guidelines on Notice Requirements of G.L. c. 180, §8A(c)*.

6. Sotheby's, *Important Old Master Paintings: The Property of the New York Historical Society (Sale 6653)*, January 12, 1995 (with auction results laid in); Sotheby's, *Important Paperweights: The Property of the New York Historical Society (Sale 6656)*, January 18, 1995 (with auction results laid in); Sotheby's, *Americana and Decorative Arts: The Property of the New York Historical Society (Sale 6661)*, January 29, 1995 (with auction results laid in).

7. In *Matter of the New York State Historical Society*, from Assurance of Discontinuance Pursuant to Executive Law Section 63(15), New York State Department of Law and Charities Division, Office of the Attorney General, New York, September 9, 1994, page 10, section 6.

8. Sotheby's, auction results laid into catalogues for sales notes in note 6.

9. Carol Vogel, "Met Museum Pre-Empts Sale of Old Master," *New York Times*, January 20, 1995.

10. "$17.6 Million for Historical Society," *Art in America*, March 1995: 29.

11. Beverly Schreiber Jacoby, "Caveat Pre-Emptor," *Museum News*, January/February 1996: 55.

12. Jacoby, 55.

13. Jacoby, 55.

14. Brooklyn Museum press release, "Brooklyn Museum Announces Landmark Costume Collection Partnership with Metropolitan Museum," December 16, 2008, www. brooklynmuseum.org/press/uploads/Costume Collection Press Release.pdf.

15. Judith Thurman, "Closet Encounters," *The New Yorker*, May 10, 2010, accessed July 15, 2011, www.newyorker.com/magazine/2010/05/10/closet-encounters.

16. Brooklyn Museum press release, 2008.

17. Dianne M. Pogoda, "Curators Mull Future of Brooklyn Museum's Costume Collection," *WWD* 159.119, June 19, 1990, p. 3.

18. Brooklyn Museum press release, "The Andrew W. Mellon Foundation Awards $3.925 Million to Brooklyn Museum for Landmark Survey of Its Historic 70,000-Object American and European Costume Collection," March 2005.

19. Carol Vogel, "Brooklyn Museum's Costume Treasures Going to the Met," *New York Times*, December 16, 2008.

20. Norman M. Feinberg, Chair of Board of Trustees of Brooklyn Museum, phone conversation with author, June 17, 2011.

21. Kevin Stayton, Chief Curator of Brooklyn Museum, phone conversation with author, June 6, 2011.

22. *Id.*

23. Harold Koda, Curator in Charge, the Costume Institute at the Metropolitan Museum of Art, phone conversation with author, July 15, 2011.

24. *Id.*

25. *American Woman: Fashioning a National Identity*, on view at the Metropolitan Museum of Art, May 5–August 15, 2010.

26. *American High Style: Fashioning a National Collection*, on view at the Brooklyn Museum, May 7–August 1, 2010.

27. Jan Glier Reeder, *High Style: Masterworks from the Brooklyn Museum Costume Collection at the Metropolitan Museum of Art* (New York: Metropolitan Museum of Art and New Haven, CT: Yale University Press, 2010).

28. "Costume Collections: A Collaborative Model for Museums," symposium held at the Metropolitan Museum of Art, May 21–22, 2010.

29. Jan Glier Reeder is the consulting curator for the Brooklyn Museum Costume Collection at the Metropolitan Museum of Art.

30. Vogel, "Brooklyn Museum's Costume Treasures Going to the Met."

31. "Brooklyn Museum—About: Mission Statement," Brooklyn Museum website, www.brooklynmuseum.org/about/mission.php.

32. Kevin Stayton, Chief Curator of Brooklyn Museum, phone conversation with author, June 6, 2011.

33. Carol Vogel, "A Silent Auction for Library's Art," *New York Times*, April 29, 2005.

34. Carol Vogel, "New York Public Library's Durand Painting Sold to Wal-Mart Heiress," *New York Times*, May 13, 2005.

35. *Id.*

36. Carol Vogel, "Eakins Masterwork Is to Be Sold to Museums," *New York Times*, November 11, 2006.

37. Stephan Salisbury, "Stunned by Sale, but Not Giving Up City and Arts Leaders Are Ready to Try to Match the $68 Million Price Tag for Eakins' Masterpiece," philly.com, November 12, 2006, articles.philly.com/2006-11-12/news/25407677_1_gross-clinic-thomas-eakins-painting.

38. Carol Vogel, "Philadelphia Raises Enough Money to Retain a Masterpiece by Eakins," *New York Times*, April 24, 2006.

39. Affidavit of James C. Donnelly, Jr., *The John Woodman Higgins Armory, Inc. v. Martha Coakley et al.* (Supreme Judicial Court Civil Action No. SJ-2013-490), December 10, 2013.

40. *Id.* at 10.

41. Covenants for the Transfer of Assets of the Higgins Armory Museum to the Worcester Art Museum, November 19, 2013.

42. Judgment, *The John Woodman Higgins Armory, Inc. v. Martha Coakley et al.* (Supreme Judicial Court Civil Action No. SJ-2013-490), December 20, 2013.

Chapter Eleven

There's No Such Thing as the Public Trust, and It's a Good Thing, Too

Donn Zaretsky

In the debates surrounding museum deaccessioning,[1] no concept plays a larger role than that of "the public trust." Deaccessioning opponents typically claim that museums cannot sell art to pay for operating costs because their collections are held in the public trust. In this chapter, I want to suggest that this claim is completely without merit. There is no such thing as the public trust—at least when it comes to works of art. "The public trust" is just a phrase opponents of deaccessioning have latched onto to advance their policy agenda.

The accepted view within the museum community is that deaccessioning is permitted to raise funds to acquire other items for the collection, but not for any other reason. This view is reflected in the ethical codes of both the American Alliance of Museums (AAM) and the Association of Art Museum Directors (AAMD).[2] Sales in violation of these rules are vehemently denounced by the museum groups and their allies in the media, and subject to severe sanction.[3]

What accounts for this view? What's so wrong with selling works and using the proceeds however the board of the museum thinks best? The answer, we are repeatedly told, is that the works are "held in the public trust" and therefore cannot be sold. For example,

- In a letter to the editor of the *New York Times*, AAM president Ford Bell identified "the essential point of museum collections," namely that "once an object falls under the aegis of a museum, it is *held in the public trust*, to be accessible to present and future generations."[4]

- In the context of the City of Detroit's ongoing bankruptcy proceedings, the *New York Times* reported that "the director of the Detroit Institute of Arts said . . . that he believed the museum's collection was 'held in the public trust' and could not be sold by the city to help pay down its multi-billion-dollar debt."[5]
- More recently, in a statement announcing sanctions against the Delaware Museum of Art for selling a work of art "to pay outstanding debt and build its operating endowment," the AAMD explained that "[w]ith this sale, the museum is treating works from its collection as disposable assets, rather than irreplaceable cultural heritage that it holds in trust for people now and in the future."[6]

In each case, the discussion proceeds in the same way. Any time an institution proposes to sell a work and use the proceeds for anything other than the purchase of more works, it is met with the argument that the work is "held in the public trust" and so may not be sold. The claim is repeated over and over again. But is it true? Is there a public trust and, if so, do museum collections belong to it?

There is, in fact, a public trust doctrine under U.S. law. As Joseph Sax put it in an influential law review article from 1970, the idea behind the doctrine is that "certain interests are so intrinsically important to every citizen" that "it is necessary to be especially wary lest any particular individual or group acquire the power to control them." So, for example, "American law courts held it 'inconceivable' that any person should claim a private property interest in the navigable waters of the United States."[7]

The most famous public trust case in American law remains *Illinois Central Railroad Company v. Illinois*.[8] In 1869 the State of Illinois made an extensive grant of property to the Illinois Central Railroad. As Sax summarizes it, the grant included "all of the land underlying Lake Michigan for one mile out from the shoreline and extending one mile in length along the central business district of Chicago—more than one thousand acres of incalculable value, comprising virtually the whole commercial waterfront of the city." Four years later, the state sought to revoke the grant, on the grounds that the original grant was in violation of the public trust in which that property had been held. The Supreme Court ruled in favor of the state and allowed the grant to be undone.

So (contrary to the title of this chapter) there is such a thing as the public trust. But notice how limited its application has been. Prof. Sax writes,

> It is clear that the historical scope of public trust law is quite narrow. Its coverage includes, with some variation among the states, that aspect of the public domain below the low-water mark on the margin of the sea and the great lakes, the waters over those lands, and the waters within rivers and

streams of any consequence. . . . Traditional public trust law also embraces parklands, especially if they have been donated to the public for specific purposes. [9]

Rivers, seas, the seashore—the sorts of things it is "inconceivable" to imagine anyone claiming a private property interest in. This is the domain of the public trust doctrine. "Certainly," as Sax notes, "the phrase 'public trust' does not contain any magic such that special obligations can be said to arise merely from its incantation." [10] Yet that is all the appeal to the public trust is in the deaccessioning context: mere incantation. Consider how little works of art have in common with the kinds of property it may make sense to think of as being held in a public trust.

First, it is not at all inconceivable that any person should claim a private property interest in them. It is in fact quite conceivable: *most* works of art are privately owned. [11] Moreover, even works held by museums are, in contrast to the rivers and seas, privately owned. It is one thing to say the State of Illinois holds the land beneath Lake Michigan in trust for the public. It is quite another to say that Randolph College, for example, holds the works it has acquired, either through purchase or donation, in trust for the public. [12] The former is government-owned property that is difficult to even imagine residing in private hands. The latter is privately owned property for which there is an active and liquid market.

Indeed, the incoherence of a public trust approach to artworks is shown by the following: Suppose I own the George Bellows painting *Men of the Docks*. It has been in my family since we bought it from the artist in 1912. No one has ever suggested—nor would anyone ever suggest—that it was inconceivable that I claim a private property interest in the painting. No one would think to argue that the painting was "held in the public trust." Now suppose I donate the painting to Randolph College—or better yet, that they buy it from me for full fair market value, using money from their endowment, or from an art-loving donor. On the logic of the AAM and the AAMD, the work is now suddenly held in the public trust. But how? By what mechanism has a piece of property that has been privately held for one hundred years been transformed into public property that can no longer be freely sold?

The answer, of course, is that it has not been so transformed. Museum collections simply are not held in the public trust. And one way we know this to be true is that museums sell works all the time. That is, the rhetoric around the rule suggests that works owned by museums can *never* be sold—recall the AAM president's claim that "the essential point of museum collections" is that "once an object falls under the aegis of a museum, it is *held in the public trust*, to be accessible to present and future generations" [13]—but the actual rule itself is that works can be sold so long as the sales proceeds are used to buy more art. It's really a use-of-proceeds rule, not a prohibition-on-sale rule. The AAMD rule is not "thou shalt not deaccession"; it's when you do deaccession, the funds received "may be used only for the acquisition of works of art."[14] Similarly, the AAM rule is "in no event shall [proceeds of sales from deaccessioning] be used for anything other than acquisition or direct care of collections."[15] In 2009, Janet Landay, the then executive director of the AAMD, told the *Philadelphia Inquirer* that selling works is a "normal part of building a collection" and "shouldn't be such a touchy subject." The "touchy part," she added, "is how the money is spent." In the same article, the president of the Pennsylvania Academy of the Fine Arts is quoted as saying that museum collections "aren't static. They aren't meant to be static."[16]

The truth is that no one—not even the museum organizations themselves—really believes the works are held in the public trust.

The title of this chapter comes from an essay by Stanley Fish, in which he argues that "abstract concepts like free speech do not have any 'natural' content but are filled with whatever content and direction one can manage to put into them." "Free speech," he says, "is just the name we give to verbal behavior that serves the substantive agendas we wish to advance."[17] The same is true of the "public trust" in the deaccessioning context: it's just the name one side of the debate gives to behavior that serves the substantive agenda they wish to advance. To say, "That work is held in the public trust," is really just another way of saying, "I don't want you to sell that work." It has no content, no meaning at all. When a museum wants to sell a work and use the proceeds for something other than acquiring new works (operating costs, capital projects, avoiding bankruptcy, etc.), we are told that the work is held in the "public trust." When it wants to sell the same work but commits to using the proceeds to buy more art, then the "public trust" drops out of the conversation. We would all be better off—the discussion regarding deaccessioning would be healthier, more honest, more rational—if the phrase played no role in the debate.

NOTES

1. Mark Gold, "Monetizing the Collection," chapter 9 in this volume.
2. See American Association of Museums, "Code Of Ethics For Museums," 2000, p. 3, www.aam-us.org/resources/ethics-standards-and-best-practices/code-of-ethics ("Proceeds from the sale of nonliving collections are to be used consistent with the established standards of the museum's discipline, but in no event shall they be used for anything other than acquisition or direct care of collections."); and Association of Art Museum Directors, "Professional Practices in Art Museums," 2011, p. 25, aamd.org/sites/default/files/document/2011Professional PracitiesinArtMuseums.pdf ("Funds received from the disposal of a deaccessioned work shall not be used for operations or capital expenses. Such funds . . . may be used only for the acquisition of works of art.").

3. See, for example, Robin Pogrebin, "Sanctions Are Ending for Museum," *New York Times*, October 18, 2010 ("When the National Academy Museum sold two important Hudson River School paintings in 2008 to pay its bills, the Association of Art Museum Directors came down hard with sanctions, making the academy a pariah in the museum world and a symbol for the evils of deaccessioning."); and Christopher Knight, "Brandeis University Issues Rose Art Museum Report," *Los Angeles Times Culture Monster Blog*, May 4, 2009 (calling proposed sale of museum art ethically "repulsive").

4. Ford Bell, "Museum Art, Held in Trust," letter to the editor, *New York Times*, March 30, 2009 (emphasis added).

5. Dave Itzkoff, "Collection of Detroit Institute of Arts Cannot Be Sold, Its Director Says," *New York Times*, May 24, 2013.

6. Statement of the AAMD, "Association of Art Museum Directors Sanctions Delaware Art Museum," June 18, 2014.

7. Joseph Sax, "The Public Trust Doctrine in Natural Resource Law: Effective Judicial Intervention," *Michigan Law Review* 68 (1970): 484.

8. 146 U.S. 387 (1892).

9. Sax, *supra* note 7, at 556.

10. See *id.* at 485.

11. See also part III of this volume.

12. Peter Dean and Bradley Bateman, *Randolph College: A Sequel, A New Relationship and More Controversy*, Handbook for Academic Museums (Boston: MuseumsEtc Ltd., 2014).

13. See *supra* note 4.

14. See *supra* note 2.

15. See *id.*

16. Stephan Salisbury, "Academy of the Fine Arts Discloses Sales of Artworks," *Philadelphia Inquirer*, January 7, 2011.

17. See Stanley Fish, *There's No Such Thing as Free Speech* (New York: Oxford University Press, 1994), p. 102.

Chapter Twelve

Endowments and Restricted Gifts

Accessible or "Hands Off"?

Anita Lichtblau, Esq.

"We have a financial emergency! May we legally use our restricted funds? What about our endowment? The Matisse print?" These questions are not uncommon for charitable organizations, including museums, especially in difficult economic times. As with many other legal questions, the answer is, "It depends!" Although recent changes in most state laws have made it easier for restrictions to be lifted or modified, in most cases, museums may not do so on their own. This essay will discuss what restricted gifts and endowments are and if, when, and how restrictions may be released or adjusted or endowment funds may be spent.

WHAT IS A RESTRICTED GIFT?

In its simplest terms, a "restricted gift" is exactly what the term indicates—a gift that is restricted in its use in some way, often forever. Indeed all gifts to a charity, which most museums are or are a part of (such as university museums), are restricted in the sense that they must be used to further the charity's charitable mission. But some gifts are subject to narrower restrictions within the museum's general charitable purposes. This type of restricted gift often presents a problem for a charity in need of additional financial resources because the original purpose may not easily be altered to meet the current financial or programmatic needs of the institution. These types of gifts are referred to in this essay as "restricted gifts."

A gift could be restricted in its purpose, such as, for example, a donation to a museum to support art classes at the museum for low-income children.

Or the gift of a historic document could be subject to the requirement that the document be displayed permanently in a particular gallery or to prohibit its sale. Or a gift could be restricted in how it is administered. For example, a donation of cash or stock could restrict spending from the principal or corpus of the gift, either permanently or for a stated period of time—this is often referred to as an endowment. Gifts may also have a combination of restrictions; for example a gift of $5 million to a museum could be restricted as to principal, with income only to be used to maintain a sculpture garden.

MAY RESTRICTIONS BE LIFTED OR MODIFIED?

This is where the "it depends" response applies. A number of different factors will determine the answer, not the least of which is which state's law applies to the gift. This area of the law is evolving quickly. On the one hand, forty-nine state legislatures (all except Pennsylvania) have passed a version of the 2006 model Uniform Prudent Management of Institutional Funds Act (UPMIFA), which among other things liberalizes rules for releasing and modifying restrictions on investment assets.[1] On the other hand, court-made law (called "common law") in some states has been moving toward giving donors greater say in whether restrictions are enforced or modified. The bottom line is that it is essential to consult with an attorney familiar with this area of law in your state as to rules concerning the release or modification of restrictions.

Nonetheless, there are certain common critical factors, such as who imposed the restriction; the type of asset given; whether the donor is alive or in existence (in the case of a donor that is an organization); the type of restriction; whether the gift instrument itself permits releasing or modifying the restriction in some circumstances; and, in some cases, the amount of the asset and the length of time that has passed since the original gift. Different categories of restricted gifts, and how those categories bear on the ability of a museum to release or modify restrictions, are described below.

BOARD-IMPOSED RESTRICTIONS

If a restriction on any type of fund or donation has been imposed only by the charity, typically by its board of directors or other governing body, and not by a donor, the gift is not considered a true restricted gift or a true endowment.[2] Therefore, the board itself may release or modify a restriction by a vote that complies with the organization's bylaws. No further approval is needed, either from the donor(s), the attorney general (or other state official charged with overseeing charitable funds), or a court, assuming that the funds or donation in question continue to be used to further the museum's charitable purpose. It is important for this type of fund to be identified in financial and corporate records as a board-created or board-restricted fund, so that latitude for later board action will be clear. In common parlance, these types of funds, if designated by the board as an endowment, are often referred to as "board endowments."

DONOR-IMPOSED RESTRICTIONS

On the other hand, if a restriction has been imposed by the donor, then a gift will be considered a true restricted gift, restrictions on which are legally enforceable and may be released or modified only under certain conditions, as discussed below. This type of restriction is often referred to as a "donor-imposed restriction." In order to be legally enforceable, the restriction must be documented in some form. Oral instructions from the donor are generally not sufficient. Typical types of documentation include

- A donor's will
- A written trust instrument
- A written gift agreement
- A deed or other document of conveyance
- Correspondence between the donor and a museum
- Check-off boxes on paper or online donation platforms

Be aware, however, that gifts subject to donor-imposed restrictions also include ones made in response to solicitations by a museum for specific purposes. For example, if a museum sends out a solicitation letter requesting donations to restore part of its collection, funds contributed in response are considered legally restricted.

GIFT INSTRUMENT PERMISSION FOR
RELEASE OR MODIFICATION

Sometimes, language within a gift instrument itself may permit releasing or modifying a restriction under certain circumstances. For example, a gift agreement may provide that funds donated to a religious museum may be used only to purchase ritual objects, unless the financial condition of the museum is so weak that funds are needed for general operating expenses, in which case up to 20 percent of the corpus of the gift may be used for such purposes. If the specific requirements in the gift instrument are met for releasing or modifying restrictions, a museum may act without further approval. Documentation of the justification for release or modification, including a legal opinion if appropriate, is advisable.

LIVING INDIVIDUAL DONORS OR ORGANIZATIONAL DONORS IN EXISTENCE

Just in the past decade, the District of Columbia, the U.S. Virgin Islands, and all states except Pennsylvania have passed a version of UPMIFA, which permits most charities[3] to release or modify a restriction if a donor consents in writing, so long as the donation continues to be used for a charitable purpose of the charity.[4] The donor must be living and competent to consent; consent from a family member or heir does not meet the requirement.

UPMIFA applies only to "institutional funds," that is, funds or other assets held for the purpose of investment; it expressly does not apply to "program-related assets," which are used to carry out a charitable mission.[5] This is an important distinction, especially for a museum. For example, a painting donated to a museum or a building housing a museum's historic collection would be considered "program-related assets," not "institutional funds." Therefore, UPMIFA would not authorize a museum to release a prohibition on selling a painting with just the donor's consent. By contrast, a donation of $500,000 originally created by the donor as a permanent endowment could be spent by the museum in its entirety in one year if the donor consented in writing. Most museum funds, including, for example, those that are restricted to spending the income for a charitable purpose, are considered "institutional funds."

The UPMIFA route to releasing or modifying restrictions applies not only to living individual donors, but also to corporate entities or trusts. Therefore, a museum could release or modify a restriction on a gift if the donor foundation consented in writing, assuming that the foundation's source for the donation had not imposed any additional restrictions on the gift to the foundation.

SMALLER GIFTS OVER TWENTY YEARS OLD

Many older museums and other charities have restricted funds donated many years ago. Often, these are smaller funds that must be separately accounted for and contain restrictions that do not make sense in today's world. Seeking court approval for release or modification of the restrictions, particularly for smaller funds, may be prohibitively expensive. UPMIFA provides flexibility by permitting a charitable institution to release or modify restrictions on smaller, older "institutional funds" by notifying, or in some states receiving the consent of, the state attorney general (or other appropriate state official), without the need for court approval. UPMIFA requires an institution to wait sixty days after notifying the attorney general before proceeding; the attorney general may take action if the proposed modification appears inappropriate.[6]

UPMIFA suggests that an eligible fund not exceed $25,000 and be at least twenty years old, but as with all UPMIFA provisions, the specific time period and amount are up to individual states. Massachusetts, for example, applies the small-gifts authorization to funds up to $75,000 but requires attorney general consent, not just notification.[7] In all cases, an institution must continue to use the funds in question in a manner consistent with the charitable purposes expressed in the gift instrument.

It is critical to review the wording of a given state's version of UPMIFA as states often vary the language from the model act. However, if the administrative approval option is available under the state law applicable to a gift, it is an excellent means of modernizing the use and management of a museum's smaller restricted funds. As with rules relating to the release or modification of restrictions with the written consent of a donor, the administrative option under UPMIFA applies only to "institutional funds," not to "program-related assets" such as works of art in a museum.

COURT-APPROVED RELEASE OR MODIFICATION OF RESTRICTIONS

If a restriction is not eligible for release or modification by any of the above means, or a donor will not consent to the release or modification desired by a museum, a museum must seek court approval if it wishes to release or modify the restriction. In that case, the museum files a complaint or petition in court, usually against the attorney general (or other appropriate state official), to seek this relief. It is advisable, even if not necessary, to notify the attorney general and seek his or her assent to the requested relief prior to filing in court.

The type of claim filed in court is typically brought as a cy pres and/or equitable deviation action. Cy pres, a term originally used in trust law, means "as near as [possible]," referring to the court's duty to adjust a purpose restriction to be as near as possible to the donor's presumed intent. Approval to change the purpose of a restricted gift is brought as a cy pres claim. A claim for equitable deviation is brought to modify the subordinate terms, typically related to the administration of a restricted gift, such as the duration or terms for spending an endowment fund. Although these doctrines traditionally applied only to trusts, more recently they have also been applied to restricted gifts to nonprofit charitable corporations and governmental entities, both under common law and UPMIFA, under the theory that the gifts create implied trusts.[8]

Under traditional trust-law principles, a court may release or modify a purpose restriction under cy pres only if it finds both that the donor had "general charitable intent" and that it is impossible, impracticable, or illegal to carry out the particular purpose articulated by the donor.[9] In that case, the court will release or modify a restriction so as to closely approximate the donor's charitable intent. On the other hand, if a court finds that the donor had "specific," rather than general, intent, but it is impossible, impracticable, or illegal to carry out the restriction as articulated by the donor, the gift will "fail"; that is, the gift will revert to the donor or his or her heirs or to a contingent beneficiary if one was named.[10]

Courts disfavor causing a gift to fail, and thereby requiring return of a gift to the donor or heirs; general intent is ordinarily found, so that the gift may continue to be used for charitable purposes. General charitable intent may be established in several ways, including the terms of other charitable gifts, provisions of the gift instrument, similar gifts to other charities, and the absence of a divesting clause in the event that specified conditions are not carried out.[11] One example of a divesting clause is a "gift over" clause that instructs that if a restriction becomes impossible or impractical to carry out by the initial charity, the gift will be transferred to a named alternative charity. Another type is a reverter clause, which provides that if the gift cannot carried out according to its terms, it reverts to the donor or his or her heirs.

Under the doctrine of equitable deviation, a court may modify subordinate terms of the gift, such as administrative provisions, if complying with them is impossible or illegal, or, due to a change in circumstances, would interfere with the accomplishment of the donor's charitable purpose.[12] Deviation modifies the means to carry out the charitable purpose, rather than the purpose itself. No finding of general charitable intent is necessary, in contrast to a cy pres claim.

A charity may bring an action under cy pres and/or equitable deviation, which are common law doctrines, or under a similar statutory provision, such as the state's version of UPMIFA, or both. Due to the overlapping nature of some of these claims, and the sometimes broader relief available under UPMIFA, it is advisable to bring claims under all of the possible causes of action.

UPMIFA loosened the traditional standard for cy pres by adding wastefulness as a criteria for releasing or modifying a restriction.[13] UPMIFA's version of equitable deviation is similar to the common law doctrine; it permits a court to modify a restriction "regarding the management or investment of an institutional fund if the restriction has become impracticable or wasteful, if it impairs the management or investment of the fund, or if, because of circumstances not anticipated by the donor, a modification of a restriction will further the purposes of the fund."[14] Again, in adopting their versions of UPMIFA, states sometimes have not followed the UPMIFA language, so it is critical to review the specific state version of UPMIFA that governs a gift and to consult with a knowledgeable attorney.

Particularly if the survival of a charitable organization is at stake, the court, and the attorney general, may be receptive to creative solutions. For example, courts have permitted the corpus of endowment funds to be "loaned" to the institution for operating expenses. As described below, a court has allowed a university museum to enter into a sharing agreement with another museum, whereby the donated art collection alternates every two years between the two museums and the proceeds from the sale of the share of the art collection are used by the university for general operations and to maintain the museum. By contrast, in a case where the court found that it was still possible to carry out the intent of the donor by displaying some although not all of the paintings, the court held that the doctrines of cy pres and deviation did not apply, and the court prohibited the sale of the paintings. [15]

ACCESSING DONOR-RESTRICTED ENDOWMENT

A donor-restricted endowment is a type of restricted gift. If a gift instrument includes very explicit instructions concerning how the funds are to be administered and spent, such as "only dividends and interest may be appropriated and spent; the principal and appreciation must be preserved in perpetuity," then the charity must follow those specific instructions. Any spending from the principal or appreciation would require court approval. However, if the gift instrument language is not that explicit, for example, "retain principal and spend income," UPMIFA permits the institution to determine on its own, taking into consideration certain factors, whether and how much spending from the endowment fund is prudent. [16]

Under the prior model act, UMIFA (Uniform Management and Investment of Funds Act), although appreciation in value, in addition to interest and dividends, could be spent from an endowment fund (unless the gift instrument explicitly said otherwise), the original value of the donation(s), or "historic dollar value" as it was termed, could not be spent. By contrast, UPMIFA permits an institution to spend the amount of an endowment fund that it determines "is prudent for the uses, benefits, purposes, and duration for which the endowment fund is established," unless a gift instrument explicitly provides otherwise. [17] UPMIFA takes the approach that prudent spending requires looking at the total assets of the endowment fund, rather than just interest, dividends, or appreciation.

UPMIFA establishes seven criteria to guide an institution in its yearly expenditure decisions from endowment funds:

1. the duration and preservation of the endowment fund;
2. the purposes of the institution and the endowment fund;
3. general economic conditions;
4. the possible effect of inflation or deflation;

5. the expected total return from income and the appreciation of investments;
6. other resources of the institution; and,
7. the investment policy of the institution. [18]

In short, UPMIFA provides greater flexibility to spend from endowment funds, without the need for approval from a court or the attorney general. If endowment spending policies and language in gift instruments have not been reviewed since the adoption of UPMIFA, it is advisable for a museum to do so.

WHAT ABOUT SELLING OR LENDING ALL OR PART OF THE MUSEUM COLLECTION?

As noted above, the UPMIFA provisions giving charities greater flexibility to release or modify restrictions without court approval apply to "institutional funds" only, not to "program-related assets." So, for example, if a museum wishes to bring in additional revenue by lending a painting to a paying exhibitor, the museum may not rely on UPMIFA to remove a restriction on lending the painting with just the donor's written consent, unless the gift instrument explicitly provides the donor with the right to do so. [19] If the donor does not reserve that right, the museum must obtain court approval to remove or modify the restriction by filing a complaint for equitable deviation and establishing that the legal criteria for that claim have been met.

Cases concerning Fisk University and the Barnes Collection, discussed below, illustrate some of the many issues that may arise when a museum attempts to sell part of its collection or otherwise modify gift restrictions in order to raise revenue. The experience at Brandeis University is also illustrative. In 2009, the trustees of Brandeis University, acting in response to the 2008 financial crash and a significant decline in the value of the university's endowment, decided to close the Rose Art Museum; transition the museum into a fine arts teaching center, studio space, and exhibition gallery; and sell the museum's art collection after necessary legal approval was obtained. [20] The Rose Art Museum, located on Brandeis's campus outside Boston, owned a significant collection of modern and contemporary art, including iconic works by Roy Lichtenstein and almost every other major American painter and sculptor of the twentieth century. The decision caused an uproar in some sectors of the community and the art world, although others defended Brandeis's decision as necessary to save its general educational mission in the face of financial distress.

The office of the state attorney general stated that it would review Brandeis's decision to sell the art. [21] A lawsuit was filed by several members of an advisory board of overseers and donors to the Rose Art Museum asking the court, among other things, to halt the closure of the museum and the sale of any artwork that was not for the purpose of purchasing new artwork. In the alternative, the plaintiffs requested, in a cy pres–type claim, that the court find that Brandeis was no longer capable of or willing to maintain the Rose Art Museum or that it had become impracticable or inappropriate that Brandeis do so, and therefore to order Brandeis to return the artwork and endowment funds to the newly created Rose Preservation Fund or another appropriate organization or individuals.[22] In June 2011, under the leadership of a new president, Brandeis settled the lawsuit, agreed to keep the Rose Art Museum open, and stated that it had no intention of selling the museum's artwork.[23]

In deciding whether to sell objects or works of art from their collections, many museums may take into consideration ethical guidelines for deaccessioning issued by various museum associations, which generally limit the use of proceeds from the sale of collections to acquisitions and in some policies, maintenance of the collection.[24] Adherence to these guidelines would therefore generally preclude sale of collection pieces to resolve financial difficulties. But guidelines are voluntary, rather than legally binding on the museums, unless they have been incorporated into a law (as they are in New York)[25] or gift instrument. A museum that violates voluntary deaccessioning guidelines, however, may face censure or sanctions by a museum association, such as a ban on loans to the museum by association members.

WHO HAS STANDING TO ENFORCE RESTRICTIONS?

A question may arise as to whether a donor or his or her family or heirs may contest the release or modification of a gift restriction. Traditionally, and it is still true in many states (at least for restricted gifts not involving charitable trusts, as opposed to charitable corporations), donors have no standing to enforce a restriction by filing a lawsuit or intervening in court proceedings by other parties seeking to modify or release the restriction. Under this rule, only a charity and the attorney general have the right to be heard on those issues, unless the donor has reserved standing or the right in the gift instrument of return of the gift if the gift terms were not followed or, in a cy pres action, if the donor lacked "general charitable intent," as discussed above. In the latter cases, the donor or his or her heirs would have a "special interest" in the disposition because they might be entitled to a return of the gift. In addition, if the gift instrument provides that the gift shall be given to a different charity if the initial charity is not able or willing to carry out the terms of the gift (commonly referred to as a "gift over"), then the latter charity's special interest would also establish its standing to contest a complaint for cy pres or deviation brought by the initial charitable recipient of the gift.

In some states, such as New York, courts have permitted a donor or donor family members to intervene in a suit or even bring a suit to enforce a restriction, particularly where the court has found that the attorney general has not acted to protect the public interest in ensuring the proper application of the charitable funds.[26] And even more recently, restatements of common law and proposals for enactment of state trust legislation have reflected standing for settlors of charitable trusts in suits to enforce trust restrictions. This apparent change in the long-held denial of standing for settlors of trusts is seen in the 2011 Restatement Third of Trusts § 94.2, which adopts the position of giving standing to settlors. The Uniform Trust Code, which provides standing at § 405, has been enacted in thirty states and the District of Columbia as of May 2014. It is therefore critical to understand the rights of donors and their families and heirs under the current state law governing a gift.

TWO EXAMPLES OF THE APPLICATION OF THE CY PRES DOCTRINE IN THE MUSEUM CONTEXT: FISK UNIVERSITY AND THE BARNES COLLECTION

Fisk University

In recent protracted cy pres litigation involving Fisk University in Nashville, Tennessee, the state appellate court ultimately permitted the university to sell a half interest in an art collection to the Crystal Bridges Museum in Bentonville, Arkansas, even though the gift of art in question was subject to a restriction that the art not be sold or exchanged. The artist Georgia O'Keeffe had donated a large collection of photographs and paintings that had belonged to her late husband, the photographer Alfred Stieglitz, as well as four additional paintings from her personal collection. Fisk University claimed that it did not have the financial resources to maintain the art collection without such a sale and that the university itself was at risk of financial failure. Under the relief ultimately requested by the university, Fisk University and the Crystal Bridges Museum were to share the artwork by displaying the entire collection at each museum on a rotating basis, and proceeds from the sale would be used in part to maintain the collection at Fisk.

In its initial 2009 decision, the appellate court reversed the lower court and held that the donor had general charitable intent to provide a charitable benefit to the university, despite the fact that O'Keeffe had a specific purpose in mind and had imposed specific restrictions. It held that, based on Stieglitz's will and letters O'Keeffe wrote to President Lyndon Johnson, the charitable intent motivating the gifts to Fisk was "to promote study of art in Nashville and the South." The court also found significant to its finding of general intent that O'Keefe had made similar gifts to several different charities at the same time. Finally, there was no divestiture clause in the gift; in other words O'Keefe did not reserve a right to have the art returned to her or her heirs if the conditions were violated. The appellate court then directed the lower court to determine whether the second prong of the cy pres test was met: Was it impossible or impracticable for Fisk to comply with the conditions of the gift?[27]

In its subsequent decision in 2011, the appellate court affirmed the lower court's finding that Fisk's dire financial condition rendered strict compliance with the gift conditions impracticable and therefore, in light of its prior holding of general intent, that cy pres relief was appropriate. The appellate court then held that the proposed sharing agreement with the Crystal Bridges Museum most closely resembled O'Keeffe's intent. The court reasoned that this proposal, as compared to proposals put forward by the attorney general, permitted the collection to be used for study by Fisk students, allowed it to remain an intact collection, gave Fisk University access to the resources of a museum to support its responsibilities relative to the art collection, and would allow the collection to be available for viewing by the public in Nashville, and in the South in general in both Nashville and Arkansas.[28]

Barnes Collection

In a highly publicized legal fight, the Barnes Foundation prevailed in its quest to move its art collection from Merion, a suburb of Philadelphia, to a new, larger building in a more accessible location in downtown Philadelphia. The Barnes Collection, consisting of priceless late nineteenth-century and early twentieth-century paintings by artists such as Cezanne, Matisse, Monet, and Renoir, was donated by Dr. Albert Barnes. The 1922 trust indenture under which the artwork was donated, which was incorporated into the by-laws of the Barnes Foundation, provided for no loans of the art and preservation of the art in the building created for that purpose and to educate students.[29] The trust indenture specifically provided that "all the paintings shall remain in exactly the places they are at the time of the death of Donor and his said wife."[30] It also limited the number of days the gallery could be open to the public—over the years courts had increased the number from one day to three and a half per week (further limited to Friday, Saturday, and Sunday by the town)—and thus limited the revenue to the Barnes Foundation.[31]

In 2002, the foundation, citing financial need, petitioned a state court to amend its charter and bylaws so as permit it to move the collection to the new location. The court, applying trust law due to the trust indenture (the Barnes Foundation is a nonprofit corporation), ultimately approved the corporation's request as an appropriate deviation from the administrative terms of the trust. In arriving at that conclusion, the court referenced Section 381 of the Restatement of Trusts (Second), which states that "a court will direct or permit the trustee of a charitable trust to deviate from a term of the trust if it appears to the court that compliance is impossible or illegal or that owing to circumstances not known to the settlor and not anticipated by him compliance would defeat or substantially impair the accomplishment of the purposes of the trust." In its initial decision, the court had held that "the present location of the gallery is not sacrosanct, and relocation may be permitted *if necessary* to achieve the settlor's ultimate purposes."[32]

The court subsequently heard much testimony from both fact and expert witnesses, including extensive analysis of the Barnes Foundation's financial condition, options for increasing revenue, anticipated cost of the relocation, and plans for the new gallery. In coming to its conclusion that deviation was necessary and that the relocation of the gallery to Philadelphia "represents the least drastic modification necessary to preserve the organization," the court made three findings. First, it found that the Barnes Foundation could not raise enough money through the sale of its nongallery assets to keep the collection in Merion and achieve fiscal stability. Interestingly, in making that finding, it disagreed with the foundation's argument that the nongallery assets could not be sold in the first place due to deaccessioning ethical guidelines. The court found that the nongallery assets were never part of a museum (they were located in another building that was never operated as a museum); rather they were works of art of an educational institution, and in any event the Barnes Collection was not even a member of the museum associations that promulgated guidelines in question.

Second, the court found that the proposed building in Philadelphia could be built within a budget of $100 million, and that therefore presumably this was a realistic option. Third, it found that the foundation's three-campus model, which required moving the gallery to a new facility in Philadelphia, was feasible, given the fundraising capability of the foundation.[33] The Barnes Collection moved to its new home in May 2012.

PRACTICE TIPS

In determining whether restricted assets may be used for purposes outside of applicable restrictions, and if so, whether additional approval from or notification to a third party is necessary, care should be taken to thoroughly examine the restrictions and the current law governing them. The first step should be to obtain any original documentation of restrictions, whether in the form of a board vote reflected in the minutes of the board meetings, a will, gift instrument, correspondence, or the museum's gift solicitation materials (the latter is something charities may not always keep good records of, but they should be kept with the donations that are made in response). Particularly if the gift is old, records may be spotty or nonexistent. Do the best you can in combing through the archives to identify any restrictions.

The next step is to have a lawyer experienced in the nonprofit field examine the applicable documentation and advise the museum on whether the law governing the gift permits the restriction to be released or modified, and if so, the process for doing so. The key factual areas of focus will be

- Is the donor living or in existence (in the case of an organizational donor) and agreeable to a modification of restriction?
- Has the asset been restricted by the board or by a donor?
- Is the asset an investment asset or a program-related asset?
- What are the amount and age of the asset?
- Is it impossible, impracticable, illegal, or, in some states, wasteful to comply with the restriction?
- Is the proposed use of the asset consistent with the general intent of the donor?

A determination can then be made as to whether releasing or modifying a restriction will require approval and if so, from whom. Even if doing so is not required, a museum may want to consult with the attorney general or notify any living donor or identifiable heirs.

NOTES

This chapter is based in part on an outline of restricted gift issues written by Richard C. Allen, a retired Casner and Edwards, LLP partner and former chief of the Charities Division of the Office of the Massachusetts Attorney General.

1. UPMIFA, which succeeded the Uniform Management of Institutional Funds Act (UMIFA), also includes guidance and standards on the management, investment, and expenditure of the institutional funds of most types of charitable organizations. The model act and comments on its provisions are available at www.upmifa.org. For an in-depth discussion of the Massachusetts version of UPMIFA, see "Management of Institutional Funds in Massachusetts" (2009) available at www.casneredwards.com/news-and-resources/resources.html.

2. UPMIFA defines "endowment" to include only endowments designated as such by donors, not by the institution itself (UPMIFA, § 2). Nor is a board-restricted gift classified in financial statements as a restricted asset; an asset that is restricted only by board action is classified as an unrestricted asset.

3. UPMFIA does not apply to trusts in which an individual or a commercial entity is a trustee. For example, it would not apply to a trust established by an individual to benefit a museum where the trustees are an individual and a local bank, but it would apply to a trust of which another charity is the trustee.

4. UPMIFA § 6(a).

5. An article further explaining the difference between "institutional funds" and "program-related assets," as those terms are used in UPMFIA can be found at uniformlaws.org/Act.aspx ?title=Prudent%20Management%20of%20Institutional%20Funds%20Act.

6. UPMIFA § 6(d).

7. Massachusetts Supreme Judicial Court Rule 1:23.

8. See *Worcester v. Directors of the Worcester Free Public Library*, 359 Mass. 601, 603 (1965); UPMIFA § 2, subsection (4) (definition of "institution").

9. See Restatement (Second) of Trusts § 399 & comment (1959); 6 A. Scott, W. Fratcher & M. Ascher, Scott and Ascher on Trusts, § 39.5, pp. 2697–2768 (5th ed. 2009).

10. See, for example, *Rogers v. Attorney General*, 347 Mass. 126 (1964).

11. *Georgia O'Keeffe Foundation v. Fisk University*, 312 S.W. 3d 1, 17 (2009)

12. See Restatement (Second) of Trusts §§ 381, 399 (1959).

13. UPMIFA § 6(c).

14. UPMIFA § 6(b).

15. *Museum of Fine Arts v. Beland*, 423 Mass. 540 (2000).

16. UPMIFA § 4.

17. UPMIFA § 4(a).

18. UPMIFA § 4(a).

19. Most donors will not reserve that right, however, because doing so might prevent a gift from being a completed gift and thus being tax deductible.

20. Brandeis University Press Release, January 26, 2009, accessible at www.boston.com.

21. Randy Kennedy and Carol Vogel, "Outcry over a Plan to Sell Museum's Holdings," *New York Times*, January 28, 2009.

22. See Complaint for Declaratory Judgment concerning the Rose Art Museum, *Rose v. Brandeis University*, No. SJ-2009-409 (SJC Single Justice July 27, 2009) WL 2428713. An amended complaint was later filed.

23. Randy Kennedy, "Brandeis Settles Suit over Proposed Art Sale," *New York Times*, June 30, 2011.

24. See for example, American Alliance of Museums' Code of Ethics for Museums (2000), www.aam-us.org/resources/ethics-standards-and-best-practices/code-of-ethics.

25. See the regulations of the New York State Board of Regents, which apply to museums established since 1890: 8 NYCRR §3.27 (c)(6).

26. For cases in which standing was granted to donors or their family members or heirs, see St. Lukes–Roosevelt Hospital Center, 723 N.Y.S. 2d 426 (App. Div. 2001); *Howard v. Administrators of the Tulane Educational Fund*, 986 So. 2d 47 (La. 2008); *L. B. Research and Education Foundation v. The UCLA Foundation*, 130 Cal. App. 4th 171, 29 Cal. Rptr. 3d 710 (Cal. Court of Appeal 2005). For an example of case denying standing to a donor, see *Carl J. Herzog Foundation v. University of Bridgeport*, 243 Conn. 1 (1997).

27. *Georgia O'Keefe Foundation (Museum) v. Fisk University*, 312 S.W.3d 1 (Tn. Ct. App. 2009).

28. In re *Fisk University*, 392 S.W.3d 582 (Tn. Ct. App. 2011).

29. In re *Barnes Foundation*, 449 Pa. Super. 81, 87 (Pa. Super. Ct. 1996) (denial of request by museum to extend tour of selected artworks).

30. In re *Barnes Foundation*, 24 Fiduciary Reptr 2d 94 (Pa. Orphans' Ct. 2004), 2004 WL 1960204.

31. *Id.*

32. *Id.*

33. In re *Barnes Foundation*, 25 Fiduciary Reptr 2d 39 (Pa. Orphans' Ct. 2004), 2004 WL 2903655.

Chapter Thirteen

The Fresno Metropolitan Museum Story

Assignment for Benefit of Creditors

Riley Walter

BRIEF HISTORY OF THE FRESNO METROPOLITAN MUSEUM

Fresno is the fifth-largest city in California and serves as the cultural and political center of the San Joaquin Valley, the richest and most productive agricultural region in the world.

The Fresno Metropolitan Museum of Art and Science ("MET") was chartered in 1979 as a nonprofit organization, and small exhibitions based on donated private collections began in 1982. The MET was initially established as a "collecting institution" dedicated to conserving and presenting the San Joaquin Valley's cultural heritage. A fundraising campaign brought in nearly $5 million and the Fresno Bee Building (circa 1922) was converted into a museum facility and became the permanent home of the MET.

The MET was open to the public from 1984 until August 2005. In 2005 the MET closed the museum facility to the public for restoration and reconstruction of the building. There were many unanticipated expenses that occurred during the construction that saw the construction budget balloon from $15 million to $28 million. The MET addressed issues such as outdated climate control systems, limited access for the physically challenged, seismic upgrades, hazardous materials abatement, new roof, landscaping, and restoration (that included both demolition and new construction) of the exterior of the historic building to its original design. The seismic retrofit was incorpo-

171

rated after the beginning of construction and is a major factor that substantially contributed to the increased costs.

In order to acquire financing to complete the project, the MET obtained a loan in 2007 that was guaranteed by the City of Fresno. The city took a deed of trust as security against all of the MET's real property to protect itself against any default by the MET. In June 2009, the city was required to pay off the bank loan at a cost of approximately $15 million.

Not only did the construction issues increase the costs, but they also resulted in a greatly extended construction period. The MET did not reopen until November of 2008. The board attempted to locate donors to help cover the remaining debt of $15 million of unpaid construction costs plus contractor claims. By 2008 capital markets had dried up to the point that refinancing the debt was not a practical option. This all occurred at a time when donations to most cultural arts institutions were declining.

In February 2009, a financial advisor was engaged to assist the MET in assessing its current financial situation, work with the board of trustees and city regarding the $15 million loan guarantee, and hopefully avoid closing the MET. After many months of limited fundraising and low attendance at prescheduled fine art exhibitions, and notwithstanding the downsizing of staff, the board of trustees determined that it was necessary to close the MET.

PREPARATION TO CLOSE MUSEUM

On October 30, 2009, the Fresno Metropolitan Museum Board of Trustees passed a special resolution appointing and designating the executive committee of the board to perform, direct, and carry out whatever was necessary to close the MET and resolve all claims against the corporation with any issues to be decided by a majority vote of the executive committee.

On December 14, 2009, the board of trustees determined that all available options had been exhausted, and voted to settle creditor claims when all assets were liquidated and the proceeds be distributed, pursuant to state law, prior to dissolving the corporation.

On December 23, 2009, a Winding Up and Dissolution of Corporation Resolution was passed by the executive committee. This resolution appointed the board president as the board's agent in the execution of all of the items listed within the resolution, including taking action on matters not specified within the resolution but consistent with the purpose of winding up and dissolving of the corporation. The board president was authorized to act on behalf of the board without the need for further authorization, unless an action needed to be taken that was substantially inconsistent with the resolution.

On January 5, 2010, the board president joined the executive director in terminating employment for the majority of staff with notifications to remainder staff that their last day would occur within ninety days. In addition, a formal announcement was made during a public press conference held in the MET courtyard.

FORMATION OF FRIENDS OF THE MET, LLC

The MET had no ability to fund the winding up and liquidation of its assets since all cash resources had been exhausted, although it was clear that an organized structured liquidation would be in the best interests of all the creditors.

The board of trustees authorized the MET to borrow up to $600,000 from the Friends of the MET, LLC, which was formed for this purpose, and to secure the loan with the MET's personal property, in order to fund the liquidating process.

MET CLOSES

The MET closed on January 5, 2010. The required State of California attorney general communication and clearance letter required of nonprofit organizations were filed and later accepted.

Liquidation of Personal Property Process

1. Auctioneer Selection: Three personal property auction houses were initially interviewed for the sale of the collection assets. Each provided a proposal with very similar fees and brief outline on how they would handle the auction. The noncollection personal property auction took place on February 17, 2010, by a local auctioneer.
2. Assignment for Benefit of Creditors: An assignee was appointed as the assignee for benefit of creditors effective April 1, 2010.

   An "assignment for benefit of creditors" (ABC) transaction is a general assignment of all assets for the benefit of all of the assignor's (MET's) creditors. A general assignment for the benefit of creditors is set forth and defined in California Code of Civil Procedure, Section 493.010 et seq. A general assignment for the benefit of creditors (1) constitutes an assignment to the assignee of all assets of assignor that are transferable and not exempt from enforcement of a money judgment; (2) is for the benefit of all of the creditors of the assignor, and (3) does not create a preference of one creditor or class of creditors over any other creditor or class of creditors.

3. The assignee took control over the assigned assets and opened operating checking and savings accounts. To ensure that funds held at the bank were insurance protected under the $250,000 FDIC limit, additional saving accounts were later opened at other banks.

Liquidation by Fine Art Auction

1. Selection Process

Prior to the appointment of the assignee, three fine art auction houses were interviewed. They included Bonhams and Butterfields, Sotheby's, and Christie's. Each auction house arrived on-site and in less than one day, each assessed the collection. A proposal of potential sale estimates, auction house fees, and plan for the most advantageous sales process was provided by each.

After a review of each proposal, a recommendation to consign with Sotheby's in New York and Bonhams and Butterfields in San Francisco was approved by the board president on March 3, 2010, and March 16, 2010, respectively, prior to the appointment of the assignee.

A total of 3,218 works and objects were consigned to be sold. Sotheby's was consigned to sell 170 fine art works and objects they valued at $5,000 or greater. Bonhams and Butterfields was consigned to sell 3,048 works and objects.

2. Original Estimate Changes

Changes in original estimates became necessary after further expert review by each auction house. There were a significant number of paintings found to be in worse condition than originally expected, works were not of the artist stated, or works were found to lack the provenance previously represented. Thus, the original auction estimates were revised downward to accommodate the value of these paintings. Each auction house was required to provide an explanation regarding any significant decrease in estimates before the assignee would approve such change.

The bidding practice by some potential buyers appeared that they were trying to take advantage of the weak economy and bid below what was expected. As such, many works and objects were sold at the reserve or closer to the lowest estimate. Total original estimates received from the auction houses ranged from $2,592,000 to $3,900,000 and changes in original estimates later decreased to $1,421,000 to $2,142,000. Overall, 136 works and objects required a change from the original estimate.

3. Schedule of Auctions

Each auction house recommended an auction schedule to realize the best return for the benefit of creditors. There were a total of twenty-nine auctions held within a fourteen-month period.

After each auction occurred, every attempt was made to sell works that did not originally sell through a one-on-one postauction sale. There were six postauction sales that netted a more positive result than had each work been listed for future auction.

4. Outcome/Results

The outcome of each auction differed to some degree from the original and/ or revised estimated value. Overall the auction results were less than estimated with the exception of a few specific works. The Asian market was the strongest and fine art, oil on canvas was the weakest. As an example, the sale of a Chinese screen that had an original estimated auction value of $50,000 to $70,000 sold for $250,000, and a fine art, oil on canvas had a revised estimated auction value of $120,000 to $180,000 sold for $85,000.

Seventy of the 170 works consigned to Sotheby's were later revalued below Sotheby's $5,000 auction value requirement, and these works were later consigned to Stair Gallery in New York to sell. The total net proceeds from all auctions totaled $1,829,765.

Fine Art Direct Sales

1. Native American Indian Basket Collection

Prior to the appointment of the assignee, the board president approved the sale of this collection to a local Native American Indian tribe providing for the future public display in the San Joaquin Valley. Bonhams and Butterfields provided an appraised value for this collection and the tribe purchased it at that value.

2. Asian Snuff Bottle Collection

The original donor's family of this collection was granted an opportunity to purchase the collection for a price equal to a net amount estimated to be raised through a live auction. Bonhams and Butterfields provided the auction value estimate for this collection, and the family purchased it from the assignee.

3. *Ansel Adams Museum Set Edition Prints*

The family of Ansel Adams brought legal action against the MET in March 2010 to prevent the sale of certain museum set edition prints. Pursuant to an agreement with the assignee, the family was granted an opportunity to purchase the collection at the fair market value. Sotheby's provided an appraised value for this collection, and the family purchased from the assignee through the trade of two Ansel Adams's prints and cash payment. The two prints received were later sold by Sotheby's at auction in October 2010.

Creditor Claims

1. *Notification*

Letters were mailed to creditors on January 5, 2010, March 8, 2010, and April 9, 2010. The April 9, 2010, communication noticed 206 creditors regarding the requirement of filing a proof of claim for any outstanding amount they believed was owed to them. All claims were due on or before May 31, 2010, in order to be allowed for consideration.

2. *Review*

In June 2010, an in-depth review of claims filed commenced by the assignee and his financial officer. A total of ninety-five claims were filed and reviewed.

Claims were categorized as either approved or disputed. All disputed claims required additional research and/or negotiations to resolve. A total of eighty-five claims were approved, two were disallowed, four were disputed, and four claims were withdrawn.

Two of the disputed claims were negotiated for acceptance in a lesser amount and one claim was settled and paid at 20 percent of the disputed amount; and, one claim, the City of Fresno, was settled by providing that it would only receive any excess funds available after all other creditors and expenses had been paid.

3. *Lawsuits*

Creditors who previously filed a lawsuit against the MET were also noticed by the assignee and required to file a proof of claim. Each of these creditors were contacted by counsel and the process was explained.

4. *Outcome/Payout*

A letter was mailed on January 20, 2011, to those creditors whose claim had been approved. A total of $1,403,486.85 was distributed to approved claims on a pro rata basis. The first of two distributions were made on June 30, 2011, in the amount of $1,050,000 with the second distribution made on or before December 19, 2011, in the amount of $353,486.98. Each claimant received 79 percent of their approved claim.

McClatchy Endowment

Included in the assets of the MET upon appointment of the assignee was the restricted Carlos K. and Phebe McClatchy Conley Art Endowment Fund ("Endowment"), totaling approximately $1.8 million. By California law, a restricted gift cannot be liquidated to fund obligations to the MET's creditors, and as such it must be passed on to another 501(c)(3) corporation that is able to carry out its purpose to the greatest extent possible. Therefore, the proper handling and transfer of the endowment became the responsibility of the assignee.

Following the filing of an application on August 9, 2010, with the Fresno County Superior Probate Court and pursuant to the court's order entered September 17, 2010, the endowment funds were transferred to the Central Valley Foundation. The foundation's board has been entrusted to carry out the donor's wishes with specific requirements and the matter remains subject to the court's continuing jurisdiction.

At about the time the assignment for benefit of creditors was being approved by the board, the board also reached agreement with the City of Fresno to convey the museum facility real property back to the city in exchange for cancellation of the indebtedness.

Once the board had approved the assignment for benefit of creditors the process began. This results in all of the assets being transferred to the assignee to be held in trust with instructions to liquidate the assets and pay the proceeds out in order of priority allowed by California law.

Creditors' Claims Process

Once the assignee was in place he sent notices to all creditors of the museum giving them ninety days to file a claim with documentation supporting the claim. The notice was clear that if a claim was not filed on time there would be no distribution.

Once all of the claims were fixed, the assignee then made a series of pro rata distributions to creditors having allowed claims. Over time creditors received 79 cents on the dollar on allowed claims.

CONCLUSION

Several lessons can be learned from utilization of this process: First, it was cheaper than a bankruptcy proceeding and the author believes that there was a higher recovery because the prices received were better than a Chapter 7 trustee would have received. It was also a faster process. Second, it was important to the board that the obligations to creditors be honored to the extent possible. Third, a key to having this process work is to carefully review the gifting documents to make sure there are no restrictions that would impede such process. Fourth, unsurprisingly, pledges do not get honored once the entity is in a process of liquidation. Last, it is a very public process. People who care about museums and art/artifacts care deeply and are very vocal. Knowing this in advance can be of assistance to public relations staff in managing media inquires about the process.

In conclusion, the Fresno MET used a little-known legal process that allowed it to honor all allowed claims in a procedure that was faster, more efficient, and less expensive than a formal bankruptcy process. As museums continue to face economic challenges in the twenty-first century, options such as the one presented and utilized by the Fresno MET should be explored.

NOTE

This chapter discusses how a struggling regional museum used a little-known legal process to resolve creditor claims against it and chronicles the closing of the Fresno Museum of Art and Science. O. James Woodward III was the assignee for benefit of creditors. He is an attorney and art collector. Riley C. Walter was insolvency counsel for the assignee. Both are headquartered in Fresno, California. All of the information in the essay regarding the Fresno Museum of Art and Science was provided by Riley Walter.

Chapter Fourteen

The Higgins Armory Museum and Worcester Art Museum Integration

A Case Study in Combining and Transforming Mature Cultural Institutions

James C. Donnelly, Jr., and Catherine M. Colinvaux

On December 31, 2013, Worcester, Massachusetts's beloved John Woodman Higgins Armory Museum closed its doors for good, ending eighty-three years of audience-pleasing displays organized around one of North America's greatest collections of arms and armor.

Three months later, on March 29, 2014, the Worcester Art Museum (WAM) opened its *Knights!* exhibition: a spectacular marriage of treasures from the John Woodman Higgins Collection and old-world masterpieces from WAM's internationally renowned collection. Shown side by side, the art elevates the armor, highlighting its grandeur and elegance and the magnificence of its craft. And the armor elevates the art, creating new and compelling connections with relevance to a broad modern audience. Severely bodiced Elizabethan women with prim headdresses are revealed as "armored" in their confining costumes as they glance side-eyed toward their metal-clad courtiers. And the courtier knights are suddenly less conclusively masculine and warlike as we see reflections of the women's finery in the tracing, gilt embellishments and wasp waists of their armor "corsets."

In the next *Knights!* gallery, helmets spanning four continents, 2,500 years, and cultures as diverse as Ancient Greece, sixteenth-century Japan, and Turkey form a "round table" of heroes under the watchful eye of a once-and-future (dark) knight in the form of Batman. In further galleries, there are spaces dedicated to children and to exhibits that juxtapose historical weaponry with reminders of modern warfare in the form of a stylized Arc de Triomphe and photographs from the Pulitzer Center on Crisis Reporting. As the Huffington Post[1] observed, the combination is a "a tour de force assemblage elevating WAM to international status" while providing a crowd-pleasing and "admirable job" of "connecting past to present and real to pop culture . . . [a]s Knights were once the 'Super-heroes' of their day."

The *Knights!* exhibit signals a revitalization of a previously purely stately WAM, most especially in WAM's approach to audience engagement and children. The opening, which included a Renaissance Faire with family-friendly offerings to engage visitors of all ages, attracted an average months' worth of visitors in its first weekend, and children flocked not just to the *Knights!* exhibition galleries, but to the entire museum in unprecedented numbers.

Yet, as successful as it has been and continues to be, *Knights!* provides only a taste of things to come. Over the next few years, the exhibit will be continually refreshed with new armor, new presentations, and new interpretative experiences, providing a laboratory and a template to learn from the best of the Higgins Armory and expand family-friendly programming across the entire museum. Within five to seven years, WAM will make a permanent home for the Higgins Collection, creating a four-thousand-square-foot multilevel gallery dedicated to its display and interpretation in ways that enhance and connect the collection to the wider world of art. At the same time, WAM will continue to expand programming to attract new audiences with an emphasis on the family audiences that traditionally loved the Higgins Armory; it will employ key Higgins Armory employees and engage a curator of arms and armor; and it will conserve, steward, and enhance the Higgins Collection in ways that were beyond the Higgins Armory's capacity.

Although a transformational triumph for WAM, the *Knights!* opening represented a bittersweet moment for the Higgins Armory. The Armory had announced only a year before the *Knights!* opening that the Armory must close, and for a grueling, final nine months, a devoted skeleton staff had labored around the clock to honor and celebrate the Armory in public exhibitions and programming while, behind the scenes, performing the myriad legal and practical tasks necessary to wind down the Armory Museum as a business and to steward the Higgins Collection to a new and worthy home.

That final year of celebrations and farewells, itself, marked the beginning of the end of a multiyear process. For more than thirty years, Higgins Armory's trustees and directors had struggled with a set of systemic, existential challenges, including lack of endowment, lack of financial support, and the extraordinary expense associated with an iconic landmark building. The decision to close was neither sudden nor accidental. It followed years of creative but ultimately unsuccessful lifesaving measures, and in that context, represented a careful, realistic appraisal of the Armory's circumstances and of the last, best opportunity to steward its collection into the future—to protect the collection itself, honor the legacy of the Higgins Armory's founder, and preserve for the people of Worcester, Massachusetts, one of their greatest treasures.

This chapter reviews the challenges that led the Higgins Armory Museum's trustees to the seemingly unthinkable decision to close a beloved institution, the hurdles that WAM trustees confronted in deciding whether it would be prudent to accept the challenges of safeguarding the Higgins Collection, and the collaboration that preserved and will eventually enhance a priceless cultural legacy. This chapter intends to describe the history and process in ways that will inform the judgment of other institutions in similar situations.

A SHORT HISTORY

If, in the words of Justice Oliver Wendell Holmes, a page of history can be worth a volume of logic,[2] then the Higgins Armory Museum is a case in point. For Worcesterites, past and present, it is almost impossible to think of the Higgins Collection of Arms and Armor as anything other than an organic, quintessential piece of Worcester history. Worcester industrialist, John Woodman Higgins, and several of his friends, founded the Higgins Armory Museum in 1928 to exhibit what had been Mr. Higgins's private collection of arms, armor, and other interesting metalwork. Mr. Higgins's love for metalwork grew out of his vocation as president and owner (together with other family members) of Worcester Pressed Steel Company, and Worcester Pressed Steel was, in turn, among the core industries, many of them involved in steel and metal working, that made Worcester an industrial capital in the nineteenth and early twentieth centuries.

In the early 1900s, Worcester Pressed Steel developed modern methods for mass-producing stamped metal objects. As the nation was preparing to enter World War I, the War Department began considering how to design and mass-produce military hardware to meet the demands of twentieth-century warfare. Making the perhaps questionable assumption that Renaissance armor could provide models, the War Department engaged Bashford Dean, the legendary first curator of arms and armor at New York's Metropolitan Museum of Art (MET), to assist in designing helmets for the modern army.[3] Mr. Dean, in turn, engaged Mr. Higgins and Worcester Pressed Steel to produce prototypes of a design derived from Renaissance helmets. The War Department ultimately rejected the historical models and settled on the more prosaic "doughboy helmet," but Worcester Pressed Steel remained an important participant in the war effort, manufacturing nearly 200,000 of the helmets by war's end.[4]

Figure 14.1. A split image of a knight and portrait of a woman, reflecting similarities in clothing design, courtesy of the Worcester Art Museum.

Mr. Higgins's involvement with the war effort and his associations with Bashford Dean transformed a preexisting interest in arms and armor into a passion, and in the postwar period, Mr. Higgins began to collect in earnest, guided in part by Mr. Dean. In the late 1920s, Mr. Higgins and his wife, Clara, traveled extensively in Europe. Although Mr. Higgins's own fortune had survived the Great Depression, the political and economic aftermath of the war forced many European noble families to sell assets, and Mr. Higgins seized the opportunity to assemble a world-class collection of arms and armor that he augmented with purchases from great American collectors such as William Randolph Hearst and Jay Gould.

According to family lore, in the mid-1920s, Clara Higgins told her husband that there was too much armor in their stately William Street home and that Mr. Higgins must find another site to store his growing collection. Mr. Higgins was prompted to action. In 1928, he, his wife, and six other relatives and friends chartered the "The John Woodman Higgins Armory, Inc." In 1929, Mr. Higgins retained a Boston architect, Joseph Leland, to give form to Mr. Higgins's own idea to create an entirely new type of building that would be beautiful and practical, but would also reveal its industrial skeleton; and by 1931, the building and museum were opened to the public: "As a correspondent to the magazine *Steel* observed at the time the museum opened, Higgins 'sought to build a structure of advanced design that in addition to its value as a place in which to work[,] might be at the same time a steel building for a steel man, a monument to the industry to which he has given his life, and to which his own products might contribute.'"[5]

Built in part with labor and technology from Worcester Pressed Steel, and colocated with the steelworks, the first two floors of the dramatic art deco building housed Worcester Pressed Steel's corporate headquarters and the top levels presented a grand, two-story faux-Renaissance "Great Hall" to house and exhibit Mr. Higgins's still-growing collection.

In 1931, when the building was complete, the John Woodman Higgins Armory Museum opened to the public with great fanfare, including a performance of the Boston Symphony Orchestra in the Great Hall. In later years, the Armory's archives include letters from celebrities of the times, including extensive correspondence from Norman Rockwell on the occasion of Mr. Rockwell's *Saturday Evening Post* cover drawing of a "knight" watchman having his coffee with one of the knights in the Higgins Armory Great Hall,[6] and a letter to Mr. Higgins from Groucho Marx, who quipped that while "there is no particular reason to bring me to Worcester, Massachusetts . . . if I ever get that far I will be happy to enroll myself as an Iron Knight, or any other knight that you may have around."[7]

For all its glory, however, the Higgins Armory Museum was always a "junior sibling" to the older, better-known Worcester Art Museum. WAM was founded in 1896 by an earlier generation of Worcester industrialists and cultural elites, and it has its own illustrious history, including an impressive list of "firsts" and notable achievements placing it at the forefront of American art museums. The museum houses renowned collections of colonial American paintings, Revere silver, American Impressionist watercolors, and early photography. As early as 1904, the Worcester Art Museum was exhibiting and collecting photography as fine art. In 1910, it became the first American museum to acquire a painting by Monet. In 1927, WAM was the first museum to bring a complete medieval building to America, and in 1932, WAM partnered with the Louvre and two other institutions in the professional excavation of Antioch, resulting in the museum having the largest and among the finest Antioch mosaics on public display. More recently, WAM originated the first exhibition to focus on Judith Leyster, a rediscovered female Dutch painter from the Golden Age.

The museum has also been a leader in art scholarship, conservation, and audience engagement. Founded in the 1930s, WAM's conservation department remains one of the most respected conservation departments in any museum, and WAM directors have a remarkable history as leaders in the art world. Four of the now famous "Monuments Men" were directors or curators of the Worcester Art Museum, including George Stout and the illustrious Francis Henry Taylor,[8] who graduated from WAM to become one of the most famous directors of the MET. Currently, WAM is among the first art museums to redefine traditional curatorial and educational boundaries to better respond to the interests of twenty-first-century museumgoers.

As this parallel history may suggest, the relationship between the Higgins Armory and WAM had elements of sibling rivalry. If the two institutions saw themselves as members of the same Worcester family, then WAM was the privileged older sibling. Indeed, in one sense, the institutions' sibling rivalry was literal: John Woodman Higgins's older brother, Aldus Higgins, was himself a successful industrialist. Aldus Higgins was president and principal owner of Norton Company, which in turn was older, larger, and more established than Worcester Pressed Steel. Although Aldus Higgins supported the Higgins Armory, he was better known in Worcester as a distinguished collector of art and a patron, benefactor, trustee, and sometime president of WAM.

Over the years, Higgins Armory and WAM collaborated on significant projects, but each sought to differentiate itself from the other in ways that siblings often do. WAM, befitting its senior status, was the more "serious" institution and became a founding member of the prestigious American Association of Museum Directors (AAMD), whose policies represent the "gold standard" in managing, exhibiting, and conserving museum collections.

Meanwhile, in contrast to its more staid, elder sibling, the Higgins Armory Museum continued to bear the personal touch of John Woodman Higgins, who (albeit with discriminating taste) purchased according to inclinations that did not necessarily correspond to current museum standards. For exam-

ple, the Armory collection included high-quality reproductions (with provenance from collections of William Randolph Hearst and Jay Gould), reflecting an era in which reproductions were collected for decorative purposes.
Similarly, Mr. Higgins's broad interest in pressed steel and decorative metalwork lead him to collect a wide variety of iron and steel objects, ancient and
modern, with no apparent relationship to one another except for the material
used in their creation. Mr. Higgins collected Roman scalpels, Dacian arm
bracelets, a Piper Cub airplane, modern mass-produced utensils, automotive
parts, and art deco forged-metal work. Other objects that did not belong in a
museum collection were also occasionally assigned accession numbers. One
notable example is Mr. Higgins's Adams-style carved wood office desk that,
although a lovely piece of furniture, has no place in a museum collection,
particularly a museum of arms and armor.

Mr. Higgins's personal touch extended to interpretation and exhibition.
He considered the steelworks, themselves, a part of the museum. Museum
visitors were encouraged to enter the factory—complete with museum labels
explaining the activities—to observe workers in action.[9] In his later years,
Mr. Higgins delighted in personally conducting tours for visitors—especially
including children who sometimes came to the museum on their own after
school to spend time with their "friend," Mr. Higgins. Norman Rockwell's
painting captures the whimsy of this era in its depiction of a museum guard
balancing a sandwich in his lap and pouring coffee from a thermos while
perched on the base of a mounted knight, the horse mannequin looking on
askance.

THE END OF AN ERA: JOHN WOODMAN HIGGINS
EXITS THE STAGE

By 1978, however, the Armory's circumstances had changed. Mr. Higgins
died in 1961. His son, Carter, who had succeeded him as president of
Worcester Pressed Steel died not long after. The Armory remained under
family control through the 1960s, but it began to focus more on arms and
armor. At the same time, tax law changes made the operation of private
museums increasingly difficult. The Armory became a private "foundation."
Although Worcester Pressed Steel could no longer fund it directly, the Armory continued to receive much of its financial support in the form of rents from
Worcester Pressed Steel, which continued to occupy the Armory building's
lower floors. Partly for tax reasons, but also to preserve the Armory's inde-
pendence and its legacy, the Higgins family sold Worcester Pressed Steel in
1971. In 1974, Worcester Pressed Steel went bankrupt, and the Higgins
Armory, which had no significant endowment, lost its most important revenue stream.[10]

NEW BEGINNINGS: THE MIXED
BLESSINGS OF INDEPENDENCE

In 1979, governance of the Higgins Armory passed for the first time to an independent board of trustees, including Higgins family and friends. The new trustees were mostly from the Worcester area, and none were collectors of arms and armor. Mr. Higgins's surviving descendants wanted the museum to continue, but neither they nor the remaining trustees filled the financial void left by the loss of the Worcester Pressed Steel rents. The Armory was running a significant annual deficit, and it was forced to consider, for the first time, how to raise money through its admissions, programming, and auxiliary museum activities. [11]

At this critical juncture, WAM made the first of several overtures to acquire the Higgins Collection. Under the WAM proposal, the two museums would have merged, and the Higgins Collection would have been placed in storage until a new building could be financed and built to house it. After six months of intensive negotiations, both the WAM and Higgins Armory boards of trustees recommended acceptance, and final merger papers were drafted. Deciding factors for the Armory trustees were the Armory's deepening financial losses coupled with fear that the Higgins Collection would be broken up and lost to the city of Worcester if the deficit continued to mount.

However, the Armory trustees' vote had been deeply divided, with one group of trustees, led by Higgins family members, strongly opposed. The dissenting trustees believed that the Armory had not made a sufficient effort to become viable as an independent institution. Under Massachusetts law, the merger could not be approved without a two-thirds vote of a much larger group of stakeholders called the "incorporators." As the incorporators' vote approached, John Higgins's two surviving children—both trustees—agreed to cover the Armory's anticipated operating deficit for the next ten years. With this additional financial assistance guaranteed, the incorporators ultimately voted down the merger.

The incorporators' vote rejecting the 1979 WAM merger proposal granted the Armory time and freedom to develop as an independent museum. Although other unsuccessful acquisition overtures followed, from both WAM and Boston's Museum of Fine Arts, Higgins Armory remained resolutely independent for another three, transformative decades.

Following leadership changes, the Higgins Armory carried on more or less successfully into the twenty-first century. Despite challenges and periodic reverses, the trustees, directors, and staff did what can fairly be described as an extraordinary job in difficult circumstances. Lacking sufficient endowment to provide substantial operating support, Higgins Armory became known for creative programming that attracted a loyal following and generated the revenue necessary to stay in business. Operations remained lean and efficient, and the Armory became "opportunistic" in the best sense: it became expert at seeking out and seizing opportunities and at making the most of its physical and human assets.

Chief among the assets was, of course, the collection of arms and armor. The Higgins Collection was (and still is) the second-largest collection of arms and armor in the Western Hemisphere, second in size only to that of the Metropolitan Museum of Art, which it nearly rivals in quality. The collection spans a period from circa 4,500 BCE to the modern era and includes objects from every continent. It is also "magnetic" in the sense that it strongly attracts visitors. After 1979, the Higgins Armory refocused on this core strength. It deaccessioned valuable art deco metalwork, and other material, that the trustees considered outside the scope of an arms and armor collection. Proceeds from such deaccessioning created a collections fund that enabled the Armory to make new purchases, further enhancing the collection.

In 1990, Higgins Armory initiated a capital campaign that raised over $2 million and allowed the museum to convert the former Worcester Pressed Steel offices into useful space for programs, a museum store, a "hands-on" gallery for children, a temporary exhibition gallery, a classroom, secure storage for those portions of the collection that were not on display, and offices for the curatorial, educational, and administrative staff. A compelling collection, engaging programming, and clever marketing ensured strong attendance. The Armory earned accreditation from the American Association of Museums (AAM).

Notwithstanding two persisting weak points (the unsuitable building and the inadequate endowment), the Higgins Armory became a stronger, more vital, and more resilient institution. Still, the Higgins trustees recognized that much more needed to be done. Although the Armory was successful by many measures, it continued to rely too heavily on revenue generated by attendance, programs, and the store.

Under the leadership of an energetic and creative new director, the trustees began to assess strategic needs in the late 1990s, which they concluded, were very substantial indeed. There was still no true endowment. Although the Armory had accumulated investments that it loosely called an "endowment," the amounts were modest and provided only limited support. The Armory struggled to make ends meet, let alone to update technology or undertake new initiatives. When times were good, the budget appeared to balance, but in reality, the Armory's finances depended largely on external events, such as the economy, which no museum can control.

The landmark Armory building was itself a part of the problem. In its unmodernized condition, it was expensive, both in terms of energy consumption and maintenance of its steel and glass exterior. Perhaps more concerning was an engineering study that revealed that the existing building could not under any foreseeable circumstances provide a suitable climate to conserve the collection.

To address these challenges, Higgins staff and trustees considered another capital campaign. They estimated the true need at $65 million. Sensing that such a large campaign was unrealistic, the Armory engaged fundraising consultants to assess the feasibility of a more modest $10 million campaign to fund essential facility and program initiatives and strengthen the Armory's endowment. Recognizing that Worcester alone could not support a campaign of even this magnitude, the study had a national scope paying particular attention to Boston and New York.

The results of the study were disappointing. The analysis indicated significant challenges, including a narrow base of existing donors, and advised the trustees to "field test" a campaign with a goal of only $5 million—just half the already pared down perception of immediate $10 million need. Even at a reduced $5 million level, the evidence of feasibility was inconclusive. Nevertheless, the trustees of the Higgins Armory resolutely embarked on the recommended $5 million campaign.

Then, as fate would have it, the events of 9/11 intervened. The aftermath of 9/11 challenged almost all nonprofit institutions, but for Higgins Armory, which had struggled even in the preceding boom times, the combined economic and societal impacts of 9/11 were devastating, both on the newly launched campaign and on day-to-day operations. A mood of uncertainty overtook the nation, affecting the Armory's audiences and funders alike. Donors became more cautious. Local foundations continued, dutifully, to offer support, but at reduced levels. Potential donors outside the Worcester area retreated, and private philanthropists retrenched. At the same time, public budgets shrank, further reducing grant opportunities and even curtailing school visits, which had become a critical revenue staple for the Armory.

In these already straightened circumstances, the financial crisis of 2008 and the Great Recession that followed were the final nails in the Armory's coffin. After years of effort, its critical needs campaign was exhausted at $2.6 million, well short of the $5 million "field test" target, and only 4 percent of the true estimated need.

THE UNPLEASANT AWAKENING: HIGGINS ARMORY CONFRONTS UNPLEASANT REALITIES

In 2008, the Armory's treasurer expressed concern that converging post-9/11 trends, compounded by the financial market crash that began in 2007, presaged serious financial challenges for the museum. In addition to the reductions in public spending that depressed visitation and the reduced philanthropic support, the Armory's already limited endowment had itself suffered a serious decline. The ongoing need to draw the same amount from its invest-ments to maintain even a lean operation was forcing the Armory to consume what endowment it had. The continuing draw served to exacerbate market losses and, if sustained, would soon deplete the Armory's investments entire-ly. In short, the combined circumstances were unsustainable and would very soon threaten the Armory's existence.

At the same time, an independent factor, ultimately as important as the economic threats, complicated matters. The Higgins Armory had been with-out a permanent director for three years. In the meantime, it had plugged along under a part-time interim head. But in mid-2008, after a long search, the Higgins Armory had engaged a new executive director. The trustees were optimistic that the new director would lead a turnaround, and hopes were raised as a temporary exhibit, mainly targeted to family audiences, proved popular and stimulated attendance. Unfortunately, the reprieve was illusory. The underlying financial challenges remained. Attempts to restart the fund-raising campaign failed. Human resources were stretched to the limit, and within a little more than two years, the new director resigned to pursue other opportunities.

At that point, Higgins Armory engaged a nonprofit consultant to become its interim director and to work with the board of trustees in charting the Armory's future. Further financial analysis led the trustees to conclude that the persistent challenges were insurmountable. The Armory's economic circumstances were unlikely to change. Existing donors had begun to express "fatigue" and question what the future could hold. Based on the fundraising feasibility study of 2004 and subsequent experience in the failed $5 million campaign, the trustees determined that it would not be prudent to begin a new campaign.

After careful deliberation, the trustees concluded that the Armory must undertake what they euphemistically called "strategic structural change."

THE HIGGINS DECISION-MAKING PROCESS: MAKING THE BEST OF A BAD HAND

Having accepted that the Higgins Armory was unsustainable as an indepen-dent museum, Armory staff and trustees worked together to establish princi-ples to guide their search for a solution for the museum and its collection. Ultimately, they settled on four "desired outcomes":

1. Provide for long-term stewardship of the Higgins Armory Museum's "core collection" by ensuring that the collection would be kept intact, valued, preserved, studied, and used;

2. Keep the core collection in Worcester if reasonably feasible, and if not, then as close to Worcester as possible;
3. Seek a partner for the core collection that would embrace a transfer of the Higgins educational philosophy and approach to interpretation; and
4. Assure that any resulting integration with another institution would be transformative and sustainable and not merely a transfer of assets.

Next, the trustees and staff identified and tested the feasibility of various alternative structures. Under some, Higgins Armory might have continued to exist in some form and partner with another institution. Under others, the Armory would close and transfer its assets after negotiating agreements to fulfill the desired outcomes. Confidential overtures tested the interest of possible strategic partners or acquiring institutions in Worcester and beyond, including not just the Worcester Art Museum, but also various colleges and universities and other cultural institutions.

Possibilities for a partnership that would allow the Armory to continue as an independent entity were quickly exhausted. No other institution was prepared to assume responsibility for the Higgins building or operate the museum as a separate campus, and the benefit of combining administrative services was insufficient to offset the Armory's fiscal challenges.

Moreover, the preliminary inquiries identified stumbling blocks that deterred other institutions. To begin with, the then-existing collection of 4,500 objects had not been refined to a "core collection" that met the standards of the Armory's own collections management policy, let alone the standards of other institutions not principally focused on arms and armor. Even if refined to a much smaller "core collection," the resources required to acquire, conserve, exhibit, and house the collection would be very substantial indeed! At first, no institution would offer more than a token exhibit while most of the collection would be stored for a decade or more pending fundraising to pay the cost of a permanent exhibit. And there was at first little willingness to consider adopting the Armory's educational and interpretational philosophy.

Despite these challenges, WAM remained the most likely prospect. After all, WAM and Higgins were members of the same "family" of Worcester cultural institutions, and WAM had unsuccessfully invited Higgins to merge on three prior occasions.

LOOKING A GIFT HORSE IN THE MOUTH: WAM REJECTS HIGGINS ARMORY'S "MODEST PROPOSAL"

Leaders of Higgins Armory approached WAM during the summer of 2011 to explore, again, the theoretical possibilities of combining the Armory with

WAM. However, the renewed courtship between WAM and the Armory at first seemed as ill fated as that of Romeo and Juliet, or perhaps more aptly, Beatrice and Benedick in Shakespeare's *Much Ado about Nothing.*

The Armory's overture came at a moment of important change for WAM. In fall 2010, WAM was considering the shape of its own future. The Great Recession had also taken its toll on WAM's investments, revealing weaknesses in WAM's other revenue streams. Despite what many institutions would consider an enviable endowment, WAM's trustees were starkly aware that they had to strengthen fundamentals—including visitation and development—in order to secure a sustainable economic future. At the same time, a beloved longtime director had announced his retirement, and WAM's board was preoccupied with the search for a successor.

In September 2011, after several months of exploratory discussion authorized by both the Armory and WAM boards of trustees, Higgins Armory's leadership presented a formal proposal to WAM's trustees to "consolidate" WAM and the Armory. Emphasizing the Armory's attraction to family and tourist audiences and the anticipated fundraising and operating efficiencies of consolidation, the Higgins proposal suggested that WAM provide gallery space to create a "Higgins at WAM." The institutions would combine operations in stages over a period of years. Ultimately, WAM would employ the equivalent of twelve former Armory employees, repurpose existing WAM galleries to house the Higgins Collection as an "Age of Chivalry" curated by Armory staff, and provide space to host the Armory's existing "Castle Quest" interactive gallery. The Armory and WAM would work together to sell or repurpose the Armory building with the realized assets supporting both institutions, and both institutions would revise their missions and philosophies to create a new harmonized entity. WAM would benefit from the additional Armory assets and from the visitation and "brand loyalty" of Higgins Armory enthusiasts. And Higgins would benefit from WAM's strong endowment and its climate-controlled galleries.

Understanding well the magnificence and attractions of the Higgins Collection, and having long been interested in a partnership with Higgins, one can imagine that the WAM trustees would have been strongly interested in the Armory's proposal. Many WAM trustees were themselves longtime residents or supporters of the city of Worcester, and it is likely they shared a sense of the importance of keeping the Higgins Collection in Worcester. The WAM trustees likely also appreciated the Armory's courage in facing its economic realities and developing an exit strategy.

At the same time, the Armory's proposal seemed to require WAM to assume significant Armory costs (including the twelve additional employees), take on large parts of the Armory's operations, give up significant gallery space to the detriment of its own collection, and reinvent itself in a new and untested model. Although WAM's revenues and visitation were not as strong as WAM desired, the Armory's proposal was conjectural, rather than the product of detailed analysis and due diligence. It seemed to require, at a minimum, possible redirection or additions to WAM's core mission, and it came, coincidentally, at the exact same meeting where the WAM trustees chose a new director—a director, who, it could be argued, should be given the opportunity to consider and direct the museum's future unfettered by an unexpected, last-minute plan to consolidate operations with another institution.

Perhaps, not surprisingly in these circumstances, the WAM trustees did not accept the Armory's proposal. Although the WAM board allowed informal conversations to continue, WAM made clear to the Armory that it was not interested in a consolidation similar to the September 2011 proposal and that even a revised approach might never be considered.

Frustrating as WAM's rejection may have been to Higgins, hindsight clearly shows it was a prudent exercise of fiduciary judgment that ultimately produced a better outcome. WAM's rejection forced a greater level of planning, ensuring that the eventual agreement was supported by thorough due diligence that addressed the needs of WAM as well as Higgins. Indeed, the process that the institutions followed after this first rejection helped WAM revitalize and "jump-start" its own mission, while allowing the Armory to meet its "desired outcome" of providing an economically secure and sustainable future for the Higgins Collection.

THE WAY FORWARD: SIBLINGS LEARN TO COLLABORATE AND RESOLVE CHALLENGES

Following WAM's September 2011 rejection, informal conversations continued. WAM's new director took over in November 2011. Within months, he and the WAM board had formulated a bold new vision statement. Trumpeting "relevance" and "sustainability," WAM sought to increase its visitation three-fold by 2020 while helping to revitalize cultural life in Worcester.

Gradually, WAM's new director was introduced to the Higgins Armory and the theoretical potential of bringing a world-class collection of arms and armor to the Worcester Art Museum. Although WAM continued to feel strongly that it could not engraft the Armory's mission, employees, and collection as an essentially freestanding museum within a museum, the new director and the WAM trustees began to consider integration possibilities that could draw on the Higgins's greatest strengths—its collection, popularity, and success at engaging audiences—in ways that would enhance WAM, improving rather than altering WAM's core mission of collecting, conserving, exhibiting, and interpreting world-class art. Thinking creatively, a first breakthrough came when WAM identified space that could potentially be

Figure 14.2. A knight displayed in the gallery at the Worcester Art Museum, courtesy of the Worcester Art Museum.

converted to arms and armor galleries without diminishing exhibit space for the WAM's own 36,000-piece collection.

At the same time, Higgins Armory scaled back its ambitions. WAM's reaction to its September 2011 proposal helped the Armory to understand that the "desired outcomes" could not be met unless the Armory's future looked significantly different from its present. Critically, the Higgins Armory began to move purposefully to hone its still-unwieldy collection to a museum-worthy "core," and it began to think not of a legal consolidation, but rather in terms of a complex gift, or asset transfer, including the core collection and a "dowry" to support it. To protect Higgins Armory's most important goals, the gift would be conditioned on fulfillment of legal covenants, including covenants on naming, use of the dowry funds, and maintenance of the Higgins legacy.

Thus focused, discussions returned to the board level. On October 23, 2012, the WAM board unanimously adopted a resolution establishing a joint committee with the Armory to identify and address the challenges of any proposed integration. As if continuing the romantic comedy theme, a rare September storm produced a travel ban that postponed an Armory board meeting. However, the Higgins board met on November 5, 2012, and adopted a nearly identical reciprocal resolution. The resolutions listed key "threshold" and "implementation" issues, which the Armory and WAM negotiated to ensure that they echoed *both* the Armory's "desired outcomes" *and* WAM's requirement that any integration not endanger, but rather strengthen, WAM's revitalized vision and sustainability goals. If, and only if, these threshold and implementation issues were met, the reciprocal resolutions obligated the Armory to give and WAM to accept and accession the Higgins core collection.

The reciprocal resolutions served several purposes. They guaranteed the Higgins Armory a home for its collection if its "desired outcomes" could be met, and they transformed WAM into a partner in seeking to achieve those outcomes. The resolutions ensured that WAM would only accept the Higgins core collection under terms that would help fuel its own "jump-start," and they created a process for leaders of both institutions to work together to explore, review, and attain shared goals.

The joint committee authorized by the reciprocal resolutions comprised the presidents, directors, and treasurers of each institution, together with several additional trustees. It began meeting even before the resolutions were finalized and continued meeting almost biweekly for several months. Early meetings established a timeline for a possible integration and identified essential issues that must be addressed before an agreement could be finalized.

The timeline emerged quickly once it became clear and could be voiced that, in order to conserve dwindling resources, the Higgins Armory must close no later than December 31, 2013. Working backward, other dates fell into place. Legal and financial due diligence must be completed as quickly as possible to identify any obstacles. Negotiations had been and remained top secret through March 2013, but the clear need to provide Higgins employees ample time to seek other employment and the necessity of obtaining a ratifying vote from the Higgins incorporators mandated a publicity plan. A budget must be developed to support fundraising and inform ultimate negotiations over the "dowry"; the deaccessioning must be completed; and a plan must be developed to dispose of the building. As the joint committee identified these issues, it formed subcommittees on legal, finance, PR/communications, and facilities (WAM) issues, and on the future of the Armory building.

Under Massachusetts law, any transfer of substantially all the assets of a Massachusetts nonprofit corporation requires approval by the office of the attorney general and the Supreme Judicial Court of Massachusetts. Recognizing that the attorney general should be apprised of the contemplated transactions well in advance of a public announcement, Higgins Armory involved the attorney general's office shortly after the reciprocal resolutions went into effect. This step proved to be critical. The attorney general's office provided guidance that informed, improved, and smoothed all of the legal processes that followed.

The joint committee also realized that it must maximize the public relations and fundraising momentum of the imminent public announcement by planning a year of farewell ceremonies at the Armory to be followed, as soon as possible after the closing, by a groundbreaking new exhibition and welcoming activities at WAM. Staffs of both institutions worked together to share and develop exhibits and programming. While WAM staff focused on preparing the transformational *Knights!* exhibit to open in March 2014, Higgins staff enhanced programming to celebrate the Higgins Armory during its final year. A special exhibit recounted the story of John Woodman Higgins and his wonderful museum. Visitors were encouraged to record their memories and thoughts, and the recordings are now part of WAM's archives.

Major donors strongly supported the transaction, recognizing that it would not only preserve the Higgins Collection, but revitalize and strengthen WAM. Within months of being advised of the integration plans, foundations and individual philanthropists pledged $6 million toward a $12 million campaign to fund the so-called Higgins integration.

Another important, albeit unplanned, benefit of the joint committee and subcommittees was the trust they created. The value of the combination became clearer to each side, but just as importantly, each side came to understand and accept that the other was motivated by legitimate fiduciary concerns; that the final agreements would have to be mutually acceptable; and that this mutual acceptability would require creativity, goodwill, and compromise. Although the process was not always easy—emotions sometimes ran high, as they do in challenging circumstances, and occasional roadblocks seemed insurmountable—the joint committee had faith they were doing something necessary, important, and transformative for their institutions and for the city, and solutions gradually emerged.

CREATING THE HIGGINS "CORE COLLECTION"

The fifteen months between the reciprocal resolutions and the closing of the Higgins Armory were busy with details of the integration absorbing nearly full-time efforts from key staff and many trustees of both institutions. Many projects were undertaken jointly, but others were institution specific.

The most important of the institution-specific activities was the Higgins Armory's refinement of the entire existing Armory collection to a core collection of objects that met the rigorous standards of the Armory's existing collection management policy. To be sure that no ethical walls were breached, WAM played no role in the deaccessioning.

The deaccessioning process began with a detailed, object-by-object review by the Armory's own expert curatorial staff, but then progressed to a formal peer review by arms and armor curators of the Metropolitan Museum of Art. The Higgins and MET curators' recommendations were then vetted by the Armory's collections committee, which itself included nontrustees with expertise in the field of arms and armor.

At each stage of the process, any object that was judged to be within the Armory's scope and worthy of remaining in a museum was retained. Only objects that did not meet preexisting collections management policy criteria were removed, including some objects that were museum quality, but not properly included in a collection of arms and armor. Doubts were resolved in favor of retaining objects that required further evaluation.

Ultimately, the recommendations resulting from this process were presented to the Higgins trustees for final approval. Deaccessioning ultimately reduced the Higgins Collection from 4,500 to 1,900 objects.

Disposition of the deaccessioned objects followed one of the three paths prescribed by the Armory's collections management policy. Although not appropriate for retention in the core collection, most of the deaccessioned objects were valuable. The Armory engaged a leading specialist auctioneer to market and sell most of the objects. Some objects that had particular historical or other significance to the Worcester community were donated to appropriate local museums, such as the Worcester Historical Society. And a few additional objects were sold to museums outside of Worcester at negotiated prices in order to keep the objects in the public domain.

THE IMPORTANCE OF PUBLIC PROCESS: BUILDING BOARD CONSENSUS AND CONDUCTING PUBLIC DISCOURSE

The reciprocal resolutions, the joint committee, and all other discussions between the Armory and WAM were, of necessity, confidential. The WAM and Armory trustees were informed, but sworn to secrecy. Knowing that the incorporators must ultimately approve any vote to close the Higgins Armory or transfer its assets, the Armory trustees had been educating the incorporators for several years about the financial challenges and need for radical change. However, the Higgins incorporators had not been told the identities of potential partners or the details of negotiations.

By February 2013, joint committee activity had advanced to a point where further progress could not be made without going public. Fundraising for the integration must begin in order to ensure funds could be received in time to assist with looming integration expenses; the public needed to be informed that fundamental change would be forthcoming; and WAM employees had to understand the goal of the work they were undertaking. As a result, the joint committee developed a tightly timed publicity "rollout" scheduled for the end of the month.

The burden of the publicity and communications fell more heavily on Higgins than WAM. The Armory advised its own employees on the morning of February 28. Later that same day, Higgins trustees and staff began to inform the Higgins incorporators through meetings and telephone calls, advising the incorporators of the Armory's anticipated December 31 closing, the reciprocal resolutions with WAM, and the work of the joint committee. On March 7, 2013, the Armory notified the public through press announcements, leaving the Armory's loyal followers nearly a year to visit and to mourn and celebrate the Higgins legacy.

Public reaction was understandably mixed. Higgins Armory was a unique and beloved institution that had touched many people in Worcester, throughout New England, and beyond. A majority sadly accepted the need for change. Some were initially skeptical of WAM's commitment to the Higgins legacy, but accepted that keeping the collection at WAM was better than dispersing it or sending it elsewhere. However, a small but determined group led by a descendant of John Woodman Higgins vociferously opposed the transaction and publicly attacked the motives and performance of the Armory's trustees and senior management.

A special meeting of Higgins incorporators was convened on February 28, 2013, to provide information without yet calling for a vote. Opponents intensified their criticism and initiated a "Save the Higgins" website and campaign to raise funds. They proposed alternatives that the Higgins board had already evaluated, but deemed imprudent. News media including the *Boston Globe* took up the story.[12]

By the Armory's annual meeting on March 27, 2013, the battle lines were drawn. But despite significant publicity, the Save the Higgins campaign had generated only $660. Financial help was *not* on the way. After passionate discussion, with news media waiting outside for word of the outcome, fifty-five of the sixty-eight incorporators who were eligible to vote approved the transaction. Ten voted against it, and three either abstained or were absent without proxies.[13]

The affirmative vote by 80 percent of all eligible incorporators comfortably exceeded the required two-thirds supermajority. However, the vote of incorporators was not the last hurdle. Through their vote, the incorporators delegated to the Armory's trustees the authority to conclude the transaction subject to obtaining covenants that satisfactorily resolved several conditions including requirements that the Higgins core collection must be accepted, managed, and conserved in accordance with WAM's policies and AAMD standards; that WAM would satisfactorily exhibit the collection, which must be publicly identified as the Higgins Armory Collection; that WAM would give appropriate consideration to hiring Armory employees; that the proceeds of Higgins noncollection assets would be earmarked to support the transaction; and that WAM would invite some Armory-approved representatives to join its own board of trustees

ALL'S WELL THAT ENDS WELL: COVENANTS AND FUND ALLOCATION AGREEMENTS

In the months following the incorporators' vote, the public response to news of the Armory's closing was remarkable. Attendance reached all-time highs, but ironically, at revenue levels that nevertheless vindicated the Higgins trustees' conclusion that increasing the already robust attendance and program revenue could not possibly fill the economic gap in the Armory's finances.

As the Armory celebrated its final months, WAM and Higgins principals negotiated the final details of the transaction. The negotiations were exhaustive, lengthy, and distinctly arm's-length. Ultimately, the agreements reached were memorialized in two documents: the "Covenants for the Transfer of Assets of the Higgins Armory Museum to the Worcester Art Museum" and an "Agreement Concerning the Allocation of Monies to be Transferred . . . to the Worcester Art Museum."

The covenants include numerous provisions that protect the Armory's legacy. They require WAM to exhibit, conserve, and interpret the core collection, identifying it as the (John Woodman) Higgins Armory Collection. WAM agrees to endow a curatorial position to focus on the Higgins collection, to recruit two trustees and a collections committee member acceptable to the Armory, and to give reasonable consideration to hiring Armory employees. The covenants provide for collecting funds so that the Higgins Armory Collection can be enhanced over time. Further, within five to seven years, WAM agrees to open a four-thousand-square-foot permanent exhibit displaying substantially the entirety of the collection.

However, the covenants are careful not to create a separate, solo Higgins museum within the larger walls of WAM. Rather, they ensure that the Higgins Collection becomes equal and integrated into the museum's collections as a whole. For example, the covenants permit Higgins objects to be displayed throughout the museum, thereby enhancing curators' ability to tell stories and draw connections between artworks. Similarly, recognizing that the best museums are fluid and that standards for interpretation evolve over time, the covenants also allow future generations of WAM leader's flexibility to reinterpret the manner in which the collection is displayed and interpreted so long as the new approaches honor the relationship of the objects and integrity of the Higgins Collection.

Within months of the Armory's closing, it was able to transfer $4.2 million under the allocation agreement, and more funds will be transferred over time. As such agreements must, the covenants and allocation agreement direct WAM's use of these monies (the Higgins "dowry"). Specifically, the documents create three new funds at WAM: (1) a Higgins Armory Collections Fund for the purchase of new objects for the Higgins Collection; (2) a Higgins Armory Curatorial Endowment to support the Higgins Collection–focused curator; and (3) a Higgins Armory General Endowment to help ensure WAM's long-term sustainability by providing additional support for operations, including increased costs resulting from the integration.

In November 2013, the Higgins and WAM boards of trustees voted unanimously to approve the covenants and allocation agreements. In December 2013, after attentive review of a substantial record, the Massachusetts attorney general—and then the commonwealth's supreme judicial court—approved the agreements. On December 31, 2013, the Higgins Armory closed as scheduled after a glorious final day of fanfare, and on March 27, 2014, the Higgins Armory Collection began its renaissance with the opening of *Knights!* at WAM. Although only a promise of things to come, *Knights!* fulfills WAM's and the Armory's commitments to one another, to their stakeholders, and to the people of Worcester, preserving and protecting the core collection, and shepherding it to new greatness.

Figure 14.3. Conservation efforts at the Worcester Art Museum, courtesy of the Worcester Art Museum

CONCLUDING OBSERVATIONS: WHAT OTHERS SHOULD CONSIDER IN SIMILAR CIRCUMSTANCES

Transactions such as this are sometimes the best and only way to preserve priceless legacies. When thoughtfully planned and carefully conducted, they can produce benefits that would be unachievable any other way. Conservation is an example, because WAM's very strong conservation resources have already allowed it to conserve bronze antiquities and leather or fabric components that Higgins did not have technical or financial resources to conserve on its own. As a result of the integration, the public is given an opportunity to see objects that Higgins could not exhibit because their condition did not allow it. Also, the final four-thousand-square-foot exhibit at WAM will use open storage to make accessible the entire 1,900-object core collection, whereas only about 450 were displayed at Higgins at any one time. In addition to offering an entirely new level of audience engagement, the collection will be accessible to scholars and curators who can take the understanding of the Higgins Collection to levels that in the past could only be imagined.

NOTES

The authors dedicate this chapter to the trustees and staffs of Higgins Armory and WAM, who were instrumental in the integration, with special tribute to Suzanne Maas, the interim director of Higgins Armory, for her courage, perseverance, and dedication to achieving the best possible result for the Armory in difficult times; Matthias Waschek, the executive director of WAM, for his vision, creativity, and brilliance in seeing and seizing the possibilities; and Clifford Schorer, Jr., the president of WAM during the integration negotiations, for his financial genius, artistic acumen, and persistent leadership.

The authors were participants in many of the events described, and this chapter is accordingly based on their own personal records and memories. It should not be viewed as representing the opinions or positions of any other person or of Higgins Armory or WAM. Any errors in describing facts and circumstances are the authors' and should not be attributed to any other person or entity.

1. M. Yolen Cohen, "The Unsung but Revolutionary Art Institutions of Massachusetts," May 12, 2014, available at www.huffingtonpost.com/malerie-yolencohen/the-unsung-but-revolution_b_5310430.html.

2. *New York Trust Co. v. Eisner*, 256 U.S. 345, 349 (1921).

3. See Peter Suciu, "American Experimental Helmets from WWI," *Military Trader*, November 30, 2011, www.militarytrader.com/military-trader-news/american-experimental-helmets-from-wwi; Charles McGrath, "Dressed to Kill from Head to Toe," *New York Times*, October 5, 2012, at C25, available at www.nytimes.com/2012/10/05/arts/design/met-show-recalls-bashford-dean-armor-curator.html?pagewanted=all; see also generally Bashford Dean, *Helmets and Body Armor in Modern Warfare* (New Haven, CT: Yale University Press, 1920).

4. Benedict Crowell (Assistant Secretary of War, Director of Munitions), *America's Munitions: 1917–1918* (Washington, DC: Government Printing Office, 1919), at 224.

5. Sara Wermiel, "A Steel and Glass Office Building and Industrial Art Museum in Worcester: Development and Historical Significance of the Higgins Armory Museum Building," a report prepared for the Higgins Armory Museum, January 2014, at 8, available at www

.higgins.org/WermielHAM.pdf, quoting William F. Holland, "Office Building of Steel and Glass," *Steel* 88 (January 22, 1931), at 35.

6. Multiple letters between Jefferson Warren (Director of the John Woodman Higgins Armory) and Norman Rockwell, August 1961–September 1962 (Higgins Armory Museum archive); see also Cover, *Saturday Evening Post*, November 3, 1962, image available at www .saturdayeveningpost.com/2013/04/12/art-entertainment/norman-rockwell-art-entertainment/ rockwells-that-dont-look-like-rockwells.html.

7. Letter from Groucho Marx to John W. Higgins, December 3, 1953, Higgins Armory Museum archive.

8. The "Monuments Men" were a joint unit of Allied Forces, formed from leading museum directors, curators, and art historians, to protect Europe's art treasures during and after World War II. They have recently been memorialized in a book and a blockbuster Hollywood movie, both called *The Monuments Men*. The character played by George Clooney in the movie is based on WAM's George Stout.

9. Kary Ashley Pardy, "An Institutional History of the Higgins Armory Museum and Its Relationship with Worcester, Massachusetts," University of South Carolina, Masters' Dissertation, 2013, at 8, available at scholarcommons.sc.edu/cgi/viewcontent.cgi?article=3523& context=etd.

10. See, for example, Mary Louise Higgins Wilding-White, "John Woodman Higgins Armory, Inc.: Important Yearly Events Outlined," c. 1986, Higgins Armory Museum archives.

11. See, for example, ibid.; see also Minutes of the [Higgins Armory] Fin. Cte. Mtg, October 18, 1978, Higgins Armory Museum archives.

12. See Geoff Edgers, "Founder's Kin Fights to Stop Higgins Armory's Closure," *Boston Globe*, March 27, 2013, available at www.bostonglobe.com/arts/theater-art/2013/03/26/final-vote-higgins-armory-closing-deal-raising-debates/l2FfLPKX6IaV7q2lyHslyM/story.html.

13. See Steven Foskett, Jr., "Incorporators Vote to Merge Collection, Close Higgins Armory Dec. 31, 2013," *Worcester Telegram & Gazette*, March 27, 2013, available at www.telegram. com/article/20130327/NEWS/303289992/0.

III

Museum Operations

INTRODUCTION: MUSEUM OPERATIONS

In addition to being guardians of unique collections with governance, finance, and collections management challenges, museums are also nonprofit organizations with some of the same operational and human resources trials as any other institution or corporation. Addressing the needs of the institution and its employees through vetting employees, by providing training for specialized duties or outsourcing responsibilities, along with generating the appropriate employment contracts and relationships are some of the functional concerns for museums.

The essays that make up this section are written by a museum security expert working in the field as well as an attorney who specializes in employment contracts for independent workers. In today's economic climate, it is becoming more common for museums to outsource some of their essential services. In doing so, museums gain access to contractors and consultants with specialized skills and expertise without having to provide benefits to these workers.[1] Good or bad, this trend is likely to continue as museums forge into the twenty-first century.

NOTE

1. N. Elizabeth Schlatter, *Museum Careers: A Practical Guide for Students and Novices* (Walnut Creek, CA: Left Coast Press, 2012), 44.

Chapter Fifteen

Employee and Independent Contractor Issues in the Museum Context

Ethan S. Klepetar, Esq.

For years, whether due to accessibility of online images and information, competing entertainment, or waning interest in cultural objects, museums have been looking for ways to cut operational costs and increase audiences and revenue. The practice of hiring independent consultants and contractors versus permanent, full-time employees has become common practice, in order to aid museums in reducing operational overhead expenses.

There are numerous differences and similarities between hiring independent contractors and permanent museum professionals, many of which will be discussed in this essay. The information and examples that follow are based on specific state laws and it is important to research and examine local state laws relevant to the community where your museum is located.

Appropriately classifying independent contractors can save museums unnecessary costs, which, for many (if not most) museums, is absolutely necessary to remain sustainable. It can be highly beneficial for museum professionals to have a basic understanding of the analysis involved in determining whether workers are employees or independent contractors.

In general, independent contractors are not entitled to the same benefits that are provided to employees; and by classifying workers as independent contractors instead of employees, the museum is not responsible for payroll taxes, unemployment insurance, workers' compensation costs, and other costs. Museums may have less liability exposure to third parties for the negligent conduct of independent contractors, whereas they are generally liable for the negligent conduct of employees.

However, misclassification of a contractor where that person could be seen as an employee can have serious consequences. There are severe penalties to deter the misclassification of employees as independent contractors. Such misclassifications can lead to liability under federal and state wage statutes, tax liability, and, in some states, like Massachusetts, even civil or criminal sanctions imposed by the attorney general.[1]

Museum administrators need to be particularly concerned about violating state and federal wage statutes. Unlike independent contractors, employees, unless they are exempt, are entitled to be paid the minimum wage and are entitled to additional compensation for working overtime.[2] An employee who is improperly classified as an independent contractor and regularly works overtime may bring a successful wage claim against his or her employer. Successful claimants, under the wage statutes, may be awarded multiple damages and attorneys' fees. In fact, a plaintiff who brings a successful wage claim in Massachusetts is *automatically* entitled to triple damages and attorneys' fees.[3] There are no special protections for museums or other nonprofits under the wage statutes. A museum is treated just like any other employer.

Museum professionals need to be sure that they are properly classified as an employee or an independent contractor in order to make sure that they are getting all of the benefits they are entitled to receive. For example, employees are more likely than independent contractors to be entitled to workers' compensation if they are injured while working. An employee can also be deprived of benefits and wages, such as vacation pay and legally required overtime compensation, by being misclassified as an independent contractor. In short, it is highly beneficial for museum professionals to understand the difference between an employee and an independent contractor, and to have a basic understanding of the analyses used to determine the proper classification of employees and independent contractors.

Unfortunately, there is no simple, black-and-white rule that can be applied in every single case to determine the proper classification of a worker. That being said, there are standards and principles that are generally applicable.

This chapter will review those general standards and principles, and show how they may be applied in a museum context to help museum professionals gain a basic understanding of this important issue and to encourage them to research local state law with regard to employment in their jurisdiction.

HOW CAN A MUSEUM PROFESSIONAL KNOW WHETHER SOMEONE IS AN EMPLOYEE OR AN INDEPENDENT CONTRACTOR?

Stated simply, the key issue in determining whether a worker is an employee or an independent contractor is the extent to which their employer controls the worker and his or her work. For employees, an employer controls not only what work they do, but the manner in which the work is done. Conversely, employers do not have control over the manner in which independent contractors do their work.

However, this standard can be difficult to apply to a specific case, as various elements are considered and applied to the facts and each case is considered on its own merits. The standard varies, depending on the decision-making entity and the jurisdiction. In other words, the proper classification of a museum professional may be different depending on whether the facts are being reviewed by the Internal Revenue Service (IRS), a state court, or an administrative agency such as the Department of Labor or a state office of workers' compensation.

Regardless of which entity is making the determination, there is some similarity in the classification considerations. For ease of discussion, and because the IRS classifications are applied uniformly throughout the country, we will focus on the types of activities the IRS examines.

There are, of course, significant tax implications involved in the proper classification of workers. An employer must withhold income taxes, withhold and pay Social Security and Medicare taxes, and pay unemployment taxes on wages paid to an employee. On the other hand, employers generally do not withhold or pay any taxes on payments to independent contractors. As a result, the IRS applies its own standard in determining whether an individual has been classified properly as an employee or an independent contractor.

The IRS standard provides a good, general background because it is applied uniformly across the United States and is based on common law principles that influence this analysis regardless of the jurisdiction. It is therefore helpful to review how the IRS determines employment classification.

The IRS uses three factors to determine who is an independent contractor and who is an employee: (1) Behavioral Control: the extent to which the employer has the right to control what the worker does and how the worker does his or her job; (2) Financial Control: whether the business aspects of the worker's job are controlled by the employer; and (3) Type of Relationship: whether the worker receives benefits typical of an employment relationship, such as vacation time, sick time, insurance benefits, and so forth. [4]

All of these factors are evaluated on a case-by-case basis, thereby determining whether a museum professional is an employee or an independent contractor. The following types of questions should be considered:

- To what extent are the worker's services an integral part of the museum's mission?
- How long has the worker been working for the museum?
- How does the worker receive his or her assignments and who determines how those assignments are performed?

- Does the worker use his or her own tools or office supplies?
- Does the worker set his or her own hours?
- Is the worker reimbursed for any purchases, materials, or supplies?
- Does the worker have his or her own office at the museum? Where does the worker work?
- Does the worker work for anyone else?
- How is the worker paid, upon completion of projects or on a regular schedule?
- Does the worker advertise independently or solely through the museum?
- Did the museum provide any training for the worker?
- What types of reports are required from the worker?
- Can the museum discipline the worker?
- Does the worker have to attend meetings at the museum?[5]

This list is not comprehensive. However, it provides a foundation for thinking about the kinds of questions and issues to consider when determining how a worker should be classified.

These questions also do not only apply to the IRS standard, but are also generally applicable whenever trying to determine whether an individual is an employee or an independent contractor.

It is also important to note two things that are *not* important in making the determination: (1) the worker's job title, and (2) whether the worker has an employment contract. The IRS wants to know the true relationship between the museum and those it hires for work. Otherwise, it would be too easy to misclassify workers. For example, a museum could make its front-desk staff independent contractors by calling them "receptionist contractors" and not providing them with employment contracts.

More information about how the IRS determines the proper classifications of workers can be found online at www.irs.gov/Businesses/Small -Businesses-&-Self-Employed/Independent-Contractor-Self-Employed-or- Employee. Also, if a museum is faced with a very close case or, for any reason, is simply not sure what the proper classification is for a given individual, a Form SS-8 captioned "Determination of Worker Status for Purposes of Federal Employment Taxes and Income Tax Withholding" may be filed with the IRS, and subsequently, the IRS will make the determination.

JURISDICTIONAL ISSUES AND TWO SPECIFIC EXAMPLES IN THE MUSEUM CONTEXT

While the IRS standard is important for tax purposes and helpful in terms of general background, it is very important that museum professionals be more familiar with the standards used in their own state.

For example, Connecticut has a particularly strict independent contractor classification standard making it much more likely that a worker be classified as an employee. In Connecticut, there is a conjunctive standard that is popularly referred to as the "ABC test."[6] Under that test, an individual is presumed to be an employee and not an independent contractor. Specifically, a worker is not considered an employee if

> [A] such individual has been and will continue to be free from control and direction in connection with the performance of such service, both under his contract for the performance of service and in fact; *and* [B] such service is performed either outside the usual course of the business for which the service is performed or is performed outside of all the places of business of the enterprise for which the service is performed; *and* [C] such individual is customarily engaged in an independently established trade, occupation, profession or business of the same nature as that involved in the service performed.[7]

The use of the word "and" means that an individual has to satisfy all three of the prongs of the ABC test in order to be considered an independent contractor.

While it is helpful to review the statute and see the standard that will be applied, it is more important to see how a court will interpret the statute in a museum context. Fortunately, the Supreme Court of Connecticut interpreted this statute in regard to whether a museum was responsible for paying a terminated worker unemployment benefits in the case *Mattatuck Museum-Mattatuck Historical Soc'y v. Administrator, Unemployment Compensation Act*, 238 Conn. at 273 (Conn. 1996).

The Mattatuck Museum-Mattatuck Historical Society operated a large exhibition hall for regional historic artifacts and art.[8] Additionally, the museum offered several artistic programs, including lectures, workshops, and arts and crafts courses.[9]

The museum hired the plaintiff to teach several art courses at the museum, but she was eventually terminated. After her termination, the plaintiff applied for unemployment compensation benefits, which the museum contested, arguing that she was an independent contractor.[10]

The administrator of the Unemployment Compensation Act found that the plaintiff was an employee, not an independent contractor, and therefore entitled to unemployment benefits. The museum appealed, all the way to the Supreme Court of Connecticut. The museum focused on prong B of the ABC test and argued the art courses were "outside the usual course of the [museum's] business."[11] After all, the museum was a historical museum that included art, but it was not an art school.[12]

However, the court, noting that the statute was intended to be applied liberally, found that the plaintiff was an employee. Initially, the court reviewed the ABC test and reiterated that "failure to satisfy any one of the prongs will render the [museum] subject to the [unemployment] act."[13] Even so, the court found that the art courses were within the museum's regular course of business and that prong B did not apply.[14]

The court explained its reasoning in detail, which provides museum professionals with an excellent summary of the kinds of facts a court will consider in determining whether a worker is an employee or an independent contractor:

> [The museum] offered the art courses on a regular and continuous basis. The record reflects the fact that the [museum] had employed instructors to teach art courses for several years. [The plaintiff] approached the [museum] with her resume because she knew that it offered art courses to the general public. Moreover, the [museum] held itself out to the public as offering art courses. The [museum] produced and distributed brochures announcing the courses, class hours, location, registration fees, and the instructors' names. Indeed, the brochure listed [the plaintiff] as a member of its "faculty," from which the general public could infer that the art courses were a regular part of the [museum's] business. Furthermore, the appeals referee found that the [museum] discounted the art courses for members in an effort to bolster its membership.[15]

As you can see, the court reviewed a number of facts to glean the nature of the relationship between the museum and the worker. Based on those facts recited above, the court found that teaching art courses was part of the museum's "regular course of business" and that the worker was an employee entitled to unemployment benefits.[16]

It is also helpful to explore a case from a different jurisdiction, using a different standard, in which the court found that the worker was an independent contractor. The Louisiana case, *Steinfelds v. Villarubia*, 53 So. 3d 1275 (La.App. 4th Cir. 2010), provides just such an example.

In that case, the plaintiff brought a workers' compensation claim against the Degas House, LLC (the "Degas House") a historic museum and guest house.[17] The plaintiff severely injured his ankle when he fell from scaffolding while doing carpentry work at the Degas House.[18] The plaintiff initially lost his claim before the Office of Workers' Compensation (OWC), but he appealed to the Court of Appeals of Louisiana.[19]

In Louisiana, there is also a presumption that workers are employees, not independent contractors. That being said, the test is not as strict as the one in Connecticut. To determine whether the employer has sufficient control over the worker to make him an employee is determined by four factors in Louisiana: (1) selection and engagement; (2) the payment of wages; (3) the power of dismissal; and (4) the power of control.[20] Unlike in Connecticut, however, "none of these factors alone is determinative of an employer/employee relationship. Rather, the totality of circumstances must be considered."[21]

Furthermore, for specifically determining whether the nature of the relationship is that of a principal and contractor, as opposed to an employer and employee, Louisiana courts consider whether (1) there is a valid contract between the parties; (2) the work being done is of an independent nature such that the contractor may employ nonexclusive means in accomplishing it; (3) the contract calls for specific piecework as a unit to be done according to the independent contractor's own methods without being subject to the control and direction of the principal, except as to the result of the services to be rendered; (4) there is a specific price for the overall undertaking; and (5) specific time or duration is agreed upon and not subject to termination at the will of either side without liability for breach.[22]

In applying these factors to the *Steinfelds* case, the court found that the plaintiff was "clearly" an independent contractor. Indeed, he "was hired to perform a single project for an agreed upon duration and specific price."[23] Furthermore, the court took into account that the plaintiff used his own tools, equipment, and materials (other than replacement boards); the Degas House exercised no control over how or when the work was performed; and there was no supervision over the plaintiff.[24]

You may think that this made the *Steinfelds* case clear cut and the court found that his claim was properly dismissed by the OWC. The plaintiff was an independent contractor and therefore was not entitled to workers' compensation benefits. Yet, the plaintiff won his appeal. While he certainly was an independent contractor, Louisiana has a special provision in its workers' compensation statute making it apply to independent contractors who are engaged in *manual labor* for a substantial part of their work time.[25] The court found that the plaintiff fell into this category and that OWC improperly dismissed his workers' compensation claim.[26]

This case not only demonstrates the facts that courts will consider in determining whether a worker is an employee or independent contractor, but also shows how important it is for museum professionals to know the applicable rules of their own jurisdiction.

CONCLUSION

It is vital for museum professionals to have a basic understanding of the difference between employees and independent contractors in their state. Not only can it help museums avoid devastating liability, but it can also help museum professionals make sure they are receiving all of the benefits to which they are entitled.

The basic difference is simple: an employer controls the work done by an employee and the manner in which it is done, whereas an employer does not exert the same control over an independent contractor. However, the proper classification of an individual as an employee or independent contractor can depend on the context of the classification and the jurisdiction in which the question is being considered. In all cases, it is a fact-specific question that must be carefully analyzed.

After gaining a basic understanding of the difference between employees and independent contractors, as well as the factors that determine the proper classification, museum professionals should review the standards that apply in their own jurisdiction. The next step for museum professionals is to review their museum's classifications and make sure they can be justified. Once the standards have been reviewed, museums should carefully articulate the employee/independent contractor designation to museum workers to avoid confusion. In addition, limitations and benefits associated with both the employee and independent contractor designations should be communicated.

NOTES

1. See 29 U.S.C. §§ 206 and 207; M.G.L. c.149, § 27C; M.G.L. c.149, § 148; M.G.L. c.149, § 148B; and, M.G.L. c.151, § 1.
2. *Id.*
3. M.G.L. c. 149, § 150.
4. See 26 C.F.R. §§ 31.3121 (d)-1 (c); 31.3306 (i)-1; and 31.3401 (c)-1; IRS Revenue Ruling, 87-41; and IRS Publication 15-A, Employer's Supplemental Tax Guide at P. 7–9.
5. *Id.*
6. See *Mattatuck Museum-Mattatuck Historical Soc'y v. Administrator, Unemployment Compensation Act*, 238 Conn. at 273 (Conn. 1996).
7. Connecticut General Statutes, § 31-222(a) (1) (B) (ii) (I) – (III) (emphasis added).
8. *Mattatuck Museum-Mattatuck Historical Soc'y,* 238 Conn. at 274 (Conn. 1996).
9. *Id.*
10. *Id.* at 275.
11. *Id.* at 278.
12. *Id.*
13. *Id.* at 277
14. *Id.* at 282.
15. *Id.*
16. *Id.*
17. *Steinfelds v. Villarubia*, 53 So. 3d 1275 (La.App. 4th Cir. 2010).
18. *Id.* at 1277.
19. *Id.*
20. La. R.S. 23:1044
21. *Steinfelds,* 53 So. 3d at 1280 (La.App. 4th Cir. 2010).
22. *Id.*
23. *Id.*
24. *Id.*
25. La. R.S. 23:1021 (7) (emphasis added).
26. *Steinfelds,* 53 So. 3d at 1284 (La.App. 4th Cir. 2010).

Chapter Sixteen

To Train or Not to Train.
Is That a Question?

The Training of Security Officers in Museums

R. Michael Kirchner, CPP

The legal issues surrounding the training of security personnel working in museums is an issue that is directly aligned with the long history of the growth of the private security industry as a whole. For the past fifty years the private security profession has grown exponentially in the United States; at present it is almost three times as large as the public law enforcement sector. Almost fifty years ago many professionals saw the need for increased control, training, and monitoring of this private security sector, and yet there has been no national move to do so. This paper will examine the existing research surrounding the issue of the training of private security personnel and look at how that relates to the use of security personnel in museums and other cultural properties in America.

A BRIEF HISTORY OF PRIVATE SECURITY IN AMERICA

In this country, the use of "private police" has fluctuated as national conditions changed. As public police forces developed during the early part of the nineteenth century, the need or call for private policing or security met a sudden decline, only to be revived with the development of a national economy in the later part of that century. As companies grew larger and became more national in scope, the need for protection of their assets intensified, and local police departments found themselves ill equipped to deal with criminals who traveled from one jurisdiction to another (Maahs and Hemmens 1998).

The majority of these "private police" included private detectives and private detective agencies. These agencies flourished until around the turn of the century when once again their popularity diminished with the expansion of public or community police departments in cities and towns across America and the creation of state and federal law enforcement agencies. It was a temporary decline, however, as increasing crime rates once again led businesses to turn to the private security sector. The needs of business and industry in America have driven the ebb and flow of the security industry.

Private security agencies remained a significant factor in law enforcement until the 1960s when they began to expand at a tremendous rate, fueled by societal crises including civil rights demonstrations, protests against the Vietnam War, and an increase in both juvenile and adult crime (Maahs and Hemmens 1998). By 1975 there were almost twice as many private security personnel as public police officers (National Advisory Committee 1976). In 2007, it was reported by the *Washington Post* that there were more than one million contract security personnel in the United States and an equal number of proprietary security officers, compared to less than 700,000 sworn police officers (Goldstein 2007).

INDUSTRY VERSUS PROFESSION

Private security has now become big business in the United States. The duties these more than two million security officers perform are as varied as the clients who employ them. Museums and nuclear power plants all employ private security officers, but for vastly different reasons and with very different expectations. Jeff Maahs and Craig Hemmens spoke to the general authority possessed by security officers when they wrote the following: "As a general rule, a security guard has the same authority as his employer in protecting the property of the employer. Security guards may even use deadly force in situations in which the property owner would as well" (Maahs and Hemmens 1998, 91). This would imply that possessing this incredible authority would carry with it the responsibility to train and be trained, in much the same manner as those in the law enforcement community. Sadly, that is not the case. There is no national standard for private security training and unequal and sometimes nonexistent statewide requirements.

With no national standard, and a wide variety of different requirements at the state level, it is easy to ignore the issue of training for private security personnel, and that is one of the factors that leads to the unfortunate perception endured by the security profession as a whole. In order for the private security field to be considered a profession, education and training are a must. In the early 1970s as the security field was growing rapidly, much was written about the future of security and the role of training and education.

Figure 16.1. Mr. Richard R. Chaney, Security Guard. Smithsonian Historic Image, by Ruel P. Tolman, 1935.

This position was stated clearly by Richard Post in 1973: "Is security a profession? No, probably not to the extent that law enforcement or many of the other areas of criminal justice are professions. . . . But, we have made a start. Things are beginning to move forward, and it is entirely possible that security may be considered the profession of the future" (Post 1978, 6). But, twenty-five years later, the hope of professionalizing the private security field still remained a vague hope, as pointed out in the following paragraph:

> Professionalism remains an empty promise without a commitment to educa-
> tion, scholarly research and development, and academic integrity. Regulatory

bodies throughout the United States have been placing heightened emphasis on education and training as part of the minimum qualifications of an applicant. The *Private Security Advisory Council*, a federally funded consortium of public law enforcement specialists and private security experts, has made numerous recommendations concerning the upgrading of educational standards. The Council notes eloquently:

> [W]hile private security is a vast crime prevention and reduction resource, it will for the most part remain only a potential resource until steps are taken to eliminate incompetence and unscrupulous conduct. Many private security personnel are only temporary or part-time employees who are often underpaid and untrained for their work. The protection of lives and property is an awesome societal responsibility, and the public interest demands that persons entrusted with such responsibilities be competent, well trained, and of good moral character. (Nemeth 1998, 36–37)

While the perception of underpaid and untrained security personnel exists, and the nation as a whole continues to shop for the lowest bid in private security, liability will exist, and that liability will spread to personnel in the private security field, and to those who employ these workers. The lack of national or statewide standards for security guards and/or security companies, has placed the responsibility on the security industry to establish professional training and education programs. Russell Bintliff says, "The security profession cannot allow inexperienced people to perform duties that call for competence. To develop and maintain a career-oriented security force, you need to develop basic and continued training that counts, and that happens when you have student-centered, performance-oriented training" (Bintliff 1992, 446).

The industry's professional associations and groups have played a distinct role in the delivery of education services. ASIS (American Society for Industrial Security) International was founded in 1955 and is one of the country's premier organizations in the security field. It has developed many training and certification programs for security officers, supervisors, and managers. The ASIS Certified Protection Professional (CPP) Program was initiated in 1977 and is the primary source of certification for security managers. Yet, certification is expensive and security officers working in entry-level positions may not qualify or choose not to pursue certification. The organizations these officers are employed by are not in a position to sponsor the certification process, as it can be costly and time consuming. This may be challenging for nonprofit organizations like museums and other cultural organizations.

So, what does this all have to do with museum security? While security officers and security companies around the country struggle with liability suits for such things as unlawful arrest, illegal detention, unreasonable use of force, does the museum world really have to worry about things like arrest, detention, and use of force? Could a museum have an employee who performs in a negligent manner when dealing with an emergency or unusual event? Do most museums even employee security guards or officers?

It is becoming common practice for museums to avoid the use of the word "security." Many museums hire "museum attendants," "safety personnel," "gallery guides," and use other phrases that avoid the stereotypical, police-type employee, in favor of customer service–oriented employees, who have safety and security responsibilities. Uniforms are often "soft," consisting of a jacket and tie or polo shirt, as opposed to the traditional uniform and related paraphernalia.

Regardless of the job title, the "duck test" applies: if it looks like a duck, and swims like a duck, and quacks like a duck, it is probably a duck. If a suit is brought forth involving the behavior of a gallery guide, and it involves a violation of a visitor's civil rights, that employee may well be judged as a security guard, regardless of official title. If a person is charged with the "protection" of the art or objects in a collection, and does not receive the proper training, it is predictable that somewhere along the line, someone will either overreact or exercise poor judgment. It is irresponsible and may even be negligent to place a person in a position of responsibility without providing the proper training required for the performance of their specific function. Charles Nemeth, chair and professor of security, fire, and emergency management at John Jay College, has spent the vast majority of his professional life in the study and practice of law and justice, the role of private sector justice in a free society, and the ethical demands on justice professionals. He spoke eloquently about negligence:

> Negligence encompasses human behavior that inflicts individual harm, injury from mistake or accident, and damages to the individual. To be negligent is to err. To err is simply to be human. Negligence is the stuff of everyday life that people fail to do with due care. Forgetting to engage auto turn signals, failing to file documents such as a tax return, misreading a right of way, or missing an important court date, all typify negligence.
>
> The whole theory of negligence operates from the measure of the average man or woman—the "reasonable person" standard. What should we expect from the average person in his or her dealings with others? . . . [Should we expect perfection?] While mistakes are part of the human equation, the law of negligence is less tolerant of gross and reckless behavior, and it surely divines its rules to fit the type of party under scrutiny. We surely expect more from doctors and lawyers than we do from janitors or construction workers. So in this sense, the average, reasonable person acts reasonably under the circumstances they live and labor under. . . .
>
> What is certain is that the security industry will be held to its own standard of professional conduct and that injuries that result will be scrutinized in accordance with our expectations of performance and due-care owed. On top

of this, the industry, like the individual, has a duty to perform and an obligation to not harm others. How the average, reasonable, security professional
carries out the task will forever be cast and recast. Beyond the Jane and John
Doe, the security operative will be held to a normative standard of performance. The measure will still be reasonableness but the setting will change
based on education, training, expertise, and occupation. In the law of negligence, the unreasonable person is needlessly careless and even reckless and
fails to take those precautions necessary to prevent injury to others. (Nemeth
1998, 136–37)

What standards of duty should apply in the assessment of security companies and security personnel? Is it not reasonable to expect that security personnel be competent in basic legal applications, or that they generally understand what techniques ensure the protection of people and property? Premise
liability suits of all kinds, which generically allege negligence—failing to
provide a safe, secure environment—besiege businesses. Even criminal conduct suffered by customers opens the door to negligence actions (Nemeth
1998). Negligence comes in many flavors, but the one important to this
discussion is that of negligent training. There is legal precedent holding
employers responsible for failing to train their employees: the U.S. Supreme
Court, in the _City of Canton v. Harris_ (1989), which held that failing to train
police officers may be the basis for managerial liability under Title 42 U.S.
Code Section 1983.

Sophisticated training can upgrade the quality and efficacy of security
personnel. Critics have long argued that required training, implemented half-
heartedly, is artificially imposed. Dennis Walters, who had a forty-nine-year
career in law enforcement and private security, authored "Training, the Key
to Avoiding Liability," in which he expressed the essential nature of training:
your security officers must be adequately trained (Walters 1985, 82). Moreover, the training they receive must be sufficiently practical to enable them to
demonstrate technical and legal competency commensurate with the duties
they perform. Classroom theory is fine, but it is not enough. Academics
should be combined with performance exercises so that officers can experience and practice methods to become confident with the techniques they may
be required to use (Walters 1985).The security industry's response to education and training has been less than enthusiastic and often more rhetorical
than substantial. While some strides are being made, procrastination on the
part of the industry, along with the lack of legislative uniformity or standards, has influenced the rigor and intensity of training.

TO TRAIN OR NOT TO TRAIN

In our current litigious society it obviously is prudent to train our public-facing personnel, regardless of their title, to deal with situations that they may actually face. We don't need to conjure up images of *Ocean's Eleven* to think about what can go terribly wrong at any museum or cultural property in the country. The director of a prestigious art museum complained to the author recently that "security consultants are always trying to convince us that we need a Vulcan Death Star hovering overhead in order to protect us." What are situations that can actually occur within a museum? Are there people who enter museums while under the influence, or who become intoxicated at a museum-sponsored event? Are there caterers, contractors, or people visiting museums who behave recklessly and place objects in danger? Are there radical people who might deface a work of art? An unusual example of what security personnel need to be prepared for is outlined in the following excerpt from an article written by Nick Madigan in the *New York Times*, on February 18, 2014:

> MIAMI—Officials at the recently inaugurated Pérez Art Museum Miami confirmed on Monday that a valuable vase by the Chinese dissident artist Ai Weiwei had been deliberately destroyed by a visitor in what appeared to be an act of protest.
>
> A spokeswoman for the museum said the incident occurred on Sunday afternoon when a local artist walked into the waterfront museum and picked up one of the vases in the [installation] titled "Colored Vases." A guard asked the man to put it down, but instead he threw it to the ground, smashing it, the spokeswoman said. (Madigan 2014)

The police were summoned and arrested a fifty-one-year-old suspect who was charged with criminal mischief and later released after posting bail. He told reporters that he planned to hold a news conference to explain his actions, but the assailant later cancelled the press event.

Incidents such as the one described above seem to be becoming more and more prevalent in the museum world. Are the security people in those museums trained to even think about incidents like this? How are they trained to respond? How should they be trained? Does museum management have reasonable expectations concerning how a security guard should act in a situation like this? What are those expectations? Do all persons involved understand that the focus of police departments is enforcement while the focus of security is voluntary compliance and conflict avoidance? These are all questions that must be explored prior to the commencement of security personnel training.

So, how should U.S. museums approach training of their security personnel? How can they assure that the guards-in-training are equipped with the necessary skills, knowledge, and judgment to perform specific job functions? First, their preparation should also be in accordance with all applicable local, state, and federal laws. Knowing that the laws vary widely from state to state makes it vitally important to verify local requirements and applicability. Second, in order to avoid liability issues, the training offered should have a direct cause/effect relationship to actual job performance and include at least the following topics:

- Use of force

  a. Unarmed security staff
  b. Armed security staff

- Unlawful search and detention
- Dealing with juveniles and other persons at risk
- Enforcing work rules and policies
- First aid
- CPR/AED
- Fire protection
- Emergency evacuation procedures

  Other training should include

- Management of aggressive behavior (MOAB)
- Patrol techniques (if applicable)
- Report writing
- Customer service training. It is the author's belief that good customer service equals good security. Practicing the principles of good customer service will go far to ensure compliance with rules, regulations, and safety procedures within the museum.

There should be a basic training program for all security employees, tailored to their varied and specific duties (i.e., gallery attendant, control center operator, overnight patrol, and fixed door post). There also should be an annual refresher course and frequent documentation of the trainings and perhaps a mentoring program. Security personnel should have adequate introduction to their job functions and opportunities to learn on the job with supervision. In addition, museum security staff should be informed about the objects that they are safeguarding and be able to assist visitors with a host of emergency and nonemergency needs.

It is only through efforts to train all frontline security personnel who regularly engage with the public, in their individual responsibilities and au-thorized responses to emergency situations, that museums will be able to shield themselves from liability concerns and better protect the objects in their care and visitors in their charge, so that museums will be safe, pleasant environments for many future generations.

BIBLIOGRAPHY

Bintloff, Russell L. (1992). *The Complete Manual of Corporate and Industrial Security*, Englewood Cliffs, NJ: Prentice Hall.

Goldstein, Amy. (2007). "The Private Arm of the Law," *Washington Post*, January 2. Retrieved from www.washingtonpost.com/wp-dyn/content/article/2007/01/01/AR2007010100665.html (July 2014).

Maahs, Jeff, and Hemmens, Craig. (1998). "Train in Vain: A Statutory Analysis of Security Guard Training Requirements," *International Journal of Comparative and Applied Criminal Justice* vol. 22, issue 1, 91–101.

Madigan, Nick. (2014). "Behind the Smashing of the Vase," *New York Times*, February 18. Retrieved from www.nytimes.com/2014/02/19/arts/design/behind-the-smashing-of-a-vase.html?_r=0.

National Advisory Committee on Criminal Justice Standards and Goals. (1976). *Private Security: Report of the Task Force on Private Security*. Washington, DC: U.S. Government Printing Office.

Nemeth, Charles P. (1998). *Private Security and the Law, Third Edition*. Retrieved from books.google.com.

Post, Richard. (1978). *Toward Rational Curriculum Development for Private Protection Services*, First National Conference on Private Security, 6.

Ross, D. L. (2000). "Emerging Trends in Police Failure to Train Liability," *Policing: International Journal of Police Strategies and Management* vol. 23, issue 2, 169–93.

Saiat, Wayne. (1982). "A Delicate Balance, The Need for Security and the Limits of Liability," *Security World* vol. 19, issue 2, 25.

Walters, Dennis. (1985). "Training—The Key to Avoiding Liability," *Security Management* vol. 29, 82.

IV

Digital Technology and Social Media in Museums

INTRODUCTION: DIGITAL MEDIA AND TECHNOLOGY

Guided tours, docent talks, and scavenger hunts have been a traditional part of the museum experience for decades. Digital technology and social media outlets have added a layer of interactivity to the museumgoer's itinerary in recent years. Scanning QR codes to obtain exhibit content, dialing up cell-tour prompts, tweeting about behind-the-scenes happenings, and posting images of photo-bombed precious art and artifacts to Instagram and Facebook have provided visitors with new ways to interface with museums and to share their experience with family and friends in real time. With swiftly changing technology a museum should keep abreast of legal concerns as an interactive experience implemented in one moment, could become obsolete in the next.

In addition to the entertainment value of digital technology, museums have also created substantial online collection databases by digitizing objects and information, making object research from afar highly achievable. With all these possibilities laid out before them, museum professionals need to educate themselves in both the possibilities and perils of social media. The articles that follow outline the swiftly changing landscape of digital technology and include topics such as an explanation of digital technology applications, the responsible use of social media, and crowdfunding as a source of revenue.

Chapter Seventeen

Social Media

Use Responsibly

Katherine E. Lewis

Social media is perhaps one of the most versatile and effective communications tools in existence, which is why museums of all sizes are working to engage and leverage different social media platforms. It is spontaneous, far reaching, and multifaceted, allowing museums to communicate directly with their existing membership and reach new audiences, and allowing those groups to communicate with one another. Social media provides an opportunity to bring people together for the same mission simultaneously.

Depending on the size of the institution, maintenance of the social media presence may be more or less challenging. However, successful integration of social media strategy into museum activities does not necessarily correlate with financial resources, thoughtful deliberation, and development of an appropriate social media strategy. One of the most misunderstood elements of social media is the level of commitment needed, which can be considerable, to launch and maintain a responsible and ultimately successful social media presence on the web.

In 2014, social media audiences grew faster than e-mail or website audiences.[1] Directors and governing boards are becoming more aware of the potential of successful social media platforms in following on-site visitors, driving website traffic, and increasing membership—which can result in increased charitable donations and revenue-generating opportunities for the museum. The 2012 Nonprofit Social Network Benchmark Report noted that while the average cost of a Facebook Like for a nonprofit is $3.50 (Twitter was $2.05), the average return value of a Facebook Like is $214.81 over the twelve-month period following the acquisition.[2] A loyal social media following is, in many ways, akin to a loyal museum membership following in years past, but perhaps more valuable in sheer volume.

Engaging the millennial generation is becoming increasingly competitive as companies in every industry vie for their attention across platforms. Therefore, education, membership, and advancement are likely to be the areas that most interest museum professionals in utilizing social media. Some museums are beginning to develop internal digital media staff positions and teams, which are also likely to be interested in social media outreach and communication platforms.

This essay is intended to be an overview of some of the most common legal concerns directly relating to the use of social media for museums. Legal issues related to social media for museums could easily be a separate publication with each area of law identified below having a dedicated chapter. This essay is not an exhaustive report on the issues, but rather a primer to get museum professionals thinking about big-picture legal concerns as they get comfortable using and maintaining a social media presence. The essay will also offer practical advice on how to approach the potential legal issues and will direct the reader to seek legal advice of local counsel throughout. A word of caution: this is a fast-paced area of both technology and law. By the time this essay is published, there will likely be new developments in either the platforms or the law, or both.

PROTECTING A MUSEUM'S NONPROFIT STATUS

Achieving 501(c)(3) nonprofit status can be just as challenging as maintaining it. What could social media have to do with your nonprofit status? As the Internal Revenue Service has stated, all the same rules that apply in the real world apply on the Internet.[3] In some contexts, however, Internet provides a variety of functional approaches to accomplish tasks that are not contemplated under existing law.[4]

There is some interesting overlap with the use of social media and the preservation of the tax-exempt status. Applying traditional tax rules to the Internet and all of the new and different abbreviated functionality that social media can be so well-known and well-liked for can be challenging. But take heart! Although the Internal Revenue Service (IRS) has not issued further guidance on nonprofit status and Internet use since 2010, there have been no significant issues in applying the single rule the IRS has disseminated to date: all the same rules apply. There are few case studies where museums have lost their 501(c)(3) status for any reason, much less for reasons related to social media use; therefore what follows is a brief exploration of the possible social media uses that may put the museum's nonprofit status at risk.

Although visions of spectacled accountants in windowless offices with feeder calculators on one side of them and tax documents on the other come to mind when we think of the IRS, their agents are perfectly capable of surfing the Internet and everything released on the Internet is discoverable by the IRS. Therefore, museums should make sure that social media use is consistent with their mission, obligations, and fiduciary responsibilities as a nonprofit organization.

There are likely to be three areas the IRS will be interested in when reviewing museum social media pages: political activity, lobbying activity, and business-related income. Back in 2000, the IRS published a request for comment in the Federal Register on nonprofit use of the Internet.[5] The agency was considering whether there was a need to issue guidance on the applicability of the Internal Revenue Code on use of the Internet. As of the date of this essay, the IRS has issued very little additional guidance in this area, but the questions put forth in the request for comment are revealing and can provide some insight into the ways in which the IRS may consider Internet and, by extension, social media use in the context of maintaining nonprofit status.

- To what extent are statements made by subscribers to a forum, such as a listserve or newsgroup, attributable to an exempt organization that maintains the forum? Does attribution vary depending on a level of participation of the exempt organization in maintaining the forum (e.g., if the organization moderates discussion, acts as editor, etc.)?[6] . . .
- What facts and circumstances are relevant in determining whether information on a charitable organization's website about candidates for public office constitutes intervention in a political campaign by the charitable organization or is permissible charitable activity consistent with the principles set forth in Rev. Rul. 78-248, 1978-1 C.B. 154, and Rev. Rul. 86-95, 1986-2 C.B. 73 (dealing with voter guides and candidate debates)?
- Does providing a hyperlink on a charitable organization's website to another organization that engages in political campaign intervention result in *per se* prohibited political intervention? What facts and circumstances are relevant in determining whether the hyperlink constitutes a political campaign intervention by the charitable organization?[7]

While all are excellent questions, the answers continue to remain unclear. In light of the uncertainty, one possible proactive approach to this problem might be to include a statement on the social media landing page explicitly asserting the content therein may contain links to third-party sites that are not under the museum's control and that the presence of these links does not indicate the museum's endorsement, sponsorship of, or affiliation with the third party or content of the linked website, including any advertisements that may be posted.

As with many highly specialized areas of law, you should always consult with an attorney in your state regarding your specific concern. For this area of specialty, the museum might consider an attorney experienced in nonprofit and tax law specifically as many issues that apply to nonmuseum 501(c)(3)s will also be applicable to museums.

TRADEMARKS AND PUBLIC IMAGE

It's crucial that the museum (1) maintain an awareness of its presence on the Internet, beyond what is on the museum website, (2) understand how the museum name and image is being used on its social media accounts, and (3) maintain control of the its public image.

Trademark law protects the association of a product or service in the consumer mind with its source. Trademark protection is about protection of the consumer, or end user. It is not in place for the protection of the business, whether for-profit or nonprofit.

Protecting the Museum Trademark

It is incumbent on the trademark holder—in this context, the museum or cultural institution—to protect and preserve that association in the public mind. So, how do we accomplish this in social media?

The museum should work to preserve continuity in its public image across social media platforms and in correspondence to the museum website. It can sometimes be challenging to preserve a consistent public image when trying to maintain several social media platforms, especially if staffing is an issue, but this can be accomplished more easily if there are fewer platforms to manage. Most nonprofit organizations only have one or two social media pages or accounts; it's more unusual to find organizations juggling ten or more accounts.[8]

Inconsistent representations of the museum name and trademark, as well as any other imbedded aesthetic in communication content, has a resulting impact on branding and intellectual property rights. In spite of the social media provider's aesthetic, a user should be able to recognize whether they are visiting the museum's official social media account.

- The museum name as it appears on its Facebook or Twitter account should be consistent with how the museum name appears in other communications and branding materials.
- Consider selecting consistent images (i.e., of the museum itself or perhaps the logo) for the social media banners that often appear across the top of the social media pages.

- The "about" page should use language that is consistent with social media pages.

Following these suggestions serves a dual purpose of strengthening the brand connection for the consumer and allowing the user to focus on the information rather than thinking about any inconsistencies.

For those just starting out, consider identifying visual indicators the museum will use in each social media platform and making sure that these are present in the creation, maintenance, and updating of each account. If the social media strategy changes or evolves, ensure that the accounts evolve together. Contemplate designing and implementing a style guide that addresses social media continuity for staff to follow. Think about looking to large organizations that are likely to have resources dedicated exclusively to social media, like television networks or large, established nonprofits like the American Red Cross for example. Pay particular attention to the selection of colors, font size, imagery, and symbols used across all social media platforms.

TREAD LIGHTLY ON THE TRADEMARKS OF OTHERS

The museum should also take care that in instances where it is working with other organizations, artists, and businesses on collaborations and/or cross-promotional opportunities that the parties have granted one another the necessary trademark licenses and permissions to allow the relationship goals to be realized, including the use of and reference to one another in social media (i.e., tweets to promote a collaborative exhibition). In many cases, organizations will specifically carve out Internet and social media use in the grant-of-license language. One particularly salient reason for this in the context of trademarks is the viral nature of social media and the need to control the use of the logo and trademark. Once certain use of the trademark is released on social media, it is very difficult, if not impossible, to correct all of the subsequent references (i.e., tweets, retweets, etc.).

RESPONDING TO PUBLIC FEEDBACK ON SOCIAL MEDIA

An important part of preserving the museum's public image is choosing how and when to respond to public feedback. Opening the museum up to social media has the potential for both positive and negative feedback. Exhibitions containing controversial subject matter, new construction and renovation projects, board member actions, and deaccessioning decisions tend to be subjects on which museum audiences have strong opinions. Positive comments are always welcome, of course, so the issue tends to revolve around how to reply to negative comments. Generally, establishing and publishing a policy statement (perhaps as part of the museum's larger terms-of-use policy for the Internet) is the best way to address this issue. When crafting this segment of your museum policy, the museum might consider the following:

- Define the type of content the museum would remove due to its offensive nature or other reasons, including content that is off topic, partisan or political, abusive, threatening, discriminatory, or obscene, infringes on the rights of others, or is otherwise unlawful.
- Provide notice that the museum monitors and reviews the discussions and postings on the social media platform.
- Reserve the museum's right to, in its discretion, edit or remove content. This would usually relate directly to how the museum defines the content it would remove under the first bullet above.

The museum may receive legitimate and respectful criticism or questions on social media. It may be very effective to use these comments as an opportunity to provide further information justifying a particular action or event, acknowledge a difficult choice, and explore the significance of a particular exhibition theme. This proactive public engagement may result in a better public image and relationship with the community.

TRUTH IN ADVERTISING

The Federal Trade Commission (FTC) regulates advertisements to the consuming public and federal law requires that ads must be truthful, not misleading, and when appropriate, backed by scientific evidence. The FTC has stated that in enforcing these laws, they apply the same standards regardless of the medium (newspapers, online, by mail, etc.).[9] The museum should be sure that in promoting museum activities, programs, gift shop offers, museum membership offers, and so forth, using social media platforms or otherwise, that the offers are truthful and not misleading.

If, after posting an offer for discounted admission, discounted memberships, or museum gift shop promotions, you discover there is an error in the posting, the best practice would be to immediately correct the posting, either by deleting it or alerting followers to the correction with a new post and to honor offers collected by customers prior to taking corrective action.

TRADE SECRETS AND CONFIDENTIALITY

Museum missions are generally focused on sharing information and providing public access to the research, resources, and collections cared for by the museum. It's no surprise that with a mission centered on sharing, that trade secrets don't often come up in conversation; however this topic is addressed in this essay because inadvertent disclosure of trade secrets via social media is a risk that should be considered.

Trade secrets are generally defined as information not generally known to the public, which gives a business a particular economic advantage. In order to be subject to protection, the business must make reasonable efforts to protect that information from disclosure. "Information" can include things like formulas, practices, processes, and so forth. Trade secret law is very state specific, and the type of information protected, as well as the effort required to protect that information, may vary by state. Perhaps it goes without saying, but nonprofit organizations, including museums, are also businesses and, depending on the institution, may have trade secrets to protect.

Unlike other forms of intellectual property, trade secrets are not registerable. In order to maintain protection of trade secrets, one must keep them confidential. The standard way to accomplish this through legal means is through confidentiality agreements, nondisclosure agreements, and noncompete agreements. The relation between the museum and the party signing the agreement will determine what agreement is most appropriate to use. There are some restrictions on the scope of noncompete and nondisclosure agreements in particular (i.e., geographic and term limits), so it's best to consult with an attorney in your area to determine the appropriate agreement and scope.

Other nonlegal methods of protection may include built-in technological security—for example, use of log-ins and passwords to access guarded information. The museum administration can also use nontechnical defenses, such as establishing special procedures or internal policies for handling the protected information.

Although perpetual, meaning protection of a trade secret will never expire, once the trade secret is out in the open there is no way to prevent others from benefiting from that knowledge and utilizing the information. The museum may have legal recourse against the disclosing party and there can be financial penalties assessed, but it can also be challenging for the museum to prove liability.

In addition to information classified as trade secret, there may be other types of information that employees and volunteers tasked with maintaining social media platforms on behalf of the museum have access to that the museum would not like released to the public. For example, when planning themes and content for future exhibitions, a museum generally wants to protect that information and is highly selective about the information released to the public and the timing of that release.

In order to protect the inadvertent sharing of trade secret and/or confidential information on social media platforms via text postings, video postings, blog content, and the like, the museum should take very specific action to

- Identify trade secret information;
- Identify confidential information;
- Consult with an attorney in your area to

  - Prepare confidentiality, nondisclosure, and noncompete agreements;
  - Determine the appropriate use for each type of agreement and the legal parameters of each agreement; and
  - Understand any limitations of each type of agreement (for example, noncompete agreements are typically unenforceable if the term is longer than one year and are not specific to a geographic region);

- Establish procedures for protecting trade secret and/or confidential information, which might include some of the following considerations:

  - Identifying individuals (employees, contractors, interns, volunteers, etc.) who will or will not have access to certain information;
  - Determine methods to identify the information (i.e., using stamps or watermarks to identify certain documents as "confidential"); and
  - Establish access barriers (i.e., log-in and password access).

- Provide training to staff, volunteers, interns, contractors, and so forth, on the procedures. Specifically address social media use in the training and provide clear instruction on what information may be released on these platforms.

USE OF MEMBER AND VISITOR INFORMATION

The first golden rule is to never use, publish, post, and so forth, any personally identifiable information (PII) in social media. PII is defined as information that can be used on its own or with other information to identify, contact, or locate a single person or to identify an individual in context. For example, PII would include name, social security number, date and place of birth, mother's maiden name, and/or biometric records, and the like. [10]

USE OF USER-GENERATED CONTENT

Turning to user-generated content, this category includes content generated by visitors to the museum (perhaps in real time), as well as those who contribute content remotely. Original content fixed in any tangible medium of expression gains copyright protection upon the moment of creation.[11] If content is protected by copyright, one must obtain permission from the copyright holder to use the content.

The industry standard for obtaining permission to use content generated by users is to include provisions in the online "terms of use" policy. Typically, the terms addressing use of user-generated content are either called out specifically in the general terms of use or laid out separately on a page dedicated exclusively to intellectual property terms and conditions. In either case, these terms of use live on the museum website, so the question becomes the following: How do you apply them to the social media platform, which has its own terms of use?

One creative way of including the museum terms of use in the social media platform may be to include a link to the museum terms of use on the museum's social media landing page. If choosing to use this method, it may be wise to review the social media platform terms of use and determine whether any of the terms and conditions conflict with those of the social media provider. For example, if social media provider terms of use state that the user retains copyright in their content and the link to the museum terms and conditions stipulates the opposite, that conflict is substantial and may negate any effort the museum has made to obtain permission to use the user-generated content. A court reviewing such a conflict may determine that in generating content on the given social media platform, albeit on the museum's landing page, the user could not reasonably be expected to also be bound by any terms other than those of the provider.

PHOTOGRAPHING THE PUBLIC

There may be cases where museum staff members wish to take photographs of the museum public spaces, including the people occupying those spaces at the time the photo is taken, and post those photos to museum social media accounts. This could be for any number of reasons, including to

- Capture users interacting with a particular display or new kind of interactive media.
- Demonstrate visitor interest in a particular object in order to post that image on its social media feed to generate interest and encourage others to visit and see the object for themselves.
- Show children participating in educational programming, in order to show some of the educational tools used in the program.
- Show members of the public using museum resources (i.e., library collections, archival documents, etc.).

- Chronicle special events such as fundraisers, museum galas, exhibit openings, and so forth, to entice participation.

Is the museum within its rights to take a photograph of visitors and use them on its website and/or its social media platforms to promote the museum mission, programming, and resources? Must the museum get permission from the visitor prior to taking the photograph? Prior to using the photograph? What does that permission look like? Are there different considerations when the subject is a child?

In order to answer the question of whether a photograph of a visitor can be used by the museum, the threshold question is whether the photograph could be taken in the first place. Photography laws differ from state to state and there is no federal rule. Generally, however, you do not need permission to take photos in public spaces. A museum gallery space would be considered public space.

There are a variety of different ways museums address this issue. Some post visible signs in the entryway of the museum that by entering the museum visitors may have their photograph taken and such photos may be used by the museum; others post photography policies online and direct museum visitors to go to the website for more information; and some take the stance that because photography in a public space is legal, no notices or policies are necessary. The right solution for your museum may vary depending on the state law where the museum is located and the risk tolerance and public relations strategy of the museum.

In the case of photographing a particular tour group, event, or adult educational program, although it may not be required by law, the museum might consider notifying the participants as a courtesy that their photograph may be taken; ask whether there are those in the group who do not wish to be photographed, and perhaps have a way to identify these people for the photographer (i.e., use a discreet sticker or pin the photographer can easily see); and make every reasonable effort to respect the wishes of the participants. If required to get permission from the participants or if the museum is unsure whether permission is required and simply wants to proceed with caution, it may be wise to have a permission form or release handy to ask people to sign.

In the case of children, museums should err on the side of extreme caution. There are many laws at both the state and federal level that protect the privacy and identity of children. Consult with a local attorney to learn more about this area of law in your state. For purposes of this discussion, if the museum wishes to take photos of children in educational programs, the best practice is to obtain prior written permission from the child's parent or legal guardian. The permission should include the intended or possible uses of the photographs, including specific reference to use in social media.

After addressing the threshold question of whether the museum could legally take the photograph, we can turn to the ability to use the resulting photograph in the museum's social media platform(s). If the photograph was taken legally and the necessary permissions, if any, were obtained, there should be no issue with using photographs of visitors in social media.

EMPLOYEES

Perhaps because social media is used just as heavily for personal purposes as for business purposes, employee use of social media has become a big topic of discussion. Also, due to the nature of social media as an informal and instantaneous method of distributing information at lightning speed to a mind-boggling number of people, the stakes are a bit higher. There are many considerations to take into account in this particular area of law. The intention of this section is merely to identify some of the most common issues.

The best practice for tackling social media use in the workplace involves drafting and implementing a social media workplace policy that addresses the following considerations:

- *Social Media Account Ownership*: For museums of any size, account ownership may be a concern. There may be more than one type of social media account to consider: the social media account for the museum and the professional account of the employee. Each category may have multiple accounts. Depending on how the social media account was set up, who pays for the account, who maintains the account, and what information is contained and posted to the account, account ownership may be a real question. The museum social media policy should consider these elements and provide clear direction to employees about ownership of the museum social media accounts. For example, if the museum is paying for the account and the purpose of the account is to promote the museum mission and programs, the policy should inform employees that the account is owned by the museum.
- *Content Ownership*: Generally, the employer owns content produced by an employee within the scope of his or her employment under the work-for-hire doctrine.[12] Whether or not the person generating the content is an "employee" for purposes of the statute, is a separate question. Regardless, the social media policy should clearly state that content created by the employee for use on museum social media accounts is owned by the museum.
- *Statements on Employee's Personal Social Media Account:* Certain statements by employees about the employer, particularly on the employee's personal social media page(s), are protected by the First Amendment. The

National Labor Relations Board (NLRB) has issued many decisions on this subject and continues to refine their position through cases on a regular basis, not always in favor of the employer.[13] The question of when an employee's speech becomes actionable by the employer is evolving and highly fact specific. Be aware that the NLRB also monitors employer social media policies to determine whether they are overly restrictive of the employee's freedom of speech.

To the extent use of social media by either the museum or the employee relates to employment actions, including hiring, disciplinary action, and termination, the museum should consult with an attorney specializing in employment law, especially if the museum is considering addressing these considerations in its social media workplace policy. This is an evolving area of law that cannot be adequately addressed in this essay.

In order for any social media policy to be effective, the museum employer should consider the following:

- Ways to make the social media policy easily accessible by all employees;
- Taking time to review the policy at the time of hire and periodically during the employment relationship;
- Educating staff, volunteers, interns, and contractors on proper uses of social media and standards of professionalism.
- Implementing and enforcing the social media policy.

VOLUNTEERS AND CONTRACTORS

Many of the same social media issues with employees exist with volunteers and contractors. The primary difference is that an employee has a special relationship with the employer that generally affords the employer more control over their behavior than a nonemployee's. In some ways, because nonemployees do not have the same level of accountability, it is more difficult to control their behavior. However, there are ways to influence a similar outcome with volunteers and contractors, primarily through creating contractual obligations that use confidentiality agreements; broadening the application of social media policy to contractors, volunteers, and interns; and incorporating work-for-hire provisions into contractor agreements.

Content Ownership

Copyright protection vests with the creator of original content from the moment of tangible fixation, regardless of the medium of expression.[14] Unlike the employee/employer relationship, work-for-hire doctrine is not automatically applied to works created by volunteers or contractors.

- *Volunteers*: "Work for hire" may not apply to volunteers. In 1989, the U.S. Supreme Court rejected the position that the "term 'employee' refers only to formal, salaried employees."[15] As tempting as it may be to apply this singular statement to volunteers, there has been no further case law on this point and so there is no clear answer to this question. However, in the context of volunteer content contributed to the museum's social media account(s), it is reasonable to look to the previously recommended terms of use to determine ownership.

- *Contractors*: Contractors are paid in return for provision of services and the relationship is generally captured by written agreement. Museums should incorporate work-for-hire provisions into agreement with contractors. If included in the contract, the work-for-hire provision would alleviate much of the doubt regarding ownership of contractor-produced content, including for social media. The work-for-hire language is not fail proof,[16] so in cases where there are specific circumstances that give rise to doubt, the museum should consult with an attorney experienced in copyright law to make a more finite determination on ownership.

Statements of Opinion on Personal Social Media Pages

Contractors and volunteers may be required to sign confidentiality agreements prior to beginning their service. Statements made by contractors and volunteers on personal pages that breach confidentiality may be actionable. However, statements of opinion on personal web pages are likely beyond the control of the museum unless the statements are false or otherwise so egregious that they would lead to a claim of defamation.

Museums often rely very heavily on volunteers to operate. Volunteers can be a transient workforce: they come and go, sometimes without much warning. It may be convenient to charge volunteers and interns with social media maintenance but there is often very little oversight. The museum should closely monitor volunteer and intern activity on the account(s), including updates and content additions.

OTHER PRACTICAL CONSIDERATIONS

In addition to the legal considerations discussed above, there are many practical considerations to think of when engaging in social media.

Manpower and Time Management: Maintaining a successful social media presence is an incredibly time-consuming venture, and caring for these accounts properly can easily be a full-time job for multiple people. Designate a staff person to manage the social media platform(s) and recognize that it is more work than it appears. This person should *not* be a temporary person, like an intern or a volunteer, but rather someone who is reliable and has demonstrated commitment to the museum.

Social Media Account Access: This area is one of the most overlooked but crucial aspects. If you cannot access your social media platform(s) you have no control over any of the issues discussed in this essay and social media suddenly becomes a big liability. Perhaps the person who either sets up, maintains, or administers the account(s) leaves the museum and fails to leave the necessary access information, which includes user names and passwords, as well as the e-mail address and corresponding e-mail account access with which the social media account is linked. Please note, this recommendation does not involve requesting access information to personal e-mail accounts. In fact, under no circumstances should a museum social media account be linked to a personal e-mail account. This might be challenge for smaller museums and cultural institutions; if so, consider creating a separate e-mail account for social media management.

FINAL THOUGHTS

- Stay involved with both the creation and maintenance of social media accounts.
- Put a staff member in charge of social media management.
- Use a museum e-mail address for social media accounts. Notifications and lost password access links are sent to this e-mail.
- Create and implement a thoughtful social media policy.
- Maintain a record of user names and passwords for each social media account.
- Utilize an exit interview process for those who have access to or maintain the accounts and include a request for the most current access information for each social media platform.

NOTES

1. "The 2014 Nonprofit Social Network Benchmark Report," NTEN: Nonprofit Technology Network, April 9, 2014, www.nten.org/research/the-2014-nonprofit-benchmarks-study, last accessed July 21, 2014.

2. *4th Annual Nonprofit Social Network Benchmark Report*, www.Nonprofit SocialNetworkSurvey.com, 2012, www.nten.org/sites/default/files/2012_nonprofit_social_networking_benchmark_report_final.pdf, last accessed July 21, 2014.

3. C. Chasin, S. Ruth, and R. Harper, *Tax Exempt Organizations and World Wide Web Fundraising and Advertising on the Internet*, Internal Revenue Circular, EO CPE Text, 2000.

4. "ABATax: Comments on Use of Internet by Exempt Organizations—I," American Bar Association website, 2001, www.americanbar.org/groups/taxation/policy/public_policy/2001_0102cmt2000_84irs_1.html, last accessed July 22, 2014.

5. "Request for Comments regarding Need for Guidance Clarifying Application of the Internal Revenue Code to Use of the Internet by Exempt Organizations Announcement 2000–84," 2000, IRS, www.irs.gov/pub/irs-tege/a2000_84.pdf, last accessed July 22, 2014.

6. See "Responding to Public Feedback on Social Media" later in this essay for suggestions regarding this inquiry.

7. "Request for Comments Regarding Need for Guidance," 2000.

8. *4th Annual Nonprofit Social Network Benchmark Report*, 2012.

9. "Truth in Advertising," Federal Trade Commission website, www.ftc.gov/news-events/media-resources/truth-advertising, last accessed July 26, 2014.

10. National Institute of Standards and Technology, U.S. Department of Commerce, Special Publication 800-122.

11. 17 U.S.C. §102.

12. 17 U.S.C. § 101.

13. National Labor Relations and Social Media website provides a very nice summary of the NLRB's role in social media in the workplace as well as general counsel memos containing discussions of recent cases that the museum may find helpful. www.nlrb.gov/news-outreach/fact-sheets/nlrb-and-social-media, last accessed August 4, 2014.

14. 17 U.S.C. §102.

15. *Community for Creative Non-Violence v. Reid*, 490 US 730, at 742, FN 8 (1989).

16. U.S. Copyright Office, *Works Made for Hire* Circular, 09/2012.

Chapter Eighteen

Digital and Information Technology in Museums

Katherine E. Lewis

Digital and information technology have become deeply integrated into the museum experience, although this is a not new phenomenon. Technology has been a part of the museum experience for a long time: audio tour guides have been used in museums since the 1950s[1] and incorporating video and sound as well as other digital media into exhibitions and collections has become standard practice. So, what kind of technology are we talking about? We are referring to the recent digital and information revolution, marked by a dramatic increase and integration of computers, communications technology, and the Internet into the museum visitor experience and operations.

Museums have typically been very traditional and conservative institutions and are not usually on the forefront of technological innovation, for good reason. Museums do not generally possess the financial or personnel resources to assume or mitigate the risks associated with uncertain technological market endeavors. As nonprofits and public stewards of precious collections that represent an important part of humanity's collective knowledge, history, and identity, museums have a strong interest in avoiding risk in order to protect their nonprofit status and their public reputations. Yet, lately we see these risk-adverse institutions inching out, sticking their toes into the tech water, testing the temperature, and coming up with some very interesting applications.

Perhaps coinciding with the recession, as museums anxiously anticipated possible tax code reforms that threatened to impact charitable donations and competed for visitors at a time when people were not traveling as much and not able to afford museum admissions as readily, there has been a distinct increase in focus on the interactive museum experience. In this climate, museums consider new ways to galvanize attendance, to demonstrate their value to a public increasingly dependent on interactive digital-content delivery, and to make their collections and programming accessible to those unable to travel to the museum in person.

How do you engage a visitor remotely, demonstrate your value, and interest them in the museum collection? Is it possible to turn that interest into a donation or contribution in lieu of or in addition to an admission? These are the types of questions that this author believes sparked the museums' interest and spurred them to explore deeper tech integration into the expression and fulfillment of their mission.

Recognizing the importance of developing digital and information technology,[2] museums have begun hiring digital media staff and some have entire departments dedicated to digital media. These departments are writing software, developing new technologies, and working with curators and museum staff to leverage social media, digitize collections, acquire and care for digital works, create new user interfaces and interactive exhibit experiences, and integrate technology into the back-of-house operations and customer management systems, similar to the SMART Museum project at the Tech Museum of Innovation in San Jose, California.[3]

For purposes of this essay, references to interactive exhibits are limited to discussion of those exhibitions or exhibition elements that have digital and IT elements, including those which collect user information or enable user-generated content, as opposed to participatory exhibitions that enable users to engage physically with the exhibit object or experience but relay little or no information.[4] There is certainly overlap: an interactive exhibition may include participatory elements; however, a strictly participatory exhibition would raise different legal concerns than one with interactive elements, including personal injury, waivers, and liability considerations—all important topics to discuss with an attorney, but not included in the scope of this essay.

This essay explores a variety of legal considerations arising in the context of digital and information technology at museums—both through the development and implementation of interactive digital exhibition elements, as well as integration into museum operations (membership, development, collections management, etc.). As software development is the primary vehicle for many of these operations, the discussion will focus on specific legal and practical issues in software-development processes and agreements.

AN INTRODUCTION

Interactive exhibitions often comprise both static and interactive components, which refers both to the exhibit objects on display as well as the components making up the overall visitor experience. Generally, there are both hardware (i.e., televisions, projectors, lights, cameras, interactive tables, etc.) and software components to consider. Hardware components typically involve sourcing the necessary equipment, purchasing, and audiovisual services as required. There may be issues of warranties and representations to consider when purchasing hardware, but we will not address those considerations. Rather, we will look to the legal and practical issues involved in purchasing and developing software for interactive exhibitions, including mobile applications, and museum operations.

PROPRIETARY SOFTWARE PURCHASE

Turning first to considerations in purchasing software from a third party for use in the museum, what follows is an overview, rather than an exhaustive list, of the terms that are of particular importance in any software service and license agreement. For clarity, we are referring to preexisting software that can be purchased from a third party, not software that has been developed by a third party for the museum.

Regardless of the relative size of the software company to the museum, it is always worth (1) reading the software terms of service and license agreements, (2) identifying terms and provisions the museum would like to negotiate, and (3) approaching the software company to ask for clarification where needed and to request modifications to the language. Do not assume that these agreements are nonnegotiable. The software company should be willing to hear out the museum's concerns and address them in the agreement.

1. *Research the Proprietor.* One of the most challenging aspects of integrating digital and information technology into the museum is its sustainability. It may be tempting to purchase software from a start-up tech company, especially when bombarded daily by media coverage of the many successful start-up stories, but look past the immediate gain to the long-term future and sustainability of the company producing the software. In the event the company is sold or goes under, what will happen to the software product the museum purchased and integrated into its systems? How will maintenance and updates be handled? Funding can be unreliable and having to implement a new software solution for a failed program may be very costly, especially taking into consideration possible data migration and implementation costs.

2. *What the Museum Is Purchasing.* The purchase of a software product does not necessarily come with a physical by-product (i.e., a software CD); rather, the purchaser often makes the transaction online and

downloads the software license directly to a computer. The purchase is confined to the download and license to use the software. Once purchased, a license or access key is usually sent by the licensor (the company who sells the software) to the licensee (the person or entity making the purchase) via e-mail and the user registers the product online.

3. *Fee Structure.* The fee structure is typically a flat fee for the initial purchase and an annual license fee. If the software company will be providing support and assistance with data migration and implementation, there will be additional fees. There may be added fees for annual maintenance and customer service plans.

4. *Term.* Many software licenses have autorenewal clauses, meaning the license is based on an annual term that renews every year automatically without any action required by either party. Depending on the software program, the intended use in the museum (including consideration of the short- or long-term anticipated use of the program), the museum might consider requesting a set term (six months, one year, etc.) with written notice of intent to renew the agreement on a mutually agreeable timeline (i.e., forty-five days prior to the end of the one-year term). This solution may not be practical for a long-term integrated software platform that the museum will likely use for the foreseeable future, like The Museum System (TMS) software, but it may be appropriate for smaller software programs that are only anticipated for use for the duration of a single exhibition or display.

5. *Internal or External Hosting.* Where will the software live, on an internal museum server or an external, third-party server? Depending on the type of data the software will collect, this question may have greater significance as part of an overall risk analysis. If the program will be collecting users' personal information (i.e., name, address, e-mail, etc.) or information that, in the aggregate, might be used to identify an individual, and it is hosted externally on a third-party server, the museum would want to take more care in understanding the terms of the software and service agreement, specifically with regard to procedures for data breaches, encryption requirements, and breach notice provisions. If the company is hosting or responsible for hosting, their ability to disclaim certain warranties is also reduced, which leads us into our next item.

6. *Warranties and Representations.* Simply put, a "warranty" is a promise that a fact is true and a further promise to indemnify the injured party if the fact is proven not to be true. For example, a software company might warrant that its software does not infringe on third-party rights. If that is later proven to be false, and the software infringes on copyright, the company would be required to indemnify the

museum. A "representation" is a statement of present or past fact that induces one party to enter into the agreement. A similar statement of noninfringement may also be called a "representation"; however there is no accompanying indemnification requirement if it later turns out the representation was false. It is common for most software licenses to come "as is" and disclaim all warranties, expressed or implied. These provisions are not usually negotiable, but depending on what the museum wants to use the software for and the proprietor's flexibility, the museum may be able to negotiate more favorable provisions.

7. *Limitation of Liability.* Many software licenses include a limitation of liability clause that usually limits to the cost of the product or some exponent thereof (i.e., three times the cost of the product license) any damages the company might pay to the museum for a failure of the product. The museum should consider whether this is appropriate based on the data it will input into the software system and the financial harm that would come to the museum if the software system failed either temporarily or permanently. If the museum paid $2,000 for the software, consider whether that would be a trivial amount in light of the risk. These provisions can be negotiated for more favorable terms.

8. *Indemnification.* Indemnification is a guarantee to pay the other party for loss or damage occurring in the future. There should be an indemnification provision in the terms and conditions promising that the company will indemnify the purchaser/licensor against any and all third-party claims of infringement. After all, the museum did not write the software and its purchase and use of the software should be protected.

SOFTWARE DEVELOPMENT

After much research, it may be that there is nothing on the market that accomplishes what the museum needs—not at all surprising in the context of exhibition content development. Many museums work with independent contractors to develop software to accomplish the goals of the particular museum, although as mentioned earlier, museums are beginning to staff software developers and digital media staff.

The challenge in software development, especially from a contracting perspective, is that many times, the museum may know generally what it would like the software to do, but these goals may change quickly to keep pace with the consuming public and the museum may not have a defined concept of the end product. Software development can be a challenging process and there are generally two methodologies, each with its own positives and negatives. What follows is a review of the two methods, descrip-

tions of the positives and negatives of each, and some suggestions on determining which methodology is best for your situation.

SOFTWARE DEVELOPMENT METHODOLOGIES:
WATERFALL AND AGILE

Waterfall Methodology

The traditional approach to software development is known as the "Waterfall
approach" and is a highly structured and linear approach to developing software. It originated in the manufacturing and construction industries.[5] This
approach is very methodical and assumes completion of one task before
advancing to the next. The typical Waterfall trajectory is as follows:[6]

1. Concept Development;
2. System Requirements;
3. Design: design software architecture and determine how to fit the new
   product into the existing architecture;
4. Implementation: software writing/"coding";
5. Testing; and
6. Maintenance.

From a legal perspective, the positives include that there is early consensus between the parties on exactly what will be delivered and when. This is
highly desirable because it leaves little room for interpretation and possible
disagreement down the road. Another positive is that under this methodology, the deliverables are clearly defined, making it very easy to measure
performance and progress against the terms of the contract.

Practically speaking, under the Waterfall methodology, museum staff typically devote less time to managing and participating in the development
process; thus meetings with the contractor are less frequent, allowing museum staff to attend to their other duties. Also, because the project has been
fully planned and thoughtfully executed from beginning to end, with many
variables having been vetted early in the process, the resulting product is
generally very well developed.

There really aren't too many legal negatives for museums under the Waterfall approach if only because the technical requirements, deliverables, payment schedules, and project management process are typically so well-de-
fined that disputes over interpretation are rare. The two likely areas of fric-
tion are (1) the museum is so dissatisfied with the end product that they
refuse to accept the final delivery, or (2) if there are changes required to the
requirements necessitating amendments to the contract, these often result in

additional and significant fees, depending upon how far along in the process the requirements change. Other possible negatives include

1. Software development is a highly specialized service area and museums do not typically have staff familiar enough with the nuances to draw up a comprehensive set of technical requirements.
2. The museum may have a goal in mind of what the software should accomplish and (perhaps) generally how the finished product should look and function, but the specifications document (usually voluminous document[s] with lots of technical language) make it difficult to visualize whether the specifications actually capture the result sought.
3. There may be prolonged periods of time between opportunities for the museum to view and test the software, during which time the museum needs may change and the developers may encounter challenges beyond their control (e.g., incompatibilities between systems requiring changes to the requirements).
4. Deviations from the established requirements can be made but are discouraged because they typically result in additional time and fees. If there is a change in the requirements, there is a resulting need to begin the workflow process (i.e., the "Waterfall") again.

The Waterfall methodology does not allow much flexibility and can take a long time to produce a finished product, by which time the technology it was based upon may be obsolete. Additionally, by the time the "new interactive experience" is ready for public consumption, the technology may be outdated and possibly uninteresting to the museum visitors. Wasted time and resources and perhaps worse, an experience that discourages future software development efforts!

Agile Methodology

"Agile methodology" is somewhat of a misnomer because it describes more of a philosophy than a methodology.[7] It is a reactionary approach to software development born of frustration with the Waterfall method. Agile acknowledges and embraces a basic truth of software development: requirements change. The process is intended to be highly customizable to the project at hand and highly flexible to accommodate evolving concepts. A primary objective of Agile is that at each iteration of the process, working software is developed. This is a stark contrast to the Waterfall method, where working software may not be delivered until much later and with far less opportunity for museum engagement and input along the way. The "Agile Manifesto" is as follows:

Individuals and interactions over processes and tools
Working software over comprehensive documentation
Customer collaboration over contract negotiation
Responding to change over following a plan. [8]

Agile implementation can take a variety of forms, similar in a way to how Waterfall can have a variety of phases depending on the complexity of the project. The following description is for illustrative purposes only and not intended to be interpreted as the "best" approach to Agile development; rather it is an example to help museum professionals understand the process in order to allow for suggestions on how to adequately protect the interests of both the museum and the developer. The terms described below give an overview of the elements in Agile development; they generally happen in the order described and then repeat as many times as necessary to complete the software development project to museum satisfaction. There are many undefined terms not captured here, so it is recommended that for a more in-depth review of the process, the museum seek out additional information to learn more.

Some Agile terminology definitions include

Product Backlog. Similar in some respects to a requirements document, but not nearly as comprehensive. Think of this as a list, in no particular order, of everything that needs to be done. If an item is higher on the product backlog, it has a higher priority. Priority is determined by the museum. This is the most important document in the development process and must be constantly updated and prioritized.

Sprint Planning Meeting. The first "sprint" planning meeting will identify priorities from the product backlog that will be treated in the first sprint (a two-week period during which the team works through items identified in this meeting to produce a functional product).

Sprint Backlog. A smaller list of items identified during the sprint planning meeting that defines the work product for the sprint.

Product Backlog Grooming. Opportunity to continually update the timeline and priorities of the product backlog.

Sprint Review Meeting. At the conclusion of the sprint, the team meets to review the sprint backlog, or the work completed and the product produced as a result of the sprint.

Scrum. Daily developer meet-ups (ten to fifteen minutes) for the duration of the sprint. Opportunity to raise issues and provide quick updates to one another (i.e., what was done yesterday, what is being done today, what will be done tomorrow). This is merely an update, not a forum to resolve issues.

With an Agile approach, because the requirements are not fully developed at the beginning and because they are subject to so many iterations of change, it can be very difficult to predict how long a particular project might last or how much it will cost. It can also be difficult to measure success objectively, again because of the lack of requirements. This type of uncertainty keeps transactional lawyers up at night. Just imagine, going to your attorney, or even pitching the idea to the museum director, and telling him or her that you have this great idea about a bit of software that will help the museum accomplish XYZ goal, but you don't really know what it will look like, how long it will take to complete, or how much it will cost.

Regardless of the lack of traditional framework of a solid software development agreement, the undeniable truth seems to be that this approach is yielding better results and happier museums. A happy museum is not likely to make breach-of-contract claims. Regardless, just because few disputes arise, does not mean that none will, or that your museum should be the test case. Therefore, what follows are a few suggestions to consider as you draft your Agile software development agreement.

1. *Acknowledge and agree to use of the Agile methodology.*
2. *Describe, to the best of your ability, what the Agile process looks like for your project.* This means, essentially, determining how your project will be managed and run day to day. For example, the process described above is one way to approach Agile development, but there are likely others depending on the company contracted. The museum may need to rely on the software developer to recommend an appropriate Agile strategy.
3. *Define the terms used.* Agile is a just that—agile, changing, evolving, and open to interpretation. Sprints may last for two weeks for some projects and three for others. Scrums may be daily or every other day, depending on the project. "Scrum masters" may not always be implemented.
4. *Identify key personnel and project roles.* Identify team members in the museum and the developer's company and determine each person's role in the sprint planning meetings, sprint reviews, scrums, product backlog grooming, and so forth. The museum level of commitment in this process is exponentially greater than in the Waterfall methodology, so the museum needs to understand fully what is expected. This process only works if all parties are engaged fully at almost every level; it is a highly collaborative process. That being said, it's not likely that the museum would participate in the daily scrum.
5. *Identify the key project documentation methods and deliverables.* The use of velocity charts and burndown charts is common in Agile, as is issue management software (e.g., Jira), which captures and tracks the

complete life of the project. This information can be exported into Excel (.xls) files or comma separated value (.csv) files. Perhaps the sprint review meetings will be summarized in PowerPoint (.ppt) files. The museum should be looking for this level of project management and should expect the developer to deliver this documentation upon request or at agreed-upon intervals. For example, perhaps the Power-Point files are delivered the day prior to the sprint review meeting, while the export files are delivered upon termination.

6. *Determine agreed-upon methods to predict term and cost.* While it can be difficult at the beginning of the project to estimate the length of time it will take to deliver the finished product and the cost, there are ways to make fairly reliable predictions of both after the conclusion of the first three or four sprints. By this time, the team should know enough about working with one another and the elements of the product that a velocity chart can be used to predict time and thus cost. In your contract, provide for a period of review for the developer to submit a velocity chart and review as a group. Amend the contract accordingly.

7. *Work product and ownership.* The contract should provide for museum ownership of all intellectual property and deliverables produced at each sprint. This is for several reasons:

   a. The product of each sprint and of the ultimate project is a work for hire. The museum pays for the service to create the product and has an expectation that the museum will own the resulting product.

   b. These forms of documentation are invaluable to the museum, especially while the project is ongoing. In the event the project is halted for a period of time or the museum terminates the contract with one developer and engages with another, these files capture a snapshot of the project progress, issues, and possible solutions. Without them, the museum may have to start from scratch.

8. *Termination.* Work with one another to determine whether and under what circumstances a party may terminate.

   a. Should the museum be able to terminate after a sprint review that demonstrates a clear failure of synthesis or success? Or should it be after a series of sprints?

   b. What happens if the project goes wrong? What does an opportunity to cure look like in Agile development? The answer to these questions is going to come from discussion between the museum and the developer.

c. May a party terminate for convenience?
d. What notice period is reasonable for termination?
e. What work product and documentation is delivered to the museum upon termination?

Which Approach Is Right for Your Museum?

Both approaches have positives and negatives. The decision on which to use may depend on the preference and availability of the museum project manager, the size of the project, the project schedule, the museum's tolerance for cost increases, and the specificity with which the museum knows how it wants the software to function. Regardless of the approach, the goal should be to have an agreement that clearly defines the relationship, the methodology, and goals, and defines deliverables.

INTELLECTUAL PROPERTY OWNERSHIP

In either Agile or Waterfall methodologies, the museum and developer should discuss and agree to all matters relating to intellectual property (IP) ownership. There are typically two categories of IP ownership that should be addressed in your software development contract: preexisting IP and newly created IP.

"Intellectual property" is broadly defined as creation born of the mind. "Intellectual property rights" are creations of the mind that are protected by law: copyright, trademark, trade secret, patent law, or some combination of one or more. In the context of software development, IP rights are commonly protected under copyright law.

"Preexisting IP" refers to intellectual property that was created and in existence before the software development project began. It could be software that was developed by a third party (this includes open-source software) and previously written software created by the developer the museum has engaged. It is common for the parties to agree that, to the extent the developer uses or incorporates preexisting software of its own into the product, the developer retains ownership of that IP. Where the developer uses or incorporates preexisting third-party software (not open source) in the product, the developer should be responsible for obtaining all necessary rights to use the copyrighted works and should warrant and represent that they have the necessary rights.

In the case of open-source software the developer should be responsible for ensuring the open-source terms and conditions are compatible with the anticipated use of the product and should deliver to the museum a summary of all implicated third-party licenses and open-source obligations, including any restrictions. For example, some open-source licenses require developers to release the resulting product under the same open-source license as the original work. This type of restriction may be completely incompatible with the museum policy. Furthermore, it may be in conflict with a restriction from other third-party software drawn upon for the same project.

Lastly, the agreement should provide an indemnification provision in which the software developer agrees to indemnify the museum in the event there are any third-party claims of intellectual property infringement.

"Newly created IP" refers to intellectual property that was not previously in existence, but was created as a result of the contract. For example, the code and documentation produced throughout the term of the contract. As discussed earlier, IP generated by the contract should be treated as a work for hire and owned by the museum. The museum is paying for the creation of the product; it is therefore correct that the museum retains ownership of both the work product and finished product. This is fairly standard in software development contracts when the product has been commissioned by the museum to achieve a particular purpose.

There may be more complex relationships, for example where the museum collaborates with the software developer to produce a product with application beyond the museum experience. In this instance, the developer may want to retain an ownership interest in the newly created IP. Consult with an attorney to determine what relationship is appropriate and to make sure that the museum is protected by the proper warranties, representations, and indemnifications necessary to mitigate as much risk as possible. Remember: sharing IP rights means sharing the risk.

FINAL THOUGHTS

One final caution: the use of software in interactive exhibits with functionality enabling the collection and storage of user information and/or enabling the creation of user-generated content, deserves careful legal consideration. It may be wise to consult with an attorney in the early stages of development, especially if using the Waterfall methodology (because it may result in changes to the requirements), to determine what, if any, warnings, notices, or policy statements need to be incorporated into the software to inform the visiting public.

NOTES

Special thanks to A. J. Carrasco for his expertise and insights on agile implementation and project management.

1. Tallon, Loic, "About That 1952 Sedelijk Museum Audio Guide, and a Certain Willem Sandburg," Musematic, May 19, 2009, musematic.net/2009/05/19/about-that-1952-sedelijk-museum-audio-guide-and-a-certain-willem-sandburg/, last accessed August 2, 2014. The Sedelijk Museum Amsterdam incorporated handheld audio guides beginning in 1952 that were developed by Philips, the Dutch electronics company, and had initially been used by the hearing impaired at cinemas.

2. An impressive number of grants are being awarded for the pursuit of digital and information technology advancement in the museums and the arts. A great example is the "SMART Museum" initiative at the Tech Museum of Innovation in San Jose, California, which aims to "track visitor engagement, personalize it and extend the learning experience beyond the museum's walls" ("Major Google.org Grant to Help Fund New The Tech Museum 'Smart Museum' Initiative," The Tech Museum of Innovation, December 14, 2011, retrieved from www.thetech.org/about-us/media-room/major-googleorg-grant-help-fund-new-tech-museum-smart-museum-initiative). Los Angeles County Museum of Art (LACMA) recently revitalized a program it began back in the 1967, Art + Technology Lab, which paired artists with technology companies in Southern California, providing grants and in-kind support to "engage in artistic practice with emerging technologies in aerospace, astrophysics, augmented reality, robots and more" (www.lacma.org/lab, last accessed August 2, 2014). The 2014 awardees have been paired with companies like Accenture, SpaceX, DAQRI, and Google (Amy Heibel, "LACMA Launches ART + Technology Lab," Unframed, December 10, 2013, lacma.wordpress.com/2013/12/10/lacma-launches-art-technology-lab/, last accessed August 2, 2014).

3. Museums and Art Law Committee. Section of Science & Technology, American Bar Association, Museums & Technology, live program, June 28, 2014.

4. *Carsten Höller: Experience*, October 26, 2011–January 22, 2012, New Museum, New York.

5. "Waterfall Model," Wikipedia, n.d., en.wikipedia.org/wiki/Waterfall_model, retrieved August 2, 2014.

6. There are several variations on the Waterfall approach that include steps for gathering the requirements, documentation, different levels of testing, and so forth. This is a generalized version of the overall process used for demonstrative purposes.

7. "Manifesto for Agile Software Development," 2001, agilemanifesto.org/, last accessed August 3, 2014.

8. *Id.* Items on the left are valued more than those on the right.

Chapter Nineteen

Crowdfunding for Museums

Alyssa L. Reiner, Esq.

WHY CROWDFUNDING?

In an era marked by coinciding economic recession and growth in annual visitor attendance,[1] museums and cultural institutions are becoming increasingly strategic about developing revenue growth via increasing membership numbers and private donations, rather than by relying on ever more uncertain corporate sponsorship and government funding.[2] The reality of cultivating more members, and more private donors, is that museums have to find new audiences for their messages, and to send those messages out to greater numbers of people and with greater frequency.

The digital revolution of the twenty-first century has enabled a major shift in the way museums employ technology and the Internet to communicate with the audiences they target. Museums have added Facebook pages, tweets, and Instagram posts to their toolkit of marketing and promotional activities. The shift toward e-mail for membership solicitations and advocacy and fundraising messages has dramatically reduced the need for frequent paper mailings to cultivate new members and donors. Electronic communication has not only increased the sheer numbers of people the museum can reach with its message, but also has provided a new tool to facilitate engagement with a generation of potential supporters who rely on technology for information and communication in a way their predecessors did not, and who may have been invisible to older, more traditional cultivation tactics. The Internet and mobile technology allow museums to reach out to the "digital natives" of the millennial generation—that culturally influential demographic born after 1980,[3] the first generation to grow up during the age of the Internet.

Crowdfunding, or fundraising by using the Internet or a similar network, looks like an ideal tool to reach large numbers of new, eager-to-be-engaged, potential donors from the "coming of age" millennial generation; millennials are avid users of social media.[4] Combining the attributes of "traditional" social media like Facebook and Twitter (whereby the user identifies his or her areas of interest; finds or follows the information, friends, and organizations that feed his or her interests; and then may choose to actively seek out opportunities to lend support to those interests),[5] and of e-mail fundraising campaigns (in which the museum identifies a very broad potential target audience for solicitations through e-mail and mailing list cultivation, and sends them direct, electronic mass mailings, which may not be positively received),[6] crowdfunding platforms draw audiences who self-identify as generally interested in project- or cause-based philanthropy, and afford museums the opportunity to "pitch" directly to a receptive audience.

WHAT EXACTLY IS CROWDFUNDING?

"Crowdfunding" is defined as the "practice of funding a project or venture by raising many small amounts of money from a large number of people, typically via the Internet."[7] Crowdfunding platforms operate via public-facing websites, which generally aggregate projects or causes in a user-friendly, eye-catching, and readily searchable manner. Sites may curate the projects they select for promotion in order to ensure that they meet site guidelines or the site's mission, or they may allow any individual or organization to initiate a request for funding. Once registered with the site, fund-seekers upload what effectively boils down to a marketing package for their projects—describing their goals, and "selling" the benefits associated with funding or participating in them.

There are two types of crowdfunding platforms, one based on an investment model, and one based on a model of donation or philanthropy. The investment or debt/equity model of crowdfunding, exemplified by such sites as AngelList and Crowdfunder.com, solicits financial backers for business start-up projects. With some variations in how the investments are solicited, managed, and applied, the basic model is the same. Backers pledge a financial investment for a stake in a business start-up; they anticipate (or at least hope for) a return on their investment as a result of the eventual success of the business, but they face the very real possibility of losing their entire investment if the business fails. This model has an extremely high level of inherent risk, and is therefore accordingly on the brink of federal regulation by the Securities and Exchange Commission.[8] Investment model crowdfunding platforms aren't appropriate for, and in fact expressly prohibit, cause-based, charitable projects.

REWARD- AND DONATION-BASED PLATFORMS

When thinking about employing crowdfunding for museums, the relevant model to consider is the donation-based platform. Sites that employ this model include Kickstarter.com, and Indiegogo.com. Within this model, platforms generally fall into two categories: project or rewards based, and cause or donation based. Kickstarter is a well-known, project-based crowdfunding platform, where project creators run funding campaigns, offering rewards or gifts to backers who pledge a donation. Kickstarter loosely curates projects; it reviews each one that's uploaded to ensure that it's a creative project in one of thirteen acceptable categories such as art, film and video, and technology, and to ensure that it has a defined, finite goal. The site also highlights aggregate pages that group projects by "featured creative communities,"[9] or individual and organizational creators that are particularly active on the site. This degree of curation enables potential backers to readily identify projects that pique their interests, but does not entail any vetting or endorsement of the likelihood of success of any particular project.

Kickstarter (through its terms of use)[10] expressly prohibits any general "causes" from seeking funding through its platform, in favor of discrete "projects." Museums can't use Kickstarter or another similar platform as a broad means to fund their missions or even their ongoing capital campaigns. Practically speaking, what this means is that Kickstarter may be a useful tool for a museum to fund a particular project or event (such as an exhibit, public program, or publication) with clear goals or benchmarks for success, and that will be completed at some fixed point in time. The Kickstarter project creator sets his or her own funding goal, and his or her campaign deadline, as well as "rewards" offered to funders pledging at certain fixed levels. If, by the campaign completion date, the project reaches or exceeds its funding goal, backers are charged for their pledges, and Kickstarter initiates the process by which the project creator will be paid (less Kickstarter's 5 percent cut of the total raised, as well as third-party payment processor's fees). Conversely, if the project doesn't reach its funding target by the deadline, no backers are charged and the project creator does not receive any money. It's an "all or nothing" approach.

Cause-based donation platforms, which as the description implies enable causes to solicit funds for their overall support rather than for discrete projects, typically do not maintain the strict "all or nothing" approach of Kickstarter and its ilk. Campaign creators may choose the "all or nothing" funding model, or they may choose to allow for flexible funding. Using the flexible funding approach, campaign creators may keep any money they raise by the conclusion of the campaign period. Indiegogo is an example of a cause-based donation platform that offers both fixed (all or nothing) and flexible funding options. For good and bad, it's a broadly inclusive crowdfunding platform.

Its campaigns are not curated at all except to the degree that they are organized into twenty-four categories on the site. Any individual and any organization can turn to a site like Indiegogo for (noninvestment) funding, from 501(c)3 registered nonprofits whose missions are to provide international humanitarian aid, to children as young as thirteen (with parental consent) looking to raise money for a school trip. Indiegogo and other cause-based platforms highlight what may be very loosely (depending on the platform) characterized as charitable causes (basically any request for funding that does not come with a debt or equity stake in the outcome), and allow backers to identify and contribute to campaigns, rather than projects, which align with their interests. As with the project-based platforms, the cause-based platforms typically employ a third-party payment processor to charge backers either when the fixed funding campaign is successfully completed, or for a flexibly funded campaign, at the moment the backer pledges a contribution.

BASIC PRACTICAL CONSIDERATIONS

It's tempting to view crowdfunding campaigns as a relatively low-cost, low-risk, and low-effort means to engage a new generation of museum donors. The decision to crowdfund, however, is not without the need for careful consideration. While most of the popular donation-based platforms (regardless of the model) have a ready audience, streamlined organization, and easy "one-click" methods to complete payment, campaigns remain, at a fundamental level, reliant on traditional models of donor development in order to succeed. On the more robust sites, at any given time there are thousands of active campaigns competing for funding. Add to that information overload facing potential donors the number of fundraising requests concurrently landing in their e-mail in-boxes[11] and competing for their attention. It's not enough for museums to take a passive approach to a crowdfunding campaign.

Museums need to drive potential donors to their campaigns, and give them reasons to support their campaign rather than any of the other projects or causes clamoring for their attention. In order for crowdfunding efforts to be successful, they should be approached in much the same thorough and deliberate manner as traditional fundraising campaigns. Goals need to be realistic and balanced against costs (in staff time, outreach expenses, marketing costs, and the opportunity cost of not using that staff and those funds to pursue other means to raise money), and museums shouldn't anticipate a financial windfall.[12]

It's critical to have an active, interested donor base likely to follow the museum to the crowdfunding site, rather than rely solely on existing site users and the hope that a campaign goes viral. Museums should employ tactics like building e-mail lists and sending campaign information directly to potential donors, sharing information and links on social media networking sites like Facebook and Twitter, and broadcasting marketing "pitch" videos through channels like YouTube. And just as traditional fundraising campaigns can reach a saturation point with targeted donors, so too can crowdfunding activities. Ultimately, museums should be aware that crowdfunding campaigns are probably not the easy route to immediate, significant fundraising windfalls, but rather that they may be one additional tool to engage a new audience—thus sowing the seeds for future fundraising successes.

LEGAL CONSIDERATIONS

Once the museum determines that a crowdfunding campaign is a good fit for its promotional and fundraising activities, the analysis isn't complete; there are a number of legal implications that must be considered. First, it's critical to understand the way the relationship between platform, donor, and museum is structured. One way to look at a crowdfunding platform is like it's an online dating service for causes—connecting interested campaigns with interested funders. Aside from telling the parties it connects that they have to behave "reasonably," the platform claims no responsibility for what they do on their date. More literally, crowdfunding websites typically stipulate, in considerable detail set forth in their terms of use, that no one can utilize the platform's services for illegal purposes (e.g., drug trafficking), engage in any activities that threaten the functionality of the platform (e.g., uploading software viruses), interfere with anyone else's use of the services, engage in any misleading or abusive behavior, or violate any laws (e.g., intellectual property laws, rights of publicity, etc.).

Crowdfunding websites, however, generally also have very thorough disclaimer and limitation-of-liability provisions that expressly detail platforms' arm's-length relationships with their users. They disclaim their responsibility for any of the content posted on the site (i.e., the accuracy of claims made by campaigns about how funds will be used and the accuracy of claims made by donors that they are capable of paying out their pledges), and any user activities. By setting up an account prior to the launch of a campaign, the museum agrees via click-through agreement that it will not hold the crowdfunding platform liable for any damages the museum sustains as a result of its use of the platform.

This legal distance between the users and operators of the platform, as dictated by the platform, starts to look even more complicated with respect to the legal relationships between the campaign creators and the backers. The platform effectively enables what appears to be a contractual relationship between the creators and the backers, yet it takes very little outward legal

responsibility for that relationship. The basic requirements for a legally binding contract between two parties are the existence of an offer to form a
contractual relationship, evidence of acceptance of that offer, and consideration or benefits to both parties for entering into the contract. The crowdfunding platform enables the museum to make an offer ("fund our project that
promises to enrich thousands of visitors"), the donor to accept ("I accept your
offer to fund the project with a pledge of fifty dollars"), and consideration to
be provided (in exchange for support for the museum's program the museum
gives the backer a tote bag or tickets to the program's opening-day events). It
does not, however, create an explicit legal connection between the parties
whereby each party expressly agrees that it will honor its responsibilities to
the other party or risk breach of contract. In the case of the relationship
between museum and donor, the elements of a contract are present as described, but there is no contract between the parties who are the beneficiaries
of the contract, because the only contracts that exist are between museum and
platform, and between funder and platform.

The missing connection is called "privity of contract." The doctrine of
privity of contract holds that a contract cannot bestow rights or impose obligations on any entity that is not a party to the contract. However, this doctrine is tempered by the concept in contract law of "third-party beneficiaries."[13] A third-party beneficiary is not a party to the contract, but is a recipient of benefits conveyed through the contractual relationship between the
other parties. A third-party beneficiary may sue to legally enforce the
contract between the primary parties, provided the contracting parties have
assented to the other's third-party beneficiary status, or by the third party's
justifiable reliance on the promise of benefit arising from the contract.[14] It is
likely that the museum, at least in the event of a failure by the backer to
complete payment on a pledge, would qualify as a third-party beneficiary to
the contract between the platform and the backer, but it is not certain. As of
the date of publication, there have been no cases testing whether a crowdfunding campaign creates third-party beneficiaries, or whether the terms and
conditions of the platform can limit the right to recover by a third-party
beneficiary.

To further muddy the waters with respect to who has responsibility to
whom in the crowdfunding arena, when the time comes for backers to pay
the amounts they've pledged to the museum's campaign, yet another party
has authority over the transaction, creating even greater distance between the
museum and the funder. Nearly all of the popular crowdfunding platforms
rely on third-party payment processors (e.g., Amazon Payments, PayPal,
etc.) to process credit card transactions. In the instance of Kickstarter, for
example, Amazon Payments acts as its third-party payment processor. While
a campaign is active, backers who make a pledge click through to the site
operated by Amazon Payments (and they are notified that they are navigating

away from Kickstarter and to Amazon), where they enter their credit card payment information, including personally identifiable information that U.S. privacy laws aim to protect from unauthorized disclosure or theft, and that information is held by the payment processor. When the campaign timeline has ended, Kickstarter notifies Amazon Payments that it should process transactions for that campaign, and only then is the backer's credit card charged. Amazon Payments processes the credit card for the pledged amount, subtracts Kickstarter's percentage from that amount, then aggregates all of the pledges for that project and subtracts a percentage for itself from that total. Only once all of the fees are subtracted, and project funds aggregated, does the museum receive payment.

This scheme creates two primary complications. The first complication is that the museum is not really the party collecting payment from the backer, and in the event of any errors in the processing, the museum can't resolve those errors and "fix" the transaction. The result of an error could be either that the backer is never charged and is unaware why, or that the backer is charged, but the museum never receives the money or any record of the pledge. In the case of the latter scenario, the backer might believe that he made a contribution to the museum, but the museum does not acknowledge it, either through the gifts or rewards promised in the campaign, or through the traditional "thank you"/donation receipt letters that follow gifts—resulting in a possible loss of goodwill that, if widespread, could be reputationally damaging.

The second primary complication arising with the use of third-party payment processors is tax related. Donors to a charitable cause or campaign have the right to income tax deductions for their donations. However, because the donor and museum are not engaged directly with one another in the transaction, accounting both for the allowable tax deductions, and for the income actually received, can be quite challenging. Platforms are not consistent with the manner in which they handle tax receipts for charitable donations. Some, like Kickstarter, do not issue receipts directly (or through Amazon Payments) to backers indicating the value of their charitable contributions. Others, like Indiegogo, do issue tax receipts "on the spot" of pledge completion. The Kickstarter model, with no receipt issued and all pledges aggregated by the payment processor, can make it difficult for the museum to ensure that each donor receives the appropriate receipt for his or her tax-deductible contribution—a responsibility that the museum will have to undertake on its own after the conclusion of the campaign. It is also important to note that for campaigns where there is a gift or reward offered at various pledge levels, donors must not claim a tax-deductible contribution for the fair market value of that portion of the pledge. Common practice is that if there is no "fair market" value to a gift—like reserved tickets to an event otherwise also open to the public—there's no deduction for the donor from the value of his or her charitable contribution, but it's advisable to check with legal counsel before informing donors of how to account for the value of rewards.

While they complicate the analysis of the risks versus rewards of crowd-funding, the issues of contract privity, third-party beneficiary status, and third-party payment processors in and of themselves are not indicators that crowdfunding is an objectionably risky financial activity. Failure by an individual backer to complete payment is not likely to result in a loss of more than a few hundred dollars, and conversely with respect to the backer as a beneficiary, failure of the museum to launch its exhibit or program, while disappointing, is not arguably a cause of financial harm at all.

A potentially higher-value (but lower-probability) financial risk to balance is that of intellectual property rights infringements. Campaign materials likely include the museum's trademarked name and logo, and copyrighted content like videos and photographs of exhibit objects; to the extent the museum is looking for funding for an innovative technology or design, a campaign might even involve patents. The terms of use for crowdfunding platforms typically stipulate that the campaign creator may only upload content whose intellectual property rights it owns, or has received permission from the owner to post. The platforms also usually stipulate that by posting such content, the campaign grants the platform rights to use, reproduce, modify, distribute, and otherwise very broadly exploit the content,[15] as well as grant users of the site the rights to exploit the content for personal, non-commercial use. In the event users of the site exploit the museum's copyrighted content (or content the museum uploaded based on permission from a third party) for commercial purposes, the only recourse the museum has against the platform that has effectively enabled the infringement by making the content accessible to the infringer, is to file a notification of infringement with the platform in accordance with the Digital Millennium Copyright Act (DMCA).[16] Remember, however, that the platform has disclaimed its liability to all of its registered users (both campaign creators and backers) such that it is not responsible for any loss or damages arising as a result of its services. Thus if the museum suffers losses either arising from the commercial misappropriation of its own intellectual property, or as a result of a third party's (e.g., the artist of a work in the museum's collections) claim that the copyright it licensed the museum for limited purposes was violated by the platform user, aside from a DMCA action by the platform to remove infringing content from elsewhere on its site, the only avenue for recovery of financial damages for infringement requires successfully suing the infringer for violation of applicable intellectual property laws.

RECOMMENDATIONS

Crowdfunding can be a useful tool for cultivating donors, and for expanding the use of, and capitalizing on, social media for marketing and promotion. The very nature of crowdfunding as an online, social media–based activity, however, can make it easy to jump into without proper due diligence. It's important to review the terms of use offered by any potential platform, and to determine (1) whether the project or cause is inconsistent with the rights and restrictions of that particular platform, and (2) how to plan and organize a campaign in order to minimize any risks associated with the terms of use. While each platform's terms will vary, and each project's need may impact the risk analysis, the following recommendations generally represent good practices.

Before jumping in,

- Determine who will have responsibility for managing any crowdfunding campaign, and ensure that it's someone capable of managing a fundraising campaign generally, not just someone who is comfortable with using social media like Twitter and Facebook.
- Carefully evaluate the outcomes you desire from your project-based or cause-based fundraising efforts, and determine whether a crowdfunding campaign will help to achieve those outcomes or will divert resources from other activities that will support them more effectively.
- Don't launch a crowdfunding campaign prematurely, without an existing online audience for your project that you have developed independently of the platform.

Once you've decided crowdfunding is right for you,

- Thoroughly review the terms of use for any crowdfunding platform under consideration to ensure that your project as envisioned will be compliant with the platform's guidelines (i.e., don't try to fit a cause-based campaign into the model of a project-based crowdfunder).
- Investigate who the third-party payment processor for the platform is, and carefully review its terms and conditions. Pay special attention not only to the payment terms, but also to the privacy policy. You will need to be prepared to react quickly to maintain goodwill with your donors in the unlikely event of a credit card breach.
- Ensure that you take adequate measures to protect your intellectual property and that of third parties entrusted to you. You should either own, or have an express license to, all of the rights you grant the crowdfunding platform with respect to the content you post. Only post content that's in the public domain, that you own outright and have determined is suitable

for widespread online dissemination, and/or for which you have permission from the owners that allows you, as well as the platform, to use the content online for very broad purposes.

- Based upon the platform's and the payment processor's terms and conditions, determine what accounting practices you will implement to handle your receipt and tracking of funds. Also, determine how you will handle the issuing of tax receipts and gift receipt notifications to donors.

When you set up your campaign,

- Consider linking to your website, and your other social media accounts for marketing and reinforcement of your message.
- Consider linking directly to your online privacy policy to disclose how you will retain and utilize any user data made available to you by the donor.
- In a manner consistent with the terms set forth by the platform, clearly indicate the contribution levels that qualify for gifts or rewards, and if possible, include a disclaimer about the amount of each contribution level (taking into consideration the value of the respective reward) that is tax deductible.
- As applicable (based on the process followed by the particular platform) include a disclaimer notifying backers that when they proceed with payment they will be directed to a third-party payment processing site, and that you have no control over the transaction when it reaches that payment processor. Here's an example of language:

> Thank you for your interest in pledging your support to Museum X. When you elect to complete your pledge, you will be directed by Platform Y to the third-party payment processing site operated by Payment Processor Z. Please be aware that you will be providing your payment data (including credit card information and other sensitive or personally identifiable information) directly to Payment Processor Z, and they will issue payment to Museum X upon further instruction from Platform Y. At no time during this process will Museum X have access to information about the status of your payment transaction. In the event of any errors or delays in processing your payment, Museum X will not have the ability to correct those errors, or otherwise assume the processing of your pledge. Please review Payment Processor Z's Privacy Policy and Terms and Conditions before proceeding with your payment; Museum X can't accept any responsibility for any privacy or data-handling risks associated with third-party payment processing, nor can it guarantee delivery of your gift in the event of a processing error that results in your pledge's not being conveyed to Museum X.

After the campaign is launched,

- Be prepared to monitor the platform website to track if and how your intellectual property is being used outside of your own campaign, whether by other users or by the platform itself. If you have any concerns about the use of your intellectual property, you should contact the platform immediately.
- Additionally, be aware of crowdfunding campaigns launched by unaffiliated third parties, which use your name or logo to falsely represent, or imply, an affiliation with you for purposes of increasing contributions or establishing credibility. Take measures as deemed appropriate by your legal counsel to curtail misuse of your trademarks.

NOTES

1. "America's Museums Reflect Slow Economic Recovery in 2012," American Alliance of Museums, 2013, p. 1, www.aam-us.org/docs/research/acme-2013-final.pdf?sfvrsn=2 ("The average increase in museum attendance in 2012 was 4.3 percent, which includes museums that had *fewer* visitors than the year before." Emphasis in original.).

2. *Id.* at 3 ("The exception to the modest revenue revival was support from government at all levels, which continued to drop: just 14 percent of museum reported increases in government support versus declining support at 35 percent of museums. This was on top of widespread declines in government support in 2009, 2010 and 2011.").

3. "Millennials in Adulthood," Pew Research Center, March 7, 2014, p. 6–7, www .pewsocialtrends.org/files/2014/03/2014-03-07_generations-report-version-for-web.pdf.

4. *Id.* (showing that "81 percent of Millennials are on Facebook," and that "[f]ully 55 percent have posted a 'selfie' on a social media site").

5. *M+R: Benchmarks 2014*, 2014, p. 39, mrbenchmarks.com ("For every 1,000 email subscribers, nonprofits have 199 Facebook fans, 110 Twitter follower, 13 mobile subscribers.").

6. *Id.* at 26 ("Average revenue per 1,000 fundraising messages delivered was $17. To put it another way, nonprofits received 1.7 cents for every fundraising message delivered.").

7. Oxford Dictionary of English, 3rd ed., s.v. "crowdfunding."

8. Crowdfunding, 78 Fed. Reg. 66,428 (November 5, 2013) (to be codified at 17 C.F.R. 200). The rules will allow for companies seeking funding to issue securities (debt or equity) to investors, and will require compliance with disclosure requirements and reporting of financial statements to protect against uninformed, high-risk investments.

9. "Discover: Curated Pages," Kickstarter.com, www.kickstarter.com/discover/curated -pages?ref=home_curated, last visited June 5, 2014.

10. "Terms of Use," Kickstarter, www.kickstarter.com/terms-of-use (last visited June 5, 2014).

11. *M+R: Benchmarks 2014*, supra note 5 at 5–6. The average nonprofit e-mail subscriber in December 2013 received seven fundraising messages, and the overall click-through response rate for fundraising messages was just 0.06 percent for the same time period.

12. "Kickstarter Stats," Kickstarter, www.kickstarter.com/help/stats, last visited May 23, 2014. As of May, Kickstarter has raised a total of $1,128,101,033, with total dollars pledged to 62,234 projects. Of those projects, most raise less than $10,000. In addition, 80,902 project were unsuccessful, meaning that the campaigns did not receive any funds from backers because of the "all or nothing" model.

1. See Restatement (First) of Contracts § 133 (1932), for a description of the three classes of third-party beneficiaries: a donee beneficiary if it appears from the terms of the promise in view of the accompanying circumstances that the promise of the promisee

in obtaining the promise of all or part of the performance thereof is to make a gift to the beneficiary or to confer upon him a right against the promisor to some performance neither due nor supposed or asserted to be due from the promisee to the beneficiary;

2. a creditor beneficiary if no purpose to make a gift appears from the terms of the promise in view of the accompanying circumstances and performance of the promise will satisfy an actual or supposed or asserted duty of the promisee to the beneficiary, or a right of the beneficiary against the promisee which has been barred by the Statute of Limitations or by a discharge in bankruptcy, or which is unenforceable because of the Statute of Frauds;

3. an incidental beneficiary if neither the facts stated in Clause (a) nor those stated in Clause (b) exist.

13. See Restatement (First) of Contracts § 133 (1932), for a description of the three classes of third-party beneficiaries:

(a) a donee beneficiary if it appears from the terms of the promise in view of the accompanying circumstances that the promise of the promisee in obtaining the promise of all or part of the performance thereof is to make a gift to the beneficiary or to confer upon him a right against the promisor to some performance neither due nor supposed or asserted to be due from the promisee to the beneficiary; (b) a creditor beneficiary if no purpose to make a gift appears from the terms of the promise in view of the accompanying circumstances and performance of the prom- ise will satisfy an actual or supposed or asserted duty of the promisee to the beneficiary, or a right of the beneficiary against the promisee which has been barred by the Statute of Limitations or by a discharge in bankruptcy, or which is unenforceable because of the Statute of Frauds; (c) an incidental beneficiary if neither the facts stated in Clause (a) nor those stated in Clause (b) exist.

14. Assent to third-party beneficiary status for the campaign creator seems a clearer avenue for the creation of third-party beneficiary status as it is the basic nature of crowdfunding system that the campaign creator is intended to receive funds pledged by backers. In order for a museum to use the concept of detrimental reliance to establish that it is a third-party benefici- ary, it would arguably have to take action based on its anticipated receipt of benefits from the campaign, and that would be both financially risky, as well as difficult to prove given the fact that the project or campaign being funded would be well into its planning stages before crowd- sourcing is appropriate or useful, and funds would have already been received from other sources.

15. Kickstarter.com, *supra* note 10. The terms of use state:

The Company [Kickstarter] will not have any ownership rights over your User Submissions. However, the Company needs the following license to perform and market the Service on our behalf and on behalf of its other Users and itself. You grant to the Company the worldwide, nonexclusive, perpetual, irrevocable, royalty- free, sublicensable, transferable right to (and to allow others acting on its behalf to) (i) use, edit, modify, prepare derivative works of, reproduce, host, display, stream, transmit, playback, transcode, copy, feature, market, sell, distribute, and otherwise fully exploit your User Submissions and your trademarks, service marks, slogans, logos, and similar proprietary rights (collectively, the "Trademarks") in connection with (a) the Service, (b) the Company's (and its successors' and assigns') busi- nesses, (c) promoting, marketing, and redistributing part of all of the Site (and derivative works thereof) or the Service in any media formats and through any media channels (including, without limitation, third-party websites); (ii) take what- ever other action is required to perform and market the Service; (iii) allow its Users to stream, transmit, playback, download, display, feature, distribute, collect, and otherwise use and publish, and permit others to use and publish, the User Submissions, Trademarks, names, likenesses, and personal and biographical materials of you and the members of your group, in connection with the provision or marketing of the Service.

16. Pub. L. No. 105-304, 112 Stat. 2860 (1998) (codified in scattered sections of 17 U.S.C.). The DMCA, which was established to address the challenges of protecting copyright online, safeguards technological measures implemented to prevent unauthorized copying of copyrighted work, and criminalizes the act of circumventing, or creating technology to circumvent, copyright on the Internet. The DMCA establishes notice and takedown procedures that websites must implement in order to address copyright infringements by users of their services.

Chapter Twenty

Rights and Reproduction

The Rapidly Changing Landscape

Julia Courtney and Katherine E. Lewis

The technology age has brought many brilliant applications to the forefront for cultural institutions and museums—beginning with cell-phone tours and increased image availability through collections databases that appear on websites of museums all over the world; touch screen, content, and image-based gallery interactive components; and the newest endeavor, open-source image programs. With the many creative ways museums are using technology to enhance visitor experience, these new open-source programs that museums are implementing on an international scale, are changing the face of research for scholars, art collectors, and students, as well as the public.

According to G. Wayne Clough, secretary of the Smithsonian Institution in Washington, DC, in *The Best of Both Worlds: Museums, Libraries and Archive in the Digital Age*, a handbook published on the Smithsonian Institution's website,

> Today's digital revolution is providing a dizzying array of tools that offer opportunities for learning institutions all over the world to become more vibrant and accessible. This revolution provides the means to share vital information, enabling people to learn more, shape informed opinions, and make decisions in their daily lives. Suddenly everyone can have access to information that previously was only available to the experts. Everyone can take part in the creative processes of institution that once were not even in public view. However, this unprecedented and continuous shift has left many institutions struggling to adapt and is forcing them to rethink how to maintain their unique qualities while at the same time adding value. Today, no organization is immune to the disruptions caused by technological innovation. [1]

Clough queries as to how museums, libraries, and archives can "prepare [themselves] to reach the generation of digital natives who bring a huge appetite—and aptitude—for the digital world?"[2] One strategy has been to hire full-time museum professionals, such as social media managers, digital technology managers, and the like, to assist rights and reproduction specialists in managing images and content for the web. The American Alliance of Museums (AAM) and Museums and the Web, as well as regional museum job databases, post positions, in institutions large and small, similar to those mentioned in increased numbers. Although many rights and reproduction specialists are reluctant to enter this growing area, as they are used to managing images and content on a smaller scale, and in a much more controlled manner, it is the wave of the future.

In response to this new phenomenon from museums, there have been many useful resources brought about by digital entrepreneurs and cultural organizations working to scrutinize public need and qualify and better manage content and images in the digital age. This illustrates the need for information.

The "explosion of the content generation and ease of distribution in the digital realm pose new challenges," said Walter G. Lehmann, who wrote the introduction for the forthcoming *Rights and Reproductions: The Handbook for Cultural Institutions.*[3] As museums work to navigate this new, all-pervasive opportunity, museum professionals who work in the rights and reproduction area are in need of best-practice guidelines and resources with which to successfully direct the trend. According to Lehmann, "rights and reproduction specialists need not become intellectual property lawyers to accomplish their jobs, but they do need accurate and up-to-date resources to help them identify legal issues."[4]

The good news is that help is on the way. Anne Young, of the Indianapolis Art Museum, is editing *Rights and Reproductions: The Handbook for Cultural Institutions*, soon to be published by the American Alliance of Museums (projected for 2015). This publication will bring substantial direction generated from case studies, art and museum law attorneys, and emerging expert museum professionals (who are effectively making image and content resources that only museums can provide) to the forefront via the World Wide Web. It will put forth new information that will assist museum professionals in following newly established best practices in this area and help them to identify potential legal issues and reduce their institution's exposure to risk.[5] According to Young, although many museums have successfully integrated their collections online and are considering executing open-source programs, the National Gallery of Art's NGA Images, Getty's Open Content program, and Yale University Art Gallery are among the forerunners in this newest endeavor, "setting the gold standard of implementing these programs."[6]

This chapter will examine the current approach to rights and reproduction issues in museums, as well as explore the implications of the rapidly changing landscape for museum professionals. Case studies of successful implementations of open-source image programs at the National Gallery of Art, Indianapolis Museum of Art, and the Yale University Art Gallery, will provide guidance on how to best approach this exciting new area of museum work. Museum professionals should consult the upcoming aforementioned publication when it becomes available for a more thorough treatment of this topic.

SEMANTICS

What do we mean when we say "rights and reproductions"? Under U.S. copyright law, copyright protection attaches at the moment an original work is fixed in tangible medium of expression,[7] also referred to as the moment of creation. The creator need not take any additional action in order to benefit from protection of the law. Once a tangible medium of expression is born, no one but its creator may reproduce, distribute, publicly perform, publicly display, or create derivative works[8] based on the original without the permission of the creator. When the term "rights and reproductions" is used, it refers to the process by which one grants and receives the necessary rights to reproduce an image for a particular purpose. Most museums now have staff dedicated to managing this process and web pages on the museum's website dedicated to this topic.

Regardless of how the transaction is made (online or hard-copy application) the act of granting and receiving copyright permissions or licenses is accomplished by contract between at least two parties and therefore has legal consequences for both parties. Depending on the institution, this document may either be called a "contract" or an "agreement." These terms are used interchangeably for the most part and as long as the underlying agreement meets the legal standards for entering a contact, both are legally enforceable instruments.[9]

Contracts may be made orally and in writing, although as a practical matter, it is best practice to treat all agreements and contracts formally and reduce the agreement to writing. This is especially true in instances where the contract governs a common revenue-generating activity that is subject to controversy, like copyright licensing. Note that a "copyright license" is not the same as a "copyright assignment." Be leery of incorporating the word "assignment" in a license agreement, unless it is to make clear that the license is not an assignment.[10]

Rights and reproductions offices will offer two types of agreements: "permissions agreements" and "license agreements." There is a very important distinction between the two: a permissions agreement generally grants permission to the requesting party to use a high-quality reproduction of the image or object, whereas a license agreement grants one or more of the copyrights in the image so that the requestor may use that image in a way that would otherwise violate the Copyright Act.

A permissions agreement generally does not grant a copyright license allowing the requestor the right to reproduce, display, or otherwise use the image. You might wonder why someone would bother to enter into a permissions agreement when they will still need to seek a license to use the image. Often permissions agreements are used for objects and images in museum collections where (1) the ownership is unknown or uncertain, or (2) the museum knows the copyright owner, but does not have the ability to grant a copyright license. While the museum may not have the ability to grant a copyright license, it does have access to the collection enabling it to produce high-resolution images. Therefore, as museums digitize their collections (by photography, 3D scanning, or otherwise) they also become the possessors of very high-quality images that can be reproduced in print publications (books, magazines, etc.), websites, films, or other commercial uses. This is an attractive revenue opportunity for museums, but it is also important to note that, in addition to museums, image houses like VARA, ARS, and Getty Images also issue permissions agreements, theoretically without the corresponding ability to grant an accompanying copyright license.

All too many times, permissions agreements are conflated inappropriately with license agreements. In some instances these hybrids are the standard forms used by a museum, perhaps the result of cobbling together multiple forms from long ago. So how can you tell whether you are getting a copyright license, permission to use a high-resolution image, or both? The main identifying feature of a permissions agreement is that it will generally include a disclaimer that states the granting institution does not warrant or represent they own the copyright and that it is the responsibility of the requesting party to identify third-party copyright owners and secure the necessary permissions to use the image. A permissions agreement will not claim to grant a copyright license.

In contrast, a license agreement will state that the one granting the license (the "licensor") owns the image and all rights associated with the image and grants to the one seeking permission (the "licensee") the right to use the image for the requested purpose. Beware a license agreement that contains a disclaimer similar to one described above as common to permissions agreements. If the licensor represents they have the legal authority to grant a license to the image, there is no legal basis for a disclaimer. Rather, the licensor should be including a representation and warranty that they are either the owner of the copyright or have the authority to grant a license to the licensee.

It is important for both the licensee and the licensor to understand the primary components of the license grant. Generally the license will identify the parties and address the following terms, which are discussed in more detail below:

- *Describe the Licensed Material* (i.e., the image name or catalogue number).
- *Exclusive or Nonexclusive.* The most common type of license in rights and reproductions is "nonexclusive," which means that the granting institution may license the same image to others for any purpose. "Exclusive license" means that the licensee is the only one who can use the copyright(s) granted in the license. Be careful to note that exclusivity can be limited to the specific copyright granted (i.e., display, performance, reproduction, etc.), or it could be an exclusive right to use in a geographic area or language, or an exclusive right to use the work in a specific medium or for a specific length of time.
- *Revocable or Irrevocable.* The most common type of license granted in rights and reproductions is "revocable," meaning that the grantor or licensor may decide at any time to revoke the license. Reasons for revoking a license include the following: the licensee violates the provisions of the license; uses the image beyond the scope of the license; or otherwise uses the image to harm the licensor's reputation. "Irrevocable" means that the license may not be revoked under any circumstances.
- *Royalty or Fees.* Typically rights and reproductions license agreements are royalty-free, although if the request is for commercial consumer product use, royalty rates may be included in the agreement. More commonly, an administrative fee (in the case of the permissions agreement) or a license fee (in the case of a license agreement) is charged per use. Fees are discussed in more depth below.
- *Term.* This refers to the period of time in which the license or permission is granted. It can be calculated by number of days, months, or years; a license may also be for the life of the exhibition or publication, or perpetual, meaning it will never end.
- *Geographic Scope.* The license or permission should include a geographic scope, which tells the requesting party whether they can use the image worldwide, or in a particular country, state, or region.
- *Rights Granted.* The license should clearly state the copyrights being granted (public performance, public display, distribution, reproduction, derivative works).
- *Approved Uses of the Licensed Material.* The license should also clearly identify the approved uses of the licensed materials, including whether commercial use, educational use, Internet and social media use, use in publications, or use in exhibitions and the like are permissible.

In the best of circumstances, a license agreement may be accompanied by delivery of a high-quality reproduction of the image or object, but not necessarily. It will vary based on the institution and the rights and reproduction department resources.

CURRENT TREATMENT OF RIGHTS AND REPRODUCTION

Most rights and reproduction departments help scholars, students, collectors, and other institutions assist those seeking digital and print reproductions of materials from vast collection, and permission to license images for personal, nonprofit, and commercial uses. Examples of these uses include publications, exhibitions, décor, television/film, Internet, and research.

Application Process

The application process usually takes a few weeks but, depending on the institution, can be expedited if circumstances warrant. By providing a thumbnail photograph, the accession number, or other identifying evidence, the inquiring party must identify the image and confirm that it exists in a museum's collection. A permission agreement will then be created upon the payment of usage fees typically detailed by the rights and reproduction specialist in the invoice/estimate. Copyrights and other proprietary rights may subsist in individuals and entities, in which case the customer is typically responsible for securing permission from those parties.

A permission agreement will be generated upon payment of usage fees and permission is not granted until the institution granting permission has countersigned the contract. Although the law may vary by state, generally a contract may only be enforced against the parties who have signed. For this reason, both the licensee and licensor typically sign licenses and permissions agreements because each has very specific legal obligations under the agreement.

As mentioned above, copyrights and other proprietary rights may subsist in individuals and entities other than the museum holding rights to the image, in which case the licensor is responsible for identifying and securing permission from those parties. Some museums will provide reasonable efforts to help the licensor identify who might own the underlying copyright, but they are not required to do so and may not have the resources available to provide assistance.

Onetime, nonexclusive permission to reproduce usually comes with several conditions including the following: that the object images that are reproduced cannot be altered without written permission, the permission-granting institution will approve color proof before the image goes to press, typically two copies of the publication must be provided to the granting institution, and the reproductions will be clearly identified by an appropriate caption and the official credit line of the granting institution, and permission fees are paid prior to usage of image in projects.

Normal turnaround is usually a few weeks after payment is received and, for a surcharge, a rush service is available in most cases. Images are usually provided in digital format in at least 300 dots per inch (dpi) for an 8.5"x11" image. Most often, digital images are provided as TIFF files unless otherwise requested. For e-mail delivery, JPEG files prove to be less cumbersome and can be requested by most institutions.

Most museums charge a fee for each image ranging from $25 to $250. Usually there is a slight discount for image requests made by nonprofit organizations. New digital images (where a high-resolution image does not yet exist so the object has to be photographed) are more costly, as the photography fee is often passed on to the requesting party. Other stipulations exist for video footage, which is usually granted short term in the form of a rental fee.

A request for Internet use might also garner additional fees. Do not assume that permission granted to use the image in an exhibit or as part of a catalogue extends to permission to use the image on the exhibit website. Generally, Internet and website use is specifically addressed in the scope of the agreement. One reason for this is because an image, once released on the Internet, is much more difficult to control than an image in hard copy.

In special situations, if an object is in need of repair before a quality photograph can be taken, some museums charge additional fees for things like conservation, repair, or cleaning. Custom scanning from slide images fall under another category in the fee structure in most museums.

Digital images are typically provided through e-mail or in a Dropbox where the image can be downloaded. In some cases, images on CD can be sent using express deliveries or the U.S. Postal Service and require a small additional fee.

RIGHTS AND REPRODUCTIONS CHALLENGES

There are certain rights and reproduction challenges facing both licensors and licensees that may have contributed to the current emerging open-content trend discussed below. Case law states that while the subjective and creative artist choices of a photographer including lighting, orientation, and perspective may contribute enough elements of original creativity to entitle a photograph of an otherwise unprotected work to be protectable under U.S. copyright law, slavish copying or photographing of an object does not entitle the creator of the derivative work (i.e., the photograph) to copyright protection because it lacks a key component of copyright: originality.[11] Therefore, it is arguable whether photographs taken by museums of collections objects in the public domain are protectable under U.S. copyright law. Among members of the public, there is a certain perceived injustice in paying for images of objects and works of art that are no long subject to copyright protection and that otherwise appear to be slavish copies of the public-domain originals. This is compounded by increased photography-prohibition policies implemented by museums across the country, which are applied equally to objects in the public domain as those currently under copyright. Visitors have little or no opportunity to photograph objects themselves and some are resentful of the restrictions.

Additionally, those (including scholars, researchers, and museums) seeking to use high-resolution images for professional publications, exhibition uses, films, and other purposes (both commercial and noncommercial) are making multiple payments for images that are subject to copyright protection. Requestors are paying for permissions agreements to get the high-resolution image and paying the copyright owner or holder for the copyright license to reproduce and use the image. It becomes a very expensive and time-consuming process.

Open-Content Programs

In order to provide a few examples of successful open-source programs we interviewed Peter Dueker, head of digital imaging services at the National Gallery of Art in Washington, DC; Anne Young, rights and reproduction specialist for the Indianapolis Museum of Art; and John French, director of visual resources, Yale University Art Gallery. Each interviewee provided an overview of their process, including the reasons they elected to move forward with the program, how long it took to implement, how many people were involved in the process, how they made it user friendly, the challenges they faced, and the benefits they enjoyed.

Peter Dueker, National Gallery of Art (NGA)

The National Gallery of Art launched NGA Images and its corresponding open-access policy in March of 2012. According to Peter Dueker, the "NGA Images and Open Access supports the educational mission of the National Gallery of Art by facilitating learning, enrichment, enjoyment, and exploration."[12]

It took NGA approximately two years for the system implementation. According to Dueker, they developed the requirements for the system prior to finalizing plans for open access that resulted in some last-minute system changes to NGA Images that fortunately the vendor was able to accommodate.

Dueker reported that NGA Images and the corresponding open-access policy involved staff from multiple gallery departments, including representatives from their legal office and imaging and visual services rights and reproductions as well as technology solutions (IT). The project was initiated and directed by Alan Newman, chief of digital imaging and visual services. Core project members included Peter Dueker, head of digital imaging services; Barbara Bernard, coordinator of visual services; and David Beaudet, technology solutions. They licensed an existing, off-the-shelf image-delivery application that was then customized to fully meet their specific requirements.

NGA has approximately 115,000 objects that are accessioned and validated for public viewing on their website (www.nga.gov). The criteria for NGA Images is that the object has been identified as presumed in the public domain and a publication quality image is available. As of November 2014, NGA had 45,000 open-access images available for download via NGA Images.

Because a project like this requires significant coordination across departments, Dueker stated that "multiple staff were involved at all stages to set project priorities and ensure the implementation was successful. We were fortunate that there was broad institutional support for the goals of open access and recognition of the importance of modernizing our rights and reproduction practices."

"Our primary requirement was to create a self-serve system that would be able to accommodate a variety of users, from novice to expert. We have two search paths—quick (simple) and advanced search for our more experienced users. We offer a quick download option so that users can obtain an image with a single click. We also provide a high-resolution download that allows users to select an image size appropriate for their use, up to 4,000 pixels on the long dimension. Additionally we provide a detailed help section that includes a technical guide for reproduction and image quality."

Only open-access images are available for direct download from NGA Images, and only if a publication-quality image is available. All other requests are sent via e-mail to a member of the visual services staff for handling. Users are responsible for obtaining any use permissions from additional rights holders.

"We are happy to see our images being utilized for both scholarly and general use. We've received very positive feedback from both the museum community and the public. We have been particularly excited to see extensive use of the site internationally. In November of 2014, we hit a major milestone with more than one million images downloaded," according to Dueker.

Since their launch in 2012, many other museums have also adopted various forms of open access and open content, which is excellent progress.

Dueker concurs, "In our view this is something that all cultural heritage institutions should be doing for their public-domain materials."

The National Gallery of Art does not charge use, permission, or image access fees. The NGA may charge processing fees to recover its costs of providing additional imaging services, such as creating guide prints, making new photographs, or customizing and formatting existing photography, whether or not the image is currently available through open access.

Anne Young, Indianapolis Museum of Art (IMA)

According to Young, the "digital age is changing the game for images and fair use. Web-based and social media have turned image use on its ear. It raises all kinds of questions about the public domain."[13] IMA has been working toward putting approximately thirty thousand to forty thousand high-resolution images of objects in their permanent collection online for pubic use as part of their open-source project. With nearly fifty-seven thousand objects in the collection, almost half of the images fall in the public domain. The remainder of the objects in the collection have copyright restrictions.

Planning

IMA had several task forces. The core task force included four people: the rights and reproduction specialist (Young), photo technician, digital info technician, and former registrar. They also used a "test task force," whose members served as consultants (twelve to fifteen people) and scrutinized usability or "user friendliness." IMA's overall staff includes about 230 employees; so minimal people were involved in the project.

Young admits that working with the software was challenging, and in the end they changed the product they were using. The core task force had to start over at one point, so they became strategic in their approach. Rather than be quick to appear online, IMA made the decision to take their time to do it right, which paid off.

Implementation

Researching the copyright restrictions took a lot of time. Before going live they had to discern between objects in the public domain and those with restrictions and be definitive about it. This work was a time-consuming component of the three-year project; IMA was redesigning their collections web pages at the same time.

To make the process user friendly, image requests come up as a button when a request to view the image in the online database is implemented. If a high-resolution image is available and the object is in public domain, there is a "download" button." If not, there is no button, or if a low-resolution image only exists, it is noted when someone tries to download the file. They used high-resolution JPEG files, which are easier for the average person to work with. If a TIFF file is required, patrons can easily request it right from the image they are viewing. A button brings them to the rights and reproduction request area. IMA also notes on its website that images have copyright restrictions so that users have the information right away. This took an enormous amount of research and confirmation for objects in the collection but, as a result of this approach, they have had no repercussions with regard to copyright use so far.

Implementation Details

IMA used Digital Assets Management software (Adobe). Three categories of image included the following:

1. Images with copyright restrictions—are on the website with a 600 dpi minimum; ARS and VARGA have 600 dpi restriction.
2. Copyright 600 dpi, no ARS or VARGA restriction—not large enough for publication; no download button
3. Images in the public domain are available for download (via button click). If the images are not available in high resolution (due to the budget for photography or just haven't been taken yet), there is no download button and website visitors are redirected to the image request area of IMA's website to facilitate a standard photo request.

Unexpected Results

IMA was surprised to find that once they stopped charging a processing fee for image requests (for high-resolution image requests, most museums charge a nominal administrative fee ranging from $100 to $500), their revenue from images actually increased dramatically and "went through the roof," instead of decreasing. This was unexpected. Young expressed that by not charging scholars, students, researchers, and other museums a processing fee IMA created a feeling of goodwill and those making requests were much more apt to pay for a high-resolution image to be taken when no images of an object were available ($100) and/or request additional images above and beyond what they initially requested. IMA then has a high-resolution image of the object it can offer in the open-source database. Young felt that people were more apt to pay for something tangible, like an image, rather than pay an administration fee. This way, they know what the money is really going toward and they feel good about their image request dovetailing with the new practices in image access. They are more likely to support scholarly endeavors and feel they are contributing so that others will have access to an image of the same object.

Their website will capture how images are being used, whether for personal, scholarly, or commercial use as it will ask for specifics when an image is downloaded. Although the IMA permits photography of objects on view in galleries and from their permanent collection, they still limit photography for special exhibits objects not in their collection, determining the photography policy on a case-by-case basis as per the lender's restrictions.

John French, Yale University Art Gallery (YUAG)

The Yale University Art Gallery officially announced its participation in open access in 2011 as part of a Yale University–wide initiative (ydc2.yale .edu/open-access-collections). Prior to open access, the gallery had been making its works available free of charge or restriction since 2009. At that time the gallery did not have an easy means of supplying files so they kept the policy quiet.[14]

French explains, "The decision why the gallery, and Yale as a whole, made the choice to go with an open-access policy for objects in the public domain spun out of a Mellon Foundation meeting held in New York City back in December 2010, with several art museum directors and their rights management point people to discuss the idea of making images available for free for scholarly purposes. It was an interesting meeting to attend as most of the directors were behind the idea of 'open access' but felt if they went to their board with the idea it would be a hard sell (mostly due to the idea of losing revenue streams). The Yale directors left the meeting feeling they were prepared to take the first step, and in fact wanted to lead the field in open access."

According to French, "campus museums have a greater capacity than their nonacademic peers to be more experimental and innovative, in part because they are protected by academic freedom, and use metrics of success that go beyond attendance or income generation."

Philosophy

The Yale University Art Gallery makes all of its images available free of charge—copyright and public domain. However, they only provide direct downloads for the public-domain work due to copyright restrictions (those sent out separately via FTP along with notice of copyright).

French stated that "one reason materials are made available for free is that we had been tracking the requests we received for many years and found that the vast majority of our requests (approximately 70 percent) were of a scholarly nature. More often than not those scholars are on a tight budget and we felt 'penalizing' them for wanting to use/promote objects from our collection was unfair given that our core mission is that of a teaching museum with an aim to enable scholarship."

"In tandem with that, the gallery also made the decision that we would not charge for new photography either. Similar to providing images for free, the feeling was that it was unfair that the first requestor would have to pay a fee for new photography, but anyone after would not. If someone is publishing or researching something from our collection, the feeling is we will then receive more attention so we should help support such projects."

Implementation

To enable the process, writing up the formal documents and outlines took close to a year. Since this was a campus-wide policy YUAG had to ensure it met all the various parties' needs and/or concerns. Internally it was not much of a hard sell as the director and governing board were behind the idea. What eventually took a little longer was setting up the mechanisms for delivering the images automatically online through YUAG's website. This required a lot of programming with its CMS, DAM, and website.

Internally at YUAG the primary people included

Director of Visual Resources: Attended meetings and sat on the campus committee of open access; internally worked to inform the staff about the changes and oversaw the backend data changes that needed to occur.

Rights and Reproductions Coordinator: Worked to change all of the forms being used for processing requests, and also was involved in internal planning for how to implement and support the change.

Art Gallery Director: Primarily his role was a support role, but also to ensure broader agreement within Yale and with the governing board.

According to French, "on campus similar parties at each cultural institution were involved in campus meetings that implemented the open-access policy and central informational website. In addition we had a general counsel representative working to review/lead the policy to ensure it did not violate any copyright laws, or at minimum addressed any concerns."

They are actively digitizing their collection so the numbers continue to grow; however, French reports that as of October 2014 YUAG had "approximately 180,000 records visible in our online collection (we do not share loans online but many are photographed). Of the 180,000 objects in the collection, 148,000 objects have images, 82,500 of those are works under copyright so only a thumbnail is shared online, 65,500 of those are public domain and freely downloadable (up to 20MB). Many objects have more than one view. The number of images online is not represented above."

"The larger challenge was efficiently working out a means to automatically deliver as many of the assets online as we could. We were fortunate to already have a robust DAM in place, which we were able to have 'feed' the online collection portion of our website [artgallery.yale.edu/collection/ search]. Unfortunately, while we were trying to implement open access, the gallery was also going through a complete website redesign, added to which the firm we hired went belly-up midway through the process, so it stalled everything."

"The gallery uses TMS for our collections database. There we record rights-related information about the individual objects. This information is pushed to our DAM (Open Text Media Manager), which stores the images of each object. The DAM has an export service which utilizes Amazon Web Services and stores derivatives of our images based on varying Object Rights Type; these triggers then feed the website appropriately. A lot of automation is built into the TMS system to automatically read object dates and make certain determinations; the others which do not fit that mold generate reports a staff person must then review and make decisions based on several factors, creation date being primary. As a general rule we display images online of copyrighted works following the AAMD [Association of Art Museum Directors] definition of a thumbnail that is 250 x 300 pixels" (aamd.org/docu ment/policy-on-the-use-of-thumbnail-digital-images-in-museum-online-initi atives).

Rewards

French reflected that the biggest reward was that "we saw a larger increase in the number of requests we typically received once we announced open access. We saw a 40 percent increase in the number of requests we were receiving. While initially this overwhelmed us staff labor-wise our automation now enables quick delivery of files. We have also seen a tendency for scholars to send us copies of their publications as a show of gratitude. We have always requested this, but it was not often accomplished. I'd like to think this change is in part due to open access. We have not seen the oft-cited fears of works showing up on shower curtains (though I might line up to buy one if they ever did!)."

Impact of Open-Source Programs

Reflecting on the case studies addressed herein, perhaps some of the best outcomes of these open-content initiatives include

- Increased research and resulting awareness of the rights and reproductions status of the institution's collection;
- Increased goodwill among the public and those who regularly seek high-resolution images for scholarly and professional purposes, resulting in increased compliance with requests for credit and publication copies; and
- Increased revenues for services related to rights and reproductions, including photography of collections objects that either did not have a high-resolution image at all or only had a low-resolution image available.

Although the revenues seem to be increasing now due to the goodwill generated among those who regularly seek reproductions, it will be interesting to see how the process evolves as these programs continue to grow and develop and museums seek to find creative revenue-generating activities that allow them to increase access to collections.

From a legal perspective, open-source programs, although an interesting trend, may not cause much of a change in the rights and reproductions landscape. As traditionally risk-adverse institutions, many museums are likely to use images of objects that are either known to be in the public domain or for which the museum owns or holds the necessary copyrights enabling it to include the image in the open-source program. Assuming that is the case, the use of images contained in these open-source programs will be governed by the terms of use published on the website. In keeping with the AAM and AAMD standards, some institutions are also making thumbnail-size images of works protected by copyright available on the Internet, but do not make them available for download.

As with similar creative commons and open-source-code repositories, not all open-source program providers are created equal. Terms may vary between institutions: do not assume that all participants in these programs will make their content available under the same terms. Always read the terms of each open-content program carefully: some may be more restrictive than others.

NOTES

1. G. Wayne Clough, *The Best of Both Worlds: Museums, Libraries and Archive in the Digital Age,* Smithsonian Institution, 2013, p. 2, accessed on November 16, 2014, www.si.edu/content/gwc/bestofbothworldssmithsonian.pdf.

2. Clough, p. 2.

3. Walter G. Lehmann, "Introduction," *Rights and Reproductions: The Handbook for Cultural Institutions*, American Alliance of Museums, projected publication date 2015, p. 1.

4. Lehmann, p. 2.

5. Lehmann, p. 5.

6. Anne Young, Rights and Reproduction Specialist for the Indianapolis Museum of Art, interview with authors, November 11, 2014.

7. 17 U.S.C. § 102.

8. 17 U.S.C. § 106.

9. Generally, although contract law varies from state to state, a contract requires four elements to be legally enforceable: offer, consideration, acceptance, and mutual intent.

10. A "copyright assignment" is the transfer of one or more of the copyright rights granted under the U.S. Copyright Act. Unlike a license, in which, the licensor retains the right to use the licensed property, an assignment is a complete transfer of the right from the assignor (the one transferring the rights) to the assignee (the one to whom the rights are transferred). Under an assignment, the assignor will no longer have the right to utilize the copyright granted without first obtaining a license from the assignee.

11. *Bridgeman Art Library v. Corel Corp.*, 36 F. Supp. 2d 191 (S.D.N.Y. 1999).

12. Peter Dueker, Head of Digital Imaging Services, National Gallery of Art, Washington, DC, interview with authors, November 14, 2014. This interview is the source of the remainder of information attributed to Dueker in this chapter.

13. Young. This interview is the source of the remainder of information attributed to Young in this chapter.

14. John French, Director of Visual Resources Yale University Art Gallery, interview with authors, November 12, 2014. This interview is the source of the remainder of information attributed to French in this chapter.

Index

abandoned property: Abandoned and
Loaned Cultural Property, 12;
Abandoned Cultural Properties Act, 11,
12; documentation, 4–5; public image,
5; questions, 4; returning, 8; staff, 5;
statutes, 5

acquisitions: antiquities, 69, 70; country of
origin, 19; due diligence, 14, 15–19;
ethics, 136; Facebook, 94, 225, 228;
firearms, 106; Nazi-looting and, 41;
ownership and, 16; proceeds of
deaccessioning, 127, 131, 153, 154n2,
165; proposals, 142, 143, 186;
provenance, 61; theft and, 13–14

Adams, Ansel, 176

aesthetic: personal taste, 37; social media
and, 228; trademark and, 228

Agile methodology: intellectual property
and, 251; manifesto, 253n7; software
development, 246, 247, 248, 249;
termination of, 250

Alcock, Thomas: collection, 18

Altmann, Maria: Foreign Sovereign
Immunities Act, 46, 48; legal theory
and, 50; obituary reference, 24n14;
Republic of Austria v. Altman, 16,
24n13, 48, 50, 52n5

American Institute of Conservation (AIC),
118

American Society for Industrial Security
(ASIS), 216

appraisers: professional, 33; value and,
27–28

Archaeological Resources Protection Act,
16

Archives of American Art, 65

art fraud: allegations, 31; Jackson Pollock,
71; John Drewe, 71; museums and, x;
Statute of Frauds, 265n12–266n13;
Wolfgang Beltracchi, 71

artifacts: Native American, 16–17, 24n17;
return of, 22, 25n42; stolen, 14, 17, 19,
23n5, 23n6

Art Loss Register, 16, 52

Association of Art Museum Directors
(AAMD): deaccessioning, 148n3, 151,
154n2; ethics, 136; guidelines for
restitution of art, 44, 70; sanctions and
Delaware Museum of Art, 155n6

attorney general: endowments and
restricted gifts, 158, 160, 163, 164, 169;
Fisk University and, 167; geography
and, 139, 146; Higgins Armory and,
194, 199; judgment, 128, 136, 165;
misclassification of employees and,
205–206; monetizing collections, 128;
museum mission and, 138, 148; New
York, 142, 147; office of, 136;
perspective of, 138; public domain and,
138, 147; public interest, 145; *Rogers v.
Attorney General*, 170n10; role of,
133n4, 138, 145; Rose Art Museum at

Brandeis University and, 164–165
attribution: artist, 60; authenticity and, 55; Calder, Alexander and, 29; Catalogue Raisonné, 30; experts, 40n1; false, 30; mistaken, 28; provenance, 70; standards and guidelines, 40n2; title changes and, 56, 60
auctions: assignment for benefit of creditors and, 173, 175; authentication and, 27; Brooklyn Museum and, 141, 142–143; catalogues, 56, 60, 65; deaccessioning and, 135, 138, 139, 140, 142, 196; due diligence and, 61–62; European, 57; expert opinion and, 33; Fresno MET Museum, 173, 174, 175, 176; Galerie Fischer, 42; Loeb Art Center at Vassar College, 140; personal property liquidation and, 173; proceeds and, 131; provenance and, 58, 62; results, 148n7, 148n8; stolen property and, 18; Waldmüller, Ferdinand Georg, painting, 60
authenticity: appraisers and, 33; Catalogue Raisonné, 30, 37; certificate of, 15, 31; curators and, 27; definition of, 28; expert opinion, 37; First Amendment and, 38; forgery and, 28–29; foundations and, 31, 32; guidelines for, 29; insurance for opinion, 34, 35; proposed statutory reform, 34, 36; provenance and, 55, 56, 57, 58, 64, 70, 71

bailment, 51
Baltimore Museum of Art (BMA), 61–62
Barnes Collection: endowments and restricted gifts, 167–168, 170n29; Fisk University and, 164
Berkshire Museum: budget, 131; deaccessioning and, 131, 132; ethics and, 132; mission, 131; overview, 130–131
best practices: Delaware Museum of Art, 131; Nazi-looted art and, 41, 52; rights and reproduction and, 270
blockbuster exhibit: art history and, 97n3; most popular, 85; traveling, 86
Boston Museum of Fine Arts: Higgins Armory and, 186; Nazi-looted art and,

45, 52n2; oldest collections, 3
Brooklyn Museum: acquisitions and, 140; costume collection, 135, 139, 141–143, 148n14, 149n17, 149n18; public domain, 147
burials: Native American, 74. *See also* interments

Cassirer, Lilly: *Cassirer v. Thesseb-Bornemisza Collection*, 52n10; Nazi-looted art and, 47, 48, 49, 50
Catalogue Raisonné, 28; authentication and, 30–31, 33; foundations and, 32; provenance and, 64
Certified Protection Professional (CPP), 216, 298
civil rights: museum security and, 214; visitors and, 217
Civil War, 23n2; weapons and, 107, 110
claimant: documentation and, 7; Fresno Museum, 176; Nazi-looted art, 41, 43, 44, 46, 52; repatriation, 80; stolen property, 20; wage statutes and, 206
collection(s): acquisition, 151; ammunition and, 110; Barnes Collection, 164, 167–168; Brooklyn Museum costume collection, 141–144, 147, 148n14, 149n17; crowdfunding, 262; deaccessioning, 153; digital technology and, 241–242, 252; donor intent, 163; ethics, 136; firearms, 99, 100, 106, 107, 112, 113, 117, 119, 120, 122; Fisk University, 166–167; found in, 3, 4, 8; Fresno Museum, 171, 173, 175–176; Higgins Armory, 145, 146, 179, 180, 183, 184, 186, 187, 189–190, 191, 192, 193, 195–196, 197, 198–200; Hildebrand Gurlitt, 42; Indianapolis Museum of Art, 270–278, 280, 281–282; inventory, 3, 4, 6, 120, 142; mission, 230; monetizing, 128, 129, 130, 131, 152; museums, 3, 4; Nazi-looted art and, 44, 62, 64, 66, 67, 68; provenance and, 55, 58, 59, 61; public inquiries, 7; public trust, 151, 152, 153; restricted gifts and, 159, 160; rights and reproduction, 269, 270, 272, 274, 275, 283; Rose Art Museum at Brandeis University, 164–165; security and, 203,

217; Springfield Science Museum, 73–74, 79, 80, 81; stolen property, 13, 15, 19, 20, 22; traveling exhibits, 86, 91, 96; undocumented, 6, 8; Worcester Art Museum, 146, 180, 184, 192, 193–194; Yale University, 21

Collections Exchange Center, 136

College Art Association, 29, 40n11

compensation: claims, 210, 211; Lilly Cassirer and, 47; office of workers compensation, 207; unemployment and, 209; workers, 205, 206

contractors: claims, 172; independent, 205–206, 208, 209, 210, 211–212; security and, 219; software development and, 232, 236, 237, 245, 246

copyright: assignment and, 284n10; Digital Millennium Copyright Act (DMCA), 262, 267n16; intellectual property and, 251; open-source image programs and, 281, 282, 283; protection, 236; rights and reproduction, 271–272, 273, 274, 275–276, 278, 279, 280; social media and, 232–233; software and, 244; trademark, 262; user-generated content and, 232, 233

corporation: endowments and restricted gifts, 161, 165, 167; McClatchy Foundation, 177; nonprofit, 177, 194, 203; Winding Up and Dissolution of Corporate Resolution, 172

Cranach, Lucas, 47, 48, 58

crowdfunding, 223, 255, 256–257; definition of, 256, 258–259, 260; recommendations, 263, 265; risk and, 262

Crystal Bridges Museum of Art, 128, 144, 166, 167

cultural property: Art Law and Cultural Property Database, 58, 69, 70; legislation and, 70; National Stolen Property Act, 18; Native American Graves and Repatriation Act, 16–18; provenance and, 57, 68; security and, 219; seizure and, 46; stolen, 13–15, 20, 22, 24n23, 24n24, 24n26

Cultural Property Implementation Act (CPIA), 69

curators: appraisers and, 33; authenticity and, 27; early, 1; firearms and, 100; guidelines, 29; independent, 86; opinions and, 28, 32, 33, 34, 35, 37, 37–39; peer review, 195; traveling exhibits and, 89; Worcester Art Museum, 184, 198, 200

customs: laws, 43; provenance and, 59–60

da Vinci, Leonardo, 32

deaccessioning: auctions and, 139; Brooklyn Museum, 142; challenges, 3; ethics, 165, 168; Higgins Armory, 194, 195; monetizing collections and, 127, 128, 131; policy, 148n3, 153; proceeds and, 132, 138, 146, 187; public domain, 135–136, 145, 146; public image and, 5, 229; public trust, 151, 153, 154

degenerate art: Nazi's and marketing of, 55; Nazi's and outlawing of, 41–42

Deursches Historishe Museum: postwar database of art, 57; restitution of art and, 49

Digital Assets Management (DAM), 279

Digital Millennium Copyright Act (DMCA), 262

documentation: abandoned property, 4; authenticity, 29; Catalogue Raisonné, 63; creditor claims, 177; cultural affiliation, 80; donor-imposed restrictions, 159; funerary objects and, 79; gift modification, 159; insurance for curators and, 35; NAGPRA grants, 78; object loans, 5; ownership and, 7, 13; photo archives, 65; provenance, 3, 15, 55, 56, 70; public image, 7; restricted gifts, 168–169; software and, 248, 249, 251, 252; source, 6

donations: crowdfunding, 255, 261; cultural institutions and, 172; endowments and restricted gifts, 159, 168; museum finances and, 125; recession and, 172, 241; social media and, 225

due diligence: crowdfunding, 263; failure, 19; Higgins Armory proposal and, 191, 192, 194; provenance and, 15, 22, 55, 59, 61; stolen property and, 14

Einsatzstab Reichsleiter Rosenberg data base, 59, 68
Egypt: Cairo Museum and King Tutankhamun exhibit, 85; Thomas Alcock collection and, 18
Elgin Marbles, 21, 25n57
endowments: board endowments, 158; Delaware Museum of Art, 152; Higgins Armory, 185, 187, 188, 198; restricted gifts, 157, 159; traveling exhibits and, 86; Worcester Art Museum, 191
experts: Alexander Calder, 29; ammunition, 110; appraisers, 33; authentication, 27–28, 29, 34, 35; Catalogue Raisonné, 30; claims against, 33, 34; digital revolution and, 269; First Amendment, 37, 38; foundations, 32; guidance, 270; Higgins Armory, 186–187, 195–196; insurance coverage for, 35; legal, x–xi; open-source programs and, 277, 282; opinions, 34, 36, 39, 75; proposed statute, 35, 36; provenance, 57; review by, 174; security, 215; stolen property and, 14; testimony of, 168
exports: antiquities, 69; laws, 17; provenance research, 70; restitution laws, 43, 46; software, 249–250; stolen property, 19
expropriation: Nazi-looted art and, 41, 46, 51

Facebook: consistency and, 228; crowdfunding, 255–256, 258, 263; images, 223; "Like" value, 225; traveling exhibits and, 94
fake: Alexander Calder, 29; authentication, 28–29; provenance, 56, 59, 71; Wolfgang Beltracchi, 71
Federal Bureau of Investigation (FBI): art crime, 24n11, 24n32; IFAR and, 65; National Stolen Art File, 16; provenance guidelines, 15; stolen art and seizure by, 18
Federal Trade Commission (FTC): truth in advertising, 230, 239n9
firearms: ammunition, 103, 104–105; antique, 100–107; collections, 1, 99–100; conservation, 112–118; display

of, 122; evolution of, 100–101; handling of, 107; legal requirements for, 106; storage and display, 118–122
First Amendment: employees and social media, 235; opinions and, 37–38
Fisk University: endowments and restricted gifts, 164, 166–167; monetizing collection, 128
Foreign Sovereign Immunities Act (FSIA): Lilly Cassirer, 48; Maria Altmann, 46–47; restitution of art, 51
forfeiture: civil, 43; Convention on Cultural Property Implementation Act, 18; stolen property, 14, 18
foundations: Alice Walton, 144; artist, 15; authentication and, 31–32; Barnes, 167–168; Catalogue Raisonné, 30; Central Valley, 177; endowments and restricted gifts, 160; First Amendment and, 38; Higgins Armory, 185, 195; Mellon, 142, 143, 280; monetization, 130; no-sue agreements, 34; opinions and, 27; statute reform and, 36
Fresno Metropolitan Museum, 171–178
Frick Art Reference Library, 59, 63, 65
funerary objects: NAGPRA and, 73; notice of intent to repatriate (NIR), 80, 81; notice of inventory completion (NIC), 79, 81; Springfield Science Museum collection, 73–74, 75, 79, 80

gallery: Austrian, 16; Barnes Foundation, 167–168; endowments and restricted gifts, 157; Higgins Armory, 187, 191; Hungarian National, 50; interactives, 269; Kapoor's, 14; *Knights!* exhibit, Worcester Art Museum, 179, 180; Knoedler, 71; National Gallery Berlin, 60; National Gallery of Art, 144; National Gallery of Art, photo archives, 65; open-source programs, 270, 276, 277, 278, 280, 281, 282; photography, 234; provenance, 15, 18, 63, 65; rights and reproduction, 271; Rose Art Museum, Brandeis University, 164; security and, 217; Stair, 175; stolen cultural property, 20; traveling exhibits and, 86, 91, 92

George Grosz: claims by heirs of, 45; *Grosz v. Museum of Modern Art*, 20, 25n43

Getty Museum: Getty Images, 272; Getty Provenance Index, 65; Getty Research Institute, 65; open-source programs, 270; ownership claims, 21, 25n54; stolen cultural property, 22

Guida Farm: human remains and, 75, 82, 82n6

Gurlitt, Hildebrand: art dealer, 55; degenerate art, 41, 55; provenance, 57

Hague Convention: photo archives, 65; provenance, 66; stolen cultural property, 17

Higgins Armory: integration with Worcester Art Museum, 179, 180–183, 184–200; public domain, 145–146, 147

Hilter, Adolph: Fuhrermuseum, 42, 66

Holocaust: assets, 44, 68; claims, 49, 55, 62; looted art work, 48

Immunity From Seizure Act (IFSA), 47

import: illegal, 17, 18; seizure of, 18; stolen property and, 15

Indianapolis Museum of Art: open-source program, 271, 276, 278–280

insurance: authentication services and, 34–35; Baltimore Museum of Art, 61; certificate of, 88, 89; firearms, 110; Fresno Museum, 174; opinions and, 28; traveling exhibits, 88, 89, 91–92, 96; unemployment and, 205, 207

intellectual property: crowdfunding, 262, 265; rights and reproduction, 270; social media, 228, 231, 233; software and, 250, 251–252

interments (burials): Native American, 73

Internal Revenue Service (IRS): independent contractors and, 207; nonprofit status protection, 226; social media, 226–227

Internet: crowdfunding and, 255–256; nonprofit status, 226; rights and reproduction, 273–274, 275, 283; social media, 226–227; stolen art resources, 16; terms of use, 229–230; trademark, 228–229; visitor experience, 241, 255–256

INTERPOL: stolen art database, 16

Klimt, Gustav, 16, 46

laches: legal defense for stolen art, 20, 45–46

Leopold Museum: Egon Scheile's *Portrait of Wally*, 64; Foreign Sovereign Immunities Act and, 46

liability: contract employees, 205, 211; crowdfunding, 259, 262; interactives and, 242; opinions and, 28; security, 216, 218, 219, 220; social media and, 231, 238; software, 245

litigation: Fisk University, 166; found in collections, 4, 7; issuing opinions and, 29, 31, 32, 34; Nazi-looted art and, 41, 43, 44, 46, 48, 49, 52; protecting opinions, 34–39; Randolph College, 128; stolen cultural property, 15, 22

looting: archaeological sites, 17, 69; Giacomo Medici and, 22; Nazi-looting, 41, 59, 66; provenance, 68

Louvre Museum: Anitoch excavation, 184; da Vinci painting, 32; documentation center, 65

management of aggressive behavior (MOAB), 220

Matisse, Henri: Barnes Collection, 167; provenance, 65

Metropolitan Museum of Art: arms and armor collection, 187; Brooklyn Museum costume collection and, 135, 141; curator of arms and armor, 181, 195; Durand painting *Kindred Spirits*, 144; purchase of Medici birthplate, 140, 142

missions: Higgins Armory and Worcester Art Museum, 191; Kickstarter and, 257; museum, ix, x, 1; social media and, 230

money: assignment for the benefit of creditors, 173–174; crowdfunding, 256, 257; deaccessioning to raise, 127, 141, 145; endowments and restricted gifts, 168; fundraising, 186; laundering, 14; public trust, 137, 153

monuments: Nubian, 85

Monuments, Fine Arts and Archives, 67
Monuments Men, 24n12, 67, 184, 201n8
Munich Central Collection Point (MCCP):
    provenance and, 57
museums: abandoned property and, 3, 4, 6,
    8; archaeological sites and, 17–18;
    crowdfunding, 255–265; curators,
    27–28; deaccessioning and public
    domain, 135–148; digital technology
    and, 241–249; due diligence and,
    15–16, 19, 20; finances and, 125–126;
    firearms in, 99, 106, 110, 118;
    independent contractors and, 205–211;
    insurance and, 34–35; monetizing
    collections, 127–132; NAGPRA and,
    73, 78; Nazi-looted art, 41–52;
    provenance and, 55, 57, 66–69, 70;
    public trust, 151–154; restricted gifts,
    15–21; rights and reproduction,
    269–283; security, 213–220; social
    media and, 225–238; statutory reform,
    36; stolen cultural property and, 13, 14,
    15; traveling exhibits and, 85–96

National Archives and Records
    Administration (NARA): provenance,
    57, 68
National Gallery of Art: open-source
    program, 276–278; photo archives, 65
National Stolen Art File, 16
National Stolen Property Act (NSPA), 18
Native American Graves Protection and
    Repatriation Act (NAGPRA): case
    study, 73–81; definition and
    compliance with, 16
Nazi: looting and, 20, 41–52; stolen
    cultural property and, 18, 21, 55,
    56–57, 56–64, 63; provenance, 59, 62,
    66–68
New-York Historical Society:
    deaccessioning and, 128, 135, 138,
    139–141, 144, 147
nonprofits: ArtStor, 142; attorney general,
    138, 194; crowdfunding, 257; digital
    technology, 241; endowments and
    restrictions, 161, 167, 169; Fresno
    Museum, 171, 173; Higgins Armory,
    188, 189; IFAR, 57; independent
    contractors, 206; public domain, 136,

137, 138; rights and reproduction, 274,
    275; security, 216; social media,
    225–229
Norton Simon Museum: Lucas Cranach
    paintings, 47, 52n7, 53n11, 58; Nazi-
    looted art, 47
no-sue agreement: curators and, 31, 34, 39
Nuremberg Race Laws, 41–42, 47

open-source programs: permissions and,
    92; rights and reproduction, 269, 271,
    276–283; software, 251
ownership: abandoned property and, 4;
    antiquities, 69–70; bailment, 51; claims,
    7, 8, 21, 45, 49, 55; content (social
    media), 236–237; conveyance of
    ownership of a child, 77; due diligence,
    19; false claims, 6; firearms, 106;
    patrimony laws, 17; permissions
    agreements and, 272; provenance, 15,
    29, 56, 57–58, 60, 62, 64; social media
    account, 235; software and, 250,
    251–252; stolen property and, 13, 14,
    16, 22, 49, 52, 55, 57; transfer of
    ownership of Brooklyn Museum's
    costume collection, 141

photographs: Higgins Museum collection,
    183; open-source programs, 276–283;
    permissions agreement, 272; policy,
    234; restrictions and, 275; traveling
    exhibits and, 92, 94
Picasso, Pablo, 36, 62–63, 72n6, 133n8
Pissarro, Camille, 21, 43
police: firearms storage and, 119; security
    training, 213–214, 217, 218, 219; stolen
    property, 61
Pollock, Jackson, 71–72
provenance: abandoned property and, 3;
    authentication and, 29;
    connoisseurship, 37; due diligence, 15,
    19–20, 22, 52; guidelines, 44, 55–72;
    NAGPRA and, 80; procedure, 29;
    resources, 67–68; suspicious, 14, 18,
    45; World War II and, 43
public domain: crowdfunding, 263;
    deaccessioning and, 135–148, 196;
    photographs and, 275, 278, 279, 280,
    281, 283; public trust, 151–153

public trust, 151–154

Quedlinburg Treasures, 67, 72n7

Randolph College: monetizing collections, 129, 130; public trust, 153
Renoir, Auguste: Barnes Foundation, 167; stolen painting and, 61
restitution: AAMD guidelines, 45; cases, 64; efforts, 42, 48, 49, 51, 67; law, 43; resources for, 59; Yale University, 50.

Schiele, Egon: Catalogue Raisonné, 64; laches defense and, 20; ownership and, 43, 45
scholars: artist foundations and, 32; authentication and, 27–28, 29, 33–34, 70; Brooklyn Museum costume collection, 141; Catalogue Raisonné, 30, 63–64; First Amendment, 37–39; Higgins Armory, 200; independent, 27; insurance, 34–36; no-sue agreements and, 34; open-source programs, 282; rights and reproduction, 269, 274, 276, 277, 279, 280
scientific testing: authentication and, 29, 30
security: firearms and, 106, 118, 119; technology and, 231; training, 213–220; traveling exhibits and, 88, 92, 94, 96
seizure: Immunity from Seizure Act, 47; Nazi-looted art and, 42, 43; U.S. government and, 18
Seurat, Georges: stolen cultural property and, 13, 14
Smithsonian Institution: photo archives, 65; rights and reproduction, 269; security guard at, 215; traveling exhibits, 86, 92
social media: account, 264; crowdfunding and, 256, 258, 263; general, 225–238, 242; photographs and, 270, 273, 278; traveling exhibits and, 94
Springfield Science Museum: collections, 73–74, 81, 82n22, 82n32; notice of intent to repatriate, 80, 82n31
statutes: abandoned property and, 8–12; deaccessioning, 137; forfeiture, 18; independent contractors and, 56; of

limitations, 44; museum property, 3–8; opinions and, 36
stolen property, 13–22, 43, 44–45

Thyssen-Bornemisza Collection: *Cassirer v. Thyssen-Bornemisza*, 48, 52n10
title. *See* ownership
trademarks: crowdfunding, 262, 265; intellectual property and, 251; public image and, 228–229
trustees: Barnes Foundation, 145; Brandeis University, 164; of collections, 7; deaccessioning and, 136, 137; Fresno Museum, 172, 173, 178; monetizing collections, 127–132; Thomas Jefferson University and, 144
Tutankhamun, King: treasures of exhibit, 85

Uniform Management and Investment Funds Act (UMIFA), 163
Uniform Prudent Management of Institutional Funds Act (UPMIFA), 158, 160–164
United Nations Educational Scientific Cultural Organization of the United Nations (UNESCO): antiquities, 69; convention, 70; National Cultural Heritage Laws database, 70; Nubian monuments and, 85; stolen cultural property and, 17, 18, 24n35

Van Gogh, Vincent, 21, 25n47, 50
Von Saher: legal precedent, 47–52, 52n7, 52n10, 53n11

Waldmüller, Georg Ferdinand, 60
wartime: claims, 46, 48, 49, 50; provenance, 45, 57, 59
Waterfall methodology software, 243–248, 249, 251, 252, 253n5
Worcester Art Museum (WAM): public domain, 145–146; transfer of Higgins Armory Collection to, 179–200
World War II: ammunition, 110; firearms, 104, 105; looting and, 16; Monuments Men, 24n12, 67, 184, 201n8; provenance research, 59–63, 64, 66–68, 72n7, 72n9; restitution litigation, 43;

stolen cultural property, 45; Task Force
on the Spoliation of Art, 44

Yale University: Art Gallery, 271, 276;
claims, 19; open-source program, 276,
280–283; public relations and, 22; *Yale
v. Konowaloff*, 21, 50

Zervos, Christian: Catalogue Raisonné of
work by Picasso, 63, 72n6

About the Editor

Julia Hollett Courtney has worked in the museum field for over twenty years. She earned a masters in art/museum education from Lesley University in Cambridge, Massachusetts, and a masters in art history and museum studies from Harvard University, in Cambridge, Massachusetts. Courtney has served as curator of art for the Springfield Art Museums in Springfield, Massachusetts (Michele and Donald D'Amour Museum of Fine Arts and George Walter Vincent Smith Art Museum) since 2006. She has conducted scholarly research and written on the collection as well as researched, organized, and designed numerous exhibits that have received national and international publicity. Courtney is a freelance writer, editor, photographer/artist, and former museum educator. She has contributed to *Antiques and Fine Art Magazine* and numerous art catalogues. She is a member of the American Association of Museums, New England Association of Museums, Association of Art Museum Curators, and the Museum and Arts Law Committee of the Section of Science and Technology Law of the American Bar Association.

About the Contributors

David Arnold earned his master of science degree from Winterthur/University of Delaware Program in Art Conservation in 1994, after which he was awarded two one-year postgraduate fellowships to work in the furniture conservation lab at Colonial Williamsburg. In 1996, he was hired by the Society for the Preservation of New England Antiquities in Waltham, Massachusetts. There he conserved wooden artifacts until the lab's closure the following year. He next served as a private conservator under contract to the National Park Service at Harpers Ferry where he treated the 360 historic firearms of the Fuller Gun Collection that is exhibited at the Chickamauga and Chattanooga National Military Park. Upon completion of the project, he moved to North Carolina to replace the general collections conservator at Tryon Palace in New Bern. A year later, Arnold was rehired permanently by the National Park Service's Springfield Armory National Historic Site to serve as its museum's first conservator. There he established the site's first formal conservation treatment program and set up its first laboratory. Both were maintained until the lab was closed in the fall of 2007. Since 2008, Arnold has worked as an objects conservator at the National Park Service's Museum Conservation Services (MCS) lab in Charles Town, West Virginia, where he treats a broad range of metal and composite-metal artifacts shipped there from sites located throughout the National Park Service system.

Catherine M. Colinvaux is the current president of the Worcester Art Museum, where she was deeply involved in the Higgins Armory integration. Previously, Colinvaux was a senior partner of a national law firm where she represented both plaintiffs and defendants in large-dollar, multijurisdiction disputes. Colinvaux served as one of the lead property insurance counsels for all aspects of the 9/11 attack on the World Trade Center. She received her

B.A. magna cum laude from Harvard and Radcliffe Colleges and her J.D. cum laude from Harvard Law School. Colinvaux has been recognized by *Massachusetts Lawyers Weekly* as a "Top Woman in Law" and by Massachusetts Super Lawyers as a Top 50 Women Lawyer, and included in *Best Lawyers in America*. In 2013, Colinvaux retired to focus on not-for-profit work.

James C. Donnelly, Jr., Esq., is a partner at Mirick, O'Connell, DeMallie, and Lougee, LLP, in Worcester, Massachusetts, focusing on business disputes and litigation. He has been a trustee or incorporator of the Higgins Armory Museum since 1986 and president from 1994 to 1997 and from 2010 to present. Donnelly is treasurer and a member of the board and executive committee of the American Antiquarian Society, a nationally renowned historical research library. He received a B.A. from Dartmouth College in 1968 and a J.D. cum laude from Boston College Law School in 1973, where he was editor-in-chief of the *Annual Survey of Massachusetts Law*. He has been selected for inclusion in *The Best Lawyers in America* in the field of corporate governance and named a Massachusetts Super Lawyer.

Dr. **Sharon Flescher** is the executive director of the International Foundation for Art Research (IFAR), a not-for-profit educational and research organization that works at the intersection of art scholarship, art law, and the public interest. She is also editor-in-chief of the award-winning *IFAR Journal*. Dr. Flescher is a graduate of Barnard College, holds M.A. degrees in both English literature and art history, and has a Ph.D. in art history from Columbia University. She also attended the Wharton Business School. Her professional career has straddled the academic, business, philanthropic, and nonprofit worlds. In addition to her work at IFAR, she is an adjunct associate professor at New York University (NYU). Prior to joining IFAR in 1998, her positions included program officer in the Museums Program of the National Endowment for the Humanities and director of grants and programs, the Equitable Foundation, a corporate philanthropic foundation.

Mark S. Gold is a partner in the law firm of Parese, Sabin, Smith, and Gold, LLP, Pittsfield, Massachusetts. He holds an undergraduate degree in economics and international studies from the American University, a law degree from Georgetown University, and a master's degree in museum studies from Harvard University. His practice includes business and corporate law, venture capital and traditional financing, and nonprofit and museum law. Mark has done considerable research and writing on the ethical rule pertaining to the use of the proceeds of deaccessioning and issues of museum governance, and has participated in panels on those topics and others at meetings of the American Alliance of Museums and regional museum associations. With

Stefanie Jandl, he was the coeditor of the two-volume *A Handbook for Academic Museums*, published in 2012 by MuseumsEtc, and the forthcoming third volume. He is a member of the board of directors of New England Museum Association.

Ivana D. Greco is an associate in the litigation department of Wiggin and Dana. Before joining Wiggin and Dana, Greco was a law clerk to Judge Faith S. Hochberg on the U.S. District Court, District of New Jersey and to Justice Anne M. Patterson on the Supreme Court of New Jersey. Greco earned her J.D., cum laude, from Harvard Law School, where she was the executive editor for the *Harvard International Law Journal,* and her B.A. from Johns Hopkins University.

David L. Hall is a partner at Wiggin and Dana, and a member of the Art and Museum Law Practice Group. He represents museums, universities, and other cultural institutions, galleries and dealers in art, private collectors, insurers, foundations, and national governments in matters relating to ownership of cultural property. In 2013, Mr. Hall retired from the U.S. Department of Justice after a twenty-three-year career as an assistant U.S. attorney. While in federal service, Mr. Hall received the Director's Award for Superior Performance, numerous Special Act Awards, and other awards and commendations from government agencies, including the FBI, CIA, DEA, and ATF. He has also been recognized with the DHS/ICE Excellence in Law Enforcement Award, the DHS/ICE International Achievement Award, and the SAFE Beacon Award. Mr. Hall served as the special prosecutor for the FBI Art Crime Team, and has extensive experience investigating and prosecuting cultural property crimes. Mr. Hall earned a B.A. from Dartmouth, an MBA from Yale, and J.D. and M.A. degrees from the University of Pennsylvania, where he was an editor of the law review.

Stefanie S. Jandl is an independent museum professional with expertise on strengthening the teaching role of academic museums within their campus communities. She has over twenty years of museum experience that includes academic outreach, exhibition planning, and collections management. She was the Andrew W. Mellon Associate Curator for Academic Programs at the Williams College Museum of Art (WCMA) in Williamstown, Massachusetts. There she helped build and strengthen the museum's academic outreach program to make the WCMA collections, exhibitions, and programs a vital interdisciplinary academic resource for Williams College faculty and students. With Mark Gold she was the coeditor of the two-volume *A Handbook for Academic Museums*, published in 2012 by MuseumsEtc, and the forthcoming third volume. She has written for *Gastronomica* and has published on the artist Man Ray. Jandl holds a B.A. in political science from the

University of Southern California and an M.A. in art history from Williams College.

A lifelong resident of Berkshire County, Massachusetts, **R. Michael Kirchner** retired as chief of police for the Town of West Stockbridge, Massachusetts in 1999, after more than twenty years in law enforcement in Berkshire County. He then worked for eighteen months as the safety manager at the Norman Rockwell Museum at Stockbridge, Massachusetts. During this time he acquired certification as a certified protection professional by ASIS International and was a charter member of the International Foundation of Cultural Property Protection (IFCPP). He has achieved certification as a certified institutional protection manager and helped to establish the New England Chapter of the IFCPP. In early 2008, Kirchner was offered the position as director of safety and security at the Harvard Art Museums. He currently holds that position at Harvard, but continues to work as a security and safety consultant. He has presented informational sessions and training seminars on physical security and emergency planning for ASIS International, American Alliance of Museums, New England Museum Association, and the International Foundation for Cultural Property Protection. He is a member of the Museum Security Committee of the American Alliance of Museums, and in 2013 was appointed vice chair of that group. Kirchner has recently cofounded a new company, Practical Management Resources, LLC, a security management–consulting firm. In 2011 Kirchner's work at Harvard was recognized by *Security Magazine,* as a member of the Security 500, a listing of the top five hundred security organizations in the country.

Ethan S. Klepetar is an attorney for the practice of Parese, Sabin, Smith, and Gold, LLP, in Pittsfield, Massachusetts. He graduated magna cum laude from Brandeis University in Waltham, Massachusetts, and received his J.D. from the University of Minnesota Law School. He lives in the Berkshires where he is dedicated to serving the community. Klepetar is proud to be the chair of the Berkshire Immigrant Center's advisory board and serves on the board of the Berkshire Museum.

Katherine E. Lewis is an attorney-advisor working in the Smithsonian Institution's Office of Contracting. She is chair of the Museum and the Arts Law Committee, organized in the American Bar Association's Section of Science and Technology, and has been a frequent speaker for American Bar Association programs as well as regional and national museum associations on legal issues facing museums, specifically as they relate to intellectual property and information technology. Katherine has published on topics including intellectual property, cultural property, social media, and copyright law. She earned her juris doctorate and master of laws in intellectual property at the

University of New Hampshire School of Law, graduated from the University of Connecticut with a bachelor of arts in art history, and is licensed to practice law in New York, Massachusetts, New Hampshire, and Washington, DC.

Anita Lichtblau is a partner in the nonprofit organizations law practice of Casner and Edwards, a Boston law firm that provides comprehensive legal advice to tax-exempt organizations and businesses and individuals involved in nonprofit matters. Her areas of legal expertise include nonprofit formation and affiliations, governance, cy pres and deviation actions, dissolutions, fundraising, lobbying and political activity, employment, and government and foundation grants and contracts. Before joining Casner and Edwards, Lichtblau served for fifteen years as both the general counsel for Action for Boston Community Development (ABCD), a large nonprofit human services organization and community action agency (CAA) that provides Head Start and other services to low-income people, and executive director of Community Action Program Legal Services (CAPLAW), a nonprofit providing legal training and technical assistance to the approximately one thousand CAAs across the country. Prior to holding those positions, Lichtblau was a senior trial attorney with the U.S. Department of Justice handling white-collar criminal cases in federal courts in New England and practiced with the Boston firm Hill and Barlow and the Washington, DC, firm Steptoe and Johnson. Lichtblau is a graduate of Harvard Law School and Cornell University, and has presented hundreds of training sessions and written numerous articles and publications on many issues relating to nonprofit organizations.

Alex MacKenzie works for the National Park Service as the curator at Springfield Armory National Historic Site in Springfield, Massachusetts. He manages one of the largest collections of American military firearms, along with archival and rare book collections focusing on the history of Springfield Armory, which operated as a government, military, small-arms factory, and research facility from 1794 to 1968. Mr. MacKenzie holds a BA in history from the University of Massachusetts, and a master's degree in archival management from Simmons College.

Nicholas M. O'Donnell is a litigation partner at Sullivan and Worcester, LLP, and the practice group leader of the firm's art and museum law group. He represents American and European museums, galleries, auction houses, and collectors in litigation on issues that range from World War II restitution claims to commercial disagreements, and advises them on transactional, intellectual property, and ethical issues. Mr. O'Donnell also advises a number of clients about the implications of deaccessioning, both for donors and museums. His Art Law Report (www.artlawreport.com) offers commentary on legal issues affecting the visual arts community. O'Donnell has spoken widely on the topic of World War II restitution litigation, including at a special conference in Heidelberg, Germany, January 2014, about the Cornelius Gurlitt affair.

Alyssa L. Reiner, Esq., is an attorney-advisor with the Smithsonian Institution. She practices transactional law with a focus on copyright transactions, particularly those involving the development and distribution of physical and digital creative content. Ms. Reiner has spoken and published on a number of topics including image licensing for museums, copyright and indigenous artworks, the impact of digital media and distribution on the entertainment and content industries, copyright and virtual museums, and the Digital Millennium Copyright Act, and online copyright-management information. Ms. Reiner is a member of the Women's Bar Association of the District of Columbia, and of the American Bar Association, serving as the chair of the Intellectual Property Section's Social Media Policy Subcommittee to the Committee on Copyright and Social Media. Ms. Reiner earned her J.D. in 1998 from the Georgetown University Law Center, and her B.A. in 1994 from Cornell University. She is admitted to practice law in Washington, DC.

Ellen Savulis is curator of anthropology at the Springfield Science Museum, Springfield, Massachusetts. She received her Ph.D. from the University of Massachusetts, Amherst. Savulis and Deborah L. Rotman edited *Shared Spaces and Divided Places: Material Dimensions of Gender Relations and the American Historical Landscape* published in 2003.

Ronald D. Spencer is chairman of the art law practice at the New York law firm of Carter, Ledyard, and Milburn, LLP. He is an expert in the legal aspects of art authentication issues and has written and edited *The Expert versus the Object: Judging Fakes and False Attributions in the Visual Arts* (2004), and edits *Spencer's Art Law Journal*.

Judith Wallace is a member of the art law group at Carter, Ledyard, and Milburn, LLP. She represents collectors, foundations, artists, and scholars in matters of art ownership, authenticity, authorship, consignment and sales, foundation governance, and other art-related matters. She writes frequently on art law issues.

Riley Walter has focused on insolvency matters since 1980 and specializes in Chapter 11 reorganization cases representing debtors. He is a certified business bankruptcy specialist accredited by the American Board of Bankruptcy, Class XIII. He is a partner in the Walter and Wilhem Law Group and an attorney and art collector. Riley Walter was insolvency counsel for the

Fresno Metropolitan Museum and worked with O. James Woodward II, the assignee for benefit of creditors. Both are headquartered in Fresno, California.

Gilbert Whittemore is admitted to the Massachusetts and Vermont bars. He has a special interest in legal issues associated with museums, especially issues arising from new technology. He has both a law degree and a Ph.D. in the history of science from Harvard and over the years has taught part-time at Harvard, MIT, and Brown University. His museum-related activity includes having served as chair of the Museum and Arts Law Committee of the Section of Science and Technology Law of the American Bar Association, advising on the drafting of statutes related to museum property in Vermont and Rhode Island, serving as a trustee of the American Precision Museum in Windsor, Vermont, and serving on the museum committee of the International Tennis Hall of Fame and Museum in Newport, Rhode Island. He currently teaches "Museums and the Law" in the museum studies program of the Harvard Extension School and has given a number of workshops to museums associations in the New England area.